Adventures of an Itinerant Imagination

Westar Studies

The Westar Studies series offers distinctive scholarly publications on topics related to the field of Religious Studies. The studies seek to be multi-dimensional both in terms of the subject matter addressed and the perspective of the author. Westar Studies are not related to Westar seminars but offer scholars a deliberate space of free inquiry to engage both scholarly peers and the public.

Adventures of an Itinerant Imagination

Essays Celebrating John Dominic Crossan on His Ninetieth Birthday

Edited by
BERNARD BRANDON SCOTT

CASCADE *Books* • Eugene, Oregon

ADVENTURES OF AN ITINERANT IMAGINATION
Essays Celebrating John Dominic Crossan on His Ninetieth Birthday

Copyright © 2025 Bernard Brandon Scott. All rights reserved. Except for brief quotations in critical publications or reviews, no part of this book may be reproduced in any manner without prior written permission from the publisher. Write: Permissions, Wipf and Stock Publishers, 199 W. 8th Ave., Suite 3, Eugene, OR 97401.

Cascade Books
An Imprint of Wipf and Stock Publishers
199 W. 8th Ave., Suite 3
Eugene, OR 97401

www.wipfandstock.com

PAPERBACK ISBN: 979-8-3852-4950-3
HARDCOVER ISBN: 979-8-3852-4951-0
EBOOK ISBN: 979-8-3852-4952-7

Cataloguing-in-Publication data:

Names: Scott, Bernard Brandon, editor.

Title: Adventures of an Itinerant Imagination : Essays Celebrating John Dominic Crossan on His Ninetieth Birthday / Bernard Brandon Scott.

Description: Eugene, OR: Cascade Books, 2025 | Series: Westar Studies | Includes bibliographical references and index.

Identifiers: ISBN 979-8-3852-4950-3 (paperback) | ISBN 979-8-3852-4951-0 (hardcover) | ISBN 979-8-3852-4952-7 (ebook)

Subjects: LCSH: Jesus Christ. | Crossan, John Dominic.

Classification: CALL NUMBER 2025 (paperback) | CALL NUMBER (ebook)

VERSION NUMBER 06/12/25

Contents

Celebrating Dom Crossan | vii

Introduction | ix

Contributors | xi

Part One   Parables and Fragments

1. On Reading Crossan | 3
   BERNARD BRANDON SCOTT

2. Gathering the Fragments of a Discourse | 20
   CHARLES W. HEDRICK

3. Parable as Challenge | 28
   DAVID GALSTON

4. Breaking Mirrors of Jesus in Africa | 34
   GLENNA S. JACKSON

5. *The Dark Interval:* An Anniversary Ode | 42
   GUERRIC DEBONA, OSB

Part Two   The Historical Jesus

6. An Interview with John Dominic Crossan | 51
   ROBERT J. MILLER

7. The Enduring Issue of Jesus: Two Quests | 63
   LANE MCGAUGHY

8. History Is Like an Unswept Room | 78
   ERIN VEARNCOMBE

9	A New Way Forward? | 82 STEPHEN J. PATTERSON
10	Unhoused and Unbound | 92 LIZ THEOHARIS
11	Encountering *The Historical Jesus:* A Transformative Moment | 96 CHAD VENTERS
12	In Search of Method | 101 BERNARD BRANDON SCOTT
13	A Scholar Schooled in the Empire of Heaven | 131 GREGORY C. JENKS
14	Rhetorical Jesus | 136 JOSEPH BESSLER
15	Logical And Lyrical | 142 ROBIN R. MEYERS
16	Deeply and Richly Listening | 147 GORDON W. G. RAYNAL

Part Three   Violence, Empire, and Civilization

17	Creation, Violence, Connection, and Community | 153 CELENE LILLIE
18	Context, Texture, Entanglement | 169 ARTHUR J. DEWEY
19	Wrestling with Divine Violence | 189 PERRY KEA
20	Crossan, Paul, and the Philosophers | 194 JOHN CAPUTO
21	Reflections on Resurrection and Redemption in Romans | 216 PAMELA EISENBAUM

Bibliography | 233

John Dominic Crossan Curriculum Vitae | 243

Celebrating Dom Crossan

John Dominic Crossan, whose biblical and historical studies are celebrated in this volume, is a key figure in the life of the Westar Institute and a significant contributor to the Jesus Seminar. With Robert W. Funk, he co-chaired the Jesus Seminar from its inception in 1989 to its final volume in 1998. Throughout the whole process, he placed the issue of the historical Jesus not only before the academic community, but, breaking free of academic restraints, he took the historical Jesus scholarship to the public. His work did not go unnoticed, attracting critics and followers alike, but that was just the beginning.

After and beyond the Jesus Seminar, Crossan stretched his talents further as he approached new issues and journeyed toward new frontiers. He wrote with great insight on Roman imperial theology out of which he forged a critique of our own imperial ambitions. It is not possible, after reading Crossan, to think that ancient history has no bearing on present reality. Crossan also has employed new insights from archaeology to expose the physical background so important to imagining the historical context of a figure like Jesus. The intimate relation of archaeology and biblical criticism is turned into a specialty with Crossan, making his writing come alive with the past's reanimation. And now, most recently, his work on the Apostle Paul is changing the way we see Paul, read Paul, and relate Paul to civilization. Once again, as Crossan brings an ancient character to life, he does not leave Paul in the past but creates, from the ancient experience of civilization, a critique of our present political order.

The relevance of Crossan's work stretches far beyond the fields in which he specializes, which is the mark of a scholar who has not lost touch with public issues. Over time, scholarship evolves, opinions change, and conclusions once felt secure can shatter under the weight of new evidence. But with great scholars the one thing that lasts is public influence. Few scholars, in their work, find a public voice that goes beyond the academy to impact everyday perceptions of the world. Crossan is one of those scholars who holds a public voice.

I am pleased to welcome such an excellent collection of essays, to thank Bernard Brandon Scott for his tireless commitment to this *festschrift* in celebration of John Dominic Crossan's ninetieth birthday, and to invite the reader to sample these diverse expressions, opinions, and critiques that highlight Crossan's many accomplishments. Some of these pieces are of a personal nature and some are more academically focused. The diversity of expression reflects the broad impact and scope of Crossan's writing. The reader will find many different points of entry into Crossan's thinking and will be grateful for these thought-provoking essays.

David Galston,
Westar Executive Director

Introduction

On January 17, 2024, John Dominic Crossan celebrated his ninetieth birthday and the Westar Institute celebrated with him. As part of that celebration Westar sponsored a year long series of programs assessing Crossan's work. Six of the papers from that celebration are part of this volume: Stephen Patterson and Brandon Scott on the historical Jesus, Celene Lillie and Arthur Dewey on violence, John Caputo and Pamela Eisenbaum on Paul. Robert Miller interviewed Crossan about his involvement with the Jesus Seminar, which he cochaired. Lane McGaughy approached this same material from a larger historical perspective.

Others were asked to write shorter reflections on Crossan's work. The editor asked them to reflect on Crossan's work by answering one of the following questions.

Crossan's most important contribution to scholarship
Crossan's most important book.
Which of Crossan's books influenced you the most?

The editor provided no other guidance other than to keep it to 1,500 to 2,500 words, a remarkable restraint for scholars. Their responses varied from scholarly assessments to personal reflections. Some have footnotes; others have none. The wide range testifies to and mirrors the sweeping vista of Crossan's own work.

I'm not sure what is the correct metaphor to describe this book. Are these essays a treasure house, a cornucopia, a garden of delights, or a mash-up? They do offer a reader expansive views from sympathetic readers assessing various aspects of Crossan's agenda. To the editor, the resulting essays exhibit a curious and intriguing interplay and harmony. Many, of course, center around the historical Jesus, Crossan's major contribution. But they approach that topic from fascinating avenues. From

Africa and homeless Americans; from aphorisms and philosophy; from the pulpit and the nurse-pastor. Perhaps a symphony led by an old rock and roller is the best metaphor.

Crossan has been not only an active, productive, and innovative scholar, but he has also been a public intellectual. In the appendix of this volume the reader will find Crossan's Curriculum Vitae. This testifies not only to his extensive publications, but also to his involvement with the public in speaking engagements, radio and TV interviews. He has surely been one of the most actively engaged biblical scholars of his generation. This CV will also serve as a resource for future scholars interested in Crossan's work—and there will surely be such scholars.

Bernard Brandon Scott, Editor

Contributors

Joseph Anthony Bessler, PhD
Robert Travis Peake Professor
Phillips Theological Seminary

John D. Caputo, PhD
Thomas J. Watson Professor Emeritus of Religion,
Syracuse University
David R. Cook Professor Emeritus of Philosophy,
Villanova University

Guerric DeBona, OSB, PhD
Professor of Homiletics
St. Meinrad Seminary and School of Theology

Arthur J. Dewey, ThD
Professor of New Testament
Xavier University

Pamela Eisenbaum, PhD
Clifford E. Baldridge Professor of Biblical Studies and Christian Origins
Iliff School of Theology

David Galston, PhD
Executive Director
Westar Institute

Charles W. Hedrick, PhD
Emeritus Distinguished Professor
Missouri State University

Glenna S. Jackson PhD
Professor Emerita, Department of Religion and Philosophy
Otterbein University

Gregory C. Jenks, PhD
Lecturer in Biblical Studies
University of Divinity, Australia

Perry Kea, PhD
Associate Professor Emeritus
University of Indianapolis

Celene Lillie, PhD
Lecturer
University of Colorado at Boulder

Lane C. McGaughy
Atkinson Professor of Religious & Ethical Studies Emeritus
Willamette University

Robin R. Meyers, PhD
Distinguished Professor of Social Justice
Oklahoma City University
Pastor First Congregational Church UCC
Norman OK

Stephen J. Patterson, PhD
George H. Atkinson Professor of Religious and Ethical Studies
Willamette University

Gordon W. G. Raynal, RN
Retired Registered Nurse
Honorably Retired Teaching Elder
Presbyterian Church U.S.A

Bernard Brandon Scott, PhD
Darbeth Distinguished Professor of New Testament Emeritus
Phillips Theological Seminary

Liz Theoharis, PhD
Executive Director
Kairos Center for Religions, Rights, and Social Justice

Erin K. Vearncombe, PhD
Assistant Professor
University of Toronto Mississauga

Chad Venters, PhD
Director, Bible Search & Rescue
Westar Institute

PART ONE
Parables and Fragments

1

On Reading Crossan

BERNARD BRANDON SCOTT

John Dominic Crossan points to adventure as a major motive in his life. It certainly describes his scholarship. Intellectually curious and honest, he constantly explores new methods and areas of research to illuminate the New Testament, early Christian writings and experience. Neither ideological nor confessional in his method, Crossan's goals are pragmatic. He is indeed adventurous, always seeking new approaches and new tools for his toolbox.

IRISH CATHOLIC

Monk and Priest

Born in Nenagh, County Tipperary, Ireland, on February 17, 1934, Crossan was baptized John Michael Edmund Crossan in the local parish. At the age of ten he went off to boarding school, not uncommon in Ireland at that time for boys of his social class. He received a good education in the classics, Latin and Greek. He appears to have prospered in this environment. When at the age of sixteen he entered the Servite[1] novitiate, he took the name, Brother Dominic. The regularity and discipline of monastic life

---

1. The Servites are a mendicant monastic order. Founded in thirteenth century, the mendicants were an innovation whereby monks who lived in community also worked outside the monastery teaching, preaching, or caring for the poor. The Franciscans and Dominicans are well-known mendicant orders.

appealed to him. "At the age of sixteen, adventure was the attraction, and from all I could see, God had going the best adventure around, and the Servites were the fastest way into it."[2]

Crossan's year-long novitiate introduced him to the monastic life and Servite practice and culture. With the novitiate, he writes, "my life changed utterly, the past disappeared almost completely, and I never even noticed its departure or missed its presence."[3] While he loved Gregorian chant, he utterly failed at it. Otherwise, the novitiate launched his adventure.

> I was now learning, with utter fascination, that adventures took place inside yourself as well. There were adventures possible within your own heart, soul, spirit, and conscience, and those more than made up for anything lost outside. I did not miss the past because the present and the future were much more exciting. I had entered monastic life for adventurous travel in a physical world and immediately encountered far more adventurous travel in a spiritual world.[4]

At the novitiate's end, Crossan emigrated to the U.S. to continue his education at the Servite seminary outside Chicago. His superiors decided he should prepare to teach biology, so he attended classes at DePaul toward that end. As he approached ordination to the priesthood in 1957, they decided his future lay in biblical studies. So after ordination, Crossan returned to Ireland to get his doctorate at St Patrick's College, Maynooth. With doctorate in hand, in 1959 he spent the next two years at the Pontifical Biblical Institute in Rome in postdoctoral studies, then from 1965–67 studying archaeology at the École biblique et archéologique française de Jérusalem (then in Jordan). Crossan praises his Servite superiors for their support of his education. In the interval between study in Jerusalem and afterwards, he taught New Testament at various Catholic seminaries and universities in the Chicago area.[5]

---

2. Crossan, *A Long Way from Tipperary*, 28.
3. Crossan, *A Long Way from Tipperary*, 58.
4. Crossan, *A Long Way from Tipperary*, 59.
5. Crossan, *A Long Way from Tipperary*, 80–86, details his educational experience under the heading of the vow of obedience. "In all those years, preordination or postordination, I was never consulted on my hopes, fears, wishes, or desires. I never expected that to happen and never missed its absence" (85).

Scholar

At age thirty-five in 1969, Crossan left the Servites and the priesthood to marry and joined the faculty of DePaul University in Chicago. This step proved as decisive and dramatic as his entrance into the novitiate at age sixteen. His public scholarship began at this point and all his important publications were to follow.

When Crossan left the Servites and the priesthood he kept his religious name, Dominic. John Michael Edmund Crossan became John Dominic Crossan. He may have left the Servites and the priesthood, but their influence stayed with him.

Crossan has discussed his reasons for leaving on several occasions.[6] He gives two reasons. "[B]y the 1960s, the monastic priesthood had become less important than biblical scholarship, and clerical celibacy had become much less important than female relationship."[7] As he puts it elsewhere, "My priestly life was spent more in the library than the parish."[8] There is, of course, almost surely a great deal more to this story than this indicates, but Crossan is entitled to his privacy. He has been honest about how scholarship drew him away from priesthood, and the love for a woman drew him away from the celibacy required for priesthood. He also had trouble with monastic obedience, especially the surrender of intellectual integrity, once he discovered the joy of intellectual inquiry.[9]

At this the time the Second Vatican Council (1962–65) unleashed a religious, theological, and liturgical ferment—surely a major influence on Crossan, the Servites, and the Catholic environment in which he was deeply embedded. In his autobiography, he writes of Vatican II in only one paragraph.

> It was bliss in that dawn to be alive and heavenly to be young, have a brand-new doctorate, and, above all, be newly specialized in biblical studies. It was especially the Bible, with its texts seen now in their particular historical situations and specific literary intentions, that was helping and even forcing a fundamental review of the Roman Catholic Tradition. But bliss for some was shock for others, and that created tensions within both

---

6. See Miller, "An Interview with John Dominic Crossan" in this volume.

7. Crossan, *A Long Way from Tipperary*, 77.

8. "Why I Left the Priesthood." https://islamchristiandebate.wordpress.com/why-i-left-the-priesthood-john-dominic-crossan/.

9. Crossan notes, "that after the publication of Paul VI's *Humanae vitae*, I' could no longer be both an obedient priest and an honest scholar," ("Bliss at Dawn," 150).

monastery and priesthood. How, in the unchanging church, could ideas and actions absolutely forbidden yesterday become acceptable today and probably normative tomorrow?[10]

Crossan left the monastic priesthood, not the Catholic Church. His argument was with the Catholic hierarchy, not Catholic faith.[11] His ethos remains profoundly catholic, with both a capital and lower case "c." From Thomas Aquinas he took the conviction that faith and reason do not conflict, so he always tries to work out that conflict. Remaining "Dom" signals his commitment to a religious vocation. He may have left the monastery, but that does not signal abandonment of the "adventurous travel in a spiritual world" that he discovered in the novitiate. "It was still there, in other words, that inaugural lure of adventure, but it was no longer centered on the priesthood but on scholarship."[12] That new adventure was the historical Jesus, absent from the Catholic agenda and only recently having gained ground among Protestant New Testament scholars. Crossan would join the chase with enthusiasm.

Crossan's Irish heritage continues as a major influence on his reconstruction of the historical Jesus.[13] Irish peasant experience in the nineteenth century informs his view of Jesus as an illiterate peasant. For Crossan, social class matters, especially in ferreting out social injustice. Some have accused him of projecting Irish experience of English colonialism onto the first-century Galilean situation. But is that projection or employing experience as a hermeneutical aid? Is Crossan only seeing his own Irish face at the bottom of well? With his usual incisiveness, he retorts, "If he [Jesus] came from a peasant hamlet, he was probably a peasant laborer. Although, of course, if it looks like a duck, walks like a duck, and quacks like a duck, it might be a camel in disguise."[14]

---

10. Crossan, *A Long Way from Tipperary*, 74. This is the only mention of Vatican II in his autobiography, surely an understatement. In "Bliss at Dawn," he remarks, "I had finished my postgraduate education just before the start of the Second Vatican Council and that my first four years of seminary teaching coincided with its proceedings," (149). This short essay does not illuminate what is in his autobiography.

11. Crossan, *A Long Way from Tipperary*, 197, for an extended discussion of this.

12. Crossan, *A Long Way from Tipperary*, 77.

13. Crossan did not become a U.S. citizen until 1990.

14. Crossan, *A Long Way from Tipperary*, xvii. See the vigorous defense of his use of his Irish experience and history (150–55).

RHETORICAL STRATEGY

Crossan's writing has been prodigious,[15] all of it well crafted. He writes with style, sensitive to the music and rhythm of language. It seems effortless. He searches for the pleasing phase that enables a reader to grasp and share his insight. Crossan presses the art of language into the service of meaning.

Simplify the Complex

Other scholars have coined the apt phrase or sentence to summarize complex phenomena. C. H. Dodd summed up Jesus' teaching on the coming of God's kingdom with the oxymoronic phrase, "realized eschatology."[16] "Eschatology" pertains to the future but "realized" says it's now. The striking juxtaposition is memorable because it makes the point without a great deal of explanation.

In an earlier generation, the French Catholic New Testament scholar, Alfred Loisy, summed up the complicated historical transition from Jesus to the Church with the phrase, "Jesus foretold the kingdom, and it was the Church that came."[17] Rudolf Bultmann's "The proclaimer became the proclaimed," is a Protestant version of Loisy's Catholic statement. The first sentence of Bultmann's *Theology of the New Testament* again summarizes this same insight. "The message of Jesus is a presupposition for the theology of the New Testament rather than a part of that theology itself."[18] This statement is economical and well put but he needed two volumes to explain it.

Crossan's rhetorical strategy coins the apt phrase or intriguing sentence that presents a reader with insight into a complex thought (e.g., the meaning of eschatology) or historical process (e.g., how the shift from Jesus to the Church occurred). This characterizes his literary style but also implements a rhetorical strategy to encapsulate his insight. Crossan spins complex ideas to linguistic gold. I have selected five topics I think central to his program that exhibit this rhetorical strategy.

---

15. Thirty-one books by my count; add to these his numerous speaking engagements. Does the man sleep?

16. Dodd, *The Parables of the Kingdom*, 35.

17. Loisy, *The Gospel and the Church*, 166 (French original 1902). The French reads: "Jésus annoncait le royaume, et c'est l'Église qui est venue."

18. Bultmann, *Theology of the New Testament*, 1:3.

About Jesus

Sayings *of* Jesus (e.g., parables) and narratives or stories *about* Jesus (e.g., healing stories) forms a basic division of Jesus material. In sorting through the origin of the narratives *about* Jesus, especially those dealing with his birth, death, and resurrection, Crossan asks whether each narrative derived from prophecy or history. He pioneered this distinction in *The Cross That Spoke* (1988), sorting through the origins of passion narratives. Crossan postulates several stages in the process. He notes, "First, there is the *historical* Passion."[19] Something happened to Jesus, but we have no evidence because the disciples fled. Then there is what Crossan terms "the *prophetic* passion," in which the separate events of an imagined passion were created from searching the scriptures: "prophecy historicized."

> Next, there is the *narrative* passion. It is almost impossible for us not to imagine this as the first phase rather than the third phase of the process. Even those who would agree that almost all the details came from prophecy, rather than history, and from theology, rather than journalism, tend to end up by saying, but, of course, it probably happened that way in any case.[20]

Such folks, in Crossan's judgment, have mistaken prophecy historicized for history remembered.

In his *The Historical Jesus* (1991), Crossan explicitly titled the section dealing with Jesus' trial and death, "Prophecy or History?"[21] In his later book, *Who Killed Jesus* (1995), he contrasts his analysis of Jesus' trial with Raymond Brown's *The Death of the Messiah* (1994). Brown admits the influence of prophecy in Crossan's terms, or Old Testament Scripture in Brown's, in the formation and construction of the trial scene. But Brown "always presumes . . . an expansion or rearrangement of received traditions based on a fairly detailed core of memory."[22] Crossan rejects this presumption based on a detailed analysis. For him, "the received tradition is not a core memory recalling what happened to Jesus under trial but a core of prophecy replacing memory's absence."[23] That leads to his

---

19. Crossan, *The Cross That Spoke*, 405.
20. Crossan, *The Cross That Spoke*, 406.
21. Crossan, *The Historical Jesus*, 368.
22. Crossan, *Who Killed Jesus?*, 117.
23. Crossan, *Who Killed Jesus?*, 117.

conclusion: "the trial is, in my best judgment, based entirely on prophecy historicized rather than history remembered."[24]

Crossan acknowledges the difficulty of conceiving that no historical memory of Jesus' trial and death has survived, but he affirms that is the case. As the gospels acknowledge, the disciples had fled, so how could an historical memory form? Instead, Crossan insists the separate events of an imagined passion were created by imaginative use of Hebrew scriptures. He summarizes this process with the memorable phrase, "prophecy historicized and history remembered."[25] Crossan's formula challenges the obviousness of a nonexistent historical memory and enables a reader to imagine another option. Even more, he makes it seem plausible.

Of Jesus

Unlike stories about Jesus, sayings *of* Jesus reflect possible historical memories. For Crossan, the parables lie at the core of the Jesus tradition and *In Parables: The Challenge of the Historical Jesus* (1973) is Crossan's first major book. Dodd's classic definition of parable has endured: "At its simplest, the parable is a metaphor or simile drawn from nature or common life, arresting the hearer by its vividness or strangeness, and leaving the mind in sufficient doubt about its precise application to tease it into active thought."[26] Crossan understands parable according to this definition in *In Parables*. His innovations emerged in other areas.

In *The Dark Interval* (1975), Crossan expands the definition of parable beyond considerations of genre or form by contrasting parable with myth. He uses the French anthropologist Claude Lévi-Strauss's structuralist understanding of myth, in which myth reconciles unreconcilable opposites, to analyze myth as story. "[I]n a mythical story, an opposition between two terms that cannot be reconciled (binary opposition), will be represented by two functional surrogates, and these replacements will allow a reconciliation or mediation which the original pair could not receive."[27]

---

24. Crossan, *Who Killed Jesus?*, 117. Dewey, *Inventing the Passion*, in chap. 6, "Memory and Midrash," makes a similar point. In *The Historical Jesus* he concludes a similar argument about the two Jesus birth stories with, "Hide the prophecy, tell the narrative, and invent the history" (372).

25. Crossan, *Who Killed Jesus?*, 1.

26. Dodd, *The Parables of the Kingdom*, 5.

27. Crossan, *The Dark Interval*, 51.

Common folktales exhibit this pattern. Crossan notes a generalized example.

> [T]he hero starts out to solve the poverty-stricken situation of himself and his family. But instead of concluding in comfortable, middle-class suburbia, he ends up marrying the king's daughter, becoming heir to the throne, and moving his family into the palace.[28]

Many Hollywood movies traffic in the same mythical plot. Horatio Alger stories and rags-to-riches narratives repeat the same plot over and over to construct the American dream:[29] if you work hard enough, you can get ahead.

For Crossan, "parable is necessary, logically, as the binary opposite of myth."[30] "Parables are supposed to overturn one's structure of expectation and therein and thereby to threaten the security of one's man-made world."[31] "Man-made world" equals myth. Or, as he phrases it elsewhere, "The surface function of parable is to create contradiction within a given situation of complacent security but, even more unnervingly, to challenge the fundamental principle of reconciliation by making us aware of the fact that *we made up* the reconciliation."[32] Crossan coins this dictum: "Myth disposes, parable proposes,"[33] four words that epitomize how myth and parable function and how they are opposed. Crossan's phrase draws a reader into his insight.

"Myth disposes, parable proposes"[34] is an important and perhaps the fundamental distinction for Crossan. It functions on several levels. First, it builds on his understanding of Jesus' parables as subverting the accepted. Then, it shifts from how a parable operates to the two different ways of telling a story. He borrows from Frank Kermonde the notion that

---

28. Crossan, *The Dark Interval*, 52.

29. See my *Hollywood Dreams and Biblical Stories*, chap. 3. So strong is this myth in American culture that we consider the poverty of the poor to be their fault.

30. Crossan, *The Dark Interval*, 63.

31. Crossan, *The Dark Interval*, 101.

32. Crossan, *The Dark Interval*, 57.

33. Crossan, *The Dark Interval*, 63.

34. "Proverb is the last word, aphorism the first word" is Crossan's aphorism that summarizes aphoristically the difference between proverb and aphorism. This distinction replicates that of myth and parable. Crossan, *In Fragments*, 25.

"Myths are the agents of stability, fictions are agents of change."[35] Crossan substitutes parable for "fiction."

Next, the two ways of telling a story, myth and parable, become ways of being in the world. This functions as an ontological principle for Crossan and defines a fundamental divide in religion. "The more useful distinction might be between mythical religion, a religion that gives one the final word about 'reality' and thereby excludes the authentic experience of mystery, and parabolic religion, a religion that continually and deliberately subverts final words about 'reality' and thereby introduces the possibility of transcendence."[36] The way of parable marks something as authentic. For Crossan, parable functions like a type of revelation breaking into the everyday world, an experience of the transcendent.

In a later book, *The Power of Parable* (2012), Crossan used the distinction between parable and myth to read the New Testament and Christianity. Its subtitle indicates its direction: *How Fiction by Jesus Became Fiction about Jesus*. The subtitle recalls a similar summary from *The Dark Interval*: "The parabler becomes parable. Jesus announced the kingdom of God in parables, but the primitive church announced Jesus as the Christ, the Parable of God."[37] Here Crossan combines Protestant and Catholic viewpoints.

For Crossan, the parables of the Treasure and Pearl summarize Jesus' parables. They "are perfect metaphors for a paradigm shift, for a tradition swerve, for a fundamental disruptive innovation."[38]

> For him [Jesus], those twin stories imagine the Great Divine Cleanup of the World as here and now present. But it is present only by divine-human participation and a divine-human collaboration. It is a treasure and a pearl demanding a transformation of the old and known past into a new and unknown future.[39]

He coins the apt phrase, "the Great Divine Cleanup of the World," for apocalyptic catastrophe, the end of the world, surrounded by doublets. Crossan then pushes it further.

35. Kermode, *The Sense of an Ending*, 39.
36. Crossan, *The Dark Interval*, 128.
37. Crossan, *The Dark Interval*, 24. "The parabler becomes parable" recalls Bultmann's "the proclaimer becomes the proclaimed," while the final sentence plays on Loisy's statement quoted above: "Jesus foretold the kingdom, and it was the Church that came."
38. Crossan, *The Power of Parable*, 135.
39. Crossan, *The Power of Parable*, 135.

> Nobody has ever summarized Jesus' challenge better than two African bishops who lived about five thousand miles and fifteen hundred years apart. "God made you without you," said Augustine of Hippo in 416. "He doesn't justify you without you." That was magnificently misquoted by Desmond Tutu of Cape Town in 1999: "St Augustine says, 'God, without us, will not; as we, without God, cannot.'"[40]

In these two quotations from two African bishops, Crossan sees the same parabolic overturn of myth that he finds in the parables of the Treasure and Pearl. The mythical version sees the Great Divine Cleanup of the World in the future and all of God's doing. Parable understands that Great Cleanup as happening now through divine–human cooperation. Augustine and Demond Tutu both subvert the *status quo* in the same way as the parables do. For Crossan, they act in an authentically Jesus way.

Crossan's expansive use of myth and parable is not without problems. He stretches the understanding of parable way beyond the original Jewish genre. His aphorism, "Myth disposes, parable proposes," functions not only as a description of how myth and parable operate and differ, but also as a heuristic and hermeneutical key to understanding what is authentic about Jesus and the tradition that follows in his wake. Parable is a unique Jewish form that quickly disappeared in the Christian tradition. I admit the power of Crossan's formulation, but can it bear the weight of this expansion? Labeling a story that subverts expectations as a parable can appear arbitrary and certainly a matter of interpretation. Many stories do that. Are they parables? Does that place them in Jesus' tradition? Crossan's sense of parable threatens to become so broad that it loses its discriminating power.

What Time Is It?

A key debate in the modern quest for the historical Jesus is Jesus' view about the coming of the kingdom of God. Was Jesus an apocalyptist who expected the coming of the kingdom in the future? Or did he think it was somehow already here? Crossan declared his position in *In Parables*. He opted for the kingdom in the present.

In dealing with eschatology or the time of the kingdom's coming, Crossan identifies three parables as paradigmatic: the Treasure, the Pearl,

---

40. Crossan, *The Power of Parable*, 135.

and the Great Fish. He cuts through the debate about the meaning of time in Jesus' preaching by identifying what he calls Jesus' attack on the "idolatry of time," his version of Dodd's realized eschatology. Not only is "idolatry of time" short and bold like Dodd's phrase but the juxtaposition of idolatry and time has a shocking element, sounding strange and arresting. This view of holy time "set Jesus against all the major religious options of his contemporaries,"[41] as a parable should.

> Jesus tells us that we do not live in firm time but on giant shifting epochs whose transitions and changes are the eschatological advent of God. It is the view of time as man's [sic] future that Jesus opposed in the name of time as God's present, not as eternity beyond us but as advent within us. Jesus simply took the third commandment seriously: keep time holy![42]

Crossan ties the presence of the kingdom to the third commandment, provocatively rephrased as, "keep time holy!" instead of keep the sabbath—one day—holy. In so doing, Crossan explains the idolatry of time without abstract digression.

He examined this issue in his *The Historical Jesus* with a cluster of sayings he entitled, "A Kingdom of Here and Now," best represented by Gos. Thom. 113 and Luke 17:20–21, he concluded:

> What is needed, then, is not insight into the Kingdom as future but a recognition of the Kingdom as present. For Jesus, a Kingdom of beggars and weeds is a Kingdom of here and now.[43]

Here again, Crossan follows the same rhetorical strategy. He avoids an abstract discussion of time but calls for insight. He expresses the kingdom as a kingdom of beggars and weeds, words that do not go together in ordinary speech. Their very unexpectedness requires that the kingdom is here and now.

Core of Jesus's Program

Three hundred and thirty-three pages into *The Historical Jesus*, Crossan concludes a long and detailed argument: "three texts are the core of the

---

41. Crossan, *In Parables*, 35.

42. Crossan, *In Parables*, 35.

43. Crossan, *The Historical Jesus*, 283. Crossan rejects "The Apocalyptic Son of Man" cluster of sayings as not from Jesus. See *The Historical Jesus*, 235–55.

argument and the place, I propose, where one can see the heart of the Jesus movement mostly clearly."[44] His whole book boils down to three texts! Crossan sums up that "core" as "the conjunction of magic and meal, miracle and table, compassion and commensality."[45] He offers the reader this nicely balanced series of doublets that brings everything in to focus. Crossan plays with a formula, helping readers to see and hear its ramifications. His triad becomes a dyad: "magic and meal, healing and eating, compassion and commensality, spiritual and material egalitarianism."[46] Then it morphs back into a triad: "dress and itinerancy, miracle and table, healing and commensality."[47] Crossan's exuberance of carefully balanced doublets helps the reader to grasp an insight into the core of the Jesus movement. Significantly, not only is it well written but easily remembered, appropriate for the oral and memorial phenomenon he summarizes. As Walter Ong has argued, to survive in an oral culture, "Think memorable thoughts."[48] Crossan brings readers into the heart of the Jesus Movement and offers them language appropriate to the insight, remaining faithful to that insight.

METHODOLOGY

Adventurous, experimental, methodical, and reflective describe Crossan's methodology. Many scholars learn their methodology in graduate school and never change.[49] That does not describe Crossan. Throughout his long career he has reflected both on how he sorts the evidence and what constitutes good evidence. His methodology has undergone several stages, all the while resting on a strong historical base.

---

44. Crossan, *The Historical Jesus*, 333. The three texts are Gos. Thom. 14:2; Saying Gospel Q 10:1; and Mark 6:7–13.

45. Crossan, *The Historical Jesus*, 332.

46. Crossan, *The Historical Jesus*, 345,

47. Crossan, *The Historical Jesus*, 349.

48. Ong, *Orality and Literacy*, 34.

49. He is disparaging of his graduate education: "The amount of the Bible that I had covered in either undergraduate or postgraduate studies was unbelievably minuscule, and even if done well in depth, was certainly not covered at all in breath. I never had a wide-sweeping survey course. And I had absolutely nothing on theory or method," "Bliss at Dawn," 149.

Catholic Formation

Crossan's education took place completely within the Catholic system. Although his superiors originally assigned him to biology so he could teach in the Servite high school, Crossan's destiny shifted before his ordination. "By then it was clear that our new biblical professor, Father Neal Flanagan, wanted me prepared for seminary teaching, but it was not at all clear that he would get what he wanted despite, or maybe even because of, the fact that *he* wanted it."[50] But Flanagan won out, and Crossan was ordered to prepare to teach biblical studies. Crossan's desires about becoming a biblical scholar are unknown and he was not consulted.[51] But surely Flanagan had spotted an aptitude for biblical study.

The late nineteenth century and early years of the twentieth century saw an opening to historical critical studies of the Bible among Catholics, especially in England, Germany, and France. The reaction of Pius X was harsh. In his Encyclical, *Pascendi Dominici Gregis*[52] (1907), he condemned modernism[53] as "synthesis of all heresies." The Holy Office issued the decree, condemning sixty-five modernist propositions.[54] Finally, an Oath against Modernism[55] was required of all priests, seminary professors, and church officials. The oath was not abolished until 1967. Alfred Loisy, the French priest, biblical scholar, and leading proponent of modernism, was excommunicated from the Church and then became a prominent professor at the Collège de France.

In 1957, Crossan began his graduate biblical studies at St. Patrick's College, Maynooth, the theological seminary of the National University of Ireland, at a time when Catholic biblical scholarship was trying to emerge from the dark night of anti-modernism. Pius XII's encyclical

---

50. Crossan, *A Long Way from Tipperary*, 84.

51. "I was commanded, but no matter how hard I try now, I cannot reconstruct any disagreement, displeasure, or even disappointment with orders from my superiors. I doubt they always ordered what I wanted, so I must presume I always wanted what they ordered" (86).

52. *Pascendi Dominici Gregis* (1907). https://www.papalencyclicals.net/pius10/p10pasce.htm.

53. Modernism attempted to reconcile Catholicism with modern thought.

54. *Lamentabili Sane* (1907). https://www.papalencyclicals.net/pius10/p10lamen.htm.

55. "The Oath against Modernism." https://www.papalencyclicals.net/pius10/p10moath.htm.

Divino Afflante Spiritu[56] (1947) opened up Catholic biblical studies and allowed Catholic scholars to translate the Bible from its original languages, not the Latin Vulgate, as had been required.[57] On the fiftieth anniversary of the encyclical, John Donahue assessed its importance, noting that "*Divino Afflante Spiritu* provided the stimulus for a development of genuine biblical scholarship within Catholicism."[58] The new biblical scholarship became a driving force at Vatican II.

Crossan's studies were conceived in this ferment. His dissertation at St. Patrick's explored *Imago Dei: A Study in Philo and St. Paul*. He emerged from his postdoctoral studies in Rome and Jerusalem[59] with a thorough grounding in the biblical languages, historical studies, historical criticism, archaeology, extensive travels in the Middle East. This education provided the foundation for all of Crossan's research and writing. He has always considered himself as first of all an historian. While the breadth of Crossan's exegetical toolbox is evident in most of his writings, *The Cross That Spoke: The Origins of the Passion Narrative* exhibits page after page of close textual analysis driving towards a comprehensive reconstruction.

A Multidisciplinary Feast

Upon leaving the priesthood in 1969 and joining the faculty of DePaul University, Crossan's publishing activity took off. He announced his arrival as a scholar with *In Parables: The Challenge of the Historical Jesus* (1967). The book inaugurates a series of experiments, some of which were short-lived. Others led to his mature method. I would list the following experiments as important milestones.

1) *Existentialism*. Crossan employed Heidegger's analysis of time to understand Jesus' eschatology in *In Parables*. Crossan's understanding of Jesus' eschatology has persisted largely unchanged; Heidegger disappeared.

2) *Structuralism*. In *The Dark Interval*, Crossan drew on Claude Lévi-Strauss' analysis of myth to understand the binary opposition of myth and parable. Again, Lévi-Strauss disappeared but the distinction

---

56. *Divino Afflante Spiritu* (1947). https://www.papalencyclicals.net/pius12/p12divin.htm.

57. The Council of Trent (1545–1563) had actually decreed that the Latin Vulgate was the only inspired text.

58. Donahue, "Biblical Scholarship."

59. See above for details.

between myth and parable developed and became fundamental to Crossan's program. Crossan also toyed with other aspects of structuralism, which gave him a certain formalism in setting up his understanding of method.⁶⁰ This is especially clear in his mature method as represented in the triple triadic structure of his methodology for Jesus research in *The Historical Jesus*.⁶¹

3) *Literary Criticism and Postmodernism*. As well as being well read in modern literature, Crossan employs secular literary criticism, evident in his analysis of metaphor, plot, and parable in *In Parables, The Dark Interval*, and *Cliffs of Fall*. This remains a permanent part of his methodological repertoire. Crossan's use throughout his corpus of an expansive sense of parable not only innovates but it functions as a type of personal literary criticism. He expands the genre of parable into a hermeneutical criterion.⁶²

4) *Comparative Literature*. I mean "comparative" in several senses. Beginning with *In Parables*, Crossan plays outside the biblical sandbox. The canon does not confine him, nor does he vest it with special status in his historical studies. He uses the parables in the Gospel of Thomas in the same way as those in the synoptic gospels. His *Four Other Gospels: Shadows on the Contours of Canon* explores the Jesus tradition beyond the canon. In *The Cross that Spoke* he argues that the origins of the passion accounts derive from a reconstructed account in the Gospel of Peter.

Crossan employs comparative literature in yet another sense by comparing Jesus's stories to other's stories. In *Raid on the Articulate*, as the subtitle indicates, he compared *Comic Eschatology in Jesus and* [Jorge] *Borges*. In another experiment, he threw his comparative net yet wider by comparing the Jesus parable of the Treasure to all the treasure stories he could find. *Finding is the First Act* demonstrated that the Jesus parable deviated from the common trove of folktales; that is, Jesus' treasure story was a parable, whereas the others were stories.

5) *Anthropological Models*. The use of various anthropological models, especially Gerhard Lenski's *Power and Privilege*, make their first appearance in Crossan's *The Historical Jesus*. Crossan's experiments come to fruition as he arrives at his mature model. Crossan's historical model

---

60. A number of his essays explicitly identify as structuralist, e.g., "Structuralist Analysis and the Parables of Jesus" and "It Is Written: A Structuralist Analysis of John 6."

61. Crossan, *The Historical Jesus*, xxviii.

62. See above, "*Of* Jesus." [X-REF]

wields the standard historical-critical tools of biblical scholarship, such as form and redaction criticism, blended with a sophisticated literary criticism, literary studies of metaphor, and cultural anthropological models in a rich reading of the text. He takes a wide view of historical method, maybe the widest possible view, neither denominational nor confessional but catholic in the root sense. Crossan's close reading is not ideological but pragmatic, in that he searches for the best tool to illuminate a text. As he has claimed, it's an adventure.

FROM THEOLOGIAN TO CULTURAL INTELLECTUAL

In shifting from being a monastic priest to university professor, Crossan also shifted over time from Catholic theologian to cultural intellectual. He once remarked that his "priestly life was spent more in the library than the parish." Crossan's scholarly publications brought him out of the ivy tower and into the public eye. He fundamentally agreed with Robert Funk, founder of the Jesus Seminar, about the ethical demand that scholarship about Jesus should take place in the open. That is why Crossan agreed to co-chair the Jesus Seminar.

The popularity of *The Historical Jesus* and *Jesus: A Revolutionary Biography* pushed Crossan into public view and his audience shifted from Catholic to public. Why would the public be interested in Jesus? Because Jesus raises fundamental questions about what it means to be a human being. Crossan was no longer asking theological questions for a Catholic audience but questions of interest to the general public. Crossan's reconstructed-historical Jesus' "strategy, implicitly for himself and explicitly for his followers, was the combination of *free healing and common eating*, a religious and economic egalitarianism that negated alike and at once the hierarchical and patronal normalcies of Jewish religion and Roman power."[63] For "Jewish religion" read "Christianity" and for "Roman power" read "American power" and one quickly sees the relevance of the historical Jesus. As Crossan observed in his autobiography, "the Jesus Wars [1990s] made it clear that historical Jesus research is open-heart surgery on Christianity, and maybe also on civilization itself."[64] He has

---

63. Crossan, *The Historical Jesus*, 422.
64. Crossan, *A Long Way from Tipperary*, 175.

made the civilizational aspect clear in his recent book *Render Unto Caesar: The Struggle Over Christ and Culture in the New Testament* (2022).[65]

In his role as public intellectual, Crossan has addressed issues such as anti-Semitism[66] and violence in the name of religion.[67] He accepts numerous speaking engagements and garners media attention in newspapers, magazines, television, and online. If Crossan's "priestly life was spent more in the library than the parish," he spends his post-priestly life as a cultural intellectual, both in the library and in public.

Crossan's long and winding adventures have taken him from Ireland to the U.S., from monk and priest to scholar and public intellectual. Throughout he has remained convinced and convincing that the historical Jesus matters, not only to historians but to Christians and the world at large. Jesus' confrontation with the Roman empire throws light on modern imperialisms. The parables of Jesus still speak to our world, but now with an Irish brogue.

---

65. He has extended this line analysis with his latest book, Crossan, *Paul the Pharisee*. Besides his usual toolkit, he employs an environmental matrix to make Paul's apocalyptic proclamation revelation to analyzing both civilization and the environmental crisis facing contemporary society.

66. Crossan, *Who Killed Jesus? Exposing the Roots of Anti-Semitism in the Gospel Story of the Death of Jesus*. Crossan had dealt with this issue in an earlier article: "Anti-Semitism and the Gospels," (1965). He wrote this article after attending the passion play at Oberammergau, Germany. Upon seeing the play "I did not know very clearly what was wrong, but something had rung terribly false as they [the gospel passion narratives] were enacted as public performance rather than read as private text." Crossan, *A Long Way from Tipperary*, 162.

67. Crossan, *How to Read the Bible and Still Be a Christian*; Crossan, *Is God Violent? An Exploration from Genesis to Revelation*.

2

Gathering the Fragments of a Discourse

CHARLES W. HEDRICK

Crossan's book, *In Fragments: The Aphorisms of Jesus*, is a landmark study of the transmissional history of Jesus' aphorisms. When it was published in 1983, aphorisms were not on the agenda of New Testament scholars. I learned about aphorisms as a distinctive linguistic form regularly used by the historical Jesus (or as Crossan refers to the broader genre, the prose miniature) from Crossan's book. At that time I had been teaching at Missouri State University for three years,[1] and was primarily worrying with projects growing out of my graduate work and only just beginning to dip my toe into historical Jesus studies.[2] I don't recall when Crossan's book came to my attention, but it would likely have been sometime around March of 1985, the first meeting of the Jesus Seminar in Berkeley, California, which I attended. His book was my first introduction to the aphorism and its importance for Jesus studies.

At the time, I wondered why I did not know more than I did about aphorisms. At no point in my graduate education do I recall aphorisms being emphasized, alongside parables, as a second distinctive utterance of the historical Jesus. Looking back today, I am prompted to think that I may well have been mistaken, and my lack of awareness was due to my own oversight. Yet a survey of the Bible dictionaries on my shelf used today in the critical study of the Bible reveals that there was only one

1. Then the school was called Southwest Missouri State University.
2. For example, I was then editing *Nag Hammadi Codices XI, XII, XIII*.

that had a separate entry on aphorism, a second-column eleven-line entry with no bibliography in *The New Interpreter's Dictionary of the Bible* (2006).³ If entries in the standard reference dictionaries used by scholars, students, and the general public may be regarded as summaries of the state of biblical scholarship on a given topic, then the conclusion seems inevitable that the aphorism, as aphorism, had not generally been accorded the same status as parables in historical Jesus studies, and in the early 1980s, New Testament scholarship was generally oblivious to the idea that Jesus was an aphorist. Crossan himself notes that "while very many books have been written on the parabolic or narrative tradition of Jesus' sayings, none has ever been written on the non-narrative or aphoristic tradition alone."⁴ The front flap of the dust jacket to *In Fragments* observes:

> Curiously enough, the greatest aphorist of all times, Jesus, often goes unrecognized as such; and, more importantly, his aphorisms—a major part of his teachings—have been largely overlooked by biblical scholars. Now, *In Fragments* offers the first comprehensive analysis of Jesus' aphorisms as an area of study distinct from but equal in importance to, his parables and dialogues.

The "prose miniature," to which aphorisms belong, is known in literary studies by several terms; each one defined slightly differently: adage, aphorism, apothegm, epigram, fragment, *gnome*, proverb, maxim, sentence (*sententia*), or saying.⁵ The definition of aphorism from C. Hugh Holman's *Handbook to Literature* (3rd ed., 1972), quoted by Crossan, scarcely distinguishes aphorism from other sayings in the prose miniature: "*Aphorism* is 'a concise statement of a principle or precept given in pointed words.'"⁶ Other definitions of aphorism are more or less

---

3. Those lacking a separate entry on aphorism are: *The Interpreter's Dictionary of the Bible* (1962), Its *Supplementary Volume* (1976); *The Anchor Bible Dictionary* (1992), but it has a short section on aphorisms in the entry on the "Teachings of Jesus," citing in part Crossan's book. There is a short single-column entry of eighteen lines on aphorism with a brief bibliography in Tate, *Interpreting the Bible*. There is a much longer entry on aphorism in Aune, *The Westminster Dictionary of New Testament and Early Christian Literature*, 36–41. To be sure, aphorisms are mentioned here and there among various entries, but only one entry that I found elevated the aphorism to a major role in the teaching of Jesus, see n11 below.

4. Crossan, *In Fragments*, viii.

5. Crossan, *In Fragments*, 3.

6. Crossan, *In Fragments*, 3. Holman's brief description had not changed in the

similar. For example: "A terse statement of a truth or dogma; a pithy generalization, which may or may not be witty."[7] "Aphorisms are concise attributed sayings that give pithy expression to an insight about life, the validity of which is generally recognized and approved."[8] "A universal truth expressed in pithy form, a maxim, proverb, or adage."[9] Aphorisms are "short metaphorical sayings of Jesus . . . compact, memorable, and provocative, they are crystallizations of insight" and "invite further insight."[10] Here are two aphorisms as examples, chosen at random from Crossan's study of what he calls fragments:[11]

> Many that are first will be last and the last first. (Mark 10:31)

> It is easier for a camel to go through the eye of a needle
> than for a rich man to enter the kingdom of God. (Mark 10:25)

Crossan briefly tracks the history of scholarship on the aphorism from the sixteenth century (Francis Bacon) into the late twentieth century (James G. Williams).[12] He finds that a great deal of difference exists between a proverb and an aphorism, both of which belong to the genre of the prose miniature. "In terms of content the aphorism's passion for contradiction leads inevitably (even if not always) to paradox 'as its ideal form of action.'"[13] The proverb transmits collective or community wisdom on the basis of ancestral authority, whereas the aphorism communicates a personal insight on the basis of individual authority.[14] The aphorism is, not infrequently, rather perplexing or unclear on its surface prompting auditors/readers to ponder it, for aphorisms trade at times in "overstatement and exaggeration, hyperbole and paradox," and even

---

seventh edition of *Handbook*.

7. Cuddon, *The Penguin Dictionary of Literary Terms*, 48.
8. Aune, *Westminster Dictionary of New Testament*, 36, 40.
9. "Aphorism," in *NIDB*, 1.188–89.
10. Borg, "Jesus, Teaching of," *ABD*, 3.807. Borg lists aphorisms along with parables as "the forms of Jesus' wisdom teaching."
11. Aphorisms are "concise, pointed, pithy sayings of never more than a few sentences." "Thus, the aphoristic form conveys universal truths in a distinctive compressed format." (Both quotations are from the front cover.)
12. Crossan, *In Fragments*, 12–25.
13. Crossan, *In Fragments*, 6, 10.
14. Crossan, *In Fragments*, 20, 25–27.

understatement.[15] Crossan concludes that in the aphorism we have a single genre, which he calls the prose miniature, gnomic discourse.[16]

His study of Jesus' aphorisms draws only on the aphorisms in Mark and Q and their parallels in Matthew and Luke and elsewhere. That leaves to be addressed in future studies other aphorisms attributed to Jesus not found in Matthew and Luke, John, the Gospel of Thomas, and elsewhere in the Jesus tradition. Crossan is not concerned at this point in his study of aphorisms with the question of originality (that is, whether the saying originated with Jesus). But his primary concern is the transmissional process of the aphoristic tradition.[17]

There is a curious exclusion from the list of numbered aphorisms that Crossan finds in Q and Mark, and their parallels. The aphoristic saying, "Let the dead bury their own dead" (Luke 9:60/Matt 8:22), is lacking an aphorism number, like other aphorisms discussed in the book. Its absence jumps-out at readers between numbered aphorisms 53 and 54 on pages 343 and 370 (*In Fragments*), and in his discussion of the aphoristic dialogues in Matt 8:19-22 and Luke 9:57-62.[18] In these dialogues Matthew has two aphorisms (*Foxes Have Holes* and *Let the Dead*) and Luke has three (*Foxes Have Holes, Let the Dead,* and *Looking Back*). Crossan never specifies why he omits the aphorism number for the saying *Let the Dead* (Luke 9:60/Matt 8:22) in his book.[19] He regards Luke 9:59-60 as dialectical dialogue rather than aphoristic dialogue, and agrees with Rudolf Bultmann, whom it struck as "improbable" (*nicht wahrscheinlich*), that the saying ever circulated as a solitary saying.[20] Nevertheless, both in form and content the individual saying in Luke 9:60/Matt 8:22 clearly fits the formal criteria Crossan himself developed for aphorisms (see note 12 above). Granted, it is a Q tradition and only singularly attested, but that does not affect the aphoristic character and style of the saying itself, even if it is integrated into a dialectical dialogue.[21] One must presume that

---

15. Crossan, *In Fragments*, 27.
16. Crossan, *In Fragments*, 20.
17. Crossan, *In Fragments*, ix.
18. Crossan, *In Fragments*, 237-44.

19. For the difference between aphoristic and dialectical traditions, see Crossan, *In Fragments*, 237. In the dialectical tradition "the saying is comprehensible only in terms of its contextual situation" and therefore "it clearly has been conceived together with it" (233, Crossan quoting Bultmann).

20. Crossan, *In Fragments*, 243; Bultmann, *Die Geschichte der Synoptischen Tradition*, 29.

21. The Jesus Seminar regarded the saying in Matt 8:22 as an authentic saying of

Crossan regards this particular saying as an aphorism that entered the Jesus tradition through "exegesis or mimesis."[22]

Aphorisms were spoken by Jesus before groups in the Roman Province of Judea and they were later recalled and repeated with both performance and interpretive variations. "In oral sensibility one speaks or writes an aphoristic *saying*, but one remembers and recalls an aphoristic *core*"[23] by means of the sense and structure of the saying. One does not necessarily remember exact words; the core of the saying is subject to compression or expansion and changes, when repeated. For example, compare the aphorism on *First and Last*: Mark 10:31; Matt 20:16; Luke 13:30; Gos. Thom. 4b.[24]

Aphorisms in the Jesus tradition appear in writing as single sayings and then are gathered in pairs that lead to interpretative interaction and verbal and thematic seepage between them. Finally, they are also gathered into clusters (more than two aphorisms included in the cluster) with similar results. Aphorisms can also be appended as conclusions to other linguistic forms, such as miracles, prayers, parables, dialogues, and stories. The individual aphoristic saying will later be gathered into aphoristic dialogues (for example, Matt 16:1–3; Luke 12:54–56; Gos. Thom. Saying 91)[25] and aphoristic stories (for example, Matt 24:1–2; Mark 13:1–2; Luke 21:5–6).[26]

Crossan's book, *In Fragments* establishes the aphorism, alongside the parable, as a classic literary form of the Jesus tradition. Crossan's study clearly distinguishes between proverb and aphorism and develops a basic terminology for the future study of aphorisms in the Jesus tradition. The book provides a platform for building a database of all the aphorisms of Jesus and for assessing the origins of aphorisms in the Jesus tradition, "of what is from Jesus, what is from exegesis, and what is from mimesis."[27]

While Crossan is not concerned in this study with issues of meaning or the function of an aphorism, it seems fair to pose the question how

---

Jesus (color of pink) at Toronto in 1989 but regarded Luke 9:60 as dubious (color of gray) at Sonoma in 1988, as reported "*The Jesus Seminar: Voting Records*," 260, 276. Nevertheless, both sayings were printed pink in Funk, *The Five Gospels*, 160 and 316.

22. Crossan, *In Fragments*, ix.
23. Crossan, *In Fragments*, 67.
24. Crossan, *In Fragments*, 42–47.
25. Crossan, *In Fragments*, 246–50.
26. Crossan, *In Fragments*, 302–7.
27. Crossan, *In Fragments*, ix.

might aphorisms work on individual auditors or readers? Some insight can be gained in answering this question from the sources that Crossan quotes approvingly or, at least, he passes them by without criticism in *In Fragments'* first chapter "The Aphoristic Genre."[28] These quotations do not construct a generic "prose miniature" but describe the aphorism's characteristics in what I take to be its most distinctive form.[29] These descriptions of aphorism track features that set it apart from other forms of the prose miniatures, particularly the proverb.

According to those sources, selected in studies from the sixteenth century to the twentieth, the aphorism is characterized by certain features that clearly impede one's ability to make sense of it. Aphorisms have the following features according to Crossan. Aphorisms are freshly original and often reflect a bold worldview (4). They are pithy statements that are not self-evident and are offered without proof or explanation (5). Every effective aphorism is characterized by contradiction of those things that appear unshakeable in authority and enjoy unquestioned general recognition (6). Every contradiction leads to paradox, a partial or ostensible contradiction, which originates from a particular experience that elicits an abundant range of insights (10). An aphorism provokes many second thoughts about distinctions that common sense thought firmly established. Its ideal form is paradox (10). Aphorisms are an invitation to ponder (15). They leave human intellect free to toss and turn and apply the aphorism to several purposes and applications (16).

The aphorism moves from the collective wisdom of the common mind to the more intense personal vision of individual challenge (20–21). The fragment pushes to the extreme possibilities latent in the aphorism (22).[30] For example, aphorism's provocative overstatement moves in the direction of the manifesto of the fragment; it does not state sober truths (23). The aphorism gives no defense of its assertion, makes no argument, and gives no explanation (25–26). The aphorism never coincides with the truth; it is either a half-truth or a truth and-a-half (27). Hence it is exaggeration, overstatement, or even understatement designed to provoke thought (27).

28. Crossan, *In Fragments*, 3–36.

29. I make this judgment because many of the sayings of Jesus in Crossan's database (Crossan, *In Fragments*, 369–71) do not reflect such a radical paradoxical character.

30. Crossan has made no distinction between aphorism and fragment, likely because the fragment pushes "to an extreme possibilities latent in the aphorism" (*In Fragments*, 22), which the aphorism also does at its most provocative (22–24).

These characteristics of the aphorism seem designed to frustrate an average auditor/reader in gaining access to what Crossan calls "the wisdom of the future."[31] At the very least they hinder easy communication between aphorist and auditors/readers. Nevertheless, the frustration and difficulty in many cases serve to lead to a serious pondering of the saying. Aphorisms "provoke a different way of seeing by jarring conventional perceptions."[32] Like its companion, the parable, which also frustrates the comprehension of auditors/readers, the aphorism points to plural significations. There are two concepts at work in an engagement with an aphorism: What the aphorist has in mind by the outrageous form of the statement, and what individual readers/auditors may take away from the aphorism. The take-away may not be what the aphorist had in mind, however, for once the aphorist has spoken, what is said belongs to auditors/readers to do with as they may. Meaning is not latent in a text, only the possibility of generating meaning. Meaning is what auditors/readers make out of a text, if they are gracious.[33] In short, aphorisms, like parables, are potentially pluri-significative.

Those who ponder the aphorism seriously will find that it challenges their already settled conclusions by presenting outlandish ideas, prompting a search for previously unthought possibilities. Here are four challenging aphorisms, in its most distinctive form, that probably originated with Jesus:[34]

> Be sly as snakes and simple as pigeons. (Matt 10:16; Gos. Thom. 39b)[35]

The saying is a paradox, "be as crafty as the con man and as gullible as his pigeon." One simply cannot be both sly and simple in the same moment. It leaves one searching for a third way between these two contradictory demands.

> Love your enemies. (Luke 6:27b; Matt 5:43–44)[36]

---

31. Crossan, *In Fragments*, 25.
32. Borg, "Jesus, Teaching of," in *ABD*, 3.807b.
33. As it so happens with parables, Hedrick, *Many Things in Parables*, 45–47.
34. See Funk et al., *The Five Gospels*. The Seminar judged these sayings to be authentic sayings of Jesus.
35. See my discussion of this aphorism in Hedrick, *Many Things in Parables*, vii–ix.
36. See my brief discussion of all four aphorisms in Hedrick, *The Wisdom of Jesus*, 83–90.

The saying puts together two words that are not used together: love and enemy. How does one love an enemy, who has made it a purpose in life to destroy you? Does one love the enemy in the same way and to the same degree that one loves family and close friends? Loving an enemy may very well result in getting someone killed. Hence, we find attempts in the biblical literature to condition what love means where enemies are concerned.[37]

> When someone snatches your outer garment, don't prevent him
> from taking your undergarment as well. (Luke 6:29b; Matt 5:40)

The saying endorses total passive resistance with respect to violence perpetrated on one's person and advocates complicity in the theft. If followed literally, one would be nude, and if one continued acting in this way, one would eventually become completely impoverished.

> Those who go hungry to fill the starving belly of another are
> blessed. (Gos. Thom. 69b)

The saying sets a very high standard for one's altruistic deeds: one feeds those who are starving even when hunger pains begin gnawing at one's own belly. What happens then, when my own resources are exhausted, and I am hungry myself? Must I continue feeding others until I become one of the starving, who depends on the kindness of others?

I yield the final word to Crossan himself:

> Both [proverb and aphorism] are short and pithy formulations. And both resolutely refuse to append any reason, argument, or explanation. But proverb gives no reason since none is necessary; it is a summation of the wisdom of the past. Aphorism, on the other hand, gives no reason because none is possible; it is the formulation of the wisdom of the future. Proverb is the last word, aphorism the first word. And the aphorist is quite content if one gets mixed up and cannot tell aphorism from proverb. But whether in form alone or content alone or in form and content together, the aphorism appears as a voice from Eden, a dictum of dawn.[38]

---

37. Hedrick, *The Wisdom of Jesus*, 88.
38. Crossan, *In Fragments*, 25.

3

Parable as Challenge

DAVID GALSTON

In *The Power of Parable*, very influential on my theology, John Dominic Crossan identifies three interpretive approaches to parables, with the first two being customary or traditional types. We can interpret parables as riddles, examples, or challenges. One interpretive approach is correct and the others false. The real question is what the parable teller intends. For Crossan the historical Jesus intends to use parables as challenges, but in the history of Christian theology, parables have invariably been interpreted as riddles and examples.

I want to focus on these three types of interpretation because, as a child, I heard the first two all the time and, even as a young theologian, I assumed that Jesus parables were mostly about examples and sometimes about riddles. Crossan convinced me that Jesus' parables are challenges, and this realization changed my theology, thus making *The Power of Parable* one of the most influential books in my life.

Interpreting the parables as riddles is one of the earliest approaches to Jesus parables because this is what the gospel writer of Mark does.[1]

---

1. Sometimes interpretating parables as riddles collapses into interpreting parables as allegories. While a riddle tries to decipher codes, or supposed codes, within the story, an allegory tries to replace the story with an entirely different configuration. Mark uses the word riddle (*parabola*) but in the case of the sower parable, Mark sees an allegory. However, riddle is an appropriate term to the extent that Mark sees each incident in the parable as a code to be deciphered. When cracked, the code points away from the everyday to a completely different world. The decoding act points the parable in the opposite direction of the parabolic intention. In this sense, parables as riddles and parables as allegories go hand in hand.

For Mark Jesus speaks in riddles to confound the outside world, but to the inside circle of followers has been given "the secret of the empire of God" (Mark 4:11). To see the parables of Jesus as primarily riddles means that the writer of Mark does not really understand what a parables is. Mark equates parable with riddle and mistakenly reduces interpretation to the act of decoding. In the parable of the sower, Mark's decoding talents are on full display when everyday images become signs for otherworldly meaning. The seeds that the sower scatters on different qualities of soil are not really seeds but the word, and the soil is not really the ground but different types of believers. Some are "good soil" and some are not. Mark uses the "word" as a decoder ring for the story.

Crossan shows how Augustine repeats the riddle approach to parables and sets a path for generations of church leaders to follow. Augustine famously decodes the parable of the Good Samaritan. Various characters and features signify divine realities hidden behind the curtain of the descriptive words. The priest and Levite who pass by the victim beaten and left for dead at the side of the road signify the "Old Testament" and its failure to provide salvation; the Samaritan who binds the wounds of the victim is indicating how God restrains sin. The Samaritan figure is Christ, obviously, and the inn to where the victim is carried to heal is no doubt the church. Augustine shows much more talent and creativity than the gospel writer Mark, but like Mark, Augustine does not really hear the parable.

Thanks to Augustine and others (Origen, for example), a riddle is a popular church way to interpret a Jesus parable. With a riddle, an interpreter needs to search for hidden signs and meanings inside the mundane story that point to a transcendental outside story. To decode the parable properly an interpreter must ascend to its true spiritual reality. The problem with the riddle approach to parables is that the theologians or the preachers must use church "kerygma" to see the hidden meaning. Jesus' parables are then forced to confess Christian dogma, which is entirely foreign not only to the parables themselves but to Jesus as a first century Jewish peasant. To be sure, in a parable something else is going on besides the literal actions of the narrative. A parable about a woman hiding leaven in three measures of flour is not about making bread, but it is wrong to exit the parable's actions to draw upon a later theology. Parables as riddles needing decoding, though common among theologians in the Christian tradition, is wrong headed.

The other equally common and equally wrong way to interpret a Jesus parable is to suppose the parable is an example. Reading parables as examples is somewhat natural because, even as children, we can understand what an example intends. It is a good thing to forgive other people and to offer a second chance. This is a significant lesson that parents will teach children. It is empowering to believe that when you make a mistake, you can learn something and try again. The precedent in the church for reading parables mainly as examples of instruction is the gift of the gospel writer Luke. In Luke, most parables serve as examples. The Prodigal Son is the story of a loser who comes home to find unexpected forgiveness, and this indicates how God forgives a sinner. The woman who loses a coin and seeks diligently to find it exemplifies the way God seeks out lost sinners and celebrates when they are found. The church, we could say, has made a living using parables as examples of what God teaches and how God expects us to act. As a preacher, I spent years using parables as examples to drive home a point. Nevertheless, a Jesus parable is not an illustration, and using Jesus parables to exemplify gospel living is another form of not hearing Jesus.

To hear a Jesus parable is to hear what Jesus intends, which point Crossan makes clear. The difficulty, of course, is to answer the question about what is intended. Crossan states that a Jesus parable is a challenge parable, and to illuminate this insight he turns with great effectiveness to the background of the Jewish wisdom tradition. The parables of Jesus belong to the genre of wisdom and are understood most appropriately as socio-political challenges that emerge from this tradition.

A challenge parable holds a prophetic edge that turns the story from everyday descriptions into political commentary. The shock of a parable lies not in the described reality but in the way reality is opened to a new horizon. The parable enters into the way things are, the way things are expected to be, and then distorts the picture. Crossan finds a key demonstration of a challenge in the story of Ruth.

In church settings, Ruth is regularly interpreted as an example parable that portrays faith to the God of Israel, but this reading misses the challenge. Ruth was a Moabite, but today that means little to the reader. More significantly, it seems to most, is that Ruth trusted her mother-in-law's God. Yet, to center Ruth's act of trust is to misidentify her and therefore to mishear what is really going on.

In Deuteronomy, Moabites are grouped with Ammonites.

> No Ammonite or Moabite shall be admitted to the assembly of the Lord. Even to the tenth generation, none of their descendants shall be admitted to the assembly of the Lord, because they did not meet you with food and water on your journey out of Egypt. (Deut 23:3–4a)

The story's literary context is the post-exilic community listening to Ezra reading the above from the Torah and decreeing that Jewish men, who remained in Israel through the exilic period, must divorce their gentile wives to re-constitute the dominance of Jewish families in the land. Probably this decree was often ignored, but it nevertheless remains recorded both in Ezra (10:19) and Nehemiah, "When the people heard the law (about Ammonites and Moabites), they separated from Israel all those of foreign descent" (Neh 13:1–2). The story of Ruth challenges customary religious prejudice with the direct claim that no less than king David, the most revered of all of Israel's kings, was the grandson of a cursed Moabite. Crossan asks his reader to "think of the book of Ruth as an example parable with a scorpion sting in its tail that turned it into a challenge parable."[2] When Ruth is taken only as an example, the story fails to shake the foundations of faith but rather merely encourages a blind faith. The poverty of misinterpreting a Jesus parable is evident in the impoverished reading of Ruth as an exemplary biblical figure.

While Crossan offers several Jesus parables to consider, I will focus on the Good Samaritan. The Samaritan parable is almost always interpreted as an example. The gospel writer Luke seems incapable of imagining other options.[3] For Luke, the story of the Samaritan answers the question, who is my neighbor? But when the parable is reframed as a challenge, the content of the story changes what we have traditionally heard. The Samaritan is not just a nice guy who does a good neighborly deed. In the proper historical context, the Samaritan is the enemy of the Jewish victim, whom he comes across lying in the ditch on the road to Jericho. The best representatives of the Jewish tradition, the people who know the Torah inside out, pass by the helpless and vulnerable body lying there before their eyes. Torah gives no excuse for passing by someone in

---

2. Crossan, *The Power of Parable*, 74.

3. Luke, almost invariably, takes parables as example stories. The lost coin is about how God searches for lost sinners, and the workers in the vineyard is about how God is generous. These parables can work that way. There is nothing wrong with searching for lost things or being generous; however, the challenge goes unheard when parables are reduced to demonstrations.

need; indeed. "Love your neighbor as yourself" (Lev 19:18) is a guiding ethical principle for the later emphasis on *mitzvot* (good deeds). The priest and Levite know the right thing but still do nothing.

Along comes a Samaritan who has every reason to hate the victim at the side of the road because, during the Hasmonean period under the leadership of John Hyrcanus, the Jews destroyed the sacred Samaritan temple at Mount Gerizim. To the Samaritans, Shechem, not Jerusalem, was God's holy city, and they, not the Jews, were God's chosen people. The violence and intolerance between Jews and Samaritans was the cultural norm. There is no reason, in the Jesus parable, to expect a Samaritan to stop and care for a Jew. In fact, we would not be surprised if the Samaritan were to stop and finish the job.

The parable becomes an embarrassment and a challenge for its original audience. After all, the Samaritans had the wrong location for the temple, the wrong holy city, and the wrong Torah. How can a Samaritan of no distinction whatever perform the Torah better than our priests and Levites? We can imagine Jesus being run out of town; we can hear the likely reaction, "Well, if you like Samaritans so much, why don't you go live with them!" The parable challenges us to break customary religious prejudice, to see our common humanity before we practice our divided religious confessions.

Crossan brings home the challenge of the Samaritan parable in ways rarely heard inside the walls of Christian churches. He states that the parable "challenges listeners to think long and hard about their social prejudices, their cultural presumptions, and, yes, even their most sacred religious traditions."[4] A challenge parable is a confrontation with our customary expectations, and if the confrontation does not occur, then both the parable and the hearer fail to hit the mark.

The long history of the church, including the gospel writers, is a sad history of misinterpreting Jesus' parables. The misinterpretations render the parables silent because the intention goes unnoticed. Hearing a parable does require some capacity, on the part of the listener, to think deeply, question sincerely, and admit honestly to prejudices and customary beliefs. Since people rarely undertake such critical self-examination, so rarely is the intention of a Jesus parable understood.

Crossan is not alone in seeing parables as challenges rather than as ethical teachings or mysterious riddles, but he is one of the most effective

---

4. Crossan, *The Power of Parable*, 62.

at making this point. Due to Crossan, I began to understand how I had misheard Jesus and, as a consequence, I was another person engaged in the practice of silencing Jesus. I am grateful to Crossan for waking me up to how a parable works, seeing the artistry involved, and allowing myself to be stung by the scorpion's tail. After Crossan, I immersed myself in other writers who could likewise "hear the parable," and I could ask, with members of the Jesus Seminar, what the world would be like, or at least the Christian tradition, if the historical Jesus was taken seriously.

The challenging voice of the historical Jesus is a challenge to the church and Christian scholarship alike. The challenge is to let Jesus speak and to prevent his provocative parables from slipping out of their disruptive intentions and falling into comfortable examples. This makes following Jesus, rather than being a Christian, a tall order for the future of the tradition, and there can be thankfulness voiced for scholars like John Dominic Crossan who attempt, and who dare, to show the way.

4

Breaking Mirrors of Jesus in Africa

GLENNA S. JACKSON

John Dominic Crossan was sitting in my Towers Hall office at Otterbein University awaiting his time to lecture. As he glanced through my bookshelf—I had nearly all his books—he asked about my parables research on the continent of Africa. As we talked, he said, "What a treasure trove of information you have." And that prompted a valuable conversation about the difference between *colonizing* other cultures' stories and insights and *sharing* other cultures' narratives and understandings. Crossan asked about my method. I answered that my basic technique was to listen and ask questions, including, "Could I/Should I talk or write about my visits and conversations with you?" All my respondents have enthusiastically supported my sharing with the rest of the world. As an example, at the end of my Fall 2000 semester of teaching a class on the Parables at Africa University in Mutare, Zimbabwe, the students shared with me two of their thoughts about our time together—a beginning and an end: 1.) They had questioned each other at the beginning of the semester: why was Prof. Jackson there because I had begun the class with, "I'm here to learn from you . . ." Jean Ntahoturi[1] summed up their early collective thoughts from the get-go with, "If you didn't already know everything, then why were you here to teach?" The fourth-year students, who were already serving churches, were accustomed to lectures, followed by a

---

1. The Rev. Ntahoturi is from Burundi, an ordained United Methodist Church pastor, and currently the Senior Grants Manager, Education Cannot Wait—Komezawige Program [in Burundi].

minute for questions, followed by absolute answers—no discussions, i.e., colonialism in the classroom.[2] 2.) On the last day of class, students thanked me for letting them know that they were contributing unique and exceptional insights to the world's understandings of Jesus' teachings and culture, and was I going to include them in presentations, teaching at Otterbein and my writing? I gave them a huge thumbs up! And then they challenged me, "OK, we are beginning to understand the importance of the historical Jesus, but what are we going to preach on Easter Sunday?!"

Incidentally, the texts I chose for the Parables Class were Westar's *The Sayings of Jesus*, *The Acts of Jesus*, and *Remedial Christianity*.[3] Because of Zimbabwe's Customs regulations, we did not get the books until the fifth week of class. Up to that point, we had been working from our Bibles only. The students were so excited to have their own "library" that they stayed up all night reading together and, to their horror, decided they needed to get rid of me! When I arrived at class the next morning, they were not standing up as usual, no customary handshake, and they did not greet me in Shona, *mangwanani akanaka* (Good Morning), but with absolute silence. All eyes were on Dzobo, spokesperson for the class.[4] I sat down. Finally Dzobo stood up and said, "Prof, we learned to respect you and to love you, but then you gave us these books." He sat down, my heart dropped to the floor and I thought, "Why do I make things so difficult?" but I said, "OK, we've got work to do. Get out your books." Twenty-four years later, I found out from Dzobo last spring that during their night of reading and scheming for my demise, he reminded his student colleagues that I would be in charge of their final grades plus I brought them chocolate every day! By the end of the semester, students were saying things like, "I can't believe Jesus said that"; "there's no way that should be colored pink." OK, "Get out your books. We have more work to do." And Tayengo[5] asked, "Can we eat the brownies now?"

---

2. Cf. Mary Ann Beavis, "Encountering the Parables," 252–54. for her evaluation of my experiential method for decolonizing the classroom.

3. Funk et al., ed., *The Five Gospels*; Funk et al., *The Acts of Jesus*; Laughlin and Jackson, *Remedial Christianity*.

4. The Rev. Dr. Samuel Dzobo now serves a traditionally black United Methodist Church in Nashville and is also the District Associate of the Holston Conference in Tennessee. He divides his time between the United States and Zimbabwe. He has been imprisoned for preaching social justice.

5. The Rev. Albano Tayengo, from Angola, is the senior pastor at Oak Haven United Methodist Church in Irving, Texas.

I went back to my faculty flat that fateful evening and got out Crossan's *In Parables: The Challenge of the Historical Jesus* (1973) to get ideas for asking the right questions that would free up African students who had been, or whose parents had been, "taught" by Western missionaries with Western misinformation and Western dogmatic prescriptions of Jesus' teachings. My gut told me that rural Africans knew more about life two thousand years ago than we Westerners could ever possibly hope to learn and the worst part was that we are not even aware that we do not know what we do not know.[6] Crossan's Preface[7] had most of what I needed, four understandings about the parables:

> 1) "Special linguisticality of Jesus' message . . . in parables: indeed [Jesus] said nothing to [his followers] without a parable."

> 2) "Reinterpretation of Jesus' parabolic intention created by the primitive church . . . [Jesus' followers got the insider's understanding of God (think 'inside joke') and the outsiders, in turn, got the insiders' understanding of] Jesus as the Parable of God."

And, of course, Crossan's first two requirements for parables studies segued into class discussions about ancient languages and 2,000 years of translations and interpretations.[8]

> 3) "Parables are only to be understood from inside their own world."

I agree with that premise and, therefore, argue that people living in poverty in today's world who lack technology, plumbing and clean water, electricity and the ability to flip a switch to change their home climate, regular paychecks, food security, and literacy can understand the parables better than those of us who have access to daily nutrition and thousands of scholarly works about Jesus. Indeed, it was my first time on

---

6. Cf. Jackson, "Learning from Africans," 9–11. Cf. also Häkkinen, *The Gospel of the Poor*, for his parallel experiences teaching and researching in poor areas of Middle Eastern countries.

7. Crossan, *In Parables*, vii–x.

8. I told The Rev. Dr. Philemon Chikafu about the class conversation and asked how he would have handled it. (He was the Chaplain and taught Hebrew Bible classes at Africa University. He died of COVID along with several other AU personnel because ventilators were not available.) He assured me that it was "about time students were exposed to the historical Jesus." He himself taught Hebrew Bible from a minimalist point of view (The Copenhagen School), but students were not so invested in the Old Testament, so did not complain.

the continent of Africa and getting to know students at Africa University and having conversations with people walking the roads as I biked every evening on the hills with older men pushing my bike to the top that I understood Jesus' saying, "Congratulations you poor! God's domain belongs to you" (Luke 6:20). They know how to survive and are the most generous of anyone I know—the less resources, the more generosity.[9]

4) "[All of] reality is parabolic."

The following understanding of the Parable of the Fig Tree (Luke 13:6–9) is a mirror of the parabolic reality of rural Zimbabwe, written by Sophirina Sign[10] in the Parables Class:

> Barrenness in our context is associated with women. Fig trees in our country are wild trees. Farmers do not grow fig trees. The trees just grow by themselves in the bush. If a woman is married she is expected to bear children. There is this concept that those with many children are the richest people. Every woman is greatly honored by the society if she bears fruits. If she fails to do so, she is regarded a cursed woman. For that reason two things are done, either of, one: the in-laws ask their son to divorce [and] marry another woman whose womb is prepared to bear fruit. Or, if the woman is to remain with her husband's family, her parents will be asked to provide a wife to the husband so that she bears offspring on behalf of the aunt or sister. Barrenness in our society is not tolerated. The main purpose of marriage is to produce children for the family. As soon as the two get married, results have to be shown. Without procreation a woman is regarded as useless within the society.[11]

---

9. Thanks to our Jesus Seminar colleague, Daryl Schmidt, we have a better understanding of the beatitudes (Matt 5:1–12/Luke 6:20–26/Thom 54; 68–69). The Greek term *makarios* that is usually translated as "blessed" has closer resonance with a translation of "congratulations." Cf. *The Five Gospels*, 292. Coincidentally, as I was looking up Daryl's article, "Fundamentally Pluralistic," I found Crossan's *Jesus* listed as the only note with Daryl writing, "When [students] get to Crossan's *Jesus: A Revolutionary Biography* at the end of the semester, they often come out fighting. I have learned to wear my verbal flak jacket for the last few sessions."

10. The Rev. Sign was the only female in the Parables Class and was often teased by her male colleagues that her *lobola* (bride price) would be worth more goats if she were to get her college degree. She chose to remain single but always has at least fourteen children living in her home. They are all orphaned children of relatives and friends because of AIDS or just sheer poverty. She is an ordained United Methodist pastor and serves the Zimbabwe East Annual Conference as the Connectional Ministerial Director and is also an adjunct lecturer at Africa University.

11. For more African interpretations of the Fig Tree, cf. Jackson, "Twenty Years of

Western commentaries tend to put this parable in a theological context of repentance, crisis, eschatology, exaggerated hope, blessing or curse and judgment, temple longevity, and so on.[12] African commentaries tend to be practical and contemporary. Crossan is close to Sign's reflection of the Fig Tree as her reality: "In Luke 13:6–9 the tree is being given one last chance to produce fruit else it will be cut down." Crossan includes this parable in "the parables of action."[13]

Crossan finishes his Preface with questions: "What is it that breaks our mirrors [of Jesus]? What can we experience in the sound of their breaking glass and what can we glimpse in the cracks of their shattering?"

What my students needed was for their mirrors of a Westernized Jesus to crack and, ironically, what I needed was for my students to break my own Westernized mirrors.[14] We experienced a lot of broken glass that semester!

Once we got some of the shattered mirrors swept up, students began reading the parables with no slate. I said, "Your assignments this semester will be to write your understanding of the parable(s) with your home village and family in mind—how would you make sense of this parable in your own culture? How are you going to preach this particular parable?" This Parables class of eight students represented four different African countries with different "official" languages (English, Portuguese, and French) and many mother tongues. I asked Julio Pinto, from Angola, and Natal from Mozambique how they studied for class and did their homework. They both replied that they first translated their English lecture notes into Portuguese, Portuguese into one of their mother tongues, then wrote their assignments in one of their mother tongues, translated them into Portuguese, and then into English.[15] The students' own experi-

Experiencing the Parables in Africa," 235–37.

12. Cf., for example, Meier, *A Marginal Jew*, 2:985; Funk et al., eds., *The Five Gospels*, 345. For a comprehensive study of The Fig Tree, cf. Scott, *Hear Then the Parable*, 331–42.

13. Crossan, *In Parables*, 82.

14. I was quite familiar with poverty. One set of grandparents lived in a poor village in southwestern Wisconsin—no indoor plumbing, unstable electricity, had to sell their horse and lived without transportation the remainder of their lives. And true to form, they were unbelievably generous with what little they did have. We grandchildren did not realize they were living in poverty until we became adults because that was our favorite place to be! Cf. Jackson, "From Hippo to Hippos."

15. Pinto died the fourth week of class. He was diagnosed with Hepatitis C and was turned down by two hospitals because he had no money. He had not told anyone that he was sick. A third hospital accepted him, but it was too late.

ences with multiple languages, ironically, shattered the mirror of biblical inerrancy.

And so, with Crossan's influence and African students' input, I developed a method called Framing the Picture with the Experiential. Crossan emphasizes the importance of watching for the interface of parable and history and uses the Passion Play at Oberammergau as an example of distinguishing the difference between the two. It was his personal experience of watching the play that brought it into focus for him.[16] It was my personal experience on the continent of Africa that gave me better frames for the pictures of life in which I had the honor of being included and are better mirrors of first-century life than our Western cultures. My method is simple and very much like any scientific method: ask questions, do traditional research, and substitute experimentation with the experiential, i.e., experience as much as possible contemporary parallel contexts from all of human history. Sakari Häkkinen agrees and makes the following parallel challenge: "[We must] think about our individual and societal attitudes toward the poor . . . and begin to see the gospel text through the eyes of the poor and oppressed. For as long as we see the poor only as subjects for whom to preach the good news, we support the problem of poverty in the world."[17]

For example, the traditional frame for the parable of the "Good" Samaritan (Luke 10:29–37) is focused on the Samaritan—how an enemy of Israel helped a first-century Judean is indeed a likely prescriptive frame. The conclusion becomes that the followers of Jesus should help anyone in need.[18] As a church organist for fifty-five years, I never once heard a sermon that did not admonish us to be like the "Good Samaritan" —and there is nothing wrong with that. The following is Ntahoturi's different and equally important understanding of the parable:

> In 1995, I was shopping in the suburb of Bujumbura [capital city of Burundi] when I heard gunfire nearby. Two soldiers were shot dead. The rebels were around. In a confused situation, I ran away in the hills. I was not alone. When we began to climb the hills, one mother realized that her five-year-old son was not with her. She was so disturbed. She decided to go back to look for him. We tried to persuade her not to go back. She refused.

---

16. Crossan, *The Power of Parable*, 1–3.
17. Häkkinen, *The Gospel of the Poor*, 5. Cf. also Jackson, "Twenty Years," 227–31.
18. Cf. Crossan, *In Parables*, 55–64, for a history of interpretation and form analysis.

"I have to go to look for my son; even if I am to die today, there is no option," she said. When she was moving around, the child saw his mother very far away. He was in rebels' hands. He started crying. The rebels suddenly saw the mother and called her to come and take the child. First, she was afraid, but she got courage, and she approached them, took the child, and ran back into the hills unharmed.[19]

According to Ntahoturi, one should frame this parable with the victim front and center in the picture rather than with the so-called good Samaritan because help comes from the most unexpected source, in this case, a soldier from the enemy tribe. Imagine a framed picture with the mother and small boy running into the Rwandan, Ugandan, or Burundian hills for safety as the focus and the enemy soldier in the background giving them a thumbs up! That prescription, 'Take help from the enemy' is really a question, 'Who are you willing to take help from—an enemy perhaps?' The Jesus Seminar includes this interpretation, but, of course, Ntahoturi had not been exposed to that; he simply knew it from his own experience.[20]

Crossan concludes, "There is nothing wrong with [differing] uses of the same parable, but they [can be] quite different ones . . . and may be due to [the gospel writers] and not Jesus. How sure can we be, then, that it was an example parable, let alone a model for all of the parables of Jesus?"[21] Crossan used three parables in Luke (Lost Sheep, Lost Coin, and Lost Son) for his argument and I observe the same in Luke's Parable of the Samaritan. One might identify with the enemy Samaritan hero or as the Judean victim—it is all about the mirror into which one is looking.

In a recent book chapter, my first sentence was, "Bob Funk was yelling at the top of his lungs and pounding on the dashboard of the pickup truck he was driving as we were on our way to Sonoma State University in California to give a lecture: 'It's obvious . . . that you've never been to Israel and probably don't even know any Jews!' I could dismiss the second

---

19. I first published this story in Jackson, "The Jesus Seminar in Africa." Uganda and Burundi were also experiencing genocide along with the more infamous Rwanda Genocide of 1994. Similar activity continues in Burundi even though this story is nearly twenty-five years old and is rarely reported in international news. Ntahoturi has also been arrested for taking an unpopular stance on social justice and has had his voting rights taken from him in the United Methodist Church hierarchy. He is still fighting in court.

20. Funk et al., eds., *The Five Gospels*, 323–24.

21. Crossan, *The Power of Parable*, 41.

part of his accusation because it wasn't true, but the first was—and served as a dramatic reminder of the need for the real thing, the experiential!"[22] So, with Otterbein University's support, I traveled to the Middle East and the continent of Africa many times—goaded and encouraged by the two New Testament giants of the twentieth and twenty-first centuries—John Dominic Crossan and Robert W. Funk. When I look into a mirror, both scholars are sitting on my shoulders. Thanks to Prof. Crossan, Africa University students made it through the Parables Class and are still serving the church. Crossan's academic importance is illustrated in his writings, lectures, and presentations and his legacy for me will be his personal influence.

---

22. Jackson, "Twenty Years," 222.

5

The Dark Interval
An Anniversary Ode

GUERRIC DEBONA, OSB

It's been fifty years now since the publication of a book on parables that became very important to me and my generation of theological students. John Dominic Crossan's *The Dark Interval: Towards a Theology of Story* (1975) posed an urgent invitation to keep company with dangerous storytellers—with Jesus at the top of the list. Now Crossan's book was hardly the first fine study of parables to cross the Rubicon and enter new literary terrain. Nevertheless, *The Dark Interval* helped enlighten a path for many of us to study the parable as story from the *inside*. As Crossan defines it, "in the parable the excitement of transcendental experience is found only at the edge of language and the limit of story and that the only way to find that excitement is to test those edges and those limits."[1]

Crossan's by now well-known "theology of limit" gave us the tools "to explore this limitation which is posed by the inevitability of life within story, of existence in this story or that but always in some story."[2] Ironically, Crossan's innovation hinted at the bifurcation afoot in the mid-1970s between biblical scholarship and praxis. While Crossan and other scholars were mining a fascinating hermeneutic in the historical Jesus, the preaching at worship across many confessions voiced a largely predictable, ubiquitously jejune interpretation of parables at the pulpit that

---

1. Crossan, *The Dark Interval*, 29.
2. Crossan, *The Dark Interval*, 2.

was mostly lifeless and, sadly, pointless. There are only so many readings of parables as derivative allegories or, worse yet, moral-example stories before preaching becomes a clichéd parody of Jesus's own storytelling. How many times would we have to sit through yet another reading of the Parable of the Talents as an ideal model of good Christian behavior with a deductive paradigm of "time, treasure and talent?" Weren't these well-intentioned preachers amassing a discourse verging on mythological Christianity? (Answer: yes). The so called New Homiletic was on the way, but not yet quite aligned with understanding the subversive tactics of the parables of the historical Jesus.

I must add that my own reading of American culture during the Reagan "Star War" years when I was a seminary student was frighteningly close to mythology as well, and rapidly eclipsing the imaginative cultural artifacts of the 1960s and 70s. During the years of the "New Hollywood," for instance, American film culture had already given us subversive, parabolic structures that proposed their own "dark intervals" of story, asking us, *teasing us* away from our national mythology into a world of fictions that were "meant to change, not reassure us."[3] Unfortunately, American cinema's disruptive film narratives of the so-called American New Wave (1967–1980), such as Robert Altman's *M*A*S*H* (1970), Roman Polanski's *Chinatown* (1974), and Martin Scorsese's *Taxi Driver* (1976) would suffer more or less the same fate that the parables of the historical Jesus encountered in Sunday proclamation: parables in the hands of the religious status quo, deploying the stories of Jesus not to *undermine* the world but to *underline* its established conventions and typology (myth) or defend its traditional boundaries (apologue). On the other hand, Crossan draws from his Irish roots to illustrate the culturally transgressive character of the parable. Imagine an IRA terrorist as the Good Samaritan. This cultural redeployment of the parable remains hardly reassuring but goes further: it imagines a unnerving tactic that opens up a future portal of potential change to the hearer. When are we going to erase the border between northern and southern Ireland? When the enemy becomes the neighbor.

I appreciate how Crossan situates the parable at the end of an arc of literary expressions, forming a polar opposite with myth at the other end of this spectrum. Demonstrating the place of the parable across an axis—myth, apologue, action, satire and parable—forms a convenient way to

---

3. Crossan, *The Dark Interval*, 39.

understand what, precisely, is at stake with the parable's hermeneutic function and its effect on the listener. But the huge distance between myth and parable reminds me of the importance placed on historical-critical methodology in the study of this literary subgenre and in the context of the historical Jesus. Absent a historical context, the parable slides down the axis into the comforting arms of myth, from which the parable is inverted, "deliberately calculated to show the limitations of myth, to shatter the world so that its relativity becomes apparent."[4] Unlike myth's reassuring effect, the parable harbors the boundaries of the "game," since the very testing of the parable's linguistic edges offers an experience of transcendence as an exciting conduit to heuristic literacy and discovery. That "play" inside the contours of story is what I found was missing from traditional approaches to parables and so necessary to parabolic cultural subversion and understanding the force of Jesus's preaching of the Kingdom. The tensive language of metaphor becomes the instrument of social and psychological change.

As I enthusiastically recall it, studying theology in the 1980s was largely the site of a lot of excitement, with the discourse on parable as a cornerstone; its practice gave me an opportunity to live inside another story, maybe even stand apart from the American culture's hegemonic narrative by studying and writing theology through something like "parabolic deeds." I certainly benefited from Bernard Brandon Scott's seminar at St. Meinrad on the parables and other takes on Jesus as a dangerous storyteller from a variety of interpreters. When I began teaching homiletics full time over twenty-five years ago, my preferred pedagogical method was informed by inductive, narrative preaching, such as the New Homiletic proposed by David J. Randolph and Fred Craddock's *As One Without Authority*, or David Buttrick's phenomenological reading of parables as metaphorical agents for social change. That list widened over the years when homiletics would become invigorated by biblical criticism of the first order, much of which focused on the parables of Jesus. This impressive list could go on and on, much of which could trace itself to *The Dark Interval* among other imaginative texts. Indeed, emergent and varied approaches to preaching had one thing in common for me: a movement away from instructional language as an "actional" model towards one that faces the hearer with a "transactional" encounter, or a preaching that finds its authority not in a mythical, didactic structure

---

4. Crossan, *The Dark Interval*, 42.

but places the historical Jesus at the center of the homiletic text. Actional communication can never be parabolic because its very nature is to deliver a message from a privileged source and, in Crossan's language, "exclude the authentic experience of mystery."[5] On the other hand, transactional communication invites the subversive world of parable because such language finds its destiny in changing the hearer as a substantial conversation partner, "to shatter the structural security of the hearer's world," or "to render possible the kingdom of God, the act of appropriation in which God touches the human heart and consciousness is brought to final genuflection."[6]

I can only imagine more broadly that Crossan's theology of story must have been extravagantly revitalizing for folks when it was released five decades ago; more significantly, it opened more than one door of Jesus as a radical interpreter of the Kingdom of God. Even if his critical (structuralist) lens may be a bit dated now, as Robert Funk points out in the revised 1988 edition of the text, *The Dark Interval* performed a valuable summation of where parable might exercise its creative energy in an understanding of the historical Jesus as a storyteller and witness to the Kingdom of God. His book was also a study of how difficult it is to receive a story of radical cultural (and religious) subversion. And then again, how easy it is to Disneyfy or bourgeoisify the challenge of living inside the sharp edges of a parabolic idiom, even when it came to the formation of the Gospels themselves. A case in point is Crossan's extended analysis of parable of The Great Feast, the revision of which did not even have to wait for the dulling emphasis of middle class, a domesticated Christianity to defang its bite; it happened already in the early stages of the formation of the canonical and non-canonical Gospels. The slippage of history and signification serve as an examples of "a classic case of the tradition's change of a parable of Jesus into an example-story and an allegory of the history of salvation."[7] So two canonical Gospels (Matt 22:1–4 and Luke 14:16–24) redact the parable as well as The Gospel of Thomas (in logion 64) and, consequently, Crossan finds that Matthew has allowed the Parable of the Evil Husbandmen to "infiltrate" a "more domestic story of the Great Feast" and allegorized the parable, while Luke and Thomas moralized it.[8] There was a reason a lot of the patristic authors like Augustine

---

5. Crossan, *The Dark Interval*, 105.
6. Crossan, *The Dark Interval*, 101.
7. Crossan, *The Dark Interval* 92.
8. Crossan, *The Dark Interval*, 96.

and John Chrysostom loved Matthew's Gospel; it was a text made for allegory.

I think that Crossan included some helpful "updating" of his early book, *In Parables: The Challenge of the Historical Jesus* (1973), by including some examples in *The Dark Interval* to demonstrate the way "myth proposes, parable disposes," outside the boundaries of the New Testament. In the Hebrew Bible, the books of Ruth and Jonah "do not intend to negate or destroy these magnificent traditions, but they do intend to remind Israel about the difference between the traditions of God and the God of the traditions."[9] The destabilization is itself the "game" that results in a parable of Boaz subverting a legal system to marry Ruth which ultimately builds a lineage to David. Then again, the call of the prophet Jonah which turns out to defy the covenant on which that election was based undermines not only the call but the mysterious voice of the one who called. It was also wise, I think, for Crossan to include Kafka and Borges as paradigmatic modern examples of parables that expose gaps in stories which, Crossan rightly suspects, "is also the start of religious experience."[10] And yet: what if this dark interval itself was to be problematized? So begins the parabolic dark interval in "Before the Law" in which religious experience—or maybe the very predictability and control of "transcendence"—turns out to be "if life were like a door intended for you alone but through which you could not enter."[11] In some sense, Borges fits the "parabler" best for Crossan's reading, since a story like "The Circular Ruins" faces us with the labyrinth of dreams, of a human dreaming into being another human, only to discover that he himself was conjured into dreamscape by someone else. Borges himself wrote about the limits of story and language itself; this "game" remains so crucial to Crossan's understanding of the parable's dynamics.

In retrospect, I might hazard an educated guess that in 1975 *The Dark Interval* lands somewhere between the last gasp of literary modernism and the emergence of postmodernity. The high modernists like T.S. Eliot, Wallace Stevens, and William Carlos William whom Crossan is fond of quoting labored to find the experience of transcendence in "the heart of darkness." At the same time, however, perhaps Crossan himself sensed that "transcendence" itself has its limits—the high modernist movement that searched for sublimity in the shadows would be replaced

---

9. Crossan, *The Dark Interval*, 52.
10. Crossan, *The Dark Interval*, 60.
11. Crossan, *The Dark Interval*, 63.

by the funhouse, pastiche and an ironic self-conscious poetic. It is easy to see here that the modern parables of Kafka and Borges become suitable onramps for the illusive highway of postmodernity or that, there is only story, and "that means there is only carefully disciplined dreaming."[12] My gratitude goes to Crossan, the literary visionary of the dynamics of story, who teased out the significance of the historical Jesus to those parabolic narratives and the *Dark Interval* itself as something like a blueprint for what was waiting to be born: the "megaparable."

---

12. Crossan, *The Dark Interval*, 67.

PART TWO
The Historical Jesus

6

An Interview with John Dominic Crossan

ROBERT J. MILLER

During the years when the Jesus Seminar was at its work (1985–1998), Crossan was frequently in the public's eye in his role as the Seminar's co-chair. The following interview provides us with an in-depth look at his participation in the Seminar and his meticulous study of the historical Jesus.

Robert Miller: How did you learn about the Jesus Seminar and how did you become its cochair with Bob Funk?

Dominic Crossan: Please allow me to answer with some necessary backstory to Bob Funk's creation of the Jesus Seminar in 1985 and to his *later* asking me to be its cochair with him. I was never, as the media often says, the Seminar's *cofounder* but simply, at Bob's invitation, its *cochair*. (In summary: *Bob*: "Would you be the cochair?" *Dom*: "Does that mean I'll have to do administrative work?" *Bob*: "No, I just want your name." *Dom*: You got it.")

I had come up exclusively through the Roman Catholic tradition as a monastic priest. My doctorate (1959) was from Ireland's national seminary and pontifical university at St. Patrick's College, Maynooth, County Kildare. Then I had two two-year diplomas, one in exegesis from the Jesuit priests at the Pontifical Biblical Institute in Rome (1959-61), and another from the Dominican priests at the École biblique et archéologique française in Jerusalem (1965-67). In other words, I received an exclusively Roman Catholic grad and post-grad education.

I had a fabulous education with my greatest *courses* not as classes but—in the archaic sense of that word—as travels all over Europe and the Middle East. In 1965-67, for example, you could take a boat easily and safely across the Persian Gulf from Iran to Iraq and similarly a taxi across Turkey from Antakya to Antalya. But, then, in August of 1968 I ran full tilt not into biblical but into papal fundamentalism. I argued on National Public Radio that Pope Paul VI was simply wrong in condemning condoms and all forms of artificial contraception as mortal sins in his recent encyclical *Humanae Vitae.*

When the ecclesiastical dust settled by the fall of 1969, I was an ex-monk and an ex-priest but happily an associate professor at DePaul University in Chicago. In terms of scholarly career, however, I had fallen between two worlds: I was well known in the Catholic tradition and the Catholic Biblical Association (CBA)—which I had joined in 1962—but not in the Protestant tradition and the Society of Biblical Literature (SBL)—although I had joined it in 1964.

Within that past situation, I compare the different fate of two simultaneous articles from 1970 to show—finally—what all that autobiography has to do with Bob Funk, the Jesus Seminar, and your question, Bob.

In 1970, I sent an article to the *Catholic Biblical Quarterly* and got no response for six months. I contacted the editor, who told me it had been rejected and that he thought he had already informed me. I took the article from its *CBQ* envelope and put it in another one to an international scholarly journal that published it unchanged.[1]

That article on Jesus' parables changed everything for me by moving my focus from the CBA—whose editors I no longer trusted—to the SBL, where my involvement was sponsored and promoted by both Norman Perrin, the SBL President in 1973, and especially by Bob Funk, SBL Executive Secretary in 1968-74, and President in 1975.

Bob proposed a Parables Seminar to the SBL and made me its chair (1972-76). He also created the journal *Semeia: An Experimental Journal for Biblical Criticism* as a complement to the *Journal of Biblical Literature.* Bob put me on its editorial board (1973-81), and I succeeded him as general editor (1981-86).

What Bob was doing in those years was, as it were, inventing the Westar Institute inside the SBL and, when he broke with the SBL in 1980, he created it outside. He had planned, for example, to create a Jesus Seminar

---

1. Crossan, "Mark and the Relatives of Jesus."

(like that earlier Parables Seminar) within the SBL but, after that break, he created it outside. When, therefore, Bob invited me to the foundation meeting of the Jesus Seminar in 1985, and later to be its cochair, *outside* the SBL, he was not starting but continuing or completing a relationship with me that went back to the early 1970s inside the SBL and was hugely important for my own scholarly career.

RM: I joined the Seminar in 1986 not because I knew much about the historical Jesus but because after attending my first meeting I was drawn in by the collaborative ambience and because the project sounded so interesting. I had completed my PhD the year before and had paid little attention to historical Jesus studies. By contrast, when the Seminar began you had already been studying and writing on the topic for years. What was it like to step into that arena with well-developed positions on some of its major topics?

DC: When I left the monastic priesthood and went to De Paul University in 1969, I decided to focus my scholarly work on the historical Jesus *through the parables*. I had been teaching Jeremias' important book on the parables[2] in seminary since my return from Jerusalem in 1967. But while I respected his exegesis of the parables, I wanted to see a credible historical Jesus rather than an incredible Lutheran Jesus speaking them. That double emphasis was already clear in the title of my first book on the subject in 1973, *In Parables: The Challenge of the Historical Jesus*.

As you mentioned, Bob, I came into the Jesus Seminar in 1985 with my own project on that subject well under way toward a first consummation with *The Historical Jesus: The Life of a Mediterranean Jewish Peasant* (1991). I thoroughly enjoyed the collegial and collaborative atmosphere of the Seminar but that was not what drew me to it—that was a happy bonus. The attraction, *ab initio*, was Bob Funk's insistence that it was *unethical* to conduct academic biblical research that was only supported so widely because of popular interest in the subject while carefully hiding what we were doing from the public.

That 1991 book on *The Historical Jesus* was intended to raise the problem of historical-Jesus *methodology* with my colleagues but, for me, any difference between its proceedings or conclusions and those of the Jesus Seminar paled into irrelevance compared to that ethical demand for publicity of discussion. It was not the collegiality of the Jesus Seminar's discussions but the publicity of its conclusions that was normative

---

2. Jeremias, *The Parables of Jesus*.

for my participation in it. (Question: has a powerful association like the SBL done enough *to publicize* its historical scholarship *against* the biblical fundamentalism that has now metastasized into Christian nationalism in the USA?)

RM: The steering committee of the Jesus Seminar decided that the first major phase of the Seminar's investigations should focus on Jesus' parables. I later realized that that decision was strategic and had important consequences. In other words, it makes a difference where you start. Can you reflect on what went into that decision and how you think it influenced the big picture of the Seminar's work?

DC: Bob Funk's focus on metaphor and on parable as metaphorical narrative was already there—and published—by the mid-1960s.

In following Bob's lead on parable as metaphor into the 1970s, I made the parables (understood as metaphors) the initial and dominant access to the historical Jesus; recall the subtitle of my 1973 *In Parables* already cited as *The Challenge of the Historical Jesus*. There I embedded Jesus' parables in a tapestry of quotations from the philosophy of metaphor and the practice of poetry, but I also justified that primary access route methodologically like this:

> The "criterion of dissimilarity"[3] . . . will apply not only to subject and content but even more especially to style and to form. One is especially interested in forms of expression which are peculiar to Jesus and with which the primitive church does not seem to be too much at home.[4]
>
> The "criterion of dissimilarity" will be applied here to the form as well as the content of Jesus' words. The interest will be on Jesus' use of metaphor in sustained parabolic mode and on how this is distinct from the usage of the primitive church and also contemporary Judaism.[5]

Later, *The Historical Jesus* (1991) trusted the "criterion of multiple independent attestation"[6] over that of "dissimilarity" for *individual* sayings because of our limited database on any given example but my 1973 use of dissimilarity in terms of parabolic "style and form" or, better,

---

3. See *Funk On Parables*. The timespan for Funk's essays is 1964–2003.

4. Crossan, *In Parables*, 5.

5. Crossan, *In Parables*, 7.

6. This criterion holds that if a saying or story in the gospels occurs in two or more early sources that are not copying from one another, it is likely to come from the historical Jesus. (Ed.)

parabolic genre and subgenre, still seems to me functionally valid: a parable story challenges the hearer(s) whereas an example story provides the hearer(s) with an illustration. the challenge to the hearer(s) of a parable story is not the illustration for the hearer(s) of an example story.[7, 8]

You also asked, Bob, how I think it—the opening to the historical Jesus initially through his parables—influenced the big picture of the Seminar's work. I cannot answer for the Seminar but only for myself, and summarily. Parables as participatory pedagogy certainly helped me understand God's Rule on Earth as a participatory theology; that the metaphor of divine intervention (from John the Baptist) was not that of divine collaboration (from Jesus the Nazarene); and that Jesus' parables to God's Kingdom fit most appropriately as medium to message.

RM: In 1986, the year after the Jesus Seminar began, you published your *Sayings Parallels: A Workbook for the Jesus Tradition*.[9] Please describe that book. Did you produce it with the Seminar in mind?

DC: The easy answer is yes, definitely. *Sayings Parallels* was produced with the Jesus Seminar in mind. The idea for the volume came from Bob Funk as the first volume of a series intended to reimagine biblical scholarship through subdivisions such as Facets, both literary and social, as well as Foundations, both with reference works and texts for comparison.

My Preface, dated December 1985, began by saying,

> Several key ideas for the form and content of this workbook derived from conversations in "The Jesus Seminar," a group of scholars who study and write, meet and discuss the development of the Jesus tradition. I am grateful to them and especially to the Seminar's convener and director, Robert W. Funk.[10]

The workbook itself was divided into four sections that correspond to four categories of "sayings": *Parables, Aphorisms, Dialogues,* and

---

7. An *example story* is one in which readers or listeners are encouraged to follow the example of a certain character. For instance, the parable of the Good Samaritan is traditionally interpreted to mean that we should imitate the Samaritan. Crossan, Funk, and many other scholars argue that interpreting this and other parables as example stories is a fundamental misunderstanding of what parables are intended to communicate. (*Ed.*)

8. Notley and Safrai, *Parables of the Sages*.

9. "If a book is worth doing, it's worth doing well. I thank most especially Char Matejovsky of Polebridge Press for acting always and successfully on that principle" (xi).

10. Crossan, *Sayings Parallels*, xi.

Stories. That last category added Jesus' words in the passion and death, resurrection, and ascension stories to the discussion of "sayings." Those four categories were also mentioned by Bob Funk in the introduction to *The Five Gospels* in 1993.[11]

Finally, a fifth category, *Miracles*, could contain "short, terse commands or comments" as sayings of Jesus. That category was "left out ... not ... because miracles are of lesser importance but because they demand and deserve an entire comparative study all to themselves."[12] Again: "As noted earlier, the fifth major category of the Jesus tradition, that of *miracles*, is not indexed in this volume for reasons of practical space and also to allow a fuller separate consideration elsewhere"[13]

In summary, for me, *Sayings Parallels* was not just preparing the database for Bob's vision of the coming *Jesus Seminar* but for my own vision of the coming *The Historical Jesus*.

RM: I notice that you put scare quotes around the word *sayings* ("sayings"). Why?

DC: Those quotation marks were intended to indicate Bob Funk's primary entrance strategy into historical Jesus research: by a focus on the "sayings." For example, the subtitle of *The Five Gospels* was *The Search for the Authentic Words of Jesus* and the dust jacket of the hardcover version had a rectangular red box asking "What Did Jesus Really Say?"

My own title and subtitle, excuse the repetition, was *The Historical Jesus: The Life of a Mediterranean Jewish Peasant* (1991)—the "life" and not just the "sayings"—and the dust jacket of that book's hardcover version had this summary: "The first comprehensive determination of who Jesus was, what he did, what he said" in that deliberate sequence, which also requires a backstory.

When my editor at HarperSanFranciso accepted *The Historical Jesus*, he requested *strongly* that I preface it with a list of the actual sayings of the historical Jesus. I pleaded *strongly* against doing that as an unacceptable narrowing of the book's title, method, and database.[14] My editor, of course, prevailed but, while giving a reluctant list, I deliberately protested up front in three different ways.

---

11. Funk et al., *The Five Gospels*, 35.

12. Crossan, *Sayings Parallel*, xiii.

13. Crossan, *Sayings Parallel*, xvi. That fifth category was never studied within the Facets and Foundations Series. See, however, Cotter, *Miracles in Greco-Roman Antiquity*.

14. Crossan, *The Historical Jesus*, see the Appendices, 427–61.

First, I titled that newly added Overture, not *The Sayings of Jesus* but *The Gospel of Jesus*. Then, I opened that Overture with this introductory phrase: "*In the beginning* was the performance; not the word alone, nor the deed alone, but, both, each indelibly marked with the other forever."[15] Next, and very, very deliberately, my overture-example was not a saying but an exorcism (with an ironic bow to Schweitzer): "He comes as yet unknown into a hamlet of Lower Galilee."[16] Finally, what followed as my own profile of Jesus as of 1991 was a carefully chosen summary followed by its expansion. All of that was my quiet authorial protest against the editorially requested thirteen-page list of sayings that followed.

At stake in all of that history is not the validity of assembling the authentic sayings of Jesus but whether that is the best entrance strategy into the "life" of that individual, his movement, and his community.

RM: I was surprised to find out that your *Sayings Parallels* was the first—and I believe still is the only—comprehensive inventory of the sayings attributed to Jesus in the early Christian centuries. I was surprised because having such an inventory seems essential to historical Jesus studies. Why do you think no one had ever compiled a collection like this?

DC: I am afraid my answer is more suspicion than information. Appendix I in *The Historical Jesus* established "An Inventory of the Jesus Tradition by Chronological Stratification and Independent Attestation." That was an open invitation for every other Jesus scholar to do likewise. The results would be necessarily divergent but that might begin creating a methodological due-process procedure for Jesus studies: "This book has to raise most seriously the problem of methodology."[17]

I thought that an "Inventory" or database of sources was a self-evident start and the basic process of due diligence. I thought that all I was adding to that self-evident due diligence (for *any* Jesus scholar) was proposing "Chronological Stratification" and "Independent Attestation." What happened, however, were multiple criticisms of this or that source or this or that date but no responses to the challenge of methodology and no proposals of alternative inventories.

None of that answers your "why" question, Bob, and that is where I have only a, possibly unfair, suspicion. Would an initial suggestion of a due-process methodology and an initial establishment of a due-diligence inventory place historical Jesus study under reason not faith, study not

15. Crossan, *The Historical Jesus*, xi.
16. Crossan, *The Historical Jesus*, xi.
17. Crossan, *The Historical Jesus*, xxvii.

dogma, and history not orthodoxy? Is that what must be avoided at all costs?

RM: The Seminar's practice of voting attracted much controversy. I was amazed that the vote of a rookie like me counted the same as that of a seasoned scholar like you. What did you think of our voting process?

DC: Our voting process was roundly mocked by both conservatives and liberals. Voting with four categories was mocked with the jibe that we thought that "truth" could be established by a vote. That method, of course, was not voting the degree of a conclusion's *veracity* but the degree of our *certainty* about it: certain, less certain, uncertain, very uncertain.

Think of this even more fundamental voting process cited by Bob Funk in 1993: "Committees creating a critical text of the Greek New Testament under the auspices of the United Bible Societies vote[18] on whether to print this or that text and what variants to consign to notes."[19] Of course and perforce! But we can go further with that exemplary parallel.

The Greek New Testament of the United Bible Societies votes according to four categories

> to indicate the relative degree of certainty in the mind of the Committee for the reading adopted as the text . . . {A} signifies that the text is certain, . . . {B} indicates that the text is almost certain, . . . {C} . . . the Committee had difficulty in deciding, . . . {D} the Committee had great difficulty in arriving at a decision.[20]

Those four rather obvious if not inevitable categories are the same basic foursome adopted by the Jesus Seminar with colored beads replacing capital letters. We spoke of those beads as red, pink, grey, black but in practice they printed out as red, purple, blue, black in *The Five Gospels*. The Jesus Seminar members *argued* from evidence what they judged to be true but *voted* to indicate how sure that argument was.

RM: In your estimation, on the whole did the Seminar judge the gospels to be more historical, less historical, or about the same as you

---

18. There are hundreds of early copies of New Testament book in Greek and these differ in hundreds of places about the exact wording. The task of comparing these variants and deciding which wordings (called "readings") are more likely to be original is known as textual criticism. In the many places where the experts on the UBS committee disagreed on which readings to adopt, they voted. (*Ed.*)

19. *The Five Gospels*, 35.

20. Metzger, *A Textual Commentary on the Greek New Testament*, 14.

judged them to be? Do you think that the Seminar was wrong about any of its major findings (as opposed to its votes on specific passages)?

DC: I think I judged the gospels to be about as historical as did the Jesus Seminar but, of course, any content proclaimed as "good news" is already honestly and explicitly an *interpretation* of history. That general agreement on gospel historicity may be of some significance because I had a very different methodology. I never started by authenticating "sayings." Think of *The Historical Jesus*' subtitle *The Life of a Mediterranean Jewish Peasant* (1991). That book started with the *Mediterranean* matrix and the *Jewish* matrix before ever getting to the *Peasant* Jesus—and his parables, aphorisms, dialogues, and stories. My theory was first to secure the historical matrix for the Jesus tradition from sources that were not committed to Jesus and only then to see whether what I (or anyone else) considered the earliest stratum of sources about Jesus fit within that matrix.

For myself, as indicated by those subtitle terms *Challenge* (1973), *Life* (1991), and everything I have written since (1991–2024)—*emphatically including any and everything about the historical Paul on Jesus as the Messiah/Christ*—the end purpose was never just what the historical Jesus said or did but what he *meant*—for then and now. Contemporary relevance was part of the historical Jesus because I found that, historically, he made claims—about, say, God's Rule on Earth—that transcended time and place. In other words, Jesus' contemporary relevance was not just a religious nicety or intra-Christian necessity but an intrinsic obligation of historical Jesus study—as with any ancient thinker who made transtemporal, translocal, transcultural claims.

RM: The Seminar worked from 1985 to 1998. Looking back from your perspective all these years later, what would you say were its most important contributions to our understanding of the historical Jesus? Looking back, do you believe there were things the Seminar should have done differently? If the Jesus Seminar were to reconvene today, what salient questions should it consider? The Jesus Seminar closed up shop twenty-eight years ago. What, if anything, do you think will endure of its work?

DC: To establish "my perspective," compare the divergent titles of two books to focus on comparative authorial intention (not on better or worse, right or wrong). I have just cited my own from 1991 and to repeat: *The Historical Jesus: The Life of a Mediterranean Jewish Peasant*. Recall another, from 1993, already footnoted but here given again in full: *The*

Five Gospels: The Search for the Authentic Words of Jesus, New Translation and Commentary by Robert W. Funk, Roy W. Hoover, and The Jesus Seminar.[6] The cover also had a small red rectangle containing in black capital letters this manifesto: "What Did Jesus Really Say?"

That latter volume is, quite frankly, a magnificent one in content and form, presentation and information, clarity and pedagogy. The five gospels of Mark, Matthew, Luke, John, and Thomas are newly translated, presented in that sequence, and the "sayings" of Jesus are printed in the four colors of those voting beads as certainly his (red), less certainly his (pink/purple), uncertainly his (grey/blue), very uncertainly his (black, of the basic text). But what *The Five Gospels* does *not* do is present a conclusion about the historical Jesus himself. Furthermore, I doubt if the Jesus Seminar could have done so.

I think the adversarial creation of a critical red-letter version (actually a four-color version) was the driving force of the Jesus Seminar for Bob Funk: "The results of the deliberations of the Seminar are presented in this red-letter edition of the five gospels" (*The Five Gospels*, p. 38; final paragraph of the Introduction). The seminar's protocols, procedures, and processes worked quite brilliantly toward that consummation because we could discuss and vote on how certain we were whether this or that saying came from the historical Jesus. But I am not sure we could have done the same on a profile—for then and now—of the historical Jesus.[21]

In summary, and again for myself, I think of a Venn Diagram in which Bob Funk and I could work together on the "sayings" of Jesus in the intersection. But the outside of that intersection was the new red-letter version for Bob and the reconstructed historical Jesus for me. If one objects that such a reconstruction was the ultimate goal of each and every member of the Seminar, I wonder was establishing "the authentic words of Jesus" the best platform from which to launch that project?

I am not proposing a new Jesus seminar nor suggesting such is even possible or advisable. But suppose the Jesus Seminar had been or was newly directed toward a reconstructed profile of the historical Jesus with never a mention of the red-letter gospel, where and how might it begin? Suppose, for example, it started with the critical fact that before the *Five Gospels* existed, the *Two Gospels* did, by the later 50s: *The Gospel according to Q* and *The Gospel according to Paul*? What would a historical Jesus

---

21. See the fourteen articles by Fellows of the Jesus Seminar in *Profiles of Jesus*, edited by Hoover. I am not sure that, say, a Profiles Seminar of those authors would, could, or should have produced a consensus historical Jesus. Maybe?

look like as reconstructed equally from, through, behind, and beneath those twin and early sources? Even if a new Jesus Seminar were never to exist, it might possibly be instructive to ponder where it should start—and whether it should end (*pace* Ray Brown and John Meier) with the burial.[22]

RM: In closing, what do you most want the public to understand about the historical Jesus?

DC: Thank you very much for that final question, Bob. It allows me to update *The Historical Jesus*' 1991 profile of Jesus and close with what I emphasize about that historical figure in 2024. Since the detailed content of my response is already available in print,[23] I will simply summarize it here, over three successive and cumulative steps: matrix, movement, and mantra.

Matrix. This step presumes the historian Josephus' discussion of the *invention* of nonviolent resistance against his homeland's first-century Romanization. That practice started with the census of 6 CE and continued afterward. Josephus terms it a "fourth philosophy" after those of the Essenes, Pharisees, and Sadducees. Moving from a short and dismissive mention in his *Jewish War* (2.118) to a long and accurate one in his *Jewish Antiquities* (18.1–10, 23–25), Josephus admits that between the violent revolts of 4 BCE and 66 CE Jewish leaders experimented with organized nonviolent resistance that explicitly accepted the possibility of communal martyrdom. That, presuming all else, is, for me now, the most significant Jewish matrix of both the Jordan-Baptism movement of John and the God's-Rule movement of Jesus.

Movement. We know that Jesus' movement was based on nonviolent resistance because both the Jewish Josephus at the end of the first and the Roman Tacitus at the start of the second century record that Jesus the Christ started a movement and was executed for it by legal Roman authority in Judea. But neither of them mentions anything about Pilate rounding up Jesus' foremost followers and crucifying them all together—think of Barabbas "and the rebels" in Mark's parabolic fiction of a violent resistance (Mark 15:7).

---

22. Raymond Brown and John Meier were prolific scholars of the first rank. Both argued that reconstructions of the historical Jesus should end with the stories of his burial.

23. Crossan, *Render Unto Caesar*. For full documentation of this brief summary, see Part Three (209–73) and especially Appendix B on "Violent and Nonviolent Response to the Romanization of Israel" (285–86).

For violent rebellion, Rome executed *both* the leaders and their major followers. For nonviolent resistance, Rome executed *only* the leaders on the presumption that their movement would die out without them—hence both Josephus and Tacitus must explain why that did not work with Jesus' movement.

In a second-century synthesis of Roman law on nonviolent resistance, "Title XXII: Concerning Seditious Persons" gave this legal precedent: "The authors of sedition and tumult, or those who stir up the people, shall, according to their rank, either be crucified, thrown to wild beasts, or deported to an island" (*The Opinions of Julius Paulus Addressed to His Son*, Book V, Title XXII.1). Hence, respectively, the fates of Jesus of Nazareth, Ignatius of Antioch, and John of Patmos.

Mantra. It is one thing to advocate helping your enemy's prostrated donkey (Exodus 23:56) or even your enemy's prostrated self (Luke 10:30–37), but why did Jesus go to that extraordinary extremity with "love your enemies" (Q/Matthew 5:44 = Luke 6:27)? Why not, "love everyone," which would include enemies but not specify them particularly? Furthermore, that human love of human enemies is a participation in the divine love of divine enemies, within the family of God (Q/Matthew 4:45 = Luke 6:35b).

In *The Five Gospels*, that former Q text was coded red and the latter was coded pink.[24] I do not know how I voted on those two sayings back then but would certainly vote red on *both* today as ultimately grounded in Jesus' vision of God's Family. Granted that, I take *love/enemies* as the mantra of Jesus' *nonviolent/revolution*. It is a motto for a movement and a movement in a motto. But why presume enemies? Do you think if you proclaim and practice Divine Rule on earth, Human Rule will go quietly into that good night?

---

24. Funk et al., eds., *The Five Gospels*, 145, 291.

1

The Enduring Issue of Jesus
Two Quests

LANE MCGAUGHY

Robert Funk opened the first meeting of the Jesus Seminar with an address entitled "The Issue of Jesus."[1] "Issue" is an expansive term, implying a much broader investigation than the modern quest for the historical Jesus. The "issue of Jesus" refers to all the traditions generated by the memory of the historical Jesus, not just to a list of his sayings or a brief sketch of his actions. Funk was calling for a thorough investigation of what he called "the Jesus tradition," both the historical person of Jesus and all the subsequent interpretations of him and the movements developed in his wake.[2] In short, for Funk the Jesus Seminar was about a thorough reassessment of the entire Christian tradition, theological as well as historical. For Funk, "the Jesus tradition" is a shorthand way of referring to the complex history of Christianity. This was the expansive scope of the Jesus Seminar's work.

THE FIRST QUEST: DOGMATIC CHRIST

Because of this larger scope, the issue of Jesus also includes what I call the quest for the dogmatic Christ—the theological project to understand the

---

1. Funk's charge to the scholars who attended the Berkeley meeting (1985) is printed in first issue of *Forum*.

2. See, for example, Funk, "From Parable to Gospel."

meaning of Jesus beginning with the late second century claim that Jesus is God's divine Son of God. This claim posed a philosophical problem for Greek-educated Gentile Christians who assumed that God is unchangeable (immutable).[3] As a result, seven ecumenical councils were convened from Nicaea I in 325 CE to Nicaea II in 787 CE to forge official church teaching about the nature of Christ that would still affirm God's immutability, while deifying Jesus. According to Jaroslav Pelikan, *only* two official dogmas were approved as a result of the seven ecumenical councils, and both focus on the nature of Christ: (1) the dogma of the Trinity (a single Godhead with three persons that includes Jesus) and (2) the dogma of the two natures of Christ (human and divine).[4] In short, Christology is at the core of Christian theology and the only theological issue, according to Pelikan, that was settled by conciliar dogmas. The issue of God is a common religious issue, while the issue of Jesus is unique to Christianity and thus its defining core. This is why the issue of Jesus is much broader than a historical reconstruction of the life of the historical figure of Jesus. Pelikan outlines the history of this broader Christological project at the core of Christianity in his *Jesus through the Centuries: His Place in the History of Culture*.[5] Given the pyramidal view of antiquity that locates the realm of the gods as rulers at the top and the human world as their servants (slaves) at the bottom, once Jesus was relocated to the heavens, his humanity was eclipsed. Jesus was worshipped as "The King of Kings" and a docetic Christology defined Christendom from the Emperor Constantine (fourth century) to the onset of anti-monarchical, democratic uprisings in the eighteenth century. As Pelikan observes, St. Francis of Assisi (early thirteenth century) was the only one who focused on the ethical practices of the human Jesus prior to the Enlightenment, though his view of Jesus was a pre-critical.

---

3. See Miles, "If Jesus Is God, What God Is He?" 1.

4. Pelikan, "Dogma," 80–82. For a thorough discussion of the origin of Christological doctrine, see Pelikan, *The Emergence of the Catholic Tradition (100–600)*, chaps. 4 and 5.

5. In 1997 Yale University Press produced a beautiful coffee-table version of Pelikan's work with two hundred colored images of Jesus.

TWIN WATERSHEDS OF THE WESTERN TRADITION

Intellectual Watershed: The Enlightenment

A radical transformation in Western intellectual history occurred in the seventeenth century. With the Age of Reason, the medieval supernatural worldview collapsed in the face of scientific discoveries that our solar system is heliocentric, dynamic, and materialistic, not geocentric, static, and luminous (non-material). The world-changing implications of the collapse of medieval supernaturalism, however, were not worked out until the eighteenth century, the Age of the Enlightenment. Mostly empty space replaced the heavily populated medieval heavens, democracies overthrew monarchies, medieval theology was challenged by Deism (laws of nature, not divine intervention) that produced the philosophy of religion, and historical criticism investigated all the cherished myths and texts from Antiquity.[6] A second quest, the quest for Jesus emerged in the context of the Enlightenment—a quest for an historical Jesus. As a result, the theological quest for the dogmatic Christ, the first quest, and the second quest, the historical quest for Jesus of Nazareth, have frequently been confused.[7]

Cultural Watershed: Industrial Revolution

A second turning point in Western civilization occurred in Great Britain with the emergence of the Industrial Revolution from 1780–1830 CE. The invention of various automated machines like the cotton gin marked the demise of medieval agrarian culture and the birth of industrialized nation-states where the power of machines displaced the manual labor of peasants and slaves. This, in turn, spawned the new disciplines of the social sciences to gauge the patterns and trends of mass groupings in industrialized societies. The empirical methodology of the social sciences meshed well with the pragmatism of popular American culture and by the beginning of the twentieth century had become the dominant analytic

---

6. For an overview of these epochal changes in the Western tradition, see Palmer and Colton, *A History of the Modern World*, chaps. VII and VIII.

7. One example is Johnson, *The Real Jesus*, who argues that an effect proves that its cause is historical: "the resurrection of Jesus . . . *can* be said to be 'historical' as an experience and claim of human beings, then and today . . ." (136).

[8] Colwell, "The Chicago School of Biblical Interpretation."

mode in the fields of sociology, political science, psychology, and anthropology. When William R. Harper established the University of Chicago as a cluster of graduate programs in 1892, he recruited Albion W. Small to establish the first sociology department in America and to launch *The American Journal of Sociology* in 1895. At the 1969 Vanderbilt Colloquium on the Chicago School of biblical interpretation, former University of Chicago President Ernest Cadman Colwell reported that the creed of the Divinity School was: "There is no sound history of Christianity except a social history, and Shirley Jackson Case was its prophet."[8] It should come as no surprise that many American New Testament scholars turned to social scientific methodology in the 1980s to update the quest for the historical.

THE SECOND QUEST: THE HISTORICAL JESUS

First Phase (1778–1906): Challenging Christology

For a critical study of the Bible to take root, Scripture must be liberated from ecclesiastical control. Johann Philipp Gabler's 1787 Altdorf lecture, "A Discourse on the Proper Distinction Between Biblical and Dogmatic Theology and the Boundaries to be Drawn for Each,"[9] inaugurates this break. Gabler limits the role of biblical theology to historical reconstruction and redefines dogmatic theology as what the Church can say about its faith, based on reason, not on scriptural revelation. After Gabler, the Bible gradually came to be understood as one of the religious texts of antiquity, subject to the same critical analysis as other ancient religious texts, and theology became philosophy of religion in the context of eighteenth-century Deism. After the divorce of biblical studies from theology, research on the Gospels became a historical search for the human Jesus and Christian origins, and theology split into apologetics (a defense of orthodox Christology) and systematics (constructions of theological systems based on philosophical arguments, not on the Bible).

Hermann Samuel Reimarus' "On the Intentions of Jesus and His Disciples," published posthumously in 1778, marks the beginning of the

---

8 Colwell, "The Chicago School of Biblical Interpretation."
9 Gabler, "Oratorio de justo discrimine theologiae biblicae."

modern quest for the historical Jesus.[10] He was the first scholar to separate the historical Jesus from the dogmatic Christ. Less often remembered, but just as important, is that Reimarus' work also marks the beginning of the historical critical study of the New Testament as a whole. All the sub-divisions of critical scholarship on the New Testament and Christian origins derive from Reimarus' distinction between the historical Jesus and the post-Easter Christ of the creeds. All the subsequent stages of New Testament scholarship have been defined by their origins in the quest for the historical Jesus.

Joseph Bessler, in his insightful and groundbreaking, *A Scandalous Jesus,* locates the issue of the historical Jesus in the much larger context of the public square. When Constantine favored and promoted Christianity, bishops were given the political power to censure public speech about religion. Those who expressed opinions that differed from the official teachings of the Church were martyred, demonized as heretics, excommunicated, or otherwise punished for betraying the true faith. When we think of regimes that censor public discourse, we normally think of modern totalitarian ideologies. But Bessler's premise is that it was official state religion ("the established Church") that monitored public discourse in the Middle Ages and punished those who challenged church dogma. In order to open the public square to free speech about religion, Christian dogma had to be challenged at its core. Here Bessler's analysis and my argument intersect. Since the core Church dogma is Christology, the quest for the historical Jesus is more than an academic exercise. It fundamentally attacks Church censorship of public discourse by challenging the foundational dogma that the "real" Jesus is the resurrected, supernatural Christ of the ancient creeds. Hence, the frequent vitriolic pushbacks against historical studies of Jesus are not surprising. History's evidence-based conclusions are direct threats to orthodox theology's control of religious discourse.

The Neoorthodox Interlude (1906–53)

Barnes Tatum[11] and others label the first half of the twentieth century as the period of the "no quest" mainly caused by Karl Barth's pushback against the of the nineteenth-century quest. Under the influence

10. Reimarus, *Reimarus: Fragments.*
11. Tatum, *In Quest of Jesus.*

of Barthian neoorthodoxy and the Papal muzzling of Catholic biblical scholarship in 1906–1907, the foundation of Christianity was located in the Apostolic faith in Jesus Christ (the kerygmatic proclamation) that emerged in the second century. This represents a revival of the pre-modern domination of dogmatic theology that Gabler had separated from biblical criticism. As a result of neo-orthodoxy's continuing influence, those who criticize the Jesus Seminar often assume "the real Jesus" is not the historical figure of Jesus but the second member of the Trinity. They thus reject Gabler's distinction between the theological and the historical quests, often in the name of a uniform, and speculative, biblical theology.

The German Connection

The roots of the critical study of the Bible reach back to the Protestant Reformation when Martin Luther trimmed the sources of religious authority to only one—the Bible (*sola scriptura*). As a result, the history of Protestant Christianity is a story of increasingly finer exegetical points producing controversies about the sole criterion for one's salvation and the grounds for denominational schisms.[12]

Jerry Wayne Brown dates the beginning of a critical approach to the Bible in America to the endowment of the Dexter Lectureship at Harvard in 1810. The donor, Samuel Dexter, declared that his gift was for the promotion of "a critical knowledge of the Holy Scriptures." The first occupant of the Dexter Lectureship was Joseph Stevens Buckminster, the pastor of the prestigious Brattle Street Congregational Church in Boston. He had read the groundbreaking works of biblical criticism from Europe and then spent 1806–07 in Germany acquainting himself with the theories of the pioneers of biblical criticism like Johann Jacob Griesbach (1745–1812).[13] Buckminster was adamant that "the American biblical student master European scholarship before he could hope to make any contribution of his own."[14] Following the example of Buckminster's pilgrimage to Germany, spending a year or two studying with leading German theologians and biblical scholars became an unofficial

---

12. A dictum of the historical theologian Ebeling: "Church history is the history of the exposition of scripture." While most histories of Christianity are institutional or political, Ebeling argued that hermeneutics is the defining force of church history. See Ebeling, "The Significance of the Critical-Historical Method for Church."

13. J. W. Brown, *The Rise of Biblical Criticism*, 10–26.

14. J. W. Brown, *The Rise of Biblical Criticism*, 25.

rite of passage for American graduate students in these two disciplines. Only recently has the American deference to German biblical scholarship begun to wane.

Second Phase (1953–72): Bridging the Divine-Human Gap

Ernst Käsemann argued in 1953 that rooting Christianity in the second century Apostolic kerygma disconnects it from history and grounds it in a docetic redeemer myth. He called for a renewal of the quest for the historical Jesus to bridge the gap between the message of the historical Jesus and neo-orthodox Christology that opened up with Barth and Rudolf Bultmann.[15] The debate that ensued after Käsemann's call for a new quest was epistemological: what is the bridge that links the historical Jesus with dogmatic claims for a supernatural Christ? Gerhard Ebeling and Ernst Fuchs, two German scholars, took up Käsemann's challenge. The former describes the historical Jesus as a "verbal occurrence" (*Wortgeschehen*) and the latter as a "speech event" (*Sprachereignis*), in light of Martin Heidegger's philosophical claim that language precedes thought and thus has the power to shape our worldviews.[16] Because Luther limited religious authority to the Bible as the only source, Ebeling and Fuchs argue that exegetical or expository sermons are the bridge between historical grounding and theological application; the "preached Word" is the point of contact, not a critical reconstruction of the historical Jesus or of Christian origins.[17] In light of this exegetical focus, Funk and others referred to the German "new quest" for Jesus of the 1950s-60s as "the new hermeneutic" because of the way the historical task was taken up into the service of theology by Fuchs and Ebeling. In a similar vein, James Robinson commented that the new questers had, in effect, substituted the term "speech event" for the theological term "salvation history."[18] As a result, the new quest faltered by 1970 because its practitioners presupposed that the only future for Jesus' message was the orthodox tradition

---

15. Käsemann, "The Problem of the Historical Jesus." For an early critique of the new quest, see Robinson, *A New Quest of the Historical Jesus*.
16. Robinson, "Hermeneutic Since Barth."
17. See Ebeling, "The Significance of the Critical Historical Method," 32–37.
18. Robinson, "Robert W. Funk and Hermeneutics, 54.

that triumphed at Nicaea and because it further assumed that the primitive kerygma is still normative for theology today.

Third Phase (1972–): The Quest Moves to America

Initial Moves

Ernest W. Saunders characterizes the post-war period of the 1950s and 60s as one of introspection and rapid change in his centennial history of the Society of Biblical Literature.[19] The SBL was dominated by conservative, mostly Protestant, Ivy League scholars. A group of younger, maverick scholars called the New Testament Colloquium set out to reform the SBL. Funk identifies James Robinson of Claremont Graduate School, Helmut Koester of Harvard Divinity School, and himself of Drew Theological Seminary as the organizers of the Colloquium.[20] Robinson refers to this ad hoc group as "the young Turks" who enlisted SBL veterans Hans Jonas, Kendrick Grobel, and Amos Wilder, to serve as their advisors and "senior sponsors" to open entrees into SBL's inner circles. After the first gathering in New York City in 1960, the Colloquium convened annually two days before the SBL annual meetings until 1969 when new SBL leadership and meeting guidelines were approved.[21]

The three founders of the Colloquium, Robinson, Koester, and Funk, were all Bultmannians and shared a common goal to introduce Käsemann's call for a new quest for the historical Jesus to an American audience. This troika divided their plans into three major assignments: (1) Robinson accepted the challenge of getting the Nag Hammadi codices liberated from the Cairo Museum and translated into English to expand research on Christian origins; (2) Koester organized a new English-language commentary series, Hermeneia, based on the German

---

19. Saunders, *Searching the Scriptures*, 41–55.

20. Funk, *Odyssey* 5:11 (unpublished memoirs dated August 10, 2002).

21. Robinson, *Evaluating the Legacy of Robert W. Funk*, 55. In 1970 the members of the NT Colloquium presented a Festshrift to Norman Perrin, *Christology and a Modern Pilgrimage*. A list of the elected members is included on p. iv: J. C. Beker, Hans Dieter Betz, Raymond E. Brown, Eldon J. Epp, Joseph A. Fitzmyer, Robert W. Funk, Victor P. Furnish, Dieter Georgi, Paul Hammer, Edward Hobbs, Hans Jonas, Helmut Koester, Robert Kraft, George MacRae, James M. Robinson, John Strugnell, Amos N. Wilder, Wilhelm Weullner. Adding Norman Perrin and Kendrick Grobel to the list brings the membership to twenty-one.

Meyer Kommentar series, to make the best of German New Testament scholarship available to North American scholars; and (3) Funk agreed to take on the organizational reform of SBL as its Executive Secretary and overhauling its publication program by creating Scholars Press. The ambition of Robinson, Koester, and Funk was to transform American New Testament scholarship by engaging it with the latest insights from Germany.

In preparation for this agenda, a series of consultations were held at Drew University in the early 1960s to introduce major German theologians and New Testament scholars to colleagues in North America. The consultations were billed as "Discussions among Continental and American Theologians" and the papers were published in a Harper & Row series *New Frontiers in Theology*. The second Drew consultation focused on the new hermeneutic and featured German scholars Fuchs and Ebeling in dialogue with Americans Robinson, Funk, Wilder, and John Dillenberger. The spotty communication gap between researchers on both sides of the Atlantic was finally bridged.

For Funk the next step was spending a year in Germany consulting directly with Käsemann, as well as other leading German theologians, about the prospects for the new quest and current German theological trends. He wrote his programmatic work, *Language, Hermeneutic, and Word of God*, on the rhetoric of parable (Jesus) and letter (Paul). Funk wanted to test firsthand the theological waters in Germany. In his 1964 essay for the Drew Consultation on Hermeneutic, Funk summed up his experience: "In Europe historical criticism has tended to become subservient to theological interests, thereby losing its critical powers; on the American side historical criticism has retained its nontheological orientation."[22] Funk remarked to me after his return that in his judgment German theology was still so constricted by Lutheran orthodoxy that it was incapable of fully addressing the quest for Jesus in the context of the modern world. The new hermeneutic began to disappear from the American scene in the late 1960s. Robinson, Funk, and Koester turned their attention to Nag Hammadi research, the reformation of the SBL, and the Hermeneia commentary series. But the eclipse of the new hermeneutic also marked something deeper that led Funk to veer away from his involvement with Robinson and Koester and move instead in the

---

22. Funk, "The Hermeneutical Problem and Historical Criticism," 166. Bessler, *Scandalous Jesus*, would expand Funk's "theological interests" to include the limits imposed on historical criticism by ecclesiastical and political powers.

direction of creating a new North American project to investigate "the issue of Jesus," that would culminate in the Jesus Seminar a decade later.

Having moved to Vanderbilt University Divinity School, Funk turned to a study of the Bible in the American tradition to relocate the quest in a new context: the secular world of modernity. He organized a colloquium at Vanderbilt in February 1969 on "The Forging of an American Theological Tradition: The Chicago School" with reflections from E. C. Colwell and James Luther Adams among others. Funk himself highlighted the socio-historical method of Shirley Jackson Case and the literary and rhetorical criticism of Amos Wilder as the precursors of a distinctive American approach to the New Testament. Funk's 1974 SBL Presidential address dealt with the Chicago School's critical approach to the Bible as the inversion of popular American religious sensibility.[23]

The SBL Parables Seminar (1973–77): Enter John Dominic Crossan

Into this mix entered an Irish ex-monk and ex-priest, John Dominic Crossan. When he joined the DePaul University faculty in 1969, he faced two daunting hurdles. As a Catholic and European, he was not connected with the network of New Testament scholars in the Society of Biblical Literature, and his chosen research area, the historical Jesus, was barely on scholarly radar screen. Crossan published an article on the parables of Jesus as metaphors, "Parable and Example in the Teaching of Jesus" in *New Testament Studies* (1972) that caught the attention of Norman Perrin and Funk, who both had written recent books on the sayings of Jesus.[24] Perrin was SBL President in 1973, and Funk was SBL Executive Secretary from 1968–73 and as SBL President in 1975. As he tackled his twin hurdles of introducing himself to American scholarship and pursuing research on the historical Jesus, Crossan could not have handpicked better sponsors. In Crossan's words,

> Each in his own way said something like this: "I really like what you're doing, and by the way, who the hell are you?" Each in his own way made certain that that I became known within the Society of Biblical Literature and the wider world of American

---

23. Funk, "The Watershed of the American Biblical Tradition."
24. Perrin, *Rediscovering the Teaching of Jesus*; Robert W. Funk, *Language, Hermeneutic, and Word of God*.

scholarship. Both promoted me although I was not their student, promoted me simply because they accepted the value of publications over institutions, ideas over pedigrees.[25]

Perrin proposed that Crossan lead a five-year SBL seminar on the parables of Jesus which seminar cemented the parables as the bedrock of the Jesus tradition.

The Jesus Seminar (1985–91)

At the 1978 SBL meeting in New Orleans, Funk proposed that the SBL sponsor a "National Seminar on the Sayings of Jesus." The first session was held at the 1979 SBL meeting in New York City. After a massive heart attack, in 1980 Funk resigned as Director of Scholars Press and created an independent publishing house, Polebridge Press. He then rebranded the SBL Seminar on the Sayings of Jesus as the Jesus Seminar with Crossan and him as cochairs.

Following the intensive work of the SBL Parables Seminar, the Jesus Seminar started its quest for the historical Jesus with an investigation of his sayings. The first meeting in 1985 focused on the inventory of sayings in Mark and Q in Crossan's *In Fragments: The Aphorisms of Jesus*. Crossan then prepared an inventory of all the sayings attributed to Jesus in the Greek Gospels in the first two centuries.[26] The work of the SBL Parables Seminar fed directly into the Jesus Seminar. The first publication of the Jesus Seminar was an introduction to the parables, *The Parables of Jesus: Red Letter Edition* in 1988.[27]

ENDURING QUESTIONS

Where to start?

The nineteenth century quest started with Jesus' deeds, Käsemann's new quest with his words, while the current third phase is divided. The Jesus Seminar started with Jesus' words, following the intensive work by many of its participants on parables, but other contemporary scholars have started with Jesus' deeds and their work is often referred to as "the

25. Crossan, *A Long Way from Tipperary*, 171.
26. *Sayings Parallels*.
27. Funk, Scott, and Butts, *The Parables of Jesus: Red Letter*.

third quest." Where one starts an argument establishes its premise and thus anticipates its conclusion.

Why did the Jesus Seminar start with Jesus' words, not his deeds? My short answer is, because Bultmann did in *The History of the Synoptic Tradition* (orig. 1921).[28] Crossan agrees that Bultmann's influence shaped the Seminar's agenda by noting that for Bultmann and the new questers only the words of Jesus mattered because for them one encounters Jesus through exegetical sermons (see above).

Parables Metaphors or Illustrations?

Whether scholars begin their reconstruction of the historical Jesus with his words or deeds, eventually the question arises, are his parables and aphorisms non-literal metaphors or simple illustrations of his message? As metaphors they hint at his vision of the kingdom of God. As simple almost childlike images, they illustrate legalistic pronouncements or theological propositions. Can illiterate peasant ears handle sophisticated metaphors or only simple illustrations?

Place of the Social Sciences?

Historical criticism has demonstrated that there is not enough evidence about the historical Jesus in the Gospels to write a full biography in the modern sense. Rather than abandoning the quest, however, many North American scholars have turned to the social sciences as offering a new methodology for their portraits of Jesus. American scholars have embraced the application of social scientific modeling as a way of sharpening our understanding of Jesus' cultural context.

Crossan has pushed beyond the focus of his earlier work on the sayings of Jesus toward a more complete account of Jesus's life that juxtaposes words and deeds. He once remarked to me that he thought this was because his initial orientation to New Testament scholarship on Christian origins was Adolf Deissmann's *Light from the Ancient East*, not Bultmann's *The History of the Synoptic Tradition*. Deissmann located Christian

---

28. McGaughy, "The Search for the Historical Jesus," 17–26. Funk mentions his hope that the results of the Jesus Seminar might become the database for a new history of early traditions about Jesus in a prospectus he sent to Charter Fellows in January 1985.

origins in the larger socio-religious context of the Greco-Roman world. This orientation opened Crossan to the cross-cultural anthropological approach which is evident in *The Historical Jesus: The Life of a Mediterranean Jewish Peasant* (1991). The sub-title illustrates this approach. He relies on the cross-cultural anthropology of Gerhard Lenski to map the social stratification of agrarian societies like that of first century Palestine. The two dominant social classes of agrarian societies, according to Lenski, are (mostly absentee) landlords (patrons) and "peasants," many of whom are treated as slaves. "Mediterranean" is the larger cultural context in which Crossan locates Jesus and alludes to the oppressive power structures of the Roman Empire that dominated life in ancient Galilee in the first century. Crossan thus assigns Jesus to the peasant class (he was clearly not an absentee landlord) under the thumb of a militaristic empire and affirms his ethnicity as Jewish. This puts Crossan's historical Jesus project on a somewhat different track from that of Funk. Crossan was quite open about his own agenda and urged his colleagues to engage him in a debate over methodology.

On May 20, 1998 Funk emailed nine Jesus Seminar Fellows who were scheduled to meet in Santa Rosa in June for a planning meeting, urging us to read Crossan's follow-up book, *The Birth of Christianity* (1989). Funk wrote: "Dom Crossan has challenged his colleagues to a debate on methodology in the quest for the historical Jesus . . . I want to urge you to read as much of *The Birth of Christianity* as you can before coming to Santa Rosa. That would enable us to share perceptions of what methodology Crossan is pursuing and whether we should undertake a discussion of his theses." Funk referred specifically to chapter 10, "The Problem of Methodology," where Crossan states his complaint:

> I have been publishing on the historical Jesus since 1969 . . . On methods, I started with historical criticism, next incorporated literary criticism, and finally added macrosociological criticism to form an integrated interdisciplinary model. When I finally published *The Historical Jesus* in 1991, I intended not just another reconstruction of Jesus but to inaugurate a full-blown debate on methodology among my peers . . . There is still no serious discussion of methodology in historical Jesus research, and the same applies to the birth of Christianity. That does not make me very proud of myself and my scholarly colleagues.[29]

---

29. Crossan, *The Birth of Christianity*, 139.

Although Funk was not persuaded that the social sciences could resolve a historical problem, Crossan's macrosociological method was widely discussed by members of the Jesus Seminar and his influence pervaded the first phase of its work. To equate the conclusions of the Jesus Seminar with Funk's agenda, as many critics have, is thus a mistake. While Funk launched the Jesus Seminar as a collaborative research project, the Seminar developed its own agenda and a variety of viewpoints were expressed in its papers and deliberations. Crossan was certainly one of several major influences on the Seminar.

Crossan regards the historical Jesus profiled by many Jesus Seminar scholars as a lifeless talking head because of its focus on his parables and aphorisms:

> As my own historical Jesus project developed in the 1980s, I was starting to focus on the life of Jesus as a whole, on words *and* deeds, on sayings *and* stories, on life as protest *and* death as execution... [T]here was something... in my own life that made it impossible any longer to think of Jesus in terms only of talk, words, or sayings, something that made it imperative to think of Jesus in terms of a total lived life.[30]

As a result of this conviction, Crossan moved beyond his early work on parables to employ this third methodology, that he calls "cross-cultural anthropology," in his attempt to embody the historical Jesus as a fully human person.

But this decision produces a different Jesus than a historical reconstruction would: a figure who is defined by his similarities with his contemporaries, rather than by his individual differences from them. Cross-cultural anthropology can describe the cultural landscape of first century Galilee, and inferences can be made about individuals in light of that environment, but it cannot verify the idiosyncrasies of a particular person. The question remains, does a generic description of first century Palestinian peasants identity the individual figure of one particular peasant, Jesus of Nazareth?

The first quest for Jesus was the dogmatic quest from the second century, through the Conciliar debates about Christology, until the Enlightenment. The methodological evolution in the second quest for an historical Jesus since the onset of the Enlightenment can be charted as follows:

---

30. Crossan, *A Long Way from Tipperary*, 177.

- First Phase: Historical Criticism
- Second Phase: Historical Criticism + Literary Criticism
- Third Phase: Historical Criticism + Literary Criticism + Social-Scientific Modeling

Crossan's challenge to the Jesus Seminar to debate methodology in the quest pivots on the question as to whether a social-scientific model can produce a historical result. To be specific, is Crossan's portrait of Jesus as a "Mediterranean Jewish peasant" a biography of Jesus of Nazareth?

8

History Is Like an Unswept Room

ERIN VEARNCOMBE

When Brandon Scott, Hal Taussig, and I were working on *After Jesus Before Christianity*, one idea upon which all three of us easily agreed (and such ideas were not necessarily many) was the meaning-making potential of a second-century CE mosaic from the dining room of a villa on the Aventine Hill in Rome. An example of a decorative motif known as "the unswept floor" (*asàrotos òikos*), the mosaic, now housed within the Vatican Museum complex, is, quite literally, garbage: it depicts the remnants of a lavish banquet, debris which is either falling, fallen, or been cast aside onto the floor. A mouse cautiously approaches a bit of walnut shell; empty oyster, clam, and snail shells sit scattered across the floor; chicken feet and lobster claws lie dismembered; berries and olive pits cast small shadows on the tiles.[1]

The Roman artist Heraklitus created this *trompe l'oeil* floor according to an originally Greek fashion, one Pliny the Elder associates with Sosus of Pergamum who, "by means of small cubes tinted in various shades . . . represented on the floor refuse from the dinner table and other sweepings, making them appear as if they had been left there."[2] The mosaic is an important entry point for many different conversations about Greco-Roman life in the first centuries of the common era. In *After Jesus*

---

1. The image can be accessed via https://www.museivaticani.va/content/museivaticani/en/collezioni/musei/museo-gregoriano-profano/Mosaico-dell-asarotos-oikos.html.

2. Pliny, *Natural History* 36.60.

Before Christianity, we refer to the image in the context of the centrality of banqueting practices in ancient Mediterranean social life. The mosaic speaks also to Roman imperial power, as many of the food scraps would have travelled from all around the Mediterranean, and beyond, to arrive in this Roman triclinium: the *Murex Brandaris* shells used in the making of imperial purple dye, for example, or ginger from India.[3] Questioning could just as easily turn from empire to education and philosophy and the intersection—or not—of this imagery with elite Roman values.

These discussions of the unswept floor would not have been possible without the work of John Dominic Crossan. Indeed, the mosaic offers a metaphor for Crossan's approach to historiography: his meticulous inquiry into the socioeconomic realities, inconvenient writings, and marginal voices from early Christ associations that traditional scholarship swept aside. Crossan finds meaning in what others have deemed disposable in our historical inheritance, "making them appear as if they had been left there," to once again quote Pliny. Crossan demands that we see the room before we sweep it.

It seems appropriate, then, that when Crossan began his address as the 2012 President of the Society of Biblical Literature, he chose to open with Walter Benjamin's words from *On the Concept of History*:

> Nothing that has ever happened should be regarded as lost for history. To be sure, only a redeemed mankind receives the fullness of its past—which is to say, only for a redeemed mankind has its past become citable in all its moments.[4]

History, for Benjamin, may be an ever-growing pile of human wreckage, but we can sift through it, brush back against it, refuse to sweep the debris aside. All historical moments hold meaning-making potential, especially those that counter our master narratives. Only when we consider the seemingly minor parts of history can we truly engage with what it means to be human.

Surely, Crossan is himself the chronicler for whom Benjamin's thesis holds true, the one who "recites events without distinguishing between major and minor ones."[5] It is a backward-looking history that distinguishes major events, a history that views the present as not just central to interpretation, but as the inevitable center. Crossan requires

---

3. See Fathy, "The Asàrotos Òikos Mosaic." 26.
4. The epigraph for Crossan's, "A Vision of Divine Justice," 5.
5. Benjamin, "Theses on the Philosophy of History," 256.

a history that moves forwards. This movement is not linear, nor is it progressive as such; it demands, simply (or not so simply), that we do not read ourselves into history, as much as that action is possible. If we are to authentically engage with the meal tradition associated with the death of Jesus, for instance, we must, Crossan tells, us "hold in abeyance two thousand years of eucharistic theology and a similar amount of Last Supper iconography."[6] We cannot start the work of history with what we think we know. We are only historians in so much as we do *not* know.

Crossan reminds us that historiography is a thoroughly human enterprise. His insistence on the inclusion of writings later called non-canonical in basic debate about the historical Jesus, for example, empowers scholars to hear voices pushed to the margins, voices that represent the vast diversity of Jesus groups, Christ associations, and so many others without name in the first two centuries of what eventually became Christianity. Crossan made no distinction between the gospels of Matthew, Mark, Luke and John and Thomas, for example, in his 1993 *The Historical Jesus: The Life of a Mediterranean Jewish Peasant*. That lack of distinction, the lack of hierarchy between writings that only later became canonical with those that, for so long, seemed lost to history, is necessary if we are to truly appreciate the fullness of our past. If we are truly interested in historical work, we cannot privilege writings that were themselves only privileged in later historical time. It does not make sense. We cannot distinguish the major and minor; we must resist the master narrative. Historiography is the work of resistance.

Crossan reminds us that this work is profoundly human. We look to the past to figure out what it means to be human. If we are to know what that means in the present, we must inquire into what that meant in the past. A redemptive history is one that considers what it is to be human. Crossan's historiography is grounded in his humanity. We cannot forget that, at its core, scholarship is meant to be people talking, one responding to another with generosity and integrity. In the first footnote of his SBL Presidential Address, Crossan references the importance of Kartsonis's volume *Anastasis: The Making of an Image*.[7] Crossan states that over the course of a decade, the volume "has been, for Sarah [Crossan] and myself, Bible and Baedeker combined—from Nevsky to Nile and Tiber to Tigris." His reference to his wife Sarah is casual and perhaps easy to overlook.

---

6. Crossan, *The Historical Jesus*. 360.
7. Kartsonis, *Anastasis*.

Here, though, we see not just the scholar at work, but the human being traveling, experiencing, learning alongside his partner. Scholarship, for Crossan, is not separate from life but deeply interwoven with it.

Through his methodical questioning of established interpretations and recognition of the collaborative nature of scholarly inquiry, Crossan has expanded how we approach historiography in studies of the early Christ associations. His work suggests that historical investigation is not merely a technical discipline but an inherently human endeavor that benefits from acknowledging the researcher's own context and limitations. Crossan's citation of Benjamin highlights how historical inquiry involves evaluating and reassessing evidence. By emphasizing a forward-working methodology that begins with context rather than conclusions, Crossan has provided biblical scholarship with analytical tools that allow for more nuanced, sometimes messy, understandings of Jesus and the diverse groups that grew up after him.

9

A New Way Forward?

STEPHEN J. PATTERSON

Everything I learned about the historical Jesus, I learned from Dom Crossan.[1]

When I joined the Jesus Seminar in 1988, I was a Jesus skeptic. I was mostly looking for colleagues with an interest in gospels, especially the Gospel of Thomas. In the first few years I think the most important thing I might have said in the seminar was, "We're out of black beads over here."[2] Gradually my principled skepticism gave way to a more nuanced, practical skepticism. Discussion of the particulars made a difference—but not a big difference. By the fall of '91, I could be found with a gray bead in hand, but only occasionally. I simply felt, given the state of the sources, scholars were very limited in what they could know about the historical Jesus.

Then Crossan published *The Historical Jesus: The Life of a Mediterranean Jewish Peasant* (1991). This changed everything. Here was a method that made sense. But more importantly, here was a content that seemed important. That is what I will discuss here: the new method and the new content Crossan brought to the conversation that revolutionized historical Jesus research.

---

1. The original context for this essay was an oral contribution to a tribute to Crossan's work in the Jesus Seminar. I have retained some of the informality and personal nature of my original remarks, *bona venia*.

2. The Jesus Seminar made a practice of voting for or against the authenticity of a saying by placing a colored bead in a box. A black bead signaled "not authentic" (a red, "authentic," a pink "maybe authentic," a gray, "probably not authentic.")

A NEW METHOD

When Crossan wrote in 1991 that historical Jesus research had become something of a scholarly bad joke,[3] he wasn't wrong. The problem was method. The New Quest[4] had made the case for the theological necessity of the historical Jesus,[5] and even the theoretical possibility,[6] but it had not produced the means. Käsemann gave the New Quest the rudiments of a method with the principle of "dissimilarity,"[7] based on the reasonable assumption that the gospels contain things that were attributed to Jesus simply because he was a revered teacher. This would have included common Jewish ideas about God or ethics and well-worn wisdom, as well as ideas about Jesus that arose later among his devoted followers. So, the New Questers considered only things that were dissimilar to common Jewish teachings, on the one hand, and to ideas Jesus' followers later had about him, on the other. They were well aware of the most obvious problem with this method: it could only yield a Jewish teacher who taught nothing Jewish and a founder figure who had nothing in common with his followers. Still, a distinctive Jesus would have to do. Dissatisfied with this approach, others relied on the presumed perspicacity of the tradition to reveal its historical roots through common sense and good judgment. The result was a flourish of diverse proposals over the next thirty years—Jesus the prophet, Jesus the Pharisee, Jesus the Hillelite, Jesus the

---

3. Crossan, *The Historical Jesus*, xxvii.

4. The New Quest refers of historical Jesus research in the middle of the twentieth century chronicled by Robinson in *A New Quest of the Historical Jesus* (1959). The New Quest is often said to have been ignited by Ernst Käsemann in a lecture delivered to an annual gathering of former students of Rudolf Bultmann in 1953 entitled, "Das Problem des historischen Jesus." It was translated and published in English as "The Problem of the Historical Jesus."

5. Käsemann argued that without due attention to the historical Jesus, Christian theology risked the ancient heresy of Docetism—the idea that Jesus the human being had no relevance for Christianity, or even that Jesus wasn't really a human being after all ("Historical Jesus," 30–34, esp. 34).

6. Robinson argued that a new conception of history found in the work of the likes of Dilthey and Collingwood—the past rendered in its significance for the present—had made the gospels less of a methodological problem than Bultmann and the early form critics had thought. The fact that they include interpretation, not just the brute facts, did not disqualify them in the least.

7. Käsemann, "The Problem of the Historical Jesus," esp. 37; Robinson embraced this principle as well (*New Quest*, 99).

revolutionary, Jesus the magician, etc.[8] The Jesus tradition was rich and diverse enough to support any of these proposals and more.

Crossan attempted to break free of this slipperiness by taking another swing at method. The result was a complicated procedure he described as a "triple triadic process"— a set of three processes, each with three components.

The first triad simply names the sort of information, or data, he was looking for. Crossan was trying to understand certain things Jesus said or did (content) in terms of a specific time and place (history), using anthropological modeling to make intrinsically foreign material intelligible (theory). There are two new things here: the use of theory (we will come back to this later) and a new approach to content. We'll start there.

Since the nineteenth century the sources for historical Jesus study had been, for the most part, the synoptic gospels, Matthew, Mark, and Luke. John was usually bracketed out. Non-canonical sources were seldom considered. These biases had rarely been challenged. Crossan decided to throw them out. Instead, he compiled an inventory of everything that might hold relevant material, which meant just about everything from the first two centuries, including the Gospel of John, as well as the gospels of Thomas, of Peter, of the Nazoreans, etc., and even non-gospel texts, like the letters of Paul or the *Didache*. Next, Crossan assigned each text a date (hewing mostly to convention) and placed it in a chronological stratum. Finally, he ear-marked material that could be found independently in two or more sources. This was the gist of Crossan's second triad.

Crossan's third triad built upon the second. Crossan now inventoried the material anew, identifying material found in the earliest stratum that is also multiply attested. This would the earliest *verifiable* corpus of material attributed to Jesus. Crossan argued that any reasonable search for authentic Jesus material should begin with this corpus. Conversely, material that was attested just once, especially if it showed up only in a source from the later strata, should be bracketed out. This meant that some of the tradition's most beloved gems, like the parable of the Samaritan, or the Prodigal Son, would never come under consideration. Indeed, they are absent from Crossan's tome.

This prioritizing of material quickly became a source of controversy. One way—the most common way—that Crossan proved up multiple attestation was with the Gospel of Thomas. With Thomas on the sidelines,

---

8. The list comes from Harrington, "The Jewishness of Jesus," whom Crossan quotes to make the point (*The Historical Jesus*, xxviii).

the words and deeds of Jesus enjoying independent multiple attestation would have consisted of just a handful of things found independently in John and the synoptics, or possibly Mark and Q. But Thomas shares dozens of sayings with the synoptic gospels. If it, like the Gospel of John, represented an autonomous stream of tradition, then suddenly dozens of sayings and parables could be assigned to that corpus of multiply attested material. Opponents complained that this gave Thomas far too much sway. If there was a Thomas version, the saying was in, if not, it was out. Of course, one could say the same for the synoptic gospels: if there was a synoptic version, the saying was in, if not, it was out. The problem for critics was that Crossan had given Thomas equal weight in the method. But Crossan saw nothing inherent in Thomas that should give it less weight. It was simply another source for identifying independently attested material.[9]

Within the synoptic nexus, of course, the earliest known writing is the lost source used by Matthew and Luke known as Q. Crossan accepted the Q hypothesis, and with it the theory advocated by several Q scholars—most notably John Kloppenborg—that the earliest parts of Q are the seven wisdom speeches that comprise the backbone of the document once you reconstruct it.[10] This includes, for example, the Q sermon, or the "Lilies of the Field" speech. If those early Q speeches can be assigned a date of roughly 50 CE, this would be our earliest datable source for Jesus material. Now, much of the material in these speeches is found independently in the Gospel of Thomas (Q's beatitudes, for example). Therefore, this paralleled material must logically predate even these Q speeches. This was critical for my own thinking about the *possibility* of the quest. If this material existed already before 50 CE, then we have a substantial corpus of Jesus's teachings from within a generation of Jesus's death and coming from people who could have known Jesus or had first-hand knowledge of what he said and did. Crossan does not make this claim, but it is true. This changed things for me. Where before I had doubted the ability of scholars ever to know anything about Jesus, now I was asked to doubt that the followers of Jesus could remember anything about him

---

9. Among those who pushed back against Crossan were many who regarded the Gospel of Thomas as late and derivative. Crossan sided with scholars who regard Thomas as an autonomous tradition, not derived from the synoptic texts (*Historical Jesus*, 427–28).

10. See Kloppenborg, *The Formation of Q*.

just twenty years after his death. That was just too much. Crossan made me a believer.

So, the method made sense. What about the results? Did they matter? That brings me to the second big thing about Crossan's work: his method gave him a way of seeing the content of the tradition in a whole new way.

A NEW CONTENT

If the triple triadic method gathered up a more extensive list of things to consider than I ever thought possible, most of it was pretty familiar: the parables, many aphorisms, some instruction and social critique, exorcisms, and the like. But Crossan's method taught him to read it differently. Just about everyone before Crossan had assembled a corpus of material and tried to interpret it by setting it in a particular historical context—the Galilee in the First Century, the Roman Empire, etc. But the Galilee in the first century is a very different place and time from the work room of the modern scholar. How could one bridge the vast hermeneutical gap separating then from now? A generation earlier, thoughtful scholars tried to bridge that gap with philosophy or theology: human beings all dwell in the common world of ideas. So, for example, in Günther Bornkamm's classic *Jesus of Nazareth* one finds chapter titles such as "The Hour of Salvation," "Repentance and Readiness," or "The New Righteousness."[11] But Crossan brought a different sensibility to his study of the Jesus corpus. When he emerged from the closely guarded world of the Roman Catholic seminary and began teaching Religion in a liberal arts college in 1969, the influence of German scholars like Bultmann and Bornkamm was receding. Instead, scholars like Crossan were influenced by conversations unfolding in the American academy, chiefly around literary criticism and cultural anthropology. Crossan's early work on aphorisms and parables reflects the former;[12] *The Historical Jesus* reflects the latter. Early pioneers of the turn to cultural anthropology in New Testament

---

11. Originally published in German in 1956, Bornkamm's text was translated into English in 1960 and became the standard text for seminary classrooms for the next 20 years.

12. In anticipation of *The Historical Jesus*, Crossan earlier offered major studies of the aphorisms (*In Fragments*) and parables (*In Parables.*)

scholarship, such as Bruce Malina[13] and Doug Oakman,[14] show up in Crossan's bibliography, as well as Thomas Carney,[15] Eric Hobsbawm,[16] Brian Wilson,[17] Gerhard Lenski,[18] Ioan Lewis,[19] and many others from the field of cultural anthropology. One can also feel the influence of Shirley Jackson Case and Shailer Matthews from the early twentieth century Chicago school.[20] From a methodological standpoint, Crossan's Jesus was very much an American Jesus.

The difference this made was profound. Instead of asking how Jesus, a Galilean peasant, might have anticipated Christian ideas about salvation or eschatology, he asked, what do peasants—for wont of a better term—actually think about? Food; land; family; sickness. These things. And they are aware of the common human experience of honor and shame; and of the distinction between clean and unclean things; and of unclean people. This is the realm of cultural anthropology, not theology. In anthropological terms, the Lord's Prayer was seen to be about food and debt, just as it says.[21] A kingdom like mustard was a like a loathsome weed, perhaps a little threatening, "something you would want in only small and carefully controlled doses."[22] The Tenants parable was not about *Jesus's* fate, but the fate of tenant farmers locked in conflict with an absentee landlord.[23] This approach freed Jesus from the burden of Christian theology to become a close and thoughtful observer of life.

Crossan's method directed him to approach the question of what Jesus *did* differently as well. Eating became central in his understanding of Jesus, inspired in part by his reading of a Claremont dissertation by Lee Klosinski[24]—yes, there are many dissertations in the bibliography of

---

13. Malina, *The New Testament World*.
14. Oakman, *Jesus and the Economic Questions of His Day*.
15. Carney, *The Shape of the Past*.
16. Hobsbawm, *Primitive Rebels*.
17. Wilson, *Magic and the Millenium*.
18. Lenski, *Power and Privilege*.
19. Lewis, *Ecstatic Religion*.
20. These figures from the original cohort at the University of Chicago Divinity School pioneered the use of sociological questions to probe the meaning of Jesus's words and deeds. See esp. Mathews, *The Social Teachings of Jesus*; and Case, *Jesus*.
21. Crossan, *The Historical Jesus*, 294.
22. Crossan, *The Historical Jesus*, 279.
23. Crossan, *The Historical Jesus*, 352.
24. Klosinski, "The Meals in Mark."

The Historical Jesus. Following Klosinski, he asked, what is the meaning of eating together? Why tell a story (the Great Feast parable) about a man who invites his friends, but ends up eating with anyone who cares to join him? This was not a story to illustrate a mythical messianic banquet to unfold at the end of time, but an exploration of what it might mean to eat with strangers in the present. And so, Crossan placed "open commensality" at the center of the Jesus tradition, a practice even more terrifying, perhaps, than the end of time.[25] In Q's so-called "mission discourse" he saw not the first missionary effort to spread the Christian word, but a practice of itinerating like Cynics, but without the typical Cynic goal of *autarcheia* (self-sufficiency). Instead, practitioners were to go out two-by-two, unequipped, so as to force them to knock on a door and say, "the Kingdom has come to you." And if they were taken in, they were to eat what was "set before them" and offer to care for the sick they might find there. The program is quite straightforward, if a little daring: form community, house by house, in bonds of trust built upon an exchange: food for care.[26] Food and health—there is nothing more basic than this when you live at subsistence level. Here was a Jesus who fit into his surroundings, at last, an historical figure teased from a text most likely at home where Jesus was at home, the Galilee.

For many critics, this Jesus was way too small. His stage was merely the Galilee, not the universe itself. For that, Crossan would have needed a missing ingredient: apocalyptic. But when Crossan got down to his base layer (Q, crossed with Thomas) apocalyptic just wasn't there. The kingdom language turned out to be sapiential rather than apocalyptic.[27] The role played by apocalypticism in historical Jesus research is sometimes overstated, but it is fair to say that for most of the twentieth century a Jesus steeped in apocalyptic eschatology had carried the day. Crossan represents a clear break with this scholarly convention: Jesus was not an apocalyptic seer. This decision took Jesus out of the canonical gospels, out of the creeds, and out of contemporary American Christian life. This, perhaps more than anything else in Crossan's work, drew objections. If you wish to make meaning from the *historical* Jesus, said Crossan, you would have to make do with a "peasant, Jewish Cynic," whose "work was

---

25. Crossan, *The Historical Jesus*, 347.
26. Crossan, *The Historical Jesus*, 332–48.
27. Crossan, *The Historical Jesus*, 292, et passim.

among the farms and villages of Lower Galilee."[28] There he observed life close in, meddled with distinctions of in and out, first and last, and peddled a kingdom of nobodies for the unclean and the shamed. His most revolutionary act was, perhaps, the way he ate—with anyone.

What could one do with such gritty material? If you wanted to do theology, it would have to be a kind of historical theology, where one begins in the fields, the kitchen, or among the graves with the demon possessed. This is what I tried to do with Crossan's Jesus in my own work, *The God of Jesus* (1998). This happened to be just the right size Jesus for my taste at the time. In the early 1990s, Deborah and I were serving a tiny church tucked in among the old federal housing projects of St. Louis. I had learned my theology in the suburbs, where a good eschatological ass-kickin' could get people to dig down into deep pockets and save a little of the world. But all of that seemed irrelevant and stupid in Christ in the City. Crossan's Jesus didn't seem stupid at all. I don't credit *Crossan* with that, by the way—except to credit him with the historical honesty to spot a foreign object in a tradition so familiar to us as to have mistaken it for our own, for centuries. If I were to summarize what I learned about Jesus from Crossan, it would be this: Jesus was a very poor person sharing with other very poor people insights about human life that might prove redemptive. To this conversation, he, I, and most scholars, are mere spectators.

AND TODAY?

When Crossan and Borg first introduced us to Lenski's model of ancient agrarian societies more than thirty years ago, we all thought, "how different." So much wealth at the very top; so many people at the bottom just subsisting on a razor thin margin; no middle class to speak of; so many "expendables." Now when I write those words I don't know if they describe better the ancient world or our own. The signs of the times are well-known: the hollowed-out towns; the tent cities; the expendables who wander the streets in a delirium that ancients would have seen as demon possession. And I needn't say how restless people have grown. In the midst of these troubles, people have turned to Jesus for answers. When angry crowds attacked the American Capitol on January 6, 2021, Jesus was everywhere—just not Crossan's Jesus. So, does historical Jesus

---

28. Crossan, *The Historical Jesus*, 421–22.

scholarship have a role to play in the unfolding crisis? Part of the sorcery of Bob Funk was that he could ensorcell us into believing that scholars could, or should, play a role. So, let's just suppose . . .

Let's take a parable and explore the consequences of its various readings for the challenges we face as a people, as a society: first, the biblical parable, then, Jesus's parable, according to Crossan.

The parable is the Tenants, sometimes called the Wicked Tenants. That tag comes from the Markan version of it, where evil tenants take over a vineyard that is not theirs, abuse those who come to collect the rent, and finally, kill the heir to the vineyard in hopes that it might be theirs. But in Mark it is not a story about vineyards and workers, but cities and saviors. In Mark's telling (Mark 12:1–12) the vineyard becomes Jerusalem; the tenants are its evil usurpers; the owner is God; and the son is Jesus. Mark saw in this parable the makings of an apocalyptic prophecy. Jerusalem was destroyed by the Romans in 70 CE because God willed it. The tenants abused the prophets and killed God's beloved Son when he came to call, and for that, they were destroyed. This is a violent, but comforting story. There are good guys and bad guys, and in the end, the bad guys get what's coming to them. God sees to it. Christians have been telling that story in one form or another for two millennia. When rioters stormed the capitol on January 6th, I am sure that something like it was playing in the background for many of them. Trump was their wronged messiah, and God would see to it that the bad guys got what was coming to them. Here is a myth of innocence and retribution, as Burton Mack might have called it.[29] That would be one way of imagining our way forward.

But C. H. Dodd had his doubts about this allegorical reading of the Tenants already in 1935.[30] Mark's historical allegory was certainly a late imposition on the original, which must have been about something else. When Thomas came along with a version devoid of Mark's allegory, Crossan helped us see that it was not originally about Jerusalem at all. But what was it about? If Jesus wasn't clairvoyant about events that would unfold forty years after his death, what sort of bard was he? Crossan asked, how would a Galilean peasant audience have responded to such a story? He answered:

---

29. I refer to Mack's 1988 work, *A Myth of Innocence*.
30. Dodd, *The Parables of the Kingdom*, 96–97.

Some: they got it right. Others: but they will not get away with it. Some: he got what he deserved. Others: but what will the father do now? Some: that is the way to handle landlords. Others: but what about the soldiers?[31]

I can imagine even more debate. *Did* they get it right? Where did they go wrong? When did rebellion go off the rails? And why? When economic arrangements push people to the breaking point, what kind of tragedy follows? Anyhow, that kind of story goes with the kind of Jesus Crossan proposed. He doesn't simplify things, he complicates them. He doesn't imagine a mythic future but examines the present under high-intensity lighting. Crossan's historical Jesus made his fellows see the world clearly and not look away. Only with that kind of unflinching honesty could he dare then to say, "Judge not, lest you be judged," or something truly arresting, like "Love your enemies."

So, what will save us, mythology or honesty? That is a question that goes back to Crossan's earliest work on the parables of Jesus. In *The Dark Interval,* Crossan confronted us with a myth-buster of a Jesus. Myth, he argued, are the stories we tell to deceive ourselves into believing everything is just fine. Parable takes off the blinders, exposes our self-deceptions, and then . . . and then . . . Well, what then? We are left in a dark interval, a little space between the collapse of the old world and the beginning of the new. In that space is a place for transcendence. There is a little eschatology in this Jesus too. It comes, though, not from the gods above, but from the strength of human imagination to see things differently and conjure a new way forward. Mythology or honesty—that is our choice, now more than ever.

---

31. Crossan, *The Historical Jesus,* 352.

10

Unhoused and Unbound

LIZ THEOHARIS

"Don't laugh folks, Jesus was a poor man."

"Baby Jesus was homeless."

"Why do we worship a homeless man on Sunday and ignore one on Monday?"

These statements have been foundational in my work organizing a movement to end poverty and homelessness, led by poor and dispossessed people in these yet to be United States. Plastered on t-shirts, posters, even religious stoles, this grassroots, poor people's movement—made up of migrant farmworkers and domestic workers organizing without labor protections, welfare rights activists and fast food workers, uninsured families, those with their water and utilities shut off, undocumented immigrants facing eviction, indigenous tribes resisting the destruction of their most holy land by multi-national corporations and so many more—has held up Jesus' material impoverishment as a source of inspiration for the 140 million poor and low-income people in the US and billions worldwide—a reality that we learned about through (and have continued to learn from) the ground-breaking work of biblical scholar and social historian, John Dominic Crossan.

When it comes to issues of poverty and their connection to Jesus of Nazareth's life and ministry, many have chosen to ignore Jesus' economic situation as well as the economic situation of the majority of people surrounding and following him, **but not Crossan**! Scholars, preachers, and parishioners have painted Jesus as a middle class, educated professional and the early Christian movement as led by those on top of society. Others have explained away the poverty and homelessness found in the gospels and excavated by social historians claiming simply that Jesus chose a "homeless lifestyle" as a Cynic philosopher and itinerant preacher, implying that people who have been born or made poor (not of their own choosing) perhaps do not have moral, political and epistemological agency to lead (like Jesus). Still others have admitted that although Jesus may have been impoverished, he overcame his poverty to become the anointed leader of his day and therefore his impoverishment was not definitive of his leadership but rather exceptional or accidental to it. Such people point out that the most important of his followers came from influential places and spaces in Roman imperial society, suggesting that the down and out should be pitied or punished—like society has long done to the poor. These interpretations and assertions, however, fail to see that this poor and homeless Jesus who led a poor people's campaign in his day was not powerful despite his poverty, he was impactful because of it.

Indeed, the pioneering analysis and detailed depiction of Jesus as an impoverished and expendable, brown-skinned, Palestinian Jewish organizer and revolutionary, born into forced migration, homelessness, and imperial overreach that Crossan has trailblazed has been a source of inspiration for so many of us.

In particular, the issue of homelessness and the Bible exemplify this issue. For years people have debated whether Jesus is calling himself homeless in Luke 9:58: "Foxes have holes and birds of the air have nests, but the Son of Man has nowhere to lay his head." In Crossan's book, *The Historical Jesus*, he asserts that that the original saying of Jesus passed down through an oral culture for generations may actually have been something more like, "Foxes have holes, birds have nest and human beings are the only ones who are homeless." So when poor and unhoused people—leaders who were taking over federally owned abandoned houses or building community through setting up homelessness encampments—heard Crossan's translation, we were blown away.

Fast forward 2000 years: homelessness started growing rapidly and changing in nature in the late 1980s forcing entire families, many of them working, to live on the streets. Since that time, because of welfare cuts, wages stagnating, rising healthcare and childcare costs, downsizing, and other neoliberal policies that have meant a death sentence for the poor, homelessness has continued to proliferate. In response, our politicians and religious leaders have marginalized and blamed the unhoused for their own impoverishment, portraying poor and unhoused people as immoral, dangerous or pitiable, even though as the richest country in human history—a nation that has at least five abandoned housing units for every unhoused person—we could and should abolish homelessness.

It should not be surprising, therefore, that poor and homeless movement leaders found comfort in God who in the form of Jesus claimed his own homelessness and empathized with the homelessness of others. This Jesus prophetically critiqued those who take and hoard the world's resources and cause others to suffer. Jesus' words and actions affirmed core slogans of the National Union of the Homeless including: 1. Homeless Not Helpless; 2. No Housing, No Peace; and 3. Power Not Pity. Crossan pioneered this new understanding of Jesus, the early Christian movement, and what is required of especially those who claim to follow Jesus to turn over the tables of injustice and bring the reign of a justice, abundance and peace here on earth! His insight gave a force and authority to the organizing unhoused leaders were doing.

Crossan boldly pictures a Jesus who was a poor, illiterate worker. He proclaims a Jesus who came to his ministry in poverty, experiencing severe dispossession by and subjugation to the Roman Empire. Jesus' social and economic position illuminates that he takes a radical stance in his teachings on and practice of economics and politics under the Roman Empire.

In the "Introduction" to *Jesus: A Revolutionary Biography*, Crossan writes, "If, for example, we are tempted to describe Jesus as a literate middle-class carpenter, cross-cultural anthropology reminds us that there was no middle class in ancient societies and that peasants are usually illiterate, so how could Jesus become what never existed at his time?"[1] Instead, Crossan concludes: "If Jesus was a carpenter, therefore, he belonged to the Artisan class, that group pushed into the dangerous space between Peasants and Degradeds or Expendables.... Furthermore, since between 95 and 97 percent of the Jewish state was illiterate at the time of Jesus, it must be presumed that Jesus also was illiterate ... like the vast majority of his contemporaries."[2]

It has been a highlight of my scholarship to learn alongside and engage with Crossan. Since I first encountered Crossan's work in the mid 1990s, I can't tell you how many places anti-poverty movement leaders

---

1. Crossan, *Jesus*, xii.
2. Crossan, *Jesus*, 25.

and I have carried the tome of *The Historical Jesus* as we travel to homeless shelters, encampments and other places of poverty. In every immersion class or graduate seminar our network has taught, we assign the work of Crossan and bemoan any seminary, faith-based community organizing program, or religious studies class that does not have multiple works by John Dominic Crossan on their syllabi. And we were beyond thrilled to be included in a series of conferences on the "New Testament and Roman Empire," convened at Union Theological Seminary at the turn of the millennium (and we got to meet our hero—Dom Crossan—at those events!)

Many of the ideas and public preaching and teaching on the counter-imperial Jesus movement that my colleagues and I have offered to grassroots groups organizing for racial justice, economic justice, gender justice, environmental justice, and peace and justice in our contemporary society have evolved from and built on the work of Crossan. This has involved developing our own Bible study connecting Crossan and Borg's book on *The Last Week of Jesus* with the last year of the Rev. Dr. Martin Luther King (and another that included Archbishop Oscar Romero). We have also illuminated key lessons on organizing from Jesus (structural building blocks that we learned about in dozens of Crossan's books) and five "M's" of his movement-building-ministry-model (message, martyrdom, miracles, media, mentoring, and missionary work) that is relevant in social justice and moral movement building work today. Crossan's work has been instrumental in a "battle for the Bible" and the movement's efforts to push back against distorted and twisted biblical interpretations and help realize a society where everybody is in and nobody is out, that lifts from the bottom so that everybody rises, and where we confront and combat Christian nationalism and the false gods of money, military and might.

Perhaps my favorite of the slogans that developed out of the National Union of the Homeless—and the namesake of one of my books—is: "we only get what we're organized to take." Thank God we have "taken" Crossan's insights and analysis. The struggle for justice, abundance for all, and peace has gained so much from them!

11

Encountering *The Historical Jesus*
A Transformative Moment

CHAD VENTERS

In 1991, John Dominic Crossan's *The Historical Jesus: The Life of a Mediterranean Jewish Peasant* first came into print and gave the world a seminal portrait of the historical Jesus. When I look back on Crossan's scholarship I am still in awe of his ability to bring sociology, anthropology, history, and textual analysis together to create an interdisciplinary vision of Jesus that, I believe, has never been surpassed. The publication of this vital study of Jesus escaped my notice at the time, primarily because I was eleven years old, and had as much interest in the historical Jesus as I did in a retirement plan. It would take another decade for me to learn that Crossan even existed, but that encounter was transformative in ways I am still coming to understand.

I entered Bible college in my early twenties, intent on spending my life as a pastor. Crossan's work was never a focus in the largely conservative school I attended, but it was during these studies that the first notion of a historical Jesus came into my purview. I had never heard of Crossan when I found *The Historical Jesus*, but being an ambitious student of the Bible, the daunting size of the nearly five-hundred-page text felt like a challenge to tackle. It became a life-changing moment that led me to become a Westar scholar.

Crossan's Overture gives a reconstructed inventory of the words that can be traced back to the historical Jesus.[1] I realized that I had never considered the need to analyze what Jesus had said using historical method. Frankly, I had never thought about applying historical method to the life of Jesus. My perception of "historical method" was like that of many idealistic Bible students: accept the New Testament gospels as fact and add historical context to the events described therein. What Crossan presented as Jesus' words was, by no means, all of the sayings of Jesus found in the gospels, and there were even saying not found in *the* gospels. My initial reaction to this inventory was not anger that he was challenging biblical authority, rather it was illuminating to see history applied to Jesus. I found myself thinking, "If we say Jesus is a historical figure, then he should be subject to the process of historical analysis." Nothing was ever the same for me after that moment.

Crossan introduced me to the controversial world of scholarly methodology. I did not grasp the intricacies of his triads and stratification, but the term "independent attestation" was revelatory. I had studied the Two Source Theory in my college gospels class but had no concept of what independent attestation meant. Independent Attestation could have been a popular early 2000s alternative band for all I knew. Crossan exhibited the fundamental issue of units being independently attested. If a unit appears in multiple documents, this does not mean it is independently attested. Crossan's reasoning, again, made complete sense. Searching for independently attested words and actions of Jesus for historical reconstruction offered a measure of protection against the possibility that an author had created sayings or deeds of Jesus. Even though I still believed in the infallibility of scripture, I understood that historical claims required historical method, and searching for Jesus should not be exempt from the application of historical method.

Crossan's book begot my interest in Jesus as a historical figure, and helped drive my desire to become a Jesus scholar. I began purchasing every historical Jesus book I could find. In addition to ensuring that Crossan was receiving steady royalties through the early 2000s, I read books by E. P. Sanders, Bruce Chilton, James M. Robinson, Marcus Borg, Paula Fredrickson, and anyone else I could find that ventured an opinion on the historical Jesus. Crossan's historical Jesus work led me to the Jesus Seminar. My first reading of *The Five Gospels* drew me deeper into questions

---

1. Crossan, *The Historical Jesus,* xi–xxvi.

of methodology, and voting on Jesus's sayings intrigued me. While the notion of scholars voting on Jesus's words and deeds did not trouble me, I found myself asking how the Jesus Seminar making modern deductions about historical matters was somehow wrong, but fourth century bishops making once-for-all decisions that all Christendom was beholden to follow was acceptable. Why did those ancient Christians have the privilege of making decisions that were perpetually binding, regardless of how the world changed? What gave them any special authority to decide anything for anybody? And I have yet to hear a good response to these questions. I was about to spend the next several years trying to introduce various church groups to Crossan and the Jesus Seminar, only to learn that those groups were not interested.

Through my twenties and early thirties, I pursued my education, while teaching in various ministries. I started working with college and young adults, leading Bible studies and learning groups, opting to push the boundaries and challenge them to consider historical method. I raved about Crossan's *The Historical Jesus* and introduced my students to the idea of methodology by discussing Crossan's approach. I learned early in the process that recommending Dom's larger *The Historical Jesus* induced a panic attack, since most were not prepared for a book longer than a Homeric epic. However, his *Jesus: A Revolutionary Biography* was more manageable and welcomed far more often. To date, I still recommend the *Revolutionary Biography* when someone wants to learn more about Jesus. I spent a semester taking a class through the findings of the Jesus Seminar, discussing independent attestation, and even having them vote on passages of the New Testament. These methods were met with mixed emotions.

Each time I sought approval to teach a class using materials from Crossan or the Jesus Seminar, there was always concern. The ever-present boogeyman of bringing historical-critical method into church was not wanting to "cause people to stumble." The fear of making people "stumble" was church code for "we don't want them questioning too much." When I was confronted about the possibility that historical analysis might cause people to question their faith, my response was always the same: "If we truly believe the Bible is 100% historically accurate, then no amount of historical scrutiny can disprove it. What are we afraid of?"

In my thirties, my audience shifted to adults. The majority of people who took my classes through the years were intrigued by the critical scholarship to which I introduced them, but others felt their faith was being attacked. I had students who left classes, sending me emails that said we were not actually studying the Bible. A friend gave me a copy of the book *Jesus Under Fire*, the fundamentalist response to the Jesus Seminar that spent an entire book airing grievances against critical scholarship that could have been summarized with the sentence, "It's in the Bible so it's all true!"[2] The reality was, and still is, that Jesus was never under fire. What Crossan and the Jesus Seminar participants were doing was nothing new, since critical scholarship did not emerge in the 1980s. The issue or problem was that they made scholarship accessible. Fundamentalists responded, "How dare they! This reaction drove me to push harder to bring critical thought to the public. Scholarship should not live in a seminary or the academy, nor should Christians be exempt from critical thought to protect dogma. Some people opted to steer clear of my classes because they were afraid such learning would just confuse their belief system. Others became adamantly supportive and I found the small but devoted niche of believers in multiple churches that wanted to be challenged.

I finished my PhD in 2018 and applied to become a Westar scholar shortly after. I attended the last in-person Westar conference in Santa Rosa before the pandemic, hoping Crossan would be there so I could express how much his work had meant to me. Though he was not in attendance, I knew I had found my people. My time working in churches was coming to an end, but my voyage with Westar was only beginning.

During that Santa Rosa meeting I met Elli Elliott. She recruited me to get involved in Westar's Bible Search & Rescue project that launched in April 2022. Early in 2023, Elli and I had the opportunity to interview Crossan for our podcast to talk about his career. I admit to a degree of nervousness meeting the living legend himself, even if it was over Zoom. One of the questions we addressed was which of Crossan's books had the greatest impact on our own scholarship. I finally had my opportunity to share with him the profound impact *The Historical Jesus* had made on me. In May of 2024, I finally met Crossan in-person at Westar's conference in Salt Lake City, and of course, I brought a copy of *The Historical Jesus* and asked him to sign it, which he graciously did. At one point during the conference, Crossan and John Caputo teased me about being too tall to be a scholar. To be fair, they are both short. In that surreal moment

---

2. Wilkins and Moreland, *Jesus Under Fire*.

I experienced the camaraderie of two incredible scholars, one of whom had been instrumental in my desire to become a scholar and join Westar.

Now almost forty-four, I have a son who is close to the age I was when Crossan's *The Historical Jesus* struck me like a proverbial bolt of lightning. Recently, I re-read the book and marveled at its precision, clarity, and relevance thirty years after its initial publication. Crossan's analysis of Jesus is a clinic on how methodology, interdisciplinary analysis, and textual analysis cohere in historical reconstruction. I still contemplate writing my own historical Jesus book, and reading Crossan's's work is a reminder of the high bar established by my Westar colleagues.

My story is not unique. Crossan has changed many lives through his scholarship. At ninety he continues to produce work that will influence generations to come. Understanding the historical reality of the Mediterranean Jewish Peasant whose existence has dramatically shaped this world is vital. The work Crossan put into establishing his historical Jesus is arguably more important now than when his book was published. The rise of Christian nationalist ideology, in conjunction with the fundamentalist embrace of the modern reimagined apocalyptic Jesus, makes the need for studying the historical Jesus more imperative by the day. *The Historical Jesus* will be read for many generations to come as people struggle with the question that Jesus is said to have asked his students, "Who do people say that I am?"

12

In Search of Method

BERNARD BRANDON SCOTT

A GOLDEN AGE

John Dominic Crossan began his studies in the 1970s on the historical Jesus and parables during a golden age for such studies. And he was a major contributor to what made that age golden. Many came to recognize that something special was happening. Marcus Borg described it as "a renaissance in Jesus studies."[1] N.T Wight titled it a third quest,[2] and James Charlesworth has written of "a renewed study of the Jesus of history."[3] E.P. Sanders boasted, "The dominant view today seems to be that we can know pretty well what Jesus was out to accomplish, that we can know a lot about what he said, and those two things make sense within the world of first-century Judaism."[4] In augurating the Jesus Seminar, Robert Funk noted, "we are entering an exciting new period of biblical, especially New Testament, scholarship."[5]

After World War II in Germany the students of Rudolf Bultmann, against the strictures of their Doctor Vater, inaugurated a new quest for the historical Jesus. The New Hermeneutic[6] and the New Quest

---

1. Borg, "A Renaissance in Jesus Studies."
2. Neill and Wright, *The Interpretation of the New Testament 1861–1986*, 379–403. I was the first one to use the phrase "Third Stage" at a session of Historical Jesus Section at the Annual Meeting of SBL in 1985. Wright was in the audience.
3. Charlesworth, *Jesus within Judaism*, 15.
4. Charlesworth, *Jesus and Judaism*, 2.
5. Funk, "The Issue of Jesus," 8.
6. Achtemeier, *An Introduction to the New Hermeneutic,* provides an excellent

for Historical Jesus originated in Germany[7] and then moved to the United States as Funk noted in his inaugural address opening the Jesus Seminar.[8] Crossan, an Irishman, came to America permanently after post-doctoral studies at the École biblique et archéologique française de Jérusalem. In 1969 he joined the faculty of DePaul University in Chicago.

The American scene quickly diverged from the German. In 1966 Funk in *Language, Hermeneutic and Word of God* offered a series of essays very much in the tradition of Bultmann and the German new hermeneutic and new quest. He attempted to rethink the categories of form criticism as applied to parables and the Pauline letters. He brought a more theoretical understanding to parable as metaphor. His exegesis of the Good Samaritan was particularly bold as he challenged the traditional understanding of the narrative as an example story and argued that it was a real parable.[9] Crossan would follow up on this suggestion.

Nineteen sixty-seven saw two major books. In the first chapter of *Rediscovering the Teaching of Jesus*[10] Norman Perrin laid out the first systematic discussion of the criteria of authenticity. His discussion has had wide influence. For him "the fundamental criterion for authenticity upon which all reconstructions of the teaching of Jesus must be built" was the criterion of dissimilarity. This criterion argued that "the earliest form of a saying we can reach may be regarded as authentic if it can be shown to be dissimilar to characteristic emphases both of ancient Judaism and of the early Church.[11] He defined two other criteria. The criterion of coherence maintained that "material from the earliest strata of the tradition may be accepted as authentic if it can be shown to cohere with material established as authentic by means of the criterion of dissimilarity."[12] Finally his third criterion was multiple attestation. "This is a proposal to accept as authentic material which is attested in all, or most, of the sources which can be discerned behind the synoptic gospels."[13] This is his least successful formulation and Perrin admits to reservations.

---

survey of this movement.

7. Käsemann, "The Problem of Historical Jesus."

8. Funk, "The Issue of Jesus," 9.

9. Funk, "The Old Testament in Parable."

10. Perrin's earlier book, *The Kingdom of God*, was more in the tradition of his teacher Joachim Jeremias.

11. Perrin, *Rediscovering*, 39.

12. Perrin, *Rediscovering*, 43.

13. Perrin, *Rediscovering*, 45.

Crossan would reformulate this criterion into his most important and powerful criterion. In Chapter 4, "Jesus and the Future," Perrin argued that the apocalyptic Son of Man saying were redactional, inauthentic.[14] This powerfully undermined the apocalyptic Jesus as these Son of Man saying were a primary piece of evidence.

Also in 1967 Dan Via's *The Parables: Their Literary and Existential Dimension* appeared. He brought the methods and insights of the New Criticism to the table. This was really a first for parable studies.[15] He divided the parables into two groups: tragic and comic parables, thus moving away from theological tropes for organizing the parables to literary categories. Crossan in this first book, *In Parables: The Challenge of the Historical Jesus* picked up on Via's work.

PROLOGUE

In the interests of honesty, I need to admit that Crossan, along with Robert Funk, has had a major influence on my own work on the parables. I first met Crossan at the first meeting the Society of Biblical Literature Parables Seminar in 1972, at the time a new format for the Society. Crossan was chair of the committee. I was a junior member and my entrance into that illustrious group was no doubt due to Funk. I have followed his career since Funk, one of my graduate school professors, alerted me to him because of our shared interest in parables. When Crossan retired from DePaul, his colleagues published a collection of essays evaluating his work, especially his then recent *The Historical Jesus*. I wrote the first essay in that collection evaluating Crossan's methodology.[16] Crossan himself appreciated the essay, at least in print.[17] I have learned from his

---

14. Perrin, *Rediscovering*, 164–73.

15. The work and influence of Amos Wilder should be acknowledged. He was the grandfather of New Testament literary studies. He was a poet and Hollis Professor of Divinity at Harvard Divinity School. His *Early Christian Rhetoric* was the tip of the iceberg of his influence. Crossan's *A Fragile Craft* was his tribute and accounting of Wilder's importance.

16. Scott, "To Impose Is Not / To Discover." While I cover much of the same material as in this essay, in the earlier essay I argued that Crossan employed both Darwinian diachronic and Saussurian synchronic models. I still think that essay is accurate, and I stand by it. In order not to repeat what I have already written, I have taken a different approach in this essay.

17. Crossan, "Responses and Reflections," 146.

work, have admired his work, and consider him the most creative New Testament scholar of his generation.

To keep this paper from becoming a very long book, like several of those on which it reports, I will focus on what I consider the two dominant problems confronting the quest for the historical Jesus.[18]

- Where to start?
- What was Jesus' position on the future or the problem of eschatology?

COMING TO A METHOD

Methodologically Crossan has been adventurous or promiscuous, depending upon your point of view.

Crossan's *The Historical Jesus: The Life of a Mediterranean Jewish Peasant* (1991), represents his mature method and, while later his interests shifted and expanded, this book established his basic method. In the 1970s Crossan initiated a number of experiments that not only established his method but also enriched it.

First Time Out

In Parables: The Challenge of the Historical Jesus (1973) was Crossan's first effort. Although at first glance it looks like his least experimental book, looks can be deceiving. His historical method was traditional, especially the form criticism. But Crossan used the new tool of redaction criticism to analyze a parable in its redactional contexts. This use of redactional criticism was imaginative and bold, moving beyond the intentions of the method's first practitioners. His analysis of the Good Samaritan is a good example. He demonstrates that the context provided by the question "who is my neighbor?" is redactional. Therefore, the narrative is not an example story, as the redactional context in Luke and the traditional parable criticism would have it, but a parable per se.[19] The precision of

---

18. I reached this conclusion in my paper "New Options in An Old Quest." An earlier version of this argument is "From Reimarus to Crossan: Stages in a Quest."

19. Crossan, *In Parables*, 57–66; Funk, "The Old Testament in Parable," was the first to argue that the Good Samaritan was not an example story but a parable. Jülicher, *Die Gleichnisreden Jesu* (1888) established the threefold division of similitudes, parables, example stories.

his redactional analysis led to a reconstruction and understanding of the narrative as parable rather than example story.

By using Martin Heidegger's categories of time to organize his discussion of the parables and the kingdom of God, Crossan avoids the traditional interpretation of the parables as eschatological or apocalyptic.[20] He does not directly attack this issue but employs Heidegger's view of time as an interpretive model. He contrasts prophetic and apocalyptic understandings of time. Apocalyptic views time as linear and sees this world coming to an end. The prophet views of time from God's viewpoint and is concerned with this world. "The question that all this raises, and raises most forcibly, is *whether Jesus is speaking out of the ancient prophetic eschatology precisely in order to oppose and deny the current apocalyptic eschatology of his contemporaries?*[21] This leads to Crossan's major thesis: "Jesus is proclaiming what might be termed *permanent eschatology*, the permanent presence of God as the one who challenges world and shatters its complacency completely."[22] With this understanding in place, he organizes the parables into three categories: parables of advent, parables of reversal, and parables of action. Jeremias' eschatological/apocalyptic interpretation has disappeared.

Crossan will reformulate and elaborate this thesis several times, but his basic position is established and will not change. This gives the kingdom of God a prophetic, not apocalyptic, interpretation and puts the parables at the center for understanding the historical Jesus.

Experiments

Crossan initiated a series of books that experimented with the ideas laid out in *In Parables*. These experiments deepened and enriched Crossan's program, often expanding it outside the then normal parameters of New Testament criticism. The reaction of the guild to these experiments was varied. But these experiments were essential for Crossan. He was not moving away from traditional New Testament criticism, but expanding it, making it more interdisciplinary. All these books except *In Fragments*

---

20. Jeremias, *The Parables of Jesus* (1972) was the standard from post-war German scholarship.

21. Crossan, *In Parables*, 26; emphasis in original. Perrin, *Rediscovering*, had challenged the authenticity of the future son of Man sayings. See above.

22. Crossan, *In Parables*, 26; emphasis in original. This is close C. H. Dodd's realized eschatology, Crossan, *The Parables of the Kingdom*, 35.

have titles from poems. "In fragments" comes from John 6:12: "Gather up the fragments that nothing may be lost."

The Dark Interval, Towards a Theology of Story marks the first experiment in the progression towards *The Historical Jesus*. It also marks a shift from *In Parables*. Without the eventual terminus of *The Historical Jesus*, one might be tempted to believed that Crossan had abandoned historical criticism for literary studies. *Dark Interval* fits into Crossan's historical Jesus studies because it makes what becomes a key distinction between parable and myth, one of the most important binaries in Crossan's repertoire. His understanding of parable derives from *In Parable* and literary criticism, while that of myth comes from Claude Levi-Strauss. Myth reconciles contradictions, while parable exposes contradictions. While Crossan's basic understanding of parable derives from his analysis of Jesus' parables, it is not limited to Jesus' parables. Crossan transmogrifies the form parable from a form critical form into a way or mode of story, making parable a heuristic device, a meta-parable.[23] *Raid on the Articulate, Comic Eschatology in Jesus and Borges* extends this insight in a comparative analysis of Jesus and Gorge Borges. This comparative analysis deepens Crossan's understanding of myth, parable, and eschatology.

In yet another form of comparative analysis, *Finding is the First Act* explores the comparative literature about treasure stories. Crossan collected enough treasure stories from a variety of cultures to elaborate its typology, which showed that Jesus' parable, a story that exposes contradictions, explodes the mythical stories of treasure stories that see treasure as a reward. As an author of a book on all of Jesus' parables, I found this book terrifying, because it indicated what I should have done for each parable. *Finding is the First Act* had a major influence on my *Hear Then the Parable* in that I tried to focus on what story Jesus was *not* telling; how his parables were reacting against storied expectations.[24]

The subtitle of *Cliffs of Fall* clearly indicates the direction of this small, but important study: *Paradox and Polyvalence in the Parables of Jesus*. This book was written in conversation with Paul Ricoeur of the University of Chicago (Crossan was at DePaul, also in Chicago). This allowed

---

23. The theological aspect of this part of his program I take to be outside my warrant. A good example of how this understanding works out in his later writings, see Crossan, *The Power of Parable*.

24. Kloppenborg, *The Tenants in the Vineyard*, follows a similar process by collecting a large amount of material dealing with ancient viticulture. His analysis remains more traditional.

Crossan yet again to expand his understanding of parable, metaphor, and paradox. This had the result of undermining the notion, traditional since Jülicher, that a parable makes a single, simple point. Crossan exploded this into polyvalence, multiple meaning. Jülicher's single point, derived from Aristotle, was his weapon against allegory with its multiple points. Crossan deftly negotiates this distinction between parable and allegory by arguing that polyvalence derives from within the parable itself as metaphor, not from outside the story as in the case of allegory. Crossan's chief parable for analysis in this case study is the Sower. Significantly, he deals with the version of the Sower in the Gospel of Thomas (9) as independent of the synoptic versions.

The title *In Fragments*[25] deliberately invokes the earlier *In Parables*. This deep and scholarly study of Jesus' aphorisms provides a major foundation for his *Historical Jesus*. Form critics had examined the aphorisms as wisdom sayings,[26] but Crossan brings his more sophisticated tools, developed in the preceding experiments, to move the discussion of aphorisms to a new level.[27] He forms a corpus of aphorisms, analyzes the form and then its elaboration into various other forms. By treating the aphorisms as a corpus, Crossan's synchronic analysis shows how the form functions as a whole, not simply as single, isolated sayings. This level of concentrated analysis raises the aphorisms to the same state and status as parables, becoming an extension of the parables. The book exhibits what I would term Crossan's mature method: collection, reconstruction, comparison, analysis.

As part of his participation in the Jesus Seminar, Crossan prepared *Sayings Parallels: A Workbook for the Jesus Tradition* (1986). This plays to his strengths as a collector, organizer and form critic. The book collects all the sayings attributed to Jesus, whether canonical or noncanonical, up to 200 ce. The sayings are displayed in parallel columns so the user can easily see the various forms that a given saying takes. This is done in as neutral a fashion as possible. "*Sayings Parallels*, then, sets out the diversity of Jesus' sayings in terms of source, genre, and version by presenting the full catalogue of the phenomenon across the designated corpus."[28]

25. Crossan, *In Fragments*.

26. Bultmann, *The History of the Synoptic Tradition*, deals with the "Logia (Jesus as the Teacher of Wisdom), 81–108.

27. Tannehill, *The Sword of His Mouth*, had opened up the literary analysis of aphorisms.

28. Crossan, *Sayings Parallels*, xv.

The *Sayings Parallels* along with *In Fragments* provided the structure for the corpus that underlies *The Historical Jesus*. During the Jesus Seminar, I used the *Sayings Parallels* extensively. My only complaint was that it did not contain the original languages. I too often had to wrestle *Sayings Parallels*, with Aland's *Synopsis* and a Coptic text of the Gospel of Thomas.

In his *Four Other Gospels: Shadows on the Contours of Canon* (1985) Crossan argued for the validity of the noncanonical tradition as evidence for our understanding of the Jesus tradition and early Christianity. The canon of the New Testament had not functioned for him as pointer to or sole receptacle for the evidence to be considered. *The Cross That Spoke: The Origins of the Passion Narrative* (1988), a brave and deeply scholarly analysis, reconstructed of the traditions that underlay the Gospel of Peter to expose the origins of the passion narrative.[29] New Testament scholarship on the whole is conservative and Crossan's forays into the noncanonical and his championing of the reconstructed "Cross that Spoke" as the origin of the passion narrative have drawn strong criticism.[30] These efforts exemplify his expansive method, skill at reconstruction, and thirst for historical understanding.

THE HISTORICAL JESUS

Inventory

The perennial question for those involved in the quest for the historical Jesus is what comes from Jesus. Various scholars have tried to solve this problem since the quest's beginning. At the beginning of the new quest, Norman Perrin systematized the criteria for determining the authenticity of sayings (see above). E. P. Sanders in *Jesus and Judaism* found the sayings tradition too problematic because it was subject to interpretation.[31] The polyvalence that Crossan rejoiced in terrified Sanders. Sanders proposed as a sure foundation a list of facts that were beyond debate. At the core of his list was Jesus' temple action which turned out to

---

29. Dewey, *Inventing the Passion* offers a competing reconstruction, but is nevertheless appreciative of Crossan's effort.

30. Brown, "The *Gospel of Peter* and Canonical Gospel Priority," offers a rousing attack on the thesis, however his attack is marred by "a reluctance to consider the possible layering of Peter and a prejudice in favor of the canonical gospels that dismisses the non-canonical." Dewey, *Inventing the Passion*, 119.

31. Sanders, *Jesus and Judaism*, 13–18.

be very debatable and much more subject to interpretation than Sanders had anticipated.[32] The Jesus Seminar took another tack. It never agreed upon criteria, although there were many discussions. Rather, scholars presented research papers on each item, discussed the papers, and then voted. This was an early form of crowd sourcing, based upon the well-established principle that the wisdom of a group is better than that of a single individual.[33]

Crossan chartered another path. At the beginning of *The Historical Jesus*, he offers "a reconstructed inventory" of all the words he thinks go back to the historical Jesus. Yet he offers a warning:

> But, as you read them [the reconstructed inventory], recall that, in the light of the preceding paragraphs, these words are not a list to be read. They are not even a sermon to be preached. They are a score to be played and a program to be enacted.[34]

The reconstructed inventory goes on for thirteen pages in small type.

How did Crossan reconstruct that inventory and what does he mean by inventory? By inventory he means "a complete declaration of all the major sources and texts, both canonical and extracanonical, to be used." Here the work done in the construction of the *Sayings Parallels: A Workbook for the Jesus Tradition* pays off. Next, each of the sources and texts must be layered chronologically. With the chronology in place, the material is arranged into levels:

- Level I 30–60 ce
- Level II 70–120 ce
- Level III 120–150 ce

This produces his stratification. Obviously, material in Level I is closer to Jesus than Level III. Crossan combined his stratification of the inventory with the criterion of multiple attestation. This criterion, as worked out by Norman Perrin, argued that material attested in multiple

---

32. See my "Holmes Is on the Case," for a critique of Sanders' position.

33. Powell, *Jesus as a Figure in History*, 81, catches this point. "What marks the Jesus Seminar as unique—probably the *only* thing that marks them as unique—is that they are a group . . . Only seventy-four scholars consented to place their names on that volume. Still, that is seventy-three more names than are associated with any of the other positions described in this book."

34. Crossan, *The Historical Jesus*, xiii.

independent sources has a high claim to be from Jesus. The logic of this criterion is that independent multiple attestation means the item must predate the independent sources in which it was found, thus pushing it earlier in the tradition, most probably oral. By valuating multiple attestation as a way to arrange the complexes from the inventory into a hierarchy, Crossan sets aside items attested in only one single source. It is important to notice what Crossan is arguing. He does not argue that single attestation means an item is not from Jesus, but rather that he is not going to use it in his analysis. For example, he obviously thinks the parable of the Good Samaritan is from Jesus, but because it only has a single attestation, he does not use it.

The Sorting Hat

In my judgment, this is Crossan's most brilliant contribution to the ongoing debate. His inventory, levels, stratigraphy, and multiple attestation created a formal model that allow various investments. You could argue about the investment, but it probably would not make a great deal of difference. For example, Crossan judges the Gospel of Thomas to be independent and in Level I. Therefore, sayings that are parallel in Thomas to those in one of the Synoptics would rate high in authenticity in Crossan's method. There are scholars who would challenge this early dating and/or its independence. I, for example, would put the Gospel of Thomas in Level II, but have concluded that it is independent of the synoptics. But such a decision would not drastically change the investment of the method. It would only rearrange it. The value of Crossan's method is that the formal investment of the stratigraphy determines what he will deal with as material with a strong claim to be from Jesus. The method sorts the material to be considered. Items that receive a high score in this method have a high claim to authenticity. To reject such a cluster, one needs a strong argument.[35] In a shift from his earlier work, Crossan is less interested in reconstructing an authentic saying than he is in understanding the core of a cluster.

Crossan's proposal did influence several members of the Jesus Seminar, but the Seminar as a whole did not adopt his method. I thought this

---

35. Crossan does in some cases argue against clusters with strong attestation. For example, Cluster 2, "Jesus' Apocalyptic Return," has items that occur in the level I and has multiple attestation. Crossan nevertheless argues against it. I deal with this cluster below.

proposal would be seriously debated and marked a real step forward. That has not proven to be the case.

Layering Method

From the beginning of his scholarly career Crossan's methodological tool bag has continuously expanded. In *The Historical Jesus* he introduces yet another tool: anthropology or social world method. He distinguishes "a macrocosmic level using cross-cultural and cross-temporal social *anthropology*, a mesocosmic level using Hellenistic or Greco-Roman *history*, and a microcosmic level using the *literature* of specific sayings and doings, stories and anecdotes, confessions, and interpretations concerning Jesus."[36] Since this tri-level analysis significantly shapes the outcome, it is important to grasp how the three levels interact.

- Top Level

    This is the level of highest abstraction. The models are multi-cultural, often from different time periods. They describe how a culture or society operates in comparison with other cultures or societies. Social world studies were making a major impact on New Testament studies at the time of the writing of *The Historical Jesus*.

- Middle Level

    This level moves from the theoretical models of the top level to the history of a particular time, in this case the Roman Empire. The Roman Empire is the mega-historical reality in which the particulars of Judaism, Jesus, and early Christianity are understood.

- Bottom Level

    At the bottom level, Crossan analyzes the clusters of his inventory.

Sociological, historical, and literary methods are brought to bear on a cluster, a broad range of skills. He moves from cross-cultural studies, to studies of the Greco-Roman world, the Roman Empire, and then to the local Galilean level. Crossan is to be commended for being clear about how his various methods interact. He is the first New Testament scholar to have worked out and proposed such a clear method. Most New

---

36. Crossan, *The Historical Jesus*, xxviii

Testament scholarship operates at the bottom level, occasionally dipping into one or the other levels. (Are we bottom dwellers?) Crossan has redefined *Sitz im Leben* from dealing with the particular life situation of the church to understanding a cluster in an ever expanding historical and theoretical context.

Crossan's three-level model establishes his book's organization. Since the anthropological model dictates brokerage as a major issue, the book is divided into three parts: Brokered Empire, Embattled Brokerage, Borderless Kingdom. This puts the Roman Empire at the book's center and has a major effect on the understanding of the kingdom of God. What the kingdom of God means in Jesus' language has been mired in the mud for centuries. Crossan reshapes this debate by making the Roman Empire the context for understanding the kingdom (empire) of God.[37] The whole book is an effort to demonstrate that the empire of God opposes the empire of Rome. This leads to a very different view of Jesus with a much stronger political emphasis than traditionally. Meals and healing become a refuge from the dangers of the Roman Empire. For most New Testament scholars, a wall runs between politics and religion. They view Jesus as a religious reformer without a political agenda. Crossan breached this wall and demonstrated that in the context of the Roman Empire the religious has inevitable political implications. Eating, healing, and speaking are both religious and political acts. They cannot be separated out.

The Core

A key cluster for Crossan is *Mission and Message*.[38] This cluster consists of seven items, three of which are from the first strata and are multi-attested. This indicates the cluster is close to Jesus. The core of this cluster brings together mission and itinerancy, "magic and meal, miracle and table, compassion and commensality."[39] The three items are Gos. Thom. 14:2; Sayings Gospel Q Luke 10:4-11(=Matt 10:7, 10b, 12-14) Mark 6:7-13. Gos. Thom. 14:2 is an excellent example of this core:

---

37. The biblical translation of *basileia* as "kingdom" instead of "empire" has obscured this relationship.

38. Crossan, *The Historical Jesus*, 434, the first cluster in the inventory.

39. Crossan, *The Historical Jesus*, 332. Crossan's analysis of this cluster runs from 332–34.

> When you go into any land and walk about in the districts, if they receive you, eat what they will set before you, and heal the sick among them.[40]

This saying is important for Crossan because the Gospel of Thomas shows no interest in healing elsewhere and yet here it is mentioned. This associates mission and itinerancy. If there is an essence (Crossan does not use this term; I do not like essences) of Jesus' program this is it. "Those three texts are the core of the argument and the place, I propose, where one can see the heart of the Jesus movement most clearly."[41] In *Jesus: A Revolutionary Biography*[42] Crossan expresses this most clearly:

> That ecstatic vision and social program sought to rebuild a society upward from its grass roots, but on principles of religious and economic egalitarianism, with free healing brought directly to the peasant homes and free sharing of whatever they had in return. The deliberate conjunction of magic and meal, miracle and table, free compassion and open commensality, was a challenge launched not just on the level of Judaism's strictest purity regulations, or even on that of the Mediterranean's patriarchal combination of honor and shame, patronage and clientage, but at the most basic level of civilization's eternal inclination to draw lines, invoke boundaries, establish hierarchies, and maintain discriminations. It did not invite a political revolution but envisaged a social one at the imagination's most dangerous depths. No importance was given to distinctions of Gentile and Jew, female and male, slave and free, poor and rich. Those distinctions were hardly even attacked in theory; in practice, they were simply ignored.[43]

---

40. In Crossan's stratigraphy, Gos. Thom. 14 comes from the first level and is independent from the synoptics. Moving it to level 2 would not change his argument. Even removing it from the cluster, i.e., denying its independent attestation, would weaken the cluster, but not by much. There would still be two other items to account for. This shows how strong this cluster is and how Crossan has not stacked the deck, or as Johnson, *The Real Jesus*, 47, has charged, "that the game is fixed."

41. Crossan, *The Historical Jesus*, 333.

42. Crossan, *Jesus: A Revolutionary Biography* is not simply a "popular" version of *The Historical Jesus*. It is more accessible, without the elaborate scholarly framework of the latter. In *Jesus* Crossan has not changed his position but has refined it. The book makes a wonderful guide to *The Historical Jesus*. But if you want the details, turn to *The Historical Jesus*. If you want the clearest expression, read *Jesus*. You might even want to read *Jesus* before reading *The Historical Jesus*.

43. Crossan, *Jesus*, 197.

In *In Parables* Crossan had side stepped the problem of the definition of the Kingdom of God in Judaism by viewing the parables as providing an experience of the Kingdom. In *The Historical Jesus* he continued the sidestepping, but he shifted from the parables to clusters which provide an enriched view of Jesus' program.

AFTERWARDS

The Historical Jesus appeared in 1991 and four years later Crossan was taking early retirement from DePaul University. One would be tempted to view *The Historical Jesus* as the culmination of his career. But in some ways, he was only getting started. He ranged beyond the historical Jesus and dug yet deeper into historical Jesus studies. He refined his method but did not shift it. *The Historical Jesus* represents his mature method.

The Birth of Christianity: Discovering What Happened in the Years Immediately after the Execution of Jesus (1998) is for me one of Crossan's more disappointing books. I have never been convinced that it delivers on its subtitle. It is more of a series of explorations than a systematic reconstruction of the period after Jesus' execution, especially in comparison with *The Historical Jesus*. Often he appears to be house cleaning, responding to criticisms, defending his positions, and at times settling scores. He dives deeply into the methodological weeds.[44] He challenges John Meier's use of the criteria of authenticity, scoring important points. He responds strongly to Raymond Brown's rejection of the independence of the Gospel of Peter.

In terms of the historical Jesus, his discussion concerning the independence of the Gospel of Thomas from the canonical tradition is important, strong, and convincing. He asks those who "have declared *every* extracanonical gospel so far discovered to be canonically dependent, on what principles might any future discovery be assessed differently? . . . Put another way: How could your position ever be falsified?"[45] This is an excellent retort. Given the current state of scholarship on extracanonical writings, one has to ask whether those insisting on the priority of the canonical texts as historical are exercising a theological prejudice. I fail to see how canon guarantees the historicity or priority of a composition. If

---

44. This book has an excellent subject index.
45. Crossan, *The Birth of Christianity*, 118–19.

you read early Christian speculations about the New Testament gospels, they got practically everything wrong: Papias, Irenaeus, Eusebius.

His chapter on Galilean Archaeology, a topic hardly dealt with in *The Historical Jesus,* is interesting in light of his collaboration with Jonathan L. Reed in *Excavating Jesus: Beneath the Stones, Behind the Texts.* Two innovations for Crossan in *The Historical Jesus* were the centrality of the Roman Empire as the opposing binary of the kingdom (or empire) of God and his use of cultural anthropology. This moved Crossan towards an interest in the material culture that had been absent in his previous work.[46] Jonathan Reed is an excellent American archaeologist with field experience in Israel.[47] The archaeology in the book is up to date and accurate. Chapter Three, "Putting Jesus in his Place" shows how the Roman Empire looks on the ground, what Jesus would have identified as the Empire's oppressive manifestations. The presence of the Empire in the Galilee was on a coin, in the houses of the rich, and in the building program of Herod Antipas first in Sepphoris and then Tiberias. In a recent Westar program, Crossan probed Antipas' motives for moving his capital from Sepphoris to Tiberias and the impact of his building program on the local peasant population. He explored how this would have affected Jesus and his group by asking if Jesus made Capernaum his base of operations to be close to Tiberias.[48] This is the empire up close and personal.

In *God and Empire: Jesus Against Rome, Then and Now* Crossan explored the hermeneutical implications of the empire of Rome versus the kingdom of God for a popular audience. This is not only historical exploration and reconstruction but also the implications for the current situation. At times Crossan's critics had mumbled about how his Irish background and experience of English oppression have colored his view of the Roman Empire. Perhaps he has equated England with Rome and read Irish resistance into Jesus and his early followers. I would be surprised if his Irish experience had not affected him. But how is that a bad thing? Perhaps the centuries of Irish struggle against English oppression enabled him to see the Jesus tradition in a way that his critics, too comfortable living in the protection of the oppressors, failed to see. *God and*

---

46. Crossan did post-doctoral studies in archeology at the École biblique et archéologique française de Jérusalem in 1965–67.

47. Reed, *HarperCollins Visual Guide the New Testament,* is my go-to recommendation for those interested in how archaeology illuminates the New Testament.

48. Crossan, "The Historical Jesus & the Galilee Boat," Westar Wednesdays, April 26, 2023.

Empire demonstrates that imperial oppression is still with us, and that Jesus' message challenges modern expressions of empire.

TWO ROADS DIVERGED

One way to view and evaluate Crossan's achievement is to compare and contrast it with its main competitor—John Meier's five-volume[49] *A Marginal Jew: Rethinking the Historical Jesus*.[50] Both were raised Roman Catholic, received Catholic educations, Crossan left the priesthood, Meier became a monsignor,[51] a rare honor for a scholar. Both taught at Catholic universities.[52] One might characterize Crossan's work as liberal and Meier's as conservative, but I do not think those categories are helpful. I prefer to view Crossan's method as expansive, at times experimental. There is a certain pragmatism in Crossan's methodological experiments. He is always looking for a new method or tool to unlock a new secret. Meier adheres to a narrowly conceived historical-critical method. Make no mistake, his method is historical.[53] He follows his mentor and model, Raymond Brown.[54] Meier's work appears encyclopedic and exhaustive, but it eschews any method other than historical. There is no literary criticism or social world method. They are either rejected or ignored. Like Sergeant Friday, he wants just the facts. "[E]very attempt will be made to keep interpretation to an absolute minimum. Our goal will be primarily

---

49. It may appear unfair to compare a multi-volume work to a single volume one, but Crossan has produced many volumes on the historical Jesus. I stacked up all the books he had written on the topic next to the five volumes of Meier and they both reached a similar height and weighed about the same. I conclude that too many trees have given their lives for the historical Jesus.

50. Meier, *The Roots of the Problem and the Person*, Vol. 1; *Mentor, Message, and Miracles*, Vol. 2; *Companions and Competitors*, Vol. 3; *Law and Love*, Vol. 4; *Probing the Authenticity of the Parables*, Vol. 5. Before Meier's untimely death on October 22, 2022, there were rumors of the sixth volume on the trial and death, the empty tomb and the resurrection. That would make sense because the structure of his multi-volume project has followed canonical gospel structure.

51. A monsignor is an Honorary Prelate of the Papal Household. He was granted this honor by Pope John Paul II in 1994.

52. It strikes me as odd that the two most important scholars of the historical Jesus are of Roman Catholic background, since until the 1970s it was a Protestant quest. Catholics have been little interested in the historical Jesus and the quest plays little (no?) role in Catholic theology.

53. At a meeting of the Catholic Biblical Association, he was very critical of Johnson's *The Real Jesus* as not historical.

54. The dedication in Vol. 3 is to Raymond Brown, In Memoriam.

the ascertaining of reliable data, not sophisticated sociological interpretation of the data via models."[55] This position is hermeneutically naïve.[56] As John Caputo has argued, "In hermeneutics, I like to say, interpretation goes all the way down."[57]

Meier is resolutely pro-canon. He has rejected every extra-canonical writing as dependent on canonical writing, as spurious, or heretical.[58] The Gospel of Thomas does not offer early independent evidence, in Meier's judgment.

Where to Start?

"Declaring the end from the beginning." (Isa 46:10)

"What we call the beginning is often the end."
(T.S. Elliot. "Little Gidding")

In the Beginning There Was Method

Crossan has reflected about method more than any other scholar investigating the historical Jesus. As we have seen, it has been an ongoing project in his writings, constantly shifting and expanding. In *The Historical Jesus*, he fully laid out both his formal method and its investment. His three triads (see above) explain both the organization of the book and the clusters from which he builds the picture of Jesus.

---

55. Meier, *A Marginal Jew*, 1:11. This comes very close to Leopold von Ranke's "wie es eigentlich gewesen ist" ("how things actually were").

56. Hunt, *History: Why It Matters* has an excellent and nuanced discussion of von Ranke and why most historians today consider that position naïve (43–45). Chapter Three, "Truth in History" is well worth reading. Hunt is the Eugen Weber Professor of Modern European History at the University of California, Los Angeles. She wrote *History: Why It Matters* because of her experience as the president of the American Historical Association.

57. Caputo, *Hermeneutics*, vii.

58. The title of Chapter 5, Vol. 1, is indicative, "The *Agrapha* and the Apocryphal Gospels." In this first volume, Meier is assessing the sources for the study of the historical Jesus. Chapter 2 deals with the Canonical Gospels, Chapter 3 with Josephus, Chapter 4 with Pagan and Jewish Sources, Chapter 5 with The *Agrapha* and the Apocryphal Gospels. This gives some indication of the importance with which he views these sources.

In his first book, *In Parables*, Crossan put the parables at the center of his reconstruction of the historical Jesus. Putting the parables at the beginning has an effect. The form parable belongs to the wisdom tradition, as Bultmann recognized.[59] Crossan argued that the parables provided an experience of the Kingdom. That is, Crossan actually allows the parable to function as a metaphor for the kingdom of God informing the hearer/reader as to what it is. The parable defines the kingdom, rather than a predetermined meaning for kingdom of God determining what the parable means. This leads to a wisdom interpretation of the kingdom. Conclusion: the parable can be interpreted apocalyptically by predetermining that the kingdom of God is apocalyptic, but starting with the parable leads to a wisdom interpretation.

In *The Historical Jesus* Crossan's starting point shifted. The macrocosmic level pointed to brokerage, which organized the book. The mesocosmic pointed to the Roman Empire, which shifted the kingdom of God into the political arena. The stratigraphy provided the clusters to be examined. This led to the conclusion: "That ecstatic vision and social program sought to rebuild a society upward from its grass roots, but on principles of religious and economic egalitarianism, with free healing brought directly to the peasant homes and free sharing of whatever they had in return."[60] This conclusion differs significantly from that of *In Parables*.

> Like a wise and prudent servant calculating what he must do in the critical reckoning to which his master summons him, one must be ready and willing to respond in life and action to the eschatological advent of God. But, unfortunately, the eschatological advent of God will always be precisely that for which wise and prudent readiness is impossible because it shatters also our wisdom and our prudence.[61]

While between *In Parables* and *The Historical Jesus* a clear line of continuity is visible, the starting point makes a real difference as indicated by these two conclusions.

---

59. Bultmann, *The History of the Synoptic Tradition*, "Logia (Jesus as the Teacher of Wisdom)," 81–108.

60. Crossan, *Jesus*, 197.

61. Crossan, *In Parables*, 119–20.

Reliable Data

Criteria

In Vol. 1 Chapter 6: *The Roots of the Problem and the Person*, Meier deals with the vexing issue of discovering what comes from Jesus. How does one attain reliable data, especially "Since these Gospels are suffused with the Easter faith of the early Church and were written from forty to seventy years after the events narrated."[62] Meier lists ten criteria, divided into two groups—primary criteria and secondary (or dubious) criteria. Each group contains five criteria. His discussion of the criteria is overall judicious. His first four criteria are Perrin's three criteria. Meier divides the criterion of dissimilarity into two separate criteria. The criterion of embarrassment, his first criterion, "focuses on actions or sayings of Jesus that would have embarrassed or created difficulty for the early Church."[63] His second criterion, "Closely allied to the criterion of embarrassment, the criterion of discontinuity . . . focuses on words or deeds of Jesus that cannot be derived either from Judaism at the time of Jesus or from the early Church after him."[64] Since these two criteria are "closely related," why do they need to be separated? Meier never makes that clear. He acknowledges a serious objection to these two criteria that "instead of giving us an assured minimum about Jesus, [they] wind up giving us a caricature by divorcing Jesus from the Judaism that influenced him and from the Church that he influenced."[65]

The final primary criterion is strange, the criterion of rejection and execution. This is a criterion that Meier has invented. He does not footnote any other scholars in regard to this criterion. "It [the criterion] does not directly indicate whether an individual saying or deed of Jesus is authentic."[66] What, then, is its purpose? "Rather it directs our attention to the historical fact that Jesus met a violent end at the hand of Jewish and Roman officials and then asks us what historical words and deeds of Jesus can explain his trial and crucifixion as "King of the Jews."

That Jesus was executed is an historical fact, but that Jewish officials were involved is highly contested. Furthermore, how sure is "King of the

---

62. Meier, *A Marginal Jew*, 1:167.
63. Meier, *A Marginal Jew*, 1:168.
64. Meier, *A Marginal Jew*, 1:171.
65. Meier, *A Marginal Jew*, 1:172.
66. Meier, *A Marginal Jew*, 1:177.

Jews" as the charge at the execution? How this criterion can deliver reliable data is not explained. The real purpose of this criterion is to allow a caricature that Meier opposes. A view of Jesus as "A tweedy poetaster who spent his time spinning out parables and Japanese koans, a literary aesthete who toyed with 1st century deconstructionism, or a bland Jesus who simply told people to look at the lilies of the field—such a Jesus would threaten no one, just as the university professors who create him threaten no one."[67] This criterion is meant to denigrate the literary criticism of the parables that Meier rejects. It forecasts his attack on the parables in Volume 5 *Probing the Authenticity of the Parables*. Given the rise of book burnings in Republican authoritarian states, the attack of dictators on poets and artists, Meier might want to rethink just how inoffensive such people are. Maybe he should consider the cases of Václav Havel or Alexander Solzhenitsyn. Or the ongoing advocacy of Pen International on behalf of imprisoned writers and poets. They seem quite capable of raising the hackles of the powerful.

Meier has a thorough discussion of criteria but does not indicate how they fit together and how they are to be used. If these are to sort out reliable data, a systematic understanding of how that can happen is called for. No such systematic understanding is brought forth. If the criteria of embarrassment and discontinuity produce such problematic results, and they are the first two primary criteria, how is the issue resolved? Meier does not say.

The Message

In his massive 1,118-page Volume 2, *Mentor, Message, and Miracles*, Meier finally gets to that reliable data. The organization of this volume is interesting. It is divided into three parts: Mentor, Message, Miracles.

Page Count

- Mentor 163
- Message 271
- Miracles 530

The disproportional treatment of miracles is evident, but even more this organization follows the gospel order. John the Baptist, Jesus'

---

67. Meier, *A Marginal Jew*, 1:177.

preaching of the Kingdom, and miracles is the early order of Mark's gospel.[68] Meier really does have a strong preference for the New Testament canon.

Meier begins his study of Jesus' message by noting, "there is no before or after. The frame and plot line of each evangelist are his own creation." From this he draws the conclusion, "Hence the major saying and deeds of Jesus during his ministry must be studied topically. The question becomes: which topic first?"[69] The reference to Jesus' ministry is typical of Meier—a traditional phrase. Even more is the studious avoidance of theory and interpretation. If there is no chronological outline to guide the arrangement of the deeds and sayings, that means that there can be no biography dependent on psychology or development. Furthermore, it suggests that a synchronic analysis would be the proper way to proceed. Instead, Meier opts for the traditional "topics," avoiding the dreaded interpretation and modern methodologies.

Kingdom of God

The first topic is the kingdom of God. Meier points to the scholarly consensus about the centrality of the kingdom of God in Jesus' message. He backs up this consensus arguing, "The criterion of multiple attestation of sources is more than satisfied." He also calls on the criterion of discontinuity. "The precise phrase 'kingdom of God' does not occur as such in the Hebrew OT, and occurrences in the deuterocanonical/apocryphal books of the OT, the OT pseudepigrapha, Qumran, Philo, Josephus, and most of the targums are rare or nonexistent."[70] After surveying early Christian literature he notes: "the frequent appearance of 'kingdom of God' on the lips of the Synoptic Jesus cannot be traced to its popularity and regular use in either pre-Christian[71] Judaism or 1st-century Christianity." The criterion of discontinuity strongly indicates that kingdom of God "faithfully reflects Jesus' own usage and emphasis. At the very least, 'kingdom

---

68. Jesus' birth, i.e., "The Origins of Jesus of Nazareth" is dealt with in Part Two of Meier, Vol. 1, *Roots of the Problem and the Person*, again following the gospel narrative.

69. Meier, *A Marginal Jew*, 2:237.

70. Meier, *A Marginal Jew*, 2:238.

71. In Meier's understanding, Jesus is the founder of Christianity and Christianity begins with Jesus. Christianity and Judaism are separate religions. This language is problematic. See Vearncombe et al., "If Not Christian, What?" in *After Jesus Before Christianity*, 11–32.

of God' was a major component of Jesus' message."[72] Here we have a piece of a reliable data.

Eschatology

One might ask at this point, since this phrase is so distinctive of Jesus, and absent in "pre-Christian Judaism" and "early Christianity," why did Jesus use it?[73] How would his audience have understood what it meant? Facing this problem, Crossan turned to the parables for his understanding of the kingdom in *In Parables* and then Rome Empire and the core clusters in *The Historical Jesus* (See above). Meier takes another tack.

> Actually, the topic of the kingdom only serves to open up the larger question of the eschatological views Jesus held; "kingdom of God" does not exhaust everything Jesus had to say (or do) about eschatology. The question of Jesus' eschatological stance pervades almost every other aspect of Jesus' ministry as well: parables, miracles, table fellowship, his call of his disciples (especially the Twelve), and the way he faced his own death.[74]

Meier has created a circular argument. Jesus' eschatology determines the meaning of the kingdom of God and "pervades" all his saying and deeds. Therefore, eschatology is the prior category. But how does one know what was Jesus' eschatology? From the deeds and sayings. Meier seems unaware that he has trapped himself. Meier is committed to an eschatological understanding of Jesus, without ever really explaining what eschatological means. This explains why he moves the parables of Jesus to Volume 5, instead of their more logical placement in the message of Jesus, Volume 2. Some of the parables begin with the formula, "The kingdom of God is like." As metaphors for the kingdom, they would seem to present primary evidence of what Jesus meant by the kingdom. But that would lead to "A tweedy poetaster who spent his time spinning out parables and Japanese koans, a literary aesthete who toyed with 1st century deconstructionism, or a bland Jesus who simply told people to

---

72. Meier, *A Marginal Jew*, 2:239

73. This question really is the unanswered question about Jesus, the issue that motivated my *Jesus, Symbol-Maker for the Kingdom*.

74. Meier, *A Marginal Jew*, 2:243.

look at the lilies of the field—such a Jesus would threaten no one, just as the university professors who create him threaten no one."[75]

Meier evades this circle by converting kingdom of God into God's kingly rule. He turns to the Old Testament and the apocryphal Old Testament to understand its occurrence there. From these he constructs his eschatological picture:

> Summing up what we have seen in the deuterocanonical/apocryphal books of the OT, we detect a persistent concern on the part of the postexilic Israel: the many members of God's people scatted among the Gentile nations (hence the word "Diaspora") or subjected to the Gentile yoke in Palestine, and the apparent inversion of what Israel expected salvation history to mean, namely, the subjugation of the Gentiles to God's people. Hope for the future naturally translates into God's gathering of all the dispersed members of his people (at times emphatically: *all* the tribes or clans) back to a liberated Jerusalem, Mt. Zion, and the temple. The once proud Gentiles will first be defeated in a great final battle; then their remnants will humbly come on pilgrimage to offer gifs to God in the Jerusalem temple.[76]

This is Jesus' eschatology: the apocalyptic myth, a word Meier does not use. "Gentiles," a distinctly Christian usage, paints the enemies in a religious way, hiding the concrete fact of the Roman empire. Meier's reconstruction of eschatology remains a religious myth disconnected from concrete investment. It is an abstraction, cobbled together from various bits and pieces. From my point of view this is the decisive passage in Meier's multi-volume work. From this point on everything is determined.

The title of chapter 15, where Meier turns to the actual message of Jesus is titled: "The Kingdom of God: God Coming in Power to Rule." The first part reads "Jesus' Proclamation of a Future Kingdom."[77] He begins the chapter by reminding the reader, "This 'tone' of the symbol around the turn of the era plus the matrix of Jesus' ministry in the eschatological message of the Baptist makes the hypothesis of an un-eschatological Jesus proclaiming an un-eschatological kingdom of God initially suspect."[78] He then remarks, "Some readers may be surprised to see that very few parables are used in the main part of my argument." Why? "[R]ecent

---

75. Meier, *A Marginal Jew*, 1:177.
76. Meier, *A Marginal Jew*, 2:251.
77. Meier, *A Marginal Jew*, 2:289.
78. Meier, *A Marginal Jew*, 2:21, 89.

scholarship, by approaching as autonomous pieces of rhetorical art, has reminded us how open is each parable to multiple interpretations."[79] And we must avoid interpretation at all costs. In a book that is exhaustively footnoted, there is no reference to that "recent scholarship." Furthermore, starting with the parables would undermine his entire eschatological scenario. Meier seems uninterested in following Jesus' clues because that might lead to interpretation. Apparently, the parables are not stable enough to lead to reliable data. Then why would Jesus have even used such an unstable form?

Thy Kingdom Come

As his first example of a future kingdom saying, Meier turns to the second petition of the Lord's prayer. He advances two arguments for the prayer being reliable data. Its original is clearly in Aramaic, but more significant in his opinion "is the simple fact that both the Matthean and Lucan traditions, for all their differences, agree on attributing the prayer to Jesus and having him specifically command his disciples to use it."[80] As impressive as this sounds, instead of it representing some fortunate agreement by Matthew and Luke, it mostly likely represents the source on which they drew. Meier appears to view Matthew and Luke as independent attestations instead of their using a common source.[81]

In dealing with the second petition, Meier reiterates that "'the kingdom of God' is simply an abstract way of speaking of God ruling powerfully as a king."[82] Since Meier clearly understands kingdom of God to be a symbol, he appears to consistently equate "symbol" with "abstract," a very confusing equation.

To his credit, Meier notes the strangeness of "come" in "thy kingdom come."[83] But then he ignores it. The whole petition is very odd. And this oddity and strangeness—kingdom and come—calls out for interpretation.

---

79. Meier, *A Marginal Jew*, 2:290.

80. Meier, *A Marginal Jew*, 2:294.

81. Meier does not deal with Didache 8, which has another version of the prayer. In Crossan's stratigraphy, this would constitute double attestation—Q (Matthew and Luke) and Didache.

82. Meier, *A Marginal Jew*, 2:298.

83. Meier consistently uses this archaic, traditional translation of the petition, as though it were somehow sacred language.

That is the point. Why else would Jesus use such odd phrases if not "to tease the mind into active thought."[84]

Meier has converted the symbol "kingdom of God" into an abstraction that means God ruling powerfully as a king. He waltzes over the oddity of "come" to rush to his conclusion: "when Jesus prays that God's kingdom come, he is simply expressing in a more abstract phrase the eschatological hope of the latter part of the OT and the pseudepigrapha that God would come on the last day to save and restore his people Israel."[85] How is this simple and how is "thy kingdom come" "more abstract" than his elaborated apocalyptic scenario? If this conclusion is not interpretation, I do not know what it is. What if "thy kingdom come" is the plea of exhausted and exasperated peasants desperate to get us out of a terrible situation of hunger and debt?

Meier's lack of theory, his aversion to interpretation, and literary or sociological methods vitiate his whole project. It represents a type of historicism that modern secular historians long ago rejected. As a result, it is nearly impossible for him to be methodologically reflective on his operations.

Crossan on Jesus and the Future

Crossan in *The Historical Jesus* approaches the issue of Jesus and the future very differently. In *In Parables* he contrasted the prophetic and apocalyptic views of time (see above for details). In *The Historical Jesus* his method dictates a different approach. His second highest attestation cluster, "Jesus' Apocalyptic Return," included six items. Therefore, it demands attention. The key question in this cluster is whether Jesus identified himself with the son of Man figure in Dan 7:13: "I saw in the night visions, and, behold, one like the Son of man came with the clouds of heaven, and came to the Ancient of days, and they brought him near before him."

The earliest stratum source in this cluster is 1 Thess 4:13–18. Paul explains to the Thessalonians what will happen at the coming of the Lord.

---

84. "At its simplest, the parable is a metaphor or simile drawn from nature or common life, arresting the hearer by its vividness or strangeness, and leaving the mind in sufficient doubt to its precise application to tease the mind into active thought." Dodd, *The Parables of the Kingdom*, 5.

85. Meier, *A Marginal Jew*, 2:299.

> For this we declare to you by the word of the Lord, that we who are alive, who are left until the coming of the Lord, will by no means precede those who have died. For the Lord himself, with a cry of command, with the archangel's call and with the sound of God's trumpet, will descend from heaven, and the dead in Christ will rise first. Then we who are alive, who are left, will be caught up in the clouds together with them to meet the Lord in the air, and so we will be with the Lord forever. (1 Thess 4:15–17)

Crossan observes that Paul does not use the son of Man for the returning judge but Lord.[86] So for Paul, son of Man is not an important title, and Paul may not know it. "In the clouds" may be (probably is) a reference to Dan 7:13.

The second item in the cluster, Mark 13:24–27, is from the second stratum. It clearly refers to Dan 7:13. "And then they will see the Son of man coming in clouds with great power and glory" (Mark 13:26). Jesus speaks of himself as the son of Man but Crossan asks, "why is the verb 'see' used for the apocalyptic judge here, although not in Paul?"[87]

Another source for this cluster from the third stratum holds the key to this puzzle.

> Behold, he is coming with the clouds, and every eye will see him, everyone who pierced him; and all tribes of the earth will wail on account of him. (Rev 1:7)

> Then I looked, and lo, a white cloud, and seated on the cloud one like a son of man, with a golden crown on his head, and a sharp sickle in his hand. (Rev 14:14)

The Revelation quotes point to Zech 12:10: "And I will pour out on the house of David and the inhabitants of Jerusalem a spirit of compassion and supplication, so that, when they look on him whom they have pierced, they shall mourn for him, as one mourns for an only child, and weep bitterly over him, as one weeps over a first-born."

Crossan can now lay out what has happened. "[T]he whole stream of tradition, far from starting on the lips of Jesus, began only after his crucifixion with meditation on Zech 12:10, then moved on to combine Dan 7:13 with that prophecy."[88] Meditative midrash on the death of Jesus produced the apocalyptic son of Man saying. Despite its early lodging in

---

86. Crossan, *The Historical Jesus*, 244.
87. Crossan, *The Historical Jesus*, 245.
88. Crossan, *The Historical Jesus*, 247.

the tradition, well before the destruction of Jerusalem, it does not go back to Jesus but originates after his execution.

TWO WAYS COMPARED

The contrast between Crossan and Meier is striking and stark.

Crossan's methodological toolkit is expansive and expanding. Meier's view of history is constricted by a nineteenth century historicist view of historical method. Method is not neutral, despite Meier's pleas. Thoughtful method requires theory and hermeneutics requires interpretation, which requires yet more theory. Whether or not one intends to interpret, interpretation happens. Method sorts data, what will be interpreted.

In my judgment, Crossan is intentional in his theory and method and clearly lays out both for the reader. Meier operates with a naïve commonsense method, or what he takes to be obvious. That commonsense approach traps him into a circular argument. Jesus was eschatological, the eschatological myth is well known from the post-exilic Jewish writings, so this is what Jesus's message means.

The starting point determines the outcome. How that starting point is determined is critical. Again, there is no neutral starting point. Crossan experimented with at least two starting points, but in his *The Historical Jesus* he settles for an elaborated theoretical model that sorts the data. The fact that it is elaborate and complex is not a negative but a virtue because it honors the material's complexity.

Meier starts with an imagined eschatological (apocalyptic) scenario derived from "deuterocanonical/apocryphal books of the OT" and applies it willy-nilly to the historical Jesus, even though he cannot find that full scenario in Jesus' language. It is clearly imposed from without.

Meier and Crossan are clearly divided on the issue of Jesus' view of the future. The common mythology of the New Testament scholarship is that Jesus was an apocalyptist. Meier is correct about that common myth. At the very beginning of the quest, Hermann Samuel Reimarus raised the kingdom of God to centrality and identified the kingdom of God with the Day of the Lord.[89] Reimarus' position became the default. David

---

89. Reimarus, *Reimarus: Fragments*; first published by Gotthold Lessing in 1774–78.

Fredrick Strauss reinforced this apocalyptic view,[90] and Albert Schweizer canonized it.[91] But there were always challengers. C. H. Dodd argued for a realized eschatology based on the parables, an important clue.[92] In 1986 Marcus Borg took a survey of the thirty "charter fellows" of the Jesus Seminar and forty-two participants in the Historical Jesus Section of Society of Biblical Literature asking the question, "Do you think Jesus expected the end of the world in his generation, i.e., in the lifetime of at least some of his contemporaries?"[93] He found the scholars closely divided on the question, with a slight lean towards the negative.[94]

This issue, too, is decided by where one starts: with the received consensus or is it open to question by re-examining the evidence?

FURTHER CONSIDERATIONS

My basic sympathy with Crossan's program is obvious. From participation in the SBL Parables Seminar, which he chaired (1972–77), his *In Parables* (1973), to the Jesus Seminar, which he co-chaired,[95] to *Historical Jesus* I have not fundamentally disagreed with the path he has followed. I was making similar methodological moves myself.

While we were methodologically compatible, we have differed on details. I have three interrelated issues that concern me.

---

90. Strauss, *The Life of Jesus Critically Examined*.

91. Schweitzer, *The Quest of the Historical Jesus*.

92. *Parables of the Kingdom*, 35. "These passages, the most explicit of their kind, are sufficient to show that in the earliest tradition Jesus was understood to have proclaimed that the Kingdom of God, the hope of many generations, had at last come" (33).

93. Borg, "A Temperate Case for a Non-Eschatological Jesus," 98. This essay coming at the beginning of the debate about Jesus' view of the future is an excellent summary of the received (German) scholarly consensus and the causes for the cracks appearing in the foundation. Borg was himself a leader in this regard.

94. "The division within the Jesus Seminar was almost exact," 99. This is interesting in light of the critics' charge that the Jesus Seminar had a fixed position in opposition to the apocalyptic Jesus. Miller, ed., *The Apocalyptic Jesus*, is an excellent resource on this issue.

95. I chaired the Parable subcommittee of the Jesus Seminar and my paper, "Essaying the Rock," provided the basis for the discussion for the two sessions in which all the parables were considered and voted on. This was the single largest block of material ever considered by the Jesus Seminar. I authored the report on that voting, the first "Red Letter" publication of the Jesus Seminar. Funk, Scott, Butts, *The Parables of Jesus*.

1. Clusters

Crossan's construction of the clusters in his inventory and the way they function with his stratigraphy and the criterion multiple independent attestation is both innovative and creative. The clusters avoid (sidestep?) the issue of looking for an original that may never have existed. Since Jesus operated in an oral environment, in the memorable words of Walter Ong, he had "to think memorable thoughts"[96] or he would have been forgotten. He must not only think memorable thoughts, but even more importantly those thoughts must be phrased in a memorable fashion. In fact, the memorable thought might have been discovered in the fashioning of memorable words. That means they must be practiced and repeated. The likelihood of a unique original is vanishingly small. Therefore, the notion of a core to a cluster is methodologically sound. Yet we can distinguish development and growth within a cluster. In Jesus' peasant prayer, "father" is clearly earlier than the Lord's prayer "Our father who is heaven." Crossan notices this. My concern is that the rules for understanding the development of the clusters are unclear and I think at times inconsistently applied. I am grateful for Crossan's development of the clusters. I think it is an advance. But I don't think we are there yet. I would like to see more reconstruction at times.

2. Great Man

At times I think there is a bit too much of a whiff of the great man theory of history. Crossan's emphasis is on Jesus, not those who surround him. Jesus was part of a group. That group tends to disappear.

3. Peasant, Oral Community

The subtitle of *The Historical Jesus* is critical for Crossan: *The Life of a Mediterranean Jewish Peasant*. I assume all these words in the subtitle are important. I want to highlight "peasant." Peasant not only indicates social class, but also that Jesus was most likely, in our terms, illiterate. He operated in an oral environment. This is not the orality of Homer, a mistake too commonly made by New Testament scholars who address orality. Jesus clearly lived in a manuscript culture where even those who do not

---

96. Ong, *Orality and Literacy*, 34.

read and write interact with writing. The great tradition finds expression in writing and manuscript, and the little tradition in the life of village peasants.[97] That little tradition is the social situation in which Crossan has located Jesus.

Given mission and itinerancy, "magic and meal, miracle and table, compassion and commensality," and egalitarianism that Crossan has argued for as the core of Jesus' program, is it really believable that Jesus was the *leader* of a group with a program? Was not the program the product of the group? Was not Jesus the product of the group? Jesus is to the Jesus tradition as Homer is to the Iliad and Odyssey.

Perhaps Jesus was started on his path to being the Christian hero because he was the one who got caught and crucified. The crucified one's name was attached to the memory.

My appreciation of Dom's work is deep and long lasting. It has been an honor to engage with it all these many years.

---

97. The distinction is from Redfield, *Peasant Society and Culture*.

13

A Scholar Schooled in the Empire of Heaven

GREGORY C. JENKS

Each of the books written by John Dominic Crossan has had its own impact on me as a scholar. More than that, his work—and the way in which he goes about his craft as a scholar—has influenced me as I have attempted to fashion my own life as an intentional working out of the sacred wisdom incarnated by that Mediterranean Jewish peasant from Nazareth.

However, the book with the most profound and sustained impact on me has been *The Historical Jesus: The Life of a Mediterranean Jewish Peasant* (1991).

My own research training as a doctoral candidate under the supervision of Professor Michael Lattke at the University of Queensland taught me to appreciate explicit methodology and the value of pursuing the original source for every idea or comment. While insufficient in and of themselves to constitute *Wissenschaft*, this dual commitment to an explicit methodology and to the quest for origins are certainly essential elements of critical scholarship. They are also attributes of Crossan's work, and especially in *The Historical Jesus*.

Matthew 13:52 asserts that every scholar who is schooled in the empire of Heaven is like some proprietor who produces from his storeroom treasures old and new." I have always appreciated that (strongly black) saying from the historical Jesus inventory, as an aspirational role description for me as a scholar.[1] For Crossan, this is no aspirational verbal sketch, but rather a simple description of both his mission (method) and his message (a nonviolent God of justice).

In citing that parable, I am aware that the various editions of the Jesus Seminar's translation of that verse shifted over time. In *The Five Gospels* (1993), the second half reads: "like some toastmaster who produces from his cellar something mature and something young." However, in the fourth edition of *The Complete Gospels* (2010), that part of the verse reads: "like some proprietor who produces from his storeroom treasures old and new."

Given Crossan's Irish flair for fashioning fine phrases in his scholarly prose, I rather appreciate the toastmaster metaphor from *The Five Gospels*. However, I suspect that translation veers too close towards paraphrase for some people, so I also can appreciate the more modest rendition in *The Complete Gospels*.

All the same, Crossan is clearly a master of the guild who delights in bringing out treasures old and new for his readers.

Crossan sets out his methodology succinctly in the prologue to *The Historical Jesus*. In just eight pages he outlines his triple triadic methodology, where each triad has its own set of three elements. Triadic thinking is deeply embedded in Crossan's work.

The first triad weaves together social anthropology, Greco-Roman history and the extant literature concerning Jesus. The second triad drills down more keenly into the literary dimension of the first triad: establishing an inventory of historical Jesus materials, offering a stratification of that inventory based on each item's probable dating, and a further filter based on the independent attestation available for each of the 522 items in that inventory.

The final triad elaborates on the outcomes of the second triad. In this phase of his method, Crossan outlines his operational procedure for pushing back towards the origins of the Jesus tradition. In a conscious imitation of sound archaeological practice, priority is given to the various strata, reflecting the dates assigned to individual items as the data is sorted chronologically. Items from stratum one (30–60 CE) enjoy a

---

1. Funk et al., ed., *The Five Gospels*, 197. The Jesus Seminar graded the various items in the historical Jesus inventory using a schema with four colors: *red* indicates a saying or an action of Jesus with a very high probability rating; *pink* indicates material that could be authentic; *grey* indicates material that is probably not authentic; while *black* indicates an item with almost no chance of being authentic.

methodological priority over items from subsequent strata: 60–80, 80–120 and 120–150 CE. While chronological proximity to the time of Jesus does not guarantee accuracy or reliability so far as critical results are concerned, it does impose a systematic rigor on the investigator. As Crossan sees it, from this first stratum we can establish "a working hypothesis about the historical Jesus that can then be tested against subsequent strata" (p. xxxii). The stratification is further refined based on attestation, with a preference for items are both early and enjoy multiple independent attestation. A logical, albeit costly consequence of that preference, is the methodological exclusion of any item with just singular attestation. No matter how precious such an item may be, such as the parable of the Good Samaritan, if it only has single attestation it is excluded from the working hypothesis, even if they can later be seen as consistent with that hypothesis. As Crossan notes (xxiii), around two-thirds of the complexes in his inventory of historical Jesus materials have only single attestation and are therefore excluded from his core data set.

No method is beyond criticism, and Crossan would be the first to concede that point. For example, if one chose to work with three strata rather than four—and set those strata as 30–75, 75–115 and 115–150 CE—then far more of the Synoptic tradition would fall within the first stratum. Of course, even so the focus on multiple independent attestation would still eliminate many of those complexes from the working data set.

Likewise, the calculation of multiple independent attestation depends on the assumptions about the existence and date of non-canonical literary materials. With characteristic candor, Crossan addresses that vulnerability directly in the first appendix in *The Historical Jesus*. Texts assigned to the first stratum include the earliest layer of the Gospel of Thomas, the Egerton Gospel, Papyrus Vindobonensis Greek 2325, Papyrus Oxyrhynchus 1224, the Gospel of the Hebrews, the Sayings Gospel Q, an early Miracles Collection, an early Apocalyptic Scenario and the Cross Gospel (an early passion narrative).

The major vulnerabilities here relate to the independence of Thomas, the existence of Q, and the existence of the Cross Gospel. If the earliest layers of Thomas and Q are assigned to a later date or denied their independence, then the data set of materials for Crossan's project would shrink dramatically. However, the critical value of Crossan's process is that his assumptions are explicit and are therefore easily recognized, debated, and evaluated. This process of ongoing peer review and critical reception is embraced by Crossan as well as being at the heart of authentic *Wissenschaft*.

Apart from Crossan's master class in critical method, *The Historical Jesus* also offered me—and thousands of others as well—an insightful and challenging account of both the message and the program of the historical Jesus.

Central to that account—deeply grounded as it is in the limited dataset of the earliest Jesus traditions that enjoy multiple independent attestation—is the concept of brokerage: the brokered empire, the embattled brokerage, and the brokerless kingdom. Another triad.

Crossan's historical analysis drew on a wide array of scholarship and was a valuable introduction to 1980s scholarship on power dynamics in ancient Mediterranean societies. He offered a perspective with its own roots in grassroots resistance, and especially Irish resistance to English occupation. The brokerless kingdom that Crossan discerned in the message of Jesus was certainly not embraced by the major protagonists at the time of the Reformation.

The vision of a brokerless kingdom remains a powerful symbol for me more than 30 years after this seminal study was published. I find Crossan's analysis of the message and program of Jesus to be both compelling and confronting.

As a priest within a sacramental faith community in the white settler colonial society of Australia, how do I engage authentically with the message and program of Jesus? How do I deploy wisdom to critique power and privilege, while offering glimpses of another way of seeing Heaven's imperial rule active among us and through us? As a priest at the Altar—or by the Font with a baby in my arms—how do I practice rituals in ways that evade the assumptions of brokerage?

In the classroom as in the nave, how do I conduct myself as a scholar schooled in the empire of Heaven? How does a brokerless seminary class function? Can there even be an Academic Dean without brokerage rights? How does an author craft their essays and monographs in such a fashion that readers are invited to imagine and implement that brokerless kingdom of which Crossan writes and of which Jesus may have spoken? For me these questions have been the gift that keeps on giving through the pages of *The Historical Jesus*, as through Crossan's other work.

In addition to his scholarship, I want to acknowledge Crossan's generous collegiality. I have always found him to be gracious and welcoming. Years before I took up my role as Associate Director of the Westar

Institute, Crossan was generous in his responses to emails from me as a junior member of the Jesus Seminar. In the years since my time in Santa Rosa, he has continued to be a valued colleague and mentor. I recall a student returning home from an international conference where they had met Crossan. They were amazed when he asked them to pass his greetings to me, once he realized they were also from Brisbane.

In particular, after my time at Westar Institute concluded, Crossan was quick to share his historical Jesus inventory with me. As a gesture of support and a very tangible expression of solidarity, he gave me permission to use the inventory with its 522 items in my own research. It was not just permission to use. He provided me with the digital files and the instruction that should anyone question my use of his intellectual property, I was simply to say that Crossan had shared the files with me and given permission for their use. Echoes of, "If anyone says to you, 'Why are you doing this?' just say this, 'The Lord needs it and will send it back here immediately'" (Mark 11:3).

Crossan's historical Jesus inventory became the core of the Jesus Database project that I developed with a few collaborators over several years. The database draws together commentary, poetry and other material related to the historical Jesus traditions. At the heart of that project was (and is) the inventory of the Jesus tradition developed by Crossan and published as part of Appendix 1 in *The Historical Jesus* (434–50).

I am immensely grateful for the scholarship to be found in *The Historical Jesus*. I am also grateful for its encouragement to pay attention to my own critical methodology as I pursue the earliest layers of the Jesus tradition in my own vocation as a scholar and a priest. Even more than that, I am grateful for the gift of a friend and mentor.

14

Rhetorical Jesus

JOSEPH BESSLER

John Dominic Crossan's *Jesus: A Revolutionary Biography* is up to something quite different from his earlier, much longer and meticulously crafted scholarly work, *The Historical Jesus: Life of a Mediterranean Jewish Peasant*. It is a different kind of engagement for a different kind of audience.[1] Crossan, himself, speaks to the difference. Near the end of his Prologue to his *Revolutionary Biography*, he writes:

> Those who wish to explore this subject in more detail and complexity may go to the much longer book on which this one is based. Fuller citation, argumentation, and documentation are available in my 1991 book *The Historical Jesus: The Life of a Mediterranean Jewish Peasant* . . . This present book is a more popular version of that one, but *it is also something more*. Every chapter contains something beyond the parent volume. And the cumulative impact of this historical biography is, I trust, more compelling and dramatic precisely because of its compact, direct presentation.[2] (emphasis added)

I want to name this "something more" that has captivated me. *Jesus'* condensed brevity suggests the intensity of the parables, sparking new connections that are at once more dramatic but also more compelling

---

1. See Walzer, "Audience in Historical Jesus Research." Walzer examines Crossan's and Wright's construction of their audiences, comparing the audiences of their more "scholarly" works with their more "popular" works.
2. Crossan, *Jesus*, xiv

than either traditional or modern attempts to capture Jesus within a wider swath of doctrinal or rational certainty. Crossan uses the various scholarly "vectors" in his analysis *to construct the sensibility of an ancient peasant audience*.³ By constructing that audience with the help of anthropological-sociological, historical research, and literary analysis, focusing on the "earliest stratum of the tradition,"⁴ depicts not some vague, generalizable historical Jesus, but a far more particular and dynamic figure, a rhetorical Jesus speaking to the very real cultural, political, and economic suffering of first-century peasants. Reduced to utter destitution, trapped within cultural hierarchies and ritual practices of exclusion, peasants, Jewish and non-Jewish alike, found themselves reduced to being mere tools, instruments of empire. Crossan's cross-vector analysis enables the contemporary reader to experience in sharp relief *both* the underlying injustice of those systemic structures and Jesus' creative and courageous engagement of them.

With his vector approach, Crossan does not attempt to get inside the historical Jesus' mind. Instead, by bringing those vectors of analysis together, he allows us to hear Jesus's words and actions differently than we had ever heard them before, namely as engaging and responding to the very real economic and cultural complexities of the first-century Galilean world.

In a section titled, "Is this not the Carpenter's son?" Crossan discusses Gerhard Lenski's anthropological theory of social stratification to situate the historical Jesus within the social structure of the time. Arguing that "any decision on Jesus' socioeconomic class must be made not in terms of Christian theology but in terms of cross-cultural anthropology,"⁵ Crossan notes that the Roman Empire was an agrarian society,

> characterized by an abysmal gulf separating the upper classes from the lower classes. On one side of the great divide were the Ruler and the Governors who together made up 1 percent of the population.... On the other side, were, above all, the Peasants—that vast majority of the population about two-thirds of whose annual crop went to support the upper classes. If they were lucky, they lived at a subsistence level ... If they were not

---

3. Crossan's methodology focuses on where "three independent vectors cross" Those vectors are: 1) "cross-cultural anthropology"; 2) "Greco-Roman, and especially Jewish history"; 3) "literary, or textual" analysis. *Jesus*, xi–xiii.
4. Crossan, *Jesus*, xiii.
5. Crossan, *Jesus*, 25.

lucky, drought, debt, disease or death forced them off their own land . . . Next came the Artisans, about 5 percent of the population, below the peasants in social class because they were usually recruited and replenished from its dispossessed members.[6]

There is much more to Crossan's depiction of Lenski's model, but he uses it to provide something of a neutral analysis of Jesus' class or social standing. He writes: "If Jesus was a carpenter, therefore, he belonged to the Artisan class, that group pushed into the dangerous space between Peasants and Degradeds or Expendables."[7]

As a result of that contextualization we, as readers, now hear Jesus' words and see his acts as positioned, strategic engagements that prompt questions, engage in debate, and press the hyperbolic foolishness of his own kingdom language to ennoble and empower peasant resistance.

Consider Crossan's treatment of the Parable of the Feast, where all those who were invited, refuse to come. Crossan writes:

> The host replaces the absent guests with anyone off the streets. But if one actually brought in *anyone off the street*, one could, in such a situation, have classes, sexes, and ranks all mixed up together. Anyone could be reclining next to anyone else, female next to male, free next to slave . . . Those events are not just ones of eating together, of simple table fellowship, but are what anthropologists call *commensality*—from *mensa*, the Latin word for "table." *It means the rules of tabling and eating as miniature models for the rules of association and socialization.* It means table fellowship as a map of economic discrimination, social hierarchy, and political differentiation.[8]

Given that understanding of the social order implied in such practices, Jesus' parable now makes a deeper kind of social and political sense. One that stirred a likely reaction. Writes Crossan,

> What Jesus' parable advocates, therefore, is an open commensality, an eating together without using table as a miniature map of society's vertical discriminations and lateral separations. The social challenge of such equal or egalitarian commensality is the parable's most fundamental danger and most radical threat . . . Since, moreover Jesus lived out his own parable, the almost predictable counteraccusation to such open commensality would

6. Crossan, *Jesus*, 25.
7. Crossan, *Jesus*, 25.
8. Crossan, *Jesus*, 68.

be immediate: Jesus is a glutton, a drunkard, and a friend of tax collectors and sinners.[9]

Commensality, Crossan notes, "was a strategy for building or rebuilding peasant community on radically different principles from those of honor and shame, patronage and clientage."[10] So, too, argues Crossan, was the Cynic-like injunction to those followers announcing the Kingdom of God, found variously in Q, in Luke, in Mark, and the *Didache*: "Do not carry money, or bag, or sandals, [or staff]; and do not greet anyone on the road" (Luke 10:4). Noting that "what Jesus is doing is located exactly on the borderline between the covert and the overt arts of resistance,"[11] Crossan shows that Jesus' practice of announcing the Kingdom of God does not simply collapse into the Cynic model. Instead, he calls special attention to the way the disciples were to carry *no* knapsack and *no* staff. In addition, they were to go "two-by-two" and were to heal the maladies of those who took them in, sharing what food they had. Crossan writes of these differences from Cynic practice:

> Since a reciprocity of healing and eating is at the heart of the Jesus movement, the idea of no staff and no knapsack is symbolically correct for the Jesus missionaries. They are not like the urban Cynics, peaching at street corner and marketplace. They are rural, on a house mission to rebuild peasant society from the grassroots upward . . . they could not and should not dress to declare itinerant self-sufficiency but rather communal dependency. Itinerancy *and* dependency: heal, stay, move on.[12]

Again, we see Crossan helping the contemporary reader to experience something of the rhetorical location of Jesus and those earliest Jesus communities in active dialogue with other movements and practices of that time and cultural space. As readers, we experience a deeper sense of the historical realness, as it were. By showing us a Jesus who needed, and sought, to situate his preaching and practice amidst the social, religious, and political tensions of that rural space, Crossan encourages an understanding of Jesus whose words and actions broke open the oppressive peace of imperial Rome.

---

9. Crossan, *Jesus*, 69.
10. Crossan, *Jesus*, 113.
11. Crossan, *Jesus*, 105.
12. Crossan, *Jesus*, 118–19.

Crossan insists that the *historical* Jesus of his book *Jesus* does not fall prey to Schweitzer's critique, namely that scholarly pursuit of the historical Jesus ends inevitably in reading one's own worldview and agenda into the past. By demonstrating how Jesus interacts with the dynamic structures, movements, and audiences of his Galilean world, Crossan gives us, again, a rhetorically situated Jesus who seeks to move and persuade his peasant audience.

Why is that important, especially to a theologian? Crossan's insistence on the historical focus of his work does not mean he has forgotten the relation between the historical Jesus and the Christ of faith in discussions of Christian theology. Indeed, he plays out the core theological agenda of the New Quest (from the late 1960s-1970s), namely, that because the creed of Chalcedon declared that Jesus was "fully God" and "fully human," theologians could begin their reflection on this mystery "from below" as well as "from above."[13] By showing us a rhetorical Jesus—one fully immersed not simply in time but in the very partial and uncertain complexities of his very small and impoverished corner of the world—Crossan has fleshed out the ambiguity and significance of a *fully human* Jesus for *theological reflection*.

In his Epilogue—which strikes me as an appropriate distance from the body of his text on the historical Jesus—Crossan states his *Christological* principle:

> Christianity must repeatedly, generation after generation, make its best historical judgment about who *Jesus was then* and, on that basis, decide what that reconstruction means as *Christ now*.[14]

By making historical reconstruction the *basis* of theological reconstruction, Crossan invites us, his readers, to *imagine* how this profoundly engaged historical Jesus in turn speaks as Christ to our time and place. Insofar as Christology is a discourse of the significance of Jesus, Crossan insists that there is no theological shortcut to reckoning with the fully historical, rhetorical Jesus, whose "work was among the farms and villages of Lower Galilee."[15] Following such a Jesus *both* then and also today, would not be about right belief" but about practices of resistance to oppression and the healing of a very broken world.

13. See my discussion of the New Quest in *A Scandalous Jesus*, 107–61.
14. Crossan, *Jesus*, 200.
15. Crossan, *The Historical Jesus*, 421–22.

Does his own historical Jesus provide any clues for how that Christological task might be informed by his work? Perhaps so. In his chapter, "The Kingdom of Nuisances and Nobodies," Crossan discusses the saying of Jesus, "Blessed are the poor," which is to say, he explains, "Blessed are the destitute." In his analysis, he links the oppression of Imperial Rome to the profound problems of injustice in our own imperial-like world.

> If we think not just of personal or individual evil, but of social, structural, or systemic injustice—that is . . . precisely the imperial situation in which Jesus and his fellow peasants found themselves . . . In any situation of oppression, especially in those oblique, indirect, and systemic ones where injustice wears a mask of normalcy or even of necessity, the only ones who are innocent or blessed are those squeezed out deliberately as human junk from the system's own evil operations. A contemporary equivalent: only the homeless are innocent.[16]

Healing this profound brokenness requires not a statement of right belief. Rather, as in the practices of Jesus that Crossan has shown us in his elaboration of the Kingdom—practices of commensality, of welcoming others by reaching beyond social hierarchies that constrain us, of seeking to undo the systemic injustices which engulf our society—Christ becomes real in the practices of living out that vision of resistance and hope. As he closes his Prologue, Crossan is aware he has not fully crossed over. He writes:

> I conclude by reproducing here an imaginary dialogue taken from an article of mine that appeared in the Christmas 1991 issue of the *Christian Century*. The historical Jesus is speaking to me.

"I've read your book, Dominic, and it's quite good. So now you're ready to live by my vision and join me in my program?"

"I don't think I have the courage, Jesus, but I did describe it quite well, didn't I, and the method was especially good, wasn't it?"

"Thank you, Dominic, for not falsifying the message to suit your own incapacity. That is at least something."

"Is it enough, Jesus?"

"No, Dominic, it is not."[17]

---

16. Crossan, *Jesus*, 62.
17. Crossan, *Jesus*, xiv.

15

Logical And Lyrical

ROBIN R. MEYERS

My favorite John Dominic Crossan story took place 15 years ago at the publishing office of *HarperOne* in San Francisco. Thanks to the encouragement of Bishop Spong, I had just signed on to write a book and was invited by my editor, Roger Freet, to visit and meet the crew. While I waited for my appointment, I noticed that the outer office was staffed by an impressive group of young women, hard at work getting some amazing books out the door.

After waiting a few minutes, one of them asked me if there was anything I needed. "No thanks, just waiting to see Roger."

"Do you need some water? Do you have any questions?"

"As a matter of fact," I replied, "there is a question I'd like to ask."

"Sure, by all means."

"Who is your favorite *HarperOne* author?"

Almost in unison, they said, "Oh, that's easy. Without a doubt, it's Dom Crossan." This was followed by giggles all around.

This did not surprise me, because I had already read several of his books and loved them. But I was surprised at the instantaneous and unanimous response.

"Why Crossan?" I followed up.

They all smiled at each other and then one of them spoke for the whole group.

"He's so cute!"

Well, there you have it. I had never thought of Crossan as cute, but Sarah certainly does. In that moment, however, I was reminded that, as it turns out, we do not respond to someone's *work*. We respond to some*one*. Dom has an impressive mind, but he is also light on his feet. He is not just the most respected historical Jesus scholar; he is also funny, and self-deprecating, and intellectually winsome. Obviously another word for this is "cute."

When asked to write a brief essay in tribute to Crossan, there was no doubt in my mind as to what his most important contribution has been. It is his whole body of work, to be sure. But as all rhetoricians know, *what* one says cannot be separated from *how* one *says* it. You can be right and yet unapproachable; you can be brilliant and yet distant; you can be a genius and a jerk. Lucky for us, Dom did not just follow his insatiable curiosity about the historical Jesus all over the Mediterranean cradle of the gospel. He also followed his heart and let us all know that in the end, Jesus was more like a "peasant Jewish Cynic" than a messiah-king. And then he invited us all to sit down and unpack this mystery together, perhaps over a stout ale, with as many jokes as bullet points—all of it to the soundtrack of his Irish brogue.

Lest this be too abstract, let me remind you that when Crossan is asked about his reasons for leaving the Catholic priesthood, he quips, "Celibacy is not what it's cracked up to be!" But then, neither was the doublethink the church insisted he accept, in particular that Aristotle's philosophy and Catholic theology fit together like the spokes of a wheel. That "reason and revelation were twin gifts from the same God, and could not be in conflict" he wrote. But when you spend more time in the library than in the sacristy, you are going to learn some things you cannot "unlearn."

In order to avoid what he called, "a conflict of interest between priestly loyalty and scholarly honesty," Crossan left the Church on good terms and never looked back. Thereafter he marched to the tune of a distinctly different drummer—a percussive soundtrack that became an animating belief. Namely, that "faith and fact, revelation and reason cannot contradict one another, unless the human mind has misunderstood either or both." Off he went to teach at DePaul University in Chicago where, like all professors, he was expected to choose a research focus. His work in the parables of Jesus had put him in contact with perhaps the most authentic utterances of Jesus, and so it was only natural that for the rest of his life (and he has already outlived most mortals), Crossan would search for the historical Jesus.

Crossan's holy trinity for understanding the historical Jesus is context, context, context. One of Crossan's operative words is "matrix." Far beyond the reported words of Jesus, Crossan wanted his readers to know that he did not just parachute in from heaven, but occupied a moment in time, a moment in Second Temple Judaism, and most importantly, a moment in the brutal occupation by the Roman Empire.

Like many historical Jesus scholars, Crossan believes that Jesus really did exist, was Jewish (which is still a surprise to many devout Christians), was not born in Bethlehem (a fiction to help fulfill prophecy) but rather in Nazareth in Galilee, had siblings, spoke Aramaic, was baptized by John (which Crossan believes is as historically certain as anything in the New Testament), had working-class disciples, taught primarily in parables, was poor, was a healer, lived under Roman occupation, had a very brief life, was crucified by Rome, and may never have been buried.

To this last point, Crossan's wrote of the crucifixion as a kind of Roman Public Service Announcement. He dared to conclude that the bodies of those crucified were left on the cross along a well-traveled road where they rotted and were picked over by birds and wild dogs. We can only imagine that as people walked by this grotesque scene, a child might ask, "What did he do?" To which any loving parent would likely respond, "Whatever it was, don't do it!"

In one significant way, however, Crossan disagrees with many historical Jesus scholars. Many believe that Jesus was an apocalyptic preacher, one whose "interim ethic" was shaped by his belief that the long-suffering evil world was soon to end, and God would intervene to punish the evil ones and reward the good with the arrival of The Kingdom of God. His mission was thus to encourage as many people as possible to be on the right side, God's side, before it was too late.

For Crossan, John the Baptist was an apocalypticist, but Jesus ends up rejecting John's vision of the Kingdom after John's death. It was not enough to await some future kingdom. What matters is that we enter a present kingdom he announced here and now. This seems rather ironic because, if Crossan is right, most Christians today act more like John than Jesus—hell, fire, and brimstone over what Crossan called "the unmediated or brokerless Kingdom of God."

As to the clash between Judaism's encounter with Greco-Roman imperialism and the peasant cynic philosopher that Crossan believes best describes Jesus, the difference is always between what people think is good and whether, in their daily lives, they actually *do* what is good. It is orthopraxy, not orthodoxy, that distinguishes the truly religious. In a world of elite religiosity and self-importance, Crossan claims that Jesus and his first followers were like "hippies in a world of Augustan yuppies."

Perhaps the most important move that Crossan made is the same one that has changed my life, and so many others in pursuit of honesty and public transparency in the scholarship of religion. In 1985, Crossan joined Robert Funk as co-chair of the "Jesus Seminar." This group of scholars not only discussed their theories of the historical Jesus, but they also *decided* by voting on the relative likelihood that certain sayings attributed to Jesus were authentic. Using colored beads that signified very likely (red), likely (pink), not likely (grey) and very unlikely (black). The media was allowed to report on this unique form of public scholarship.

I remember being called into a meeting once at the university where I teach and asked by a religion professor if I had ever heard of the Jesus Seminar. I could tell by his tone of voice that the inquisitor found it blasphemous. Aware that I was hanging out with radicals in the Westar Institute, my colleague said, "Robin, how can you abide by scholars who dare to vote on what Jesus said?" It was futile trying to explain that this was not exactly what the Jesus Seminar did. In this man's mind, everything Jesus said was in red, and the gospel of John was as historically accurate as the gospel of Mark.

When Crossan published his breakthrough book in 1991, *The Historical Jesus: The Life of a Mediterranean Jewish Peasant*, it got mentioned in the *New York Times* and rose to the top of the religion best-seller list. A briefer version, *Jesus: A Revolutionary Biography*, is my choice for Crossan's most important book and the one that influenced me the most. Without sacrificing scholarship, Crossan made his essential findings accessible to non-scholars, which may be the most important, and least-practiced skill in the academy. His success is grounded in his accessibility, the power of his words, and the credibility of his personality. Without watering down his research, he made clear to his readers that the Jesus we think we know is almost certainly not the historical Jesus. This was blasphemy to some. But to countless others, it was liberating. Because let's face it, the supernatural Jesus of developed doctrine can be worshipped, but he cannot be followed. We cannot walk on water, but then neither could Jesus, unless he knew where the stones were.

After reading so many of Crossan's books, including the ones he co-authored with Marcus Borg, I am indebted to him as a scholar, but also as a person. His favorite words and phrases, the "matrix," the "drag of normalcy," "distributive justice," and God as a "householder" just to mention a few, have become a treasured part of my own vocabulary. His deep understanding of the essential call for Christians to be nonviolent has renewed my belief that Jesus was a pacifist, even as it has sharpened my dismay at the armies of "Christian soldiers" that march into battle singing hymns.

As Christian Nationalists move into the West Wing, and we prepare for the plutocracy that is replacing democracy, the words and legacy of John Dominic Crossan are more important now than ever. His body of work will outlast the dark times through which we are passing and will help reset a new generation devoted to the unconditionality of justice. For this we can be grateful that John Dominic Crossan was not only logical, but lyrical. Long after we have forgotten the words, we will still be humming the tune.

16

Deeply and Richly Listening

GORDON W. G. RAYNAL, RN

John Dominic Crossan has always had a concern for the general reader. His *The Essential Jesus* (1998) is an excellent example. His earlier more academically oriented works on the sayings of Jesus, *In Parables: The Challenge of the Historical Jesus* (1973), and *The Dark Interval: Towards a Theology of Story* (1975) are splendid examples of Crossan's meticulous scholarship, and books that I have returned to again and again in my own study of the historical Jesus. Since the only thing we have directly from Jesus are his words, his voiceprint, those two academically oriented volumes show Crossan's command of Jesus' language, and his mastery of the web of literary, historical, anthropological, sociological and theological thinking that are a must to truly understand Jesus' wisdom sayings and stories. Those two academic books lay out the careful methodology that Crossan has crafted, and in my view, they are the two most important academic works he has written. I want to highlight *The Essential Jesus*, because this brief volume helps readers understand the power of Jesus' artistry, and it highlights Crossan's literary abilities and sensibilities.

JESUS' ARTISTRY

Wisdom sayings and stories are sensory-evocative forms of human communication intended to foment active intrapersonal and interpersonal engagement. In this short work Crossan illustrates a deep and playful engagement with what Jesus actually said. Crossan's own playfulness moves away from tiresome concern for exact wording or literal interpretation. Further his creativity frees one from the allegorizing Jesus' language that we see in the gospels and the later tradition and highlight the direct sense-arousing nature of wisdom sayings.

By laying out the aphorisms and parables one at a time with no commentary, the book's format invites a reader to be aroused afresh in hearing the word-bomb and the word-balm nature of Jesus' gift. In addition, the use of ancient art works related to Jesus' sayings function to keep the reader focused on their senses. Together, words and images on a page become invitations to hear and to see. And then, in terms of format, Crossan moves from sensory hearing to the sayings and stories being rich resources for feeling and thinking after one has read each saying and seen each image. The value of this approach is wonderful because it assists one to actively engage in listening, then wondering, feeling, thinking, and pondering founded in the distinctive voiceprint of a man who lived two millennia ago. This little book invites you to as sit on the porch and look at the world through the lens of Jesus' startling gift.

CUMULATIVE EFFECT

Crossan's succinct introduction, the layout of the ninety-three sayings with the images, and his own commentary on each saying paints a compelling verbal portrait of the man, Jesus of Nazareth. This volume gets to Jesus' essential talent, the essential brilliance, and the essential power his gift still has for every day of living. Jesus' word-bombs and word-balms work to invite a fresh and refreshing hearing of Jesus. While many books on Jesus and the earliest years of Christianity overwhelm the reader with the ideas and beliefs of their authors, even though this is a work of serious historical and theological reflection, it invites one to think about Jesus and his impact upon his own times and upon history ever after.

As a Presbyterian pastor whose task it was to preach and teach from the Bible, some two decades ago I spent a year inviting my congregation to listen to Jesus. Not being shackled with the lectionary and the tight control it puts on reading the Bible, and thinking about Jesus in particular, this exercise of inviting people to listen to Jesus was a delightful challenge to me as a preacher and proved to be a helpful gift for my listeners. In this exercise of sustained listening, this book proved enormously valuable. Crossan's playful imagination served to help us to listen more broadly and more deeply to Jesus himself. Some of my sermons sought to open up Jesus' world and help the congregation understand the Jesus' context. Other sermons simply invited my listeners to try to grasp the power of Jesus' words for their own lives, and their own personal contexts, and the larger social contexts of the twentieth-first century. The NRSVue translates Matthew 10:40 as "Whoever welcomes you, welcomes me, and whoever welcomes me, welcomes the one who sent," while Crossan imaginatively renders it:

> To listen to you or to listen to me,
> is not to hear us
> but to hear the God who sent us both.

This example shows how freeing Crossan's playful imagination is. As a resource for preaching, I cannot say enough what a gift it was to be invited into deep listening and imagining.

I invite you to read or re-read this short book. For me it epitomizes Crossan's own unique skills in helping others to deeply and richly listen. Crossan can help in this because he also listens deeply and richly. *The Essential* Jesus demonstrates how his personal gift with words point not to himself, but back to the man of Galilee two millennia ago. *Let anyone with ears, listen!* (Mark 4:9 NRSVue), or per Crossan's tart rendition:

> You have heads, use them.

PART THREE
Violence, Empire, and Civilization

17

Creation, Violence, Connection, and Community[1]

CELENE LILLIE

Questions of violence have been central to my investigations into the history of Christianity over the course of the last twenty years. As I reflect on this, it's no surprise that these initial inquiries came in the wake of September 11th and the second Iraq War. And it was these inquiries into the world of ancient Christianity that led me to the scholarship of John Dominic Crossan.

In the days after September 11th, I was surprised by my curiosity to understand in a new way my Christian roots. I was completing an undergraduate degree at a Buddhist institution, and while I loved my education and the way it entwined with Buddhist thought, I had an impulse to understand more about Christianity. While I was drawn to understand Christianity in new ways, the Christian valence of post-September 11th rhetoric—from promoting military retaliation to the incendiary language of "the axis of evil"—as a justification for retributive violence deeply disturbed me. Some of the many questions that arose were: Is this what Christianity was really about? What does Christianity think about violence? How did and does the Christian tradition address it? What does Judaism say about violence? How did Jewish thought influence the teachings of Jesus? What does Jesus actually say about violence?

---

1. Many thanks to Brandon Scott for his meticulous editorial work—it has certainly made this a better piece. As always, any faults or oversights are mine alone.

Alongside school, I worked at a large independent book store and was slightly embarrassed by my newfound, or re-found, interest in Christianity. I would pretend to shelve books in the Christianity section to hide the fact that I was actually browsing for authors who might help me gain insight into the questions I longed to answer. And, of course, among the authors I encountered on those shelves was John Dominic Crossan. Crossan opened a world that I could have hardly imagined—a world of rigor and wonder, where the work of doing Christian history occasioned possibilities for curiosity and questioning. While my questions concerning violence and Christianity were not specifically answered, I encountered the possibility, particularly through Crossan's writings, where, if not answers, better questions could be found.

Crossan's influence would follow me as I began graduate studies—his work on parables greatly influencing my readings of the Gospel of Mary for my Masters' thesis. His work also played a large role in my thinking about the context of empire—not only in terms of the Christian Testament, but during my doctoral studies in extracanonical texts as well. Additionally, I had the great privilege of working with him through Hal Taussig's project, *A New New Testament*,[2] as well as in my work after graduation with the Tanho Center.[3] It is hard to find the right words to express the ways in which Crossan has influenced and shaped my thinking and scholarship.

For this occasion, I want to focus on Crossan's book *How to Read the Bible and Still be a Christian*. Alongside this, I will explore some of my own contemplations and questions that Crossan's work has inspired. I want to address two areas in particular. First, how Crossan's myriad insights into the Genesis creation narrative connect to my own work on the retellings of Genesis from Nag Hammadi. Second, and related to this, the ways in which community and interconnection—the ways in which we interact and support one another, the way our lives are bound with that of others, human and nonhuman—might help us think about the practice of nonviolence.

---

2. Taussig, ed., *A New New Testament*.

3. A small non-profit committed to educating the public on a wide variety of early Christian literatures.

GENESIS AND ITS RETELLINGS: KNOWLEDGE, VIOLENCE, AND CIVILIZATION

One of the things I have found particularly striking is that the thematics Crossan identifies in terms of the canonical Genesis narrative are also found in the retellings of Genesis from the Nag Hammadi codices: the Reality of the Rulers, the Secret Revelation of John, and On the Origin of the World. In these retellings, however, these thematics are recast in a mytho-logic that addresses their contemporary, i.e. Roman, situation.[4] While I cannot address all of Crossan's insights, I find it fascinating that his contemporary interpretations of Genesis parallel certain types of ancient exegesis of it. Far from traditional notions of original sin that cry out for punitive responses, both Crossan's and Nag Hammadi's interpretations of Genesis highlight how violence was not a part of the divine plan for the world.

Crossan situates the Genesis 1–9 stories within a Mesopotamian and ancient Israelite "matrix," to use his term, showing how these narratives of the world's beginning are inextricably linked with their contemporary contexts.[5] He connects the trees of life and knowledge from the garden of Eden with motifs from and responses to the Epic of Gilgamesh: the "tree of life" signifying the immortal realm of the gods as contrasted with the mortal realm of humans; and the "tree of knowledge of good and evil" giving humanity a conscience and morality.[6] Crossan then turns to the story of Cain and Abel, showing how, "Genesis 4 is not just about the original instance of fratricidal violence but about the primordial origins of escalatory violence—or sin." He emphasizes that the first time "sin" is invoked is not in the Garden of Eden, but rather when Cain slays Abel.[7] The escalatory violence instigated by this fratricide becomes the template for the violence that marks civilization and society.[8]

Crossan's definition of "original sin" is an important takeaway from his investigation. He argues that:

---

4. The core retelling of the first six or so chapters of Genesis in these stories seems to date to the second half of the second century CE, as Irenaeus refers to a version of it in his *Against Heresies*.

5. See Crossan, *How to Read the Bible*, especially Part II: "Civilization," 41–72.

6. Crossan, *How to Read the Bible*, 44–56.

7. Crossan, *How to Read the Bible*, 66.

8. Crossan, *How to Read the Bible*, 64.

> "Sin" did not happen in the garden due to disobedience or sexual indiscretion (in fact the word "sin" in not mentioned at all in Genesis 1–3), but rather takes place when Cain kills his brother Abel in Genesis 4.
>
> "'[S]in' in Genesis 4 is not a flaw in creation but in civilization, a fault not in nature but in culture."
>
> "[O]riginal sin is not about individuals and sex but about communities and violence."
>
> "Sin is not inescapable or irresistible, 'you will rule over it,' says God in Genesis 4:7, as a divine wager on the human conscience."[9]

These are the very themes found in the retellings of Genesis from Nag Hammadi.

"Sin did not happen in the garden due to disobedience or sexual indiscretion"

While the basic narrative of Genesis retellings most likely dates to the mid-second century, well before Augustine's articulation of "original sin," precursors to this doctrine are found in writings of those such as 1 Timothy, Irenaeus, and Tertullian. For example, 1 Tim 2:9–15 emphasizes that it was not Adam but Eve who "was deceived and became a transgressor" hence sealing her subordinate status and necessitating salvation through silence and childbirth. Irenaeus, in 3.22.4 of *Against Heresies*, compares the virginal purity of Mary, the mother of Jesus, with Eve arguing that Eve's disobedience and unbelief are "unknotted" through Mary's obedience and faith. Notions such as these are extended in a text like Tertullian's *On the Apparel of Women* where, in instructing women what to wear as to protect the eyes and desires of men, he states:

> Do you know not that each of you is an Eve? God's sentence on your gender lives even in our times, and so it is necessary that the guilt must also continue. You are the one who opened the devil's door; you unsealed the forbidden tree; you first betrayed the divine law; you are the one who enticed him [Adam] whom the devil was too weak to attack. How easily you destroyed man,

---

9. Crossan, *How to Read the Bible*, 67 (my summary of Crossan's "four conclusions").

the image of God! Because of the death which you brought upon us, even the Son of God had to die.[10]

1 Timothy stresses disobedience and salvation through motherhood, while Irenaeus contrasts the disobedience of Eve with the purity of Mary. Tertullian takes these a step further, stressing not only Eve's disobedience but emphasizing the connection between her seductive sexuality (particular through dress in the rest of his treatise) and the necessity of Jesus's death. Of course, Tertullian does not relegate the guilt of Jesus's death to Eve alone, but to all who bear the mark of her gender.

These are the types of interpretations of Genesis that the retellings from Nag Hammadi seem to be pointedly addressing. For example, in On the Origin of the World, Eve is not a transgressor but rather an emissary from the divine realm: she brings life to Adam and salvation to humanity. In this retelling the rulers of the world think they are gods—much like the Roman emperors. When these rulers discover that there are more powerful divine beings than themselves, including Eve, they try to capture these divine beings and their power through violence (in this case sexual violence). In On the Origin of the World, "sin"[11] is the violation of Eve through the rulers' violence; violence brought about by the misunderstandings and ignorance of the rulers in their quest for power. Sin, here, has nothing to do with Eve's actions but with the violent transgressions of the rulers of the world.

"'Sin' in Genesis 4 is not a flaw in creation but in civilization, a fault not in nature but in culture"

The notion that sin is not a flaw in creation but rather in civilization is also reflected in the Nag Hammadi retellings of Genesis, though framed in a different way. The retellings use the two creation narratives found in Genesis (the first in Gen 1:1—2:3 and the second in Gen 2:4—3:34) to contrast the divine realm of the true God with that of the false rulers of the material world. In the Secret Revelation of John, for example, the divine realm corresponds to the first creation narrative as it describes the

10. Tertullian, *On the Apparel of Women* 1.1, as quoted in Phipps, "Eve and Pandora Contrasted," 42.

11. I put this in quotation marks as the word "sin" is not used in this particular portion of the text. The word only occurs once in the Coptic (*nobe*) in 103:12–14 when the ruler mistakenly declares "I am God, and there is no other besides me," thus "he sinned against all the immortals."

true God in apophatic terms and the divine realm that emanates from him as embodying the attributes of harmony and concord.[12] This divine realm is then juxtaposed with the material world of the rulers, which corresponds to the second creation narrative found in Gen 2:4—3:34. Part of the retellings' interpretational strategy is tied to the two different names for God used in the two different tales of creation. Genesis 1:1–2:3 uses the Hebrew *Elohim*, which the Greek translates as *theos* (god); Gen 2:4–3:24 employs *Yahweh* which is translated in Greek as *kyrios* (lord or master). Significantly, *kyrios* is not simply an honorific, but the word could refer to everyone from a head of household to a paterfamilias to the emperor himself.[13] In this way, the texts critique the Roman system by contrasting the harmonious realm of *Elohim*/*theos*/god and yoking the rulers of the world, who mis-frame themselves as gods and saviors and who claim to be harbingers of peace rather than purveyors of violence, with the *kyrios*/lord of Gen 2:4—3:24.

The retellings of Genesis, then, use the second narrative of creation to explore the violent flaws of civilization and specifically show the ways in which they differ from the divine realm. This difference is most clearly seen in the rulers' rape of Eve and its parallels to Roman conquest. When the rulers of the world realize that they are not the highest or most powerful gods they decide they will try to seize this power by literally seizing Eve—who in On the Origin of the World, rather than being derivative of Adam, is a powerful being from the divine realm. The rulers' seizure and rape of Eve has strong intertextual resonances not only with Rome's founding narratives, including Mars' rape of Rhea Silvia and the Roman's rape of the Sabine women, but also with Rome's ideology of conquest.[14]

The retellings of Genesis further critique civilization noting the ways in which civilization and culture, through the influence of the rulers, are the very things that lead humanity astray. For example, On the Origin of the World says, "when the seven rulers were cast down from their heaven

---

12. On the creation of the divine realm see Secret Revelation of John BG 27.1—36.15//III 9–14.9//II 4.22–9.24//IV 6.24–14.6; and King, *Secret Revelation*, 90, 125, 159–60.

13. See King, *Secret Revelation*, 157–73; and Lillie, *The Rape of Eve*, particularly 241–71.

14. See Lopez, *Apostle to the Conquered*; and Lillie, *The Rape of Eve*, particularly Chapter One, for the connection between rape, Rome's founding narratives, and Roman conquest. Chapters 3 and 4 deal with the connection of these and other Roman narratives with the stories of the rulers' rape of Eve as found in the three retellings of Genesis in Nag Hammadi.

down to earth, they created for themselves angels, numerous, demonic, to serve them. The latter taught humankind in many kinds of error and magic and potions and idol worship and spilling blood and altars and temples and sacrifices and libations to all the daemons of the earth . . ." (124.4–12). Here, On the Origin of the World specifically connects the worship of gods who are not gods (i.e. idols) with the machinations of the worldly rulers, emphasizing that these actions are actually errors. The Reality of the Rulers, on the other hand, underscores the emotional and mental effects of the rulers' rule over humanity. It states that the rulers "threw humanity into great distraction and a life of grief, so that their people might be devoted to worldly things necessary to stay alive and might not have the time to be occupied with the holy spirit" (91.7–11). With these lines, Reality of the Rulers gestures toward the way in which empire and civilization under the rulers keep humanity in their thrall. It also names the grief and hardship required to keep this system in place. In comparison, the Secret Revelation of John has the most pointed and clear critique of civilization. In a parallel to Genesis 6, the text says that the children of the Chief Ruler disguise themselves as the husbands of the daughters of humans, having sex with them and:

> filling them with the spirit of darkness, which they mixed with them and with wickedness. They brought gold, silver, a gift, and copper and iron and metal and every sort of thing belonging to these classes. And they beguiled the human beings who had followed them into great anxiety by leading them astray into much error. And they grew old without having enjoyment. They died without having found any truth and without having known the God of Truth. And thus the whole creation became enslaved forever, from the foundation of the world until now. (II 29.15–30.7)

The Secret Revelation of John concretely connects wickedness with riches (gold, silver, gifts, and copper) with the metals necessary to acquire these through conquest and war (iron and other metals). The text also stresses the mental, emotional, and physical tolls of this system and its attendant anxiety, joylessness, and enslavement.

While the retellings' pessimism and critique of empire and civilization has often been interpreted as a critique of materiality and the material realm, it is crucial to stress that this is not account for the complexity in the texts. For example, in each of the texts "nature"[15] plays a positive and central role. For example, both the serpent and the tree of knowledge play a central role in aiding humanity and their ability to discern the manipulative and violent nature of the rulers. This is most clearly evident in On the Origin of the World where the serpent is an emissary of the divine realm, calling Eve to eat from the tree. Both the serpent and the tree have a positive valence and, by eating the fruit Eve and Adam become partner and "they loved each other. When they saw that those who molded them had the form of beasts, they loathed them. They knew much" (118.24–119.18). In On the Origin of the World, the serpent and the tree bring recognition of the true nature of the rulers and their violent machinations as malevolent—it is the civilization, the order brought by the rulers that is flawed; it is "nature" that allows these flaws to be recognized, to be known.

> "[O]riginal sin is not about individuals and sex but about communities and violence"

Again, though framed differently than Genesis, the retellings make it clear that the "sins" of humanity lie in the structures that promote hierarchy, power differentials, and violence. On the Origin of the World's recasting of Genesis shows this clearly. As noted earlier, when the rulers realize there are beings more powerful than themselves they concoct a plan to entrap these divine beings—particularly here a divine being called "the Adam of Light"—by creating an earthly "Adam." They are worried that this Adam of Light will ruin and take over their world so they "create a human being out of earth according to the image of our body and according to the likeness of this being [the Adam of Light], to serve us, so that when he sees his likeness he might fall in love with it. Then he will no longer ruin our work, and we shall make those born from the light our slave for this entire age" (112.25—113.5).[16] When they make their Adam, they are unable to enliven him, so the divine realm creates an "instructor," Eve, to give Adam life. Eve is the one who ultimately breathes into him, making Adam alive (113.6—116.8).

---

15. I place nature in quotation marks here to emphasize any type of false dichotomy or separation between humanity and nature.

16. Cf. Gen 1:26–27.

CREATION, VIOLENCE, CONNECTION, AND COMMUNITY

The rulers become even more distraught seeing Eve's live-giving power, and make a plan to seize and capture her so that her power might be theirs. The rulers say:

> Come, let us grab her and cast our sperm into her so that she becomes defiled and unable to ascend to her light. And those who she bears will be subject to us. But let us not tell Adam, for he is not one of us. And let us bring a sleep over him, and teach him in his sleep that she came from his rib so that the woman might be subjected, and he may be lord over her. (116,8–25)[17]

The text makes clear that the subjugation of Eve is not simply about her but rather about the subjugation of all humanity that will issue forth from their violence against her. Additionally, the notion that Eve is derivative of Adam, and thus woman subject not only to the rulers but to man, is cast as a lie through which the rulers might amass more—if illegitimate—power and authority. While sex is at the center of this narrative, this is not a narrative about consensual sex or sexuality. This is a narrative about violence and the subjugation of the human community by unjust rulers.

"Sin is not inescapable or irresistible, 'you will rule over it,' says God in Genesis 4:7, as a divine wager on the human conscience"

The Genesis retellings also emphasize that "[s]in is not inescapable or irresistible." As explored above, sin/violence is a product of the desire for rule, power, and domination. In these retellings, Eve's (and Adam's) eating of the fruit from the tree of knowledge points the way out. Through eating the fruit, their relationship is not signified by the rule of one over the other but rather by Eve and Adam's partnership and love. As Crossan emphasizes in his analysis of the original Genesis narrative, in the retellings, Adam and Eve become the model for ethical knowledge of good and evil, and the right or just action that flows from that knowledge.[18] Yet despite this acquisition of moral knowledge by Eve and Adam, the rulers still exert their influence on humanity as it is fruitful and multiplies,

---

17. Cf. Gen 2:21–22; 3:16.
18. Crossan, *How to Read the Bible*, 54–56.

bringing the trappings of civilization—hierarchy, power, material wealth, perceived scarcity—and its attendant violence.[19]

As Crossan notes in Genesis, and was explored previously, these retellings insist that the rulers' violence is not an inherent quality of nature, but a part of the structures humanity has created. The Nag Hammadi narratives emphasize that violence—particularly hierarchical violence (cast as sexual violence)—is not part of the divine plan. The divine plan—a reflection of the divinity itself—emphasizes help, care, partnership, and community. This is seen in the ways in which Wisdom-Sophia and Eve care for humanity and in the equal partnership between Eve and Adam. These texts are not simply advocating for an intellectual ethic, but, as On the Origin of the World states, "Indeed by their actions and their knowledge each one will make their origin known."[20]

GENESIS AND INTERDEPENDENCE

In *How to Read the Bible and Still be a Christian*, Crossan explains how God's distributive justice is part and parcel of creation itself as described in Gen 1:1—2:4.[21] In organizing creation around the weekly Sabbath, sabbath year, and Sabbath jubilee—cites of rest and restoration—Crossan argues that "in the biblical tradition nonviolent distributive justice is not a command *by* God but is the character *of* God."[22] Alongside Crossan's work, I'd like to explore some of the ways we can see the thread of distributive justice woven with notions of interdependence. By interdependence, I refer to the ways in which human beings, or any part of creation, are not independent islands, but rather the reality that the life and being of one is always intwined with and constituted by the life and being of others. In her research, which uses biology as a way to argue for the interdependent reality of being, Kriti Sharma state it this way: "By and large, we think that interdependence just means '*independent* objects *interacting . . .*' Instead, what these [biological] data may be suggesting is that our world is not composed of independent entities at all."[23] In the following

---

19. Secret Revelation of John II 28.32–30.11; BG 72.11–75.10; On the Origin of the World 123.4-24; Reality of the Rulers 91.7-11.

20. On the Origin of the World 127.14-17, *How to Read the Bible*.

21. See particularly Crossan, *How to Read,* chap. 5 "Creation and Covenant," 75–88.

22. Crossan, *How to Read the Bible,* 78; italics in original.

23. Sharma, *Interdependence,* 2; italics in original.

sections, I explore how notions of interdependence might undergird the call to nonviolent distributive justice not only Genesis, but in books like Leviticus and the teachings of Jesus as well.

In traditional interpretations of the creation narrative, humans are framed as creation's "pinnacle." Human self-centeredness certainly plays a role in this assumption—as well as that fact that humans are created in the divine image (Gen. 1:26). (Though as Crossan quips—who actually does their best work on Friday afternoon?[24]). Crossan notes that because humanity is created in the divine image, the responsibility of stewardship for the whole of creation is predicated on using the template of God's distributive justice.[25] I would also argue that the placement of human creation last emphasizes this stewardship—humanity is *dependent* on all that was created before it to survive; the rest of creation has no need of humanity for its own survival. Through the very nature of creation, the fate of humanity and all that lives and breathes and creeps and crawls, all that grows and flourishes, air, water, and earth, are inextricably related. And when the profundity of this interrelationship is fully realized, acts of violence become an impossibility. This is because if our very being is dependent upon the beings of others, that we are "*mutually constituted . . . existing at all only due to [our] dependence on other things*,"[26] violence against another—not just human others—is ultimately violence against ourselves.[27]

The retellings of Genesis, in particular, emphasize the reciprocal implications of violence. When the rulers of the world rape Eve, both On the Origin of the World and the Reality of the Rulers underscore that through inflicting this heinous harm, the rulers actually convict

---

24. Crossan, *How to Read the Bible*, 76–77.

25. Crossan, *How to Read the Bible*, 78–79.

26. Sharma, *Interdependence*, 2; italics in original.

27. It is important to note two references here. The first is Caruth's, *Unclaimed Experience*, 1–9, where she talks about the literary characters of Tancred and Clorinda from Torquato Tasso's *Jerusalem Liberated*. In Caruth's telling, Tancred becomes traumatized, i.e. is subject to psychic wounding, after unknowingly killing his beloved Clorinda in battle. In this story, it is the wounder that experiences the wound of wounding, i.e. the repercussions of his own act of violence. I note that this reading does not address the power dynamics and responsibility of the perpetrator (here or in Caruth), but nevertheless points to an interdependent dynamic between the wounder and the wounded. This dynamic can also be found in PTSD and moral wounding literature in terms of those involved in war, for example. The second work of note is Butler's, *The Force of Non-Violence*, where she provides a thorough-going critique of notions of individualism in the face of violence and nonviolence.

themselves—the violence they perpetrate reverberates back on them.[28] In these reverberations we see notions of Crossan's treatment of escalatory violence, and also cyclical violence and intergenerational trauma. Escalatory violence is often times the result of violence begetting violence and upping the ante in retributive response. The cyclical and intergenerational nature of violence is succinctly rendered in the adage, "hurt people hurt people"—and it is only through rehumanizing people and resacrilizing the world on which humanity is dependent that parity and peace become possible.

As Crossan notes, we are privy to the possibility of peace in visions like those found in Isaiah and Micah where lions lie down with lambs and swords are refashioned into plowshares and war will no longer be learned.[29] Crossan grounds this vision of peace in God's distributive justice, which he links to the notion of Sabbath and the very structure of creation—again, as Sabbath extends to the Sabbath year, which in turn extends to the Jubilee as outlined in Leviticus 23 and 27.[30] All of God's creation—from humans to animals to plants to the earth itself—has a right to rest and release (Lev 25). People cannot own creation which has an inherent freedom, they are simply stewards of it. As God states in Lev 25:23: "The land shall not be sold in perpetuity, for the land is mine; with me you are but strangers and sojourners."[31] The use of the Hebrew *ger* in this verse, translated as "strangers," is striking as it forms an intertextual connection not only with the narrative arc of the Torah, but with God's law of ethical action towards others. In Gen 15:13 God tells Abraham that his descendants will be strangers in the land of Egypt, enslaved and oppressed for four-hundred years. Once set free, God continually reminds the Israelites of their enslavement in Egypt as a call to the ethical treatment of strangers in their own land: "You shall not wrong or oppress a stranger, for you were strangers in the land of Egypt" (Exod 22:21); "You shall not oppress a stranger; you know the heart of a stranger, for you were strangers in the land of Egypt" (Exod 23:9); "When a stranger resides with you in your land, you shall not oppress the stranger. The

---

28. Reality of the Rulers 89.27–30, "And they defiled her abominably. And they defiled the seal of her voice, and so they convicted themselves through the form they had shaped in their own image." On the Origin of the World 117.12–14, "And they erred. They did not know they defiled their own body. The authorities and their messengers had defiled the likeness in every way."

29. Crossan, *How to Read the Bible*, 77; Crossan, *Render unto Caesar*, 30–31.

30. Crossan, *How to Read the Bible*, 78–80.

31. Crossan, *How to Read the Bible*, 22–23, 80.

stranger who resides with you shall be as the citizen among you; you shall love the stranger as yourself, for you were aliens in the land of Egypt" (Lev 19:33–34). Those who we consistently try to other, to make into an oppositional "they," are, in fact, us.

This last quotation from Leviticus, in turn, links with the Jesus tradition. Mark 12:28–34 tells of an encounter between Jesus and a scholar who asks him which commandment is the greatest. Jesus answers, "The first is, 'Hear, O Israel: the Lord our God, the Lord is one; you shall love the Lord your God with all your heart, and with all your soul, and with all your mind, and with all your strength.' The second is this, 'You shall love your neighbor as yourself.' There is no other commandment greater than these" (Mark 12:29–31). The Jesus Seminar was skeptical about attributing these words to Jesus. They noted that this framing of the law is found in the teachings of the Rabbi Hillel who taught at the end of the first century BCE and beginning of the first century CE. These verses from Deut 6:4–5 and Lev 19:18 were circulating in the ancient milieu and are also quoted by Paul in Gal 5:14, so whether they were said by Jesus or not, they were certainly in his matrix. In the Gospel of Luke, a similar encounter to the one found in Mark 12:29–31 frames the parable of the "Good Samaritan" (Luke 10:25–35, a story voted pink by the Jesus Seminar).[32]

What I find fascinating in this Lukan juxtaposition of the "greatest commandment" and the parable of the "Good Samaritan" is how Lev 19:18 ("You shall not take vengeance or bear a grudge against any of your people, but you shall love your neighbor as yourself") is concretely yoked with Lev 19:33–34 ("When a stranger resides with you in your land, you shall not oppress the stranger. The stranger who resides with you shall be to you as the citizen among you; you shall love the stranger as yourself, for you were strangers in the land of Egypt."). In the Lukan parable, the stranger exemplifies the ethic of loving neighbor and stranger, stretching the bounds of societal norms of who deserves care and concern.

JESUS, INTERDEPENDENCE, AND COMMUNITY

The question of who is worthy of care and concern is central to the message of Jesus. As a Galilean Jew, marginalized by the dominant culture,

---

32. See Funk et al., eds., *The Five Gospels*, 36–37, for information on the Jesus Seminar's voting.

Jesus uses his marginalization to create networks of community and care. Through these networks, he stretches the boundaries of societal norms to create the already/not yet world of God's kingdom/empire based on nonviolence and distributive justice, rather than on the violence inherent to Caesar's empire. Crossan underscores the juxtaposition between Jesus' "world" and Pilate's/Caesars in John 18:36 where Jesus says, "My kingdom/empire is not from this world. If my kingdom/empire were from this world, my followers would be fighting to keep me from being handed over . . ."[33] But what did this nonviolent world look like?

Jesus's table community put this new world on display. The gospels narrate that Jesus ate with "sinners and tax collectors,"[34] and in stories like the feeding of the 5000, Jesus sets the stage for those who are generally thought of us unworthy of rest and leisure to recline with one another and eat their fill.[35] Additionally, as God makes God's "sun rise on the evil and on the good, and sends rain on the just and the unjust," Jesus extends not only his feeding program but his healing program as well to include the enslaved of centurions[36] and the daughters of Syrophoenicians.[37] These stories show how loving enemies and prayer for those who persecute you (Matt. 5:44; Luke 6:27–28) are not just intellectual exercises but actions by which one's ethics will be known. Jesus' extension of himself and his programs beyond societal norms gives rise to community which is further exemplified in his prayer. The Matthean version of this prayer says:

> 6:9 All of you pray, then, like this:
> Our Father in heaven,
> sacred be your name.
> 10 Your empire come,
> Your will be done,
> as in heaven also on earth.
> 11 Give us today our daily bread.
> 12 And set free our debts
> as also we have set free our debtors.
> 13 And do not bring us to the time of trial,
> but rescue us from the evil doer.

---

33. Crossan, *How to Read the Bible*, 170; Crossan, *Render Unto Caesar*, 245–47
34. Mark 2:15–16; Matt 9:10–11; 11:19; Luke 5:29–30; 7:34; 15:2.
35. Mark 6:30–44 and parallels.
36. Matt. 8:5–13; Luke 7:1–10.
37. Mark 7:24–30; cf. Luke 15:21–28, here a Canaanite woman.

CREATION, VIOLENCE, CONNECTION, AND COMMUNITY

> 14 For if you all forgive people their transgressions,
> your heavenly Father will also forgive you all;
> 15 but if you all do not forgive people,
> neither will your Father forgive your transgressions.

Much in this prayer deals with distributive justice, but what I want to highlight is the lack of a single singular pronoun. This prayer is about all of us together and none of us apart. Put another way, the prayer of Jesus is never about me, but always about us. This links to the kingdom/empire as both within and among us.[38] Like *ruach* or *pneuma*—the pregnant words in Hebrew and Greek gesturing toward breath, wind, and spirit—the empire of God exists within and among and between. And like breath, wind, and spirit, the empire of God is the very thing that connects individuals with one another and their world, the very thing that creates community.

The Gospel of Matthew also attributes sayings to Jesus such as: "For where two or three are gathered in my name, I am there among them" (18:20) and "Truly I tell you, just as you did it [fed, welcomed, clothed, cared for, visited] to one of the least of these who are my siblings, you did it to me" (25:40). In these ways, Jesus brings the communal and interconnected reality of being and action in clear focus. When folks gather together in community, Jesus is there; when folks extend themselves to those in need, Jesus is there. It is also important to remember that the communal and interconnected reality of being and action is also highlighted by Matthew in the reverse:

> [F]or I was hungry and you gave me no food, I was thirsty and you gave me nothing to drink, I was a stranger and you did not welcome me, naked and you did not give me clothing, sick and in prison and you did not visit me.' Then they also will answer, 'Lord, when was it that we saw you hungry or thirsty or a stranger or naked or sick or in prison, and did not take care of you?' Then he will answer them, 'Truly I tell you, just as you did not do it to one of the least of these, you did not do it to me.'
> (Matt 25:42–45)

---

38. Here I note the ambiguity of the Greek preposition *entos* which can be translated as within or among, Luke 17:21. And, thanks to Brandon Scott for also reminding me of parallels in Gos. Thom. 3: "Jesus said, 'If your leaders say to you, "Look, the empire is in the sky," then the birds of the sky will precede you. If they say to you, "It is in the sea," then the fish will precede you. Rather, the empire is within you and it is outside you.'" And 113: "His disciples said to him, 'When will the empire come?' 'It will not come by looking for it. It will not be said, "Look, here!" or "Look, there!" Rather, the Father's empire is spread out upon the earth, and people don't see it.'"

This emphasis on community strongly correlates with Crossan's analysis of the Jewish population's nonviolent and communal resistance in the first centuries BCE and CE. In these protests, young and old, men and women, participated together.[39] This continues to be a feature of resistance to empire within the Jesus movement as Pliny the Younger, governor of Bithynia and Pontus in the early second century CE, remarks decades later: The Christian community there, led by two enslaved women, consisted of young and old, men and women, enslaved and free.

CONCLUSION

Although the events of September 11th and its aftermath led to my initial questions concerning violence and Christianity, our contemporary times give renewed urgency to these questions and connections. A friend recently recounted a conversation where her interlocutor told her that working for peace was naïve. She responded, if peace is so naïve, so easy, why haven't we accomplished it already?

I find myself returning to her words again and again, thinking about the difficultly and courage and tenacity working for peace, equity, and justice demands. I find Crossan's work so valuable in these moments because, in his search for historical insight, he opens up spaces for us to think more clearly and act more consciously in our contemporary settings. Crossan's questions about nonviolence, ethics, and community help me to think about what it means to live in this very interconnected contemporary world—his questions help me ask my own questions, help me struggle to find my own answers, and always remind me that the most fruitful place to engage this work is in community.

---

39. Crossan, *How to Read the Bible*, 143–50; Crossan, *Render unto Caesar*, chap. 11–12, 211–37.

18

Context, Texture, Entanglement

ARTHUR J. DEWEY

*In gratitude to Dom Crossan
il miglior fabbro
Dante, Purg. 26, 248*

In honoring the enduring scholarly contributions of John Dominic Crossan, it is helpful to focus on his work through a particular critical lens. By scanning his work through the theme of the Bible and Violence, we can begin to detect the weight and worth of his scholarly effort.

My reflection starts by noting three main points:
    First, history matters.
    Second, meaning is spun.
    Third, we are responsible for our interpretations.

And I shall conclude my reflections by exploring the entangling implications of Crossan's critical understanding of one notorious passage, that of Matthew's Blood Curse.[1]

---

[1] Matt 27:24–25 and John 8:44–47 form the double helix of the virus of anti-Judaism and anti-Semitism. Around these two passages other material from both the Hebrew Scriptures and the Christian Writings have been entwined to produce a lethal combination that has been active since the second century ce. Taken out of their original context and read without any historical and rhetorical nuance, these passages have provided historically the foundation for the killing and extermination of Jews through the centuries. The recent killing of Jews at the Tree of Life Synagogue, Pittsburgh, PA, (October 2018) was another somber demonstration of how words become weaponized. I deal only with the Matthaean material. For more on John 8 and the Tree of

A VISUAL CLUE

Before highlighting the creative work of Crossan, consider this cover of *National Geographic*.[2] The image depicts Jesus with a crown of thorns, stripped to the waist, standing on a balcony with Pilate presenting him to the people. When I first saw this magazine near the checkout counter of my local grocery store, I was immediately attracted. *National Geographic* is renowned for its photography and richly elaborated maps. Since the magazine headline reads "Jesus and the Origins of Christianity," you might presume that will deliver the historical materials about Christian origins. However, upon opening the magazine, you are hard pressed to find out who has done the research. At the same time, while the photography is first-rate, it seems that the images have been seen before. In fact, as an overall narrative emerges, it conveys little more than what is usually rounded up and displayed as the origins of the Jesus Movement.

The magazine makes it difficult to find out who is responsible for this production. The only person named was Jean-Pierre Isbouts, who is described as having studied Greek and Latin before pursuing graduate studies in archaeology, art history and musicology at Leiden University. He completed his doctoral research on the nineteenth-century architectural firm of Carrère & Hastings at Columbia University in New York. As his biographical page[3] indicates Isbouts has been greatly absorbed in producing documentaries and other artistic endeavors. Nothing there to indicate that he has any critical control over the material he gathers together. Nor was there anything in the magazine to suggest that he was aware of any of the cutting New Testament research.

Perhaps most telling is the cover itself. It is actually a cut and paste from the 1880 painting of Antonio Ciseri, entitled "Ecce Homo." Isbouts has manufactured the entire volume from this cut and paste process. This has been his modus operandi as an artistic producer, as one can see from his vita. But what is most disconcerting is that there is no attempt at distinguishing fact from art. Rather, the artwork fills in the gaps

---

Life Synagogue, see my "Shattering the Sabbath's Peace," Oct 30, 2018, https://www.westarinstitute.org/blog/shattering-the-sabbaths-peace.

2. To view this cover, go to: https://www.natgeosubscriptions.com/product-page/jesus-and-the-origins-of-christianity-11-11.

3. http://www.jpisbouts.org/biography.

in supporting what usually serves as the traditional narrative. Furthermore, the realistic style of Ciseri bolsters the impression that this is what happened.[4]

Antonio Ciseri, *Ecce Homo*, 1871 (in the public domain via Wikimedia Commons. Source/Photographer: SIKART dictionary and database. SIAR inventory number 57336. https://commons.wikimedia.org.

The cover maintains what Crossan and others have called "the longest lie."[5] The realistic style of the painting does nothing to question those who populate the painting (from Pilate to the crowds in the distance), nor to ask the prior question: was there ever was a trial? It plays into the growing cultural habit of looking at things through a camera lens, the still world of the photograph. The sheer rhetorical force of the cover avoids nuanced questions by getting people interested in quickly following up with the selection provided inside. The cover, thus, functions as a

---

4. Or, as Pope, now Saint, John Paul commented on Mel Gibson's *Passion of the Christ*, "It is what it was." https://www.catholicnewsagency.com/news/378/pope-john-paul-endorses-the-passion-of-christ-with-five-simple-words#:~:text=The%20Pope's%20response%20was%3A%20%22It,accused%20of%20being%20anti%2DSemitic.

5. Or, the "longest hatred," the 'big lie." See Wistrich, *Antisemitism*. What is unspoken in the painting of Ciseri is the response of the crowd. And with that response comes the justification for the persecution and killing of Jews.

"come on" and "cover-up," tacitly carrying forward whatever prejudices the readers and the designer of this volume possess. The magazine reinforces what has already been spread throughout the culture. This allows the lurking transmission of the virus of anti-Semitism to continue without a word, without anyone thinking.

History Matters

Crossan's work on the death of Jesus is crucially important. He has made enormous contributions to this tragic material. Few scholars have done so much for so long. My own research has intersected with his on this question. More specifically, *Who Killed Jesus? Exposing the Roots of Anti-Semitism in the Gospel Story of the Death of Jesus* (1995) demonstrates some of key and critical contributions Crossan has made in biblical scholarship.

Who Killed Jesus is a relatively short book in comparison to some of Crossan's other work. But it shows Crossan in the white heat of a critical conversation with Raymond Brown's ambitious study: *The Death of the Messiah. From Gethsemane to the Grave: A Commentary of the Passion Narratives in the Four Gospels* (1994). Brown's main intention in his study is to provide a redactional presentation of the canonical passion narratives. He is aware of the historical questions that dog this material. He uses as much historical data as can be adduced. He nimbly moves between historical witnesses and the gospel passages. Clearly, however, Brown is not engaged in a ceaseless search for a factual basis of the material he is investigating. He acknowledges that the lines of evidence often get quite thin, and all a historian is left with are popular constructions and traditions that seem to fade away. Often, at this juncture he will conclude that the matter or event is "not impossible" or that it is "not implausible" for it to be the case. But Brown would be hard pressed to go much further with those loose ends.

In sum, Brown's *Death of the Messiah* is an encyclopedic attempt at rendering a commentary on the canonical passion narratives. He presents what would appear to many to be the final word on the matter. By moving from passage to passage, with a keen indulgence on each line, and a constant eye towards any historical data that might throw light on the commentary, Brown appears to take the measure of historical and Christian evidence. Brown plows on with his commentary with his primary concern to deliver redactional results. This is what each of the four canonical writers intended to communicate to their particular communities. His use of correlating materials from ancient history to firm up his argument adds to his ongoing argument of plausibility. Still, even when Brown finds no specific correlation, he presses on to make sense of the Gospel writer's intent.

Brown's willingness to settle for what is plausible or likely does not sit well with Crossan. While Brown may contend that a passage may have had some small historical nucleus, its actual detection often exceeds the commentator's grasp. I would argue Brown employs a common sense understanding of historical research. He can imagine earlier historical data, but the evidence in hand cannot be teased out to get a firm grasp of that earlier tradition. In some ways Brown reads evidence on the model of the photograph.[6] Unless the evidence is sharp, in clear black or white, one can make no sense of it. It is relegated to the indistinct or out of focus past. The researcher's task is to arrange the still life as presented.

But is the evidence that easily defined? What are the grounds for making a judgment? Crossan, dissenting, notes:

> Historical scholarship is not called to absolutes or to certitudes but only to its own best reconstructions given accurately, honestly, and publicly. Even in our courts, with life and death in the balance, our best judgments are "beyond a reasonable doubt." We seldom get to beyond any doubt. But, in the end judgments must be made, and most historical judgments are based on "this is more plausible than that rather than "this is absolutely certain" or "that is absolutely wrong." None of this allows us to hedge or to fudge or to hide behind double negatives like "not implausible" or "not impossible."[7]

Crossan dares to ask what is more probable in probing the evidence. Brown wants to detect things as they are, as if the text was a photographic plate. If the facts can't be seen, then the text becomes opaque. If the text cannot deliver clear data, beyond any doubt, then what can be known? Crossan sagely asks whether Brown's well-used double negative

---

6. For many contemporary readers of the Bible the narrative conveys "what happened." Just as a photograph captures a scene, a text reflects the facts. However, this is an assumption that only emerges in the nineteenth century. Moreover, it avoids asking whether the texture of the text suggests other possibilities of interpretation. What is the text is uttering the dreams or creative constructions of a long dead community?

7. Crossan, *Who Killed Jesus?*, x.

conclusions (not implausible, not impossible) are actually ways of wiggling out of giving some defensible answer?[8] Both Brown and Crossan agree that history matters. Crossan, however, does not let Brown slip away from the responsibility historical investigation entails.

Meaning Is Spun

Because history matters, Crossan adds a new wrinkle to the conversation. He does not treat the evidence in a commonsense fashion. The text is not a simple reflection or replica of fact. Crossan makes an important distinction concerning the nature of the evidence at hand. Paying attention to the use of scripture by the gospel writers, detecting brief and suggestive moves, Crossan asks whether the passion narratives are best characterized as examples of prophecy historicized or history remembered? With this distinction Crossan exposes a major assumption by Brown regarding *the understanding of memory*. Brown not only approaches the evidence as a modern document, but even more he never investigates how the ancients made meaning, how they remembered. He seems unconcerned to get a feel for the *texture of the text*. He does not notice that the material from the outset is a weaving together of words and images, sound and hope, the old and the new. In his drive for clarity, Brown does not conceive of the possibility that the evidence in hand needs other ways of detection, that these remnants of ancient memory are crafted and woven.[9]

Crossan, on the other hand, in *Who Killed Jesus* uncovers that the earliest passion narrative comes from working with scriptural quotes. In attempting to make sense of the fate of Jesus, the words of Israel's sacred writings were first cited and then transformed into narrative. Another name for this process is midrash. Words give birth to a meaningful construction. For Crossan the evidence he encounters is not a simple mass of documentation that demands correlation, confirmation and an isomorphic relation to facts. Rather the composition is the result of a Jewish craft of memorable weaving—the warp and woof of memory and tradition. He titles this prophecy historicized. Scriptural citations are intrinsic to the early layers of memory work.

---

8. Crossan, *Who Killed Jesus?*, x

9. This is where the work of Lee and Scott, *Sound Mapping the New Testament*, is so crucial. Greek composition was literally a weaving of sound and sight.

In each chapter of *Who Killed Jesus* Crossan shows a masterful hand and eye on the texture of the material. He has a better feel than Brown for the material evidence. He does not provide us with an encyclopedic catalog of possibilities and references, as does Brown. Rather, Crossan stays on the scent, continues to feel the pulse of the material. He demonstrates that each gospel writer is creatively carving out a narrative. He also shows that they are doing it with an understanding of memory that is not that of a documenter. Rather, this is midrashic memory, where scripture is spun into scene and story.

Such a composition from midrashic memory terrorizes those who want certitude and facts. The basis of the passion narratives evolves out of what we today would term fiction?[10] This is tantamount to heresy for those who want their religion neat, neither shaken nor stirred. This may be the basic reason that Brown took great exception to Crossan's thesis of the "Cross Gospel."[11] He sees in Crossan's compositional theory "little to recommend."[12] According to Brown the Gospel of Peter is a derivative, secondary composition that amalgamates various and hazy memories, oral echoes of the canonical tradition. Crossan's reversing the lines of transmission completely and making the case that a version of the Gospel of Peter is the origin of the passion narrative tradition completely undermine *The Death of the Messiah*'s encyclopedic construction.

We should not be surprised that Crossan makes this critical move. He has in his work on parables demonstrated his penchant to detect how a saying works.[13] While Brown and others call a halt to the historical basis on the passion passages (beyond which there are dragons!), Crossan dares to get the feel of the evidence, even if it means recasting the ways in which one envisions the growth of the early Jesus traditions. He has seen that a commonsense analysis does not catch some fundamental clues. Crossan envisions that other people, especially in another time, go about remembering and making meaning in different ways.

---

10. Early work on the biological understanding of memory assumed that memory was passive, with the brain receiving impressions. However, neurological advances soon found that, even on a cellular level the brain actively constructs memory through synapse growth among neurons.

11. Crossan, *The Cross that Spoke*.

12. R. E. Brown, *The Death of the Messiah*, 2:1321. Of course, to admit the cogency of Crossan's thesis would undermine Brown's entire historical configuration of early Christianity, as well as much of his research.

13. Crossan, *The Dark Interval*.

We Are Responsible for Our Interpretations

The recognition of different ways of remembering reveals an ethical dimension. As interpreters we are entangled in our own presumptions and must make a concerted effort to detect the other side of the conversation. This effort to understand is truly a matter of fairness—to whoever originally constructed this material. In paying attention to the way the material is crafted we see another instance of the medium is the message. The "how" allows us to touch on the "what." As interpreters we are engaged on a number of levels. It is not a simple assessment of fact but of recognizing that we need to use our imaginations to become aware of how meaning is crafted by another. We fail in interpreting if we do not see, therefore, how memory is constructive and that humans remember in ways that are different and active. Remembering is not a simple passive event, but an active construction from the cellular to the personal to the cultural and back again.

Brown is well aware that the passion narrative has carried a memory load, much of which is loathsome and lethal.[14] However, in not wanting history to be an obsession in his investigation,[15] Brown overlooks the possibility that handling the evidence demands an even more intensive and sensitive historical approach, whereby one can detect the way in which the ancients delivered their memories. Such detection may lead to significantly different historical consequences.

ENTANGLEMENT: THE BLOOD CURSE OF MATTHEW

Matthew 27:24-25 is one of the most lethal passages in the New Testament:

> Now when Pilate could see that he was getting nowhere, but that a riot was starting instead, he took water and washed his hands in full view of the crowd and said, I'm not responsible for this man's blood. That's your business!"
> In response all the people said, "So, smear his blood on us and on our children.

---

14. R. E. Brown, *The Death of the Messiah*, 1:383-97.
15. R. E. Brown, *The Death of the Messiah*, 1:24.

Brown brings a cautious response to this material. He is, of course, aware of the havoc these verses have had throughout the history of Jewish-Christian relations.[16] But he does not simply dismiss the material because moderns find it offensive, but considered the possibility that some people in Matthew's time would "share this attitude."[17] Moreover, Brown views this section to be the "most effective theatre among the Synoptics."[18]

The overall scene for this material—the trial—Brown considers historical.[19] Mark has built upon a historical kernel: Pilate sentenced Jesus to die on charge of being king of the Jews.[20] Mark provides a kerygmatic dramatization of scriptural citations reserved in tradition.[21]

When Brown turns to Matthew's version, he declares:

> In terms of historicity let me observe that I think that this episode represents a Matthean composition on the basis of a popular tradition reflecting on the theme of Jesus' innocent blood and the responsibility it created . . . Some of the elements that went into such tradition were quite old, and there may have been a small historical nucleus; but the detection of that nucleus with accuracy is beyond our grasp.[22]

Brown observes that the language used ("I'm not responsible for this man's blood. That's your business!") by Pilate is unusual. Why would a Roman magistrate employ Jewish terms of responsibility? Evidently, because this material has percolated up from those earlier popular Jewish traditions, that unfortunately fall outside any sure historical grasp. Further, Brown mentions that in Matthew's curious perspective, juxtaposing how the "people" accept responsibility for Jesus' death, while all others in the story are trying to avoid being entangled in it.[23]

---

16. R. E. Brown, *The Death of the Messiah*, 1:831.
17. R. E. Brown, *The Death of the Messiah*, 1:832.
18. R. E. Brown, *The Death of the Messiah*, 1:832.
19. This is not unlike the assumptions that readers would make of the *National Geographic* cover mentioned earlier.
20. R. E. Brown, *The Death of the Messiah*, 1:725.
21. R. E. Brown, *The Death of the Messiah*, 1:730. In essence, the Markan Passion Predictions serve as generative elements.
22. R. E. Brown, *The Death of the Messiah*, 1:833.
23. R. E. Brown, *The Death of the Messiah*, 1:837–39. The dramatic irony that the Matthaean audience would hear in the words of the people who do not understand the full import of what they are saying is not an issue for Brown.

His concluding remarks are telling. Brown asks whether "Matthew would extend the responsibility and punishment beyond his own time to the indefinite future."[24] After noting there may be some in the Matthaean community he invokes the notion of God's sovereignty to forgive and to break the chain of guilt by recalling that the last supper in Matthew Jesus refers to his blood—for the forgiveness of sins.[25]

In sum, Brown considers the Blood Curse verses reflect the concerns of the Matthean community vis-à-vis their Pharisaic rivals. In that sense the historicity comes from that late first century competition. Yet, Brown leaves open the possibility that this passage is derived from some earlier, popular expression. It remains for the reader of Brown to determine how plausible these arguments appear.

Crossan takes a different approach. While both Brown and Crossan see Matthew dependent on the Markan Trial narrative, for Crossan Mark is not a historical account. Rather, he contends that:

> The Trial is, in my best judgment, based entirely on prophecy historicized rather than history remembered. It is not just the *content* of the trial(s) but the very *fact* of the trial(s) that I consider to be unhistorical.[26]

While Brown is content to consider this material in terms of plausibility and verisimilitude, Crossan asks if that is the best the investigator can do? Should we be content with leaving a modicum of possibility that this scene has a very early origin? Crossan takes away all such speculation by arguing there was no trial. His argument in *Who Killed Jesus?* lays out what he considers to be the earliest layer of the Gospel of Peter, namely the Cross Gospel. The trial as a scene emerges not from some indecipherable popular tradition but from the construction of a scene from the Hebrew Writings. Prophetic texts become historicized.[27] Psalm 2:1[28] forms

---

24. R. E. Brown, *The Death of the Messiah*, 1:839.

25. This is a theological solution (a *deus ex machina*?) offered almost in desperation by Brown. If he had considered how the Gospel of Matthew might have been heard by the original community, where the ironic echo from the Last Supper words could be felt in the crowds "taking the blame," he could have argued that Matthew had indeed provided a more compassionate understanding of the crowd's declaration.

26. Crossan, *Who Killed Jesus?*, 117.

27. Examples of this midrashic activity. Notice the "prophetic layer" of Peter that Denker, *Die theologiegeschichtliche Stellung*, detected: Gos. Pet. 1:1/Ps 2:1; Isa 50:6, Zech 12:10/Gos. Pet. 3:4; Isa 53:12/Gos. Pet. 4:1a; Isa 50:7, 53:7/Gos. Pet. 4:1b; Ps 22:18/Gos. Pet. 4:3; Ps 69:21/Gos. Pet. 5:2; Ps 22:1/Gos. Pet. 5:5a.

28. Ps 2:1 "Why do the nations conspire and the peoples plot in vain?"

the basis of the construction of the trial scene in the Cross Gospel, which in turn receives a Markan reduplication. The use of irony in the choice of Barabbas precedes the Matthew's irony noted by Brown.[29]

The author of the Cross Gospel was not trying to remember what had happened but wanted to produce a dramatic actualization. Past and present would conjoin for consumption beyond the scribal level. As Crossan puts it,

> Some anonymous genius took these diverse scriptural fulfillments and historicized them into a story of what happened to Jesus but did it so that those events were actualized in the most recent experiences of the Christian community, and that interaction of past and present was presented in a popularized format. There is no historization without actualization and popularization, not in Peter and not in the canonical passion accounts either.[30]

Here is another way of using memory. Scribal attention to prophetic texts can generate meaning for the present situation. This is not a documentary memory. Nothing here for historical museums or filing cabinets. Rather, such prophetic lines are actionable, ready to come alive in the present to throw light on a particular community's situation. It does not motion backwards but carries meaning forward. By being alert to oddities or curious combinations, Crossan has detected historical elements and factors that could not be absorbed through the usual historical categories.

Considering this, Crossan speaks to the Blood Curse passage. First, Crossan disagrees with Brown over the historicity of the trial scene. While Brown would see the Jewish demands for crucifixion and Roman declarations of innocence to be "plausible," Crossan regards this as Christian propaganda. This makes sense in the first century when Jesus communities were relatively powerless, marginal and disenfranchised. But what are we to make of Matthew's particular addition (Matt 27:24–25)? Crossan concludes:

> I cannot find any detailed historical information about the crucifixion of Jesus. Every item we looked at was prophecy historicized rather than history recalled. There was one glaring

---

29. Crossan makes a strong case that the "fingerprints of Mark" are all over this passage. The doubling, creative parallelisms and the use of irony are not lost on him. Crossan, *Who Killed Jesus?*, 110–12.

30. Crossan, *Who Killed Jesus?*, 95.

exception. The one time the narrative passion broke away from its base in the prophetic passion, that is, from the single composite trial in Psalm 2, was to assert Jewish responsibility and Roman innocence. But those motifs were neither prophecy nor history but Christian propaganda, a daring act of public relations faith in the destiny of Christianity not within Judaism but within the empire. In a way that *was* history, not past history but future history.[31]

In effect, the blood curse material, the clamor for execution and the assertions of innocence are later propaganda efforts. But is that all that can be said to do justice to this passage?

A Deeper Entanglement

Crossan's argument that the passion narrative was generated from historicizing prophetic citations can be deepened by asking whether the earliest level of the Gospel of Peter suggests more memory work. Here I differ from Crossan's view on the earliest level of Peter. While we have written and debated these issues and I have learned much from our encounters, I do not now intend to pursue our differences. But I contend that not only is there a layer under the Cross Gospel, but that it follows a specific genre. Both Crossan and I used George Nickelsburg's *Resurrection, Immortality and Eternal Life in Intertestamental Judaism*, a thoroughgoing review and reconstruction of the Tale of Suffering and Vindication of the Innocent One. Nickelsburg demonstrates that the story was widespread in intertestamental Judaism.[32]

The overarching story pattern detected by Nickelsburg can be summarized as follows:

> The actions and claims of a just person provoke his opponents to conspire against him. This leads to an accusation, trial, condemnation, and ordeal. In some instances this results in his shameful death. The hero of the story reacts characteristically, expressing his innocence, frustration, or trust in prayer, while there are also various reactions to his fate by characters in the tale. Either at

---

31. Crossan, *Who Killed Jesus?*, 159.

32. One can see examples of the ordeal and vindication of the innocent even in the book of Daniel with Daniel and the lions' den and the three young men in the fiery furnace. Judith's story is another, as well as the heroic suffering and death of the seven brothers, mother, and Eleazar in 4 Maccabees.

the brink of death or in death itself the innocent one is rescued and vindicated. This vindication entails the exaltation and acclamation of the hero as well as the reaction and punishment of his opponents.

Nickelsburg elaborated the various components of this tale.[33] These are the usual components of the story:

a *Reason* given for the situation

a *Conspiracy* is formed against the Innocent One

an Accusation

a Trial

Helpers who are in sympathy with the Innocent One the innocent makes a *Choice*

which occasions the *Condemnation* and *Ordeal*

a Protest

an expression of *Trust* by the innocent

Reaction by others occurs

a Rescue

an Exaltation

followed by more *Reactions*, and *Acclamation Vindication* of the innocent

Punishment and *Confession* by those who opposed the innocent one

The various passion stories exhibit how they not only use this overarching frame but also add or subtract from the various possible components. Noticing that the Tale has a trial component helps us to see why there is a trial for Jesus. Brown considers that this was plausible, i.e., historical. Crossan denies it happened but that the trial comes from historization of prophetic citations. Now the story pattern of the Innocent Sufferer includes a trial as a component and thus accommodates such prophetic historizations. In my *Inventing the Passion* I have argued that the structure of the Tale of the Innocent provides the memory space for

---

33 Crossan has argued that the Trial scene arises from the prophetic material (Ps 2) that has been historicized. By recognizing the genre of the structure encompassing these prophetic memories, one can see that a Trial scene was a crucial and expected component of the Tale of the Suffering Innocent One.

the prophetic citations and the organizing principle for constructing the passion narrative.[34]

Matthew, therefore, does add to the Markan source,[35] and each addition is drawn from the elements of the Tale's overarching structure. The writer of Matthew recognizes the overarching memory structure of the Tale of Suffering and Vindication of the Innocent One and continued to write out of it.[36] Clearly the selection of this memory space indicates that the author was convinced that Jesus died unjustly and chose this scribal structure that deals precisely with the unjust deaths of the innocent. In response to the shock and awe of Jesus' crucifixion, some followers refused to forget that man and began to use the fictive structures already composed within the Jewish wisdom tradition.

The author of the earliest layer of Peter had already taken the side of the oppressed in choosing to construct this narrative along the story lines of that tradition.[37] Mark and Matthew continue in this conviction. This story was never meant as an objective report; rather it offered hope in the shadow of devastation. Scavenging this material for cold, hard factoids misses the mark.

The letter from Pilate's wife (Matt 27:19) then is not simply an additional aspect to the narrative but another testimony to Jesus' innocence. Likewise, the Blood Curse verses (Matt 27:24–25) present another declaration (albeit cowardly) of Jesus' innocence and an illustration of opposition by those who want Jesus crucified. Thus, the writer portrays Pilate as washing his hands, thereby declaring he is "not responsible for this man's blood" (Matt 27:24). All the people in the crowd respond, "So, smear his blood on us and on our children" (Matt 27:25). From the perspective of Matthew's community, the people have not chosen wisely. They have

---

34. Dewey, *Inventing the Passion*.

35. For a complete list see Dewey, *Inventing the Passion*, 123–25. Note especially Matt 27:3–10 This insertion, detailing the death of Judas, reinforces the judgment upon the one who opposed the Innocent One. Matt 27:19 This brief insertion further underscores the innocence of the victim. Matt 27:24–25 Once more the innocence of the victim is maintained, along with the dramatic irony of the scene. Matt 27:40b, 43 Those who oppose the victim taunt him with the sarcastic use of the title of "God's son." This title reflects the material in Wisdom of Solomon 2. Matt 27:51b–53 This insertion further elaborates the reaction to the death of the Innocent One.

36. Each writer of the passion narratives was aware of this memory structure that authorized each to select rhetorically what would speak to that particular writer's concerns and audience.

37. As such, the author joined the ranks of those before him in carrying forward the question of the suffering of the innocent.

not perceived Jesus' innocence. Instead, they chose the wrong "Jesus," "a notorious prisoner" (Matt 27:16). They rejected the "Anointed One" for an unlikely stand-in. Even the Roman official declared Jesus' innocence. To which the people ironically state that they will be responsible for Jesus' death.[38]

From the point of view of Matthew's community, living in the period after the Jewish War, the Jewish people obviously had received retribution for Jesus' execution. The Temple had been destroyed and Jerusalem sacked and plundered. The Gospel of Mark already had linked the death of Jesus to the destruction of the Temple.[39] The gospel of Matthew maintains this connection and expands it. It started the trend towards lessening Roman involvement or responsibility in Jesus' execution with Pilate's washing of his hands. At the same time, the onus of responsibility is shifted not only onto Jewish leaders but also on the people themselves. The people within the scene have unknowingly implicated themselves in Jesus' fate.[40]

For many of the members of Matthew's community clearly the Jews in this scene bear the responsibility for Jesus' death. It was on their lips. Those who read this gospel literally and without a sense of historical context continue to use this quote as proof of Jewish guilt and a reason why Jews throughout history are "cursed." They cursed themselves when they said, "So, smear his blood on us and on our children." They knowingly rejected Jesus and for that they continue to suffer from a cursed condition.

But is it that clear? On a simple literal level, the "cursed" condition would have applied to the crowd (and their children) before Pilate at that time. By the time Matthew was written in the late first century that "judgment" had been rendered on those who experienced the sack of Jerusalem. In other words, the people had "taken their hit." A literal interpretation of the scene thus actually misses the dramatic capacity of the material.

Mark had already infused with irony this dramatic scene before Pilate.[41] Matthew carries this irony forward. The crowd in Mark and Mat-

---

38. Each of these items are components of the Tale of the Innocent Sufferer. See Crossan, *Who Killed Jesus?*, 110–12.

39. See Dewey, *Inventing the Passion*, 80.

40. Within this scene the people sarcastically declare that they will be responsible for Jesus' death. They do not see what Matthew's community holds: Jesus was innocent.

41. The crowd unwisely chooses the insurrectionist over the innocent one (Mark 15:15).

thew do not perceive the implications of their judgments. However, from the perspective of the Markan and Matthaean communities, the crowd appears to miss what the later Jesus communities knew: Jesus is the Innocent One. The declaration of the crowd in Matthew further underscores this ironic position which is intensified even more when one considers how this scene sounds written after the destruction of Jerusalem.

Why does Matthew intensify this dramatic irony?

- Is Matthew "rubbing it in" against fellow Jews who did not share the conviction that Jesus was the Anointed One?
- Is this gospel the beginning of an inter-Jewish dispute that will ultimately develop into anti-Judaism and then anti-Semitism?
- Is Matthew trying to spin the death story of Jesus away from any Roman involvement?

Two factors must be considered. First, Matthew employs the story frame of the Suffering Innocent One. The intensification of this story focuses sharply on "the people." Does this focus mean that the Matthean Jewish group[42] was condemning those who disagreed with them over Jesus' status as the Anointed One? It would appear so, except for the very words put on the people's lips by the writer: "So, smear his blood on us and our children." We have already noted the dramatic irony from the perspective of the Gospel writer and community: the Matthaean community recognizes that the crowd do not know what they are saying. There is more here than simply realizing that the words presaged the tragic fall of Jerusalem. The people called for Jesus' blood to be smeared on them. On first blush, it means that they will be responsible for his life. Yet we cannot forget that this gospel carried echoes of its oral performance. In fact, the last time that blood was mentioned before this section came at the final meal of Jesus and his disciples.

> He also took a cup and gave thanks and offered it to them, saying, "Drink from it all of you, for this is my blood of the covenant

---

42. Pilate's declaration of Jesus' innocence and washing his hands reframes the death of Jesus. Historically Jesus was executed by a Roman official. Years later, when the two Jewish groups, the Pharisees and the Matthaean community, competed to speak for the vanguard of what was left of the Jewish people, Jesus' followers sought to downplay the fact that their original leader was executed by the Romans. In determining who would speak for the Jews, turning to a community whose leader they had liquidated by Rome was a hard sell.

which has been poured out for many for the forgiveness of sins." (Matt 26:27–28)

Matthew alone adds the phrase "for the forgiveness of sins" (Matt 26:28c). Matthew has taken over the Markan language wherein the death of Jesus has been cast as a hero's death. The Markan Jesus dies, like other Jewish heroes, for many. But in Matthew the outpouring of Jesus blood, that is, his death, brings the possibility of forgiveness. This outpouring in blood echoes the scene in Exodus, where Moses seals the people in God's covenant:

> Moses took the blood and dashed it on the people, and said, "See the blood of the covenant that the Lord has made with you in accordance with all these words." (Exod 24:8)

Matthew's Jewish perspective implies a second irony embedded in this passage. Not only do the people fail to see what they are saying but, from Matthew's community's vantage, the people are unwittingly calling for the blood of Jesus, that is, *the forgiveness of the covenant*, to fall on them. The writer of Matthew is actually offering to his fellow Jews the opportunity to recognize in those ironic words the possibility of life and forgiveness. *The emphasis of this scene is not upon a harsh condemnation of fellow Jews but an offer of forgiveness and reconciliation.* The Matthaean community is trying to win over fellow Jews to the Jesus cause. Their refusal to accept Jesus could be turned around and his death could become their occasion of God's forgiveness.

Sadly, there is a third ironic note to be heard from this scene. Later, when the readers of Matthew's gospel are no longer Jewish but Gentile, the reading is heard quite differently. The attempt at reconciliation by the Matthaean community with fellow Jews was a failure. Subsequently the very scene used by the Matthaean community to suggest the possibility of reconciliation actually became one of the foundation stones in the bastion of antisemitism. What was once a literary instrument employed to speak subtly to fellow Jews soon became a lethal weapon with which to justify the hatred and killing of Jews.

One Final Entanglement

If one were to follow my argument about the earliest level of Peter,[43] there is a poignant point to be made. The original level does indicate that the people lead the "lord" away to death. But the fragment ends, not in condemnation, but in repentance. The earliest level attempts to reconcile two sides of a mixed gentile/Jewish community. It spoke to those who carried the stigma or sense of inferiority (i.e., not being Jewish) as well as to those Jews who had not understood what Jesus was about. At that original level this narrative was attempting to turn a mixed community into a new association by removing the social stigma and shame that went hand in hand with social negotiation in the first century. The full-bodied telling of the story of the vindicated Innocent One concretizes the possibility of imaginatively crossing social boundaries first in the narrative and then in social interaction. Those who saw themselves as inferior, within the pyramidal power structure of the Roman world, who were understood as less than human, saw in such constructions a way to reframe *their* existence and future. It was never a question of reporting the story of the death of Jesus. No one was interested in handing on some

---

43. Dewey, *Inventing the Passion*, chap. 9. Here is what I consider the earliest layer.

2 3cAnd he turned him over to the people on the day before the Unleavened Bread, their feast. 3 They took the lord and kept pushing him along as they ran; and they would say, "Let's drag the son of God along, since we have him in our power." 2And they threw a purple robe around him and sat him upon the judgment seat and said, "Judge justly, King of Israel." 3And one of them brought a crown of thorns and set it on the head of the lord. 4And others standing about would spit in his eyes, and others slapped his face, while others poked him with a rod. Some kept flogging him as they said, "Let's pay proper respect to the son of God." 4 And they brought two criminals and crucified the lord be- tween them. But he himself remained silent, as if in no pain. 2And when they set up the cross, they put an inscription on it, "This is the king of Israel." 3And they piled his clothing in front of him; then they divided it among themselves, and gambled for it. 4But one of those criminals reproached them and said, "We're suffering for the evil that we've done, but this fellow, who has become a savior of humanity, what wrong as he done to you?" 5And they got angry at him and ordered that his legs not be broken so he would die in agony. 5 It was midday and darkness covered the whole of Judea. They were confused 2And one of them said, "Give him vinegar mixed with something bitter to drink." And they mixed it and gave it to him to drink. 3And they fulfilled all things and brought to completion the sins on their head. 4Now many went about with lamps, and, thinking that it was night, they laid down. 5And the lord cried out, saying, "My power, (my) power you have abandoned me." When he said this, he was taken up. 6And at that moment, the veil of the Jerusalem temple was torn in two. 6 And then they pulled the nails from the lord's hands and set him on the ground. And the whole earth shook and there was great fear . . . 8 1bEverybody was moaning and beating their breasts, and saying "If his death has produced these over- whelming signs, he must have been entirely innocent."

factual account for posterity. Rather, the construction of the story of the fate of Jesus breached the myths that dominated the social world of the first century.

As we consider the possible ramifications of this detection of layers within the passion narratives, it becomes clear that engagement and commitment generated this material. This was not some cold-eyed assessment nor a remote reportage. It was a matter of life and meaning.

CONCLUDING THOUGHTS AND ANOTHER IMAGE

As I conclude this appreciation of and engagement with the scholarly insights of Dom Crossan, it is clear that, in his imaginative and committed work, Dom Crossan has been no spin doctor, no apologist for the status quo. He has not evaded the hard and complicated questions. Rather he has had the courage to ask about the very assumptions of the material investigated. He has been able to detect that the evidence regarding the narratives of the death of Jesus requires the capacity to cross into the imagination and memory of the first century. He has made us aware of the complicated texture of the texts. He did not settle for a commonsense resolution but disclosed the warp and woof of an ancient construction. In so doing he has brought us closer to the active memory work of the early Jesus movement.

It seems that the original image of "Ecce Homo" from the *National Geographic Magazine* has actually been lingering in the background of this paper. The usual assumption of the bible reader and even of some biblical scholars that the text like a photograph replicates the facts has been directly countered by Crossan's nimble and sensitive reading of the passion evidence. This has led him to see that the death narrative of Jesus was an attempt not to represent the facts but to find meaning with the imaginative traditions and tools available. By applying a "more difficult reading" Crossan challenges us to see how those early generations of Jesus followers wrestled with the very meaning of Jesus' death.

I close now with another image. It is time to move away from the representational assumptions of many modern readers to an appreciation of the splendid complexities of different memories. I offer the painting of Marc Chagall: *Exodus*. Here the solidarity of the crucified one with his people in the frantic motion of Exodus is quite marked. It presents a memory of hope unfolding in the onrush of history. Please view Mark Chagall's *Exodus*, at https://www.wikiart.org/en/marc-chagall/exodus-1966.

19

Wrestling with Divine Violence

PERRY KEA

If I were to name Crossan's most important scholarly work, it would probably be *The Historical Jesus: The Life of a Mediterranean Jewish Peasant* (1991). Crossan's stratification of the traditions about Jesus combined with his employment of anthropological and historical models yielded a coherent and compelling reconstruction of Jesus, making it the standard for Historical Jesus research.

However, I want to call attention to a book that is important because of the issue it addresses. It exposes a different side of his work. Crossan's *How to Read the Bible and Still be a Christian: Struggling with Divine Violence from Genesis Through Revelation* appeared in 2015. He explains that he wrote this book based on the many interactions he has had with church members when invited to speak about his views on the historical Jesus. "Q&A sessions after church lectures *always* raised theological issues involving Christian faith and practice"[1] Repeatedly, in these sessions, Crossan's picture of Jesus as a non-violent resistor to Roman imperial violence (abetted by high priestly collaboration) ran into questions about Jesus' own alleged violence (e.g., Jesus' driving out the money changers from the Temple) and the Book of Revelation's description of the conquering Christ who destroys God's enemies (Rev 19:11–21). While Crossan addresses these two texts quickly in his first chapter, he observes that the conversation did not stop there.

---

1. Crossan, *How to Read the Bible*, 7; italics original.

As Crossan explains, these questions about a nonviolent or violent Jesus led to even more questions about the biblical view of God. How does one account for the apparently bipolar vision of God in the Bible—a God of violent retributive justice or a God of nonviolent distributive justice?[2] As Crossan puts it, "How, then, are we to act against injustice and violence—nonviolently or violently"?[3] Given that both perspectives are *in* the Christian Bible[4] itself, how can Christians decide? Dealing openly with this conflict is why I regard this as one of Crossan's most important books. He begins with a problem that nags at contemporary Christians and then proposes a way of working through this problem "by imagining the Bible as a whole—as a completed volume, as an organized unity, and as an integrated totality."[5] He chooses to respect the Christian Bible as a revelation and guide for the lives of Christians.[6] *How to Read the Bible* thus becomes a work of constructive biblical theology. On display are Crossan's considerable historical critical skills, but here put into the service of articulating a theology, an understanding of God, rooted in the Christian Bible.

In *How to Read the Bible* Crossan tracks what he calls the rhythm of divine assertion and human civilization's subversion across many biblical texts and historical contexts. We see this, for example, in chapter 2. He begins with the Jubilee Year of liberation text in Leviticus 25. This tradition imagines the land as belonging to God, not others, but which God freely distributed to the various tribes and clans. This is an example of God's distributive and restorative justice. But human greed and injustice subverted the Jubilee Year legislation.

Crossan cites the story of Naboth's Vineyard as an extreme example (1 Kgs 21). He observes that the normal way of subverting divine goodness was through the process of land being mortgaged and foreclosed.

---

2. Crossan, *How to Read the Bible*, 16–18.

3. Crossan, *How to Read the Bible*, 20.

4. Crossan recognizes the problem of applying the term "Christian Bible" to the Hebrew Canon. He describes his use of the term as "simply descriptive of that set of sacred scriptures extending from Genesis through Revelation" (18). He implies that the first "Christians'" appropriation of the Hebrew scriptures was organic because they were Messianic Jews. If they had not been, "that usage would have been conceptual theft, textual plagiarism, and cultural looting" (18).

5. Crossan, *How to Read the Bible*, 20.

6. Crossan is aware of the need to make his case to non-religious people too, something he does in other recent books and public lectures. He begins to address this additional audience in the Epilogue of this book.

As a result, ancestral lands and the gifts they provided were lost. Crossan calls the familiar coercive ways humans subvert the intended goodness of creation the "normalcy of civilization."[7]

At the end of chapter 2, after his two exploratory probes into the Bible, Crossan identifies the norm that will guide him through rest of his study.

> How do we Christians know which is our true God—our Bible's violent God, or our Bible's nonviolent God? The answer is actually obvious. The norm and criterion of the Christian Bible is the biblical Christ . . . God is violent if Christ is violent, and God is nonviolent if Christ is nonviolent.
>
> But which Christ do we mean? The nonviolent Jesus riding on the peace donkey in the Gospel, or the violent Christ riding on a white warhorse in Revelation?
>
> If, for Christians, the biblical Christ is the criterion of the biblical God, then, for Christians, the historical Jesus is the criterion of the biblical Christ (italics his).
>
> My proposal in this book is that *the same individual* (italics his) studied as the Jesus of history by academic research and accepted as the Christ of faith by confessional belief is the norm and criterion of the Christian Bible.[8]

This is very clear, but as readers might anticipate, a problem for Crossan's position is that there is more than one reconstruction of the Jesus of history. For example, some scholars favor the view that the historical Jesus subscribed to an apocalyptic world view. By contrast, Crossan's reconstruction of the Jesus of history roots him in Israel's wisdom tradition. His Jesus speaks of a God "who causes rain to fall on the just and the unjust," who calls upon his audience to love their enemies and pray for their persecutors. The God described in Israel's wisdom tradition and in the teaching of Jesus is the one who created a good world and provided it with abundant resources.[9] This is the God who operates on the basis of nonviolent distributive justice.[10] The apocalyptic Jesus of other historical reconstructions speaks of a God who, at the end of the present

---

7. Crossan, *How to Read the Bible*, 24.

8. Crossan, *How to Read the Bible*, 34–35.

9. Crossan treats the issue of nonviolent distributive justice or violent retributive justice in the wisdom tradition in chapter 8.

10. Crossan's case for a nonviolent Jesus is most fully developed in chapter 10. In chapter 11 he tracks how and why early sources (such as Q) changed the picture of a nonviolent Jesus to one that is more congenial to retributive violence.

age, intervenes to punish and destroy humans who exploit and oppress the weak. This God imposes violent retributive justice for offenses against God's people. Given the difference between these two reconstructions of Jesus, one could question the wisdom of making the Jesus of history the "norm and criterion of the Christian Bible." For that reason, some scholars would prefer the biblical Christ as that norm, although as Crossan (and others) have pointed out, the biblical Christ has several faces. As Crossan makes clear, the pattern of nonviolent distributive justice *asserted* in some parts of the Gospel tradition and then *subverted* by violent retributive justice in other parts, constitutes an ongoing tension within the Christian Bible. As we have had to learn over and over, there is no reading of scripture without presuppositions. Or as the deconstructionists would say, it's interpretation all the way down.

For the remaining chapters, Crossan tracks the "recurrent rhythm between the biblical version of God's nonviolent distributive justice and God's violent retributive justice" throughout the Bible.[11] In each chapter, Crossan contextualizes his selected biblical texts within their cultural and historical contexts. By situating each example within those contexts, Crossan finds explanations for the assertion/subversion process. For example, in discussing Israel's prophetic tradition (chapter 7), he explains and demonstrates how Israel's understanding of its covenant with God was affected by the Assyrian empire's preference for extremely violent sanctions toward rebellious vassal states. "Far too much of Assyrian imperial theology entered Israelite covenantal theology."[12]

One of the things I admire about this book is Crossan's honesty and his hermeneutical vision. He recognizes and declares consistently that the Christian Bible contains both a vision of a nonviolent God and one of a violent God. He does not run from this but seeks to understand it. In the process, he seeks a solution. Each chapter of the book contributes to the construction of this solution, which is laid out with great clarity in the book's Epilogue. There Crossan draws out the implications of making the historical Jesus the norm and criterion of the biblical Christ, and by extension, of the Christian Bible and Christian faith. Crossan develops a metaphor based on his study of Christian iconography.[13] He calls it the Biblical Iconic Focus. He draws upon iconographic representations

---

11. Crossan, *How to Read the Bible*, 28.

12. Crossan, *How to Read the Bible*, 115.

13. This work is reflected in his 2018 book, written with his spouse Sarah Crossan, *Resurrecting Easter*.

in very old churches that indicate to him how the Old Testament and New Testament narratives find their center and norm in Christ.[14] In the final pages of this book, Crossan points to the direction he would take to help Christians read the Bible. He holds onto the necessary relationship between "justice" and "love." "Justice without love may end in brutality, but love without justice must end in banality."[15]

Crossan's *How to the Read the Bible* offers contemporary Christians a critical and constructive way of reading the Bible and identifying its center. For this reason, I consider this a highly valuable and important book.

---

14. Crossan, *How to Read the Bible*, 241–43.
15. Crossan, *How to Read the Bible*, 245.

20

Crossan, Paul, and the Philosophers

JOHN CAPUTO

The aim of *Paul as Pharisee: A Vision of Post-Civilization* is both historical and theological, that is, to wrest free the Paul of the authentic letters from what the subsequent tradition has made of Paul, not only in the later history of the Church but in the New Testament itself, in the deutero-Pauline letters and the Acts of the Apostles. The latter in particular is admonished by Crossan for its bald attempt to rob Paul to pay Peter, to Romanize the radical *ekklesia* Paul is describing, to soften the edges of Paul and begin the long history of Constantinism that scars institutional Christianity.[1] Paul, he thinks, is a radical thinker, with revolutionary views about "civilization," the odious ways of the world in which human beings subject one another—by race (Greeks and Jews), class (master and slave), and gender (male and female). Against this, Paul proposes what Crossan calls, in the subtitle of the book, *A Vision of Post-Civilization*, meaning a radical egalitarian and non-violent community in the Messiah, the "kingdom of God," not the *imperium Romanum*. Paul dared to challenge the rule of the Roman Empire itself in a letter written to the Romans, telling the powers of this world their days are numbered and that by executing God's chosen one, these dark powers had signed their

---

1. Thankfully, Pauline scholarship has returned in a critical and disciplined way to the authentic letters to sort out Paul's actual views from what later generations tried to do with him. But autobiographical material should not get a pass either. As Crossan points out, the "I" can get in the way of the "we." Autobiographers might be tempted to cast themselves in the best possible light, a hero for the cause, surrounded by enemies, betrayed by friends, snake-bitten and ship-wrecked, fighting the good fight.

own death warrant. The rule of the God of Israel was at hand, not only as future coming but as something that had already begun in the crucifixion and resurrection of Messiah Jesus, the "first fruits" of which are already found in the resurrection. The kingdom of God is already open for business.

The title of the book, *Paul the Pharisee*, reflects Crossan's thesis that Paul's experience of the risen Messiah is pretty much responsible for what would later become what we call "Christianity." This is the notion that the Messiah suffered a martyr's death at the hands of the powers of darkness and was raised from the dead by the power of God, thereby inaugurating the advent of God's rule on earth. This narrative, described by Gustaf Aulén in 1930 in a famous book as *Christus Victor*,[2] is uniquely Paul's—not to be found in the Q-gospel or in the *Didache*—because *Paul is a Pharisee*, among whom the resurrection of the dead at the end of time, the final judgement of collective humankind, is a central feature, and is sharply to be distinguished from individual ascension or *apotheosis*, which was a feature of the ancient world generally.

Beyond its meticulous historical detective work, Crossan's book is also a crossing, a cross-over, a border-crossing from history to theology and from theology to philosophy. Paul thinks that a Big Being called God is going to raise up every person who has ever lived in order to subject them to a final judgment, deciding whether to reward them forever, maybe show them mercy, or subject them to a punishment that will make them wish they were not raised up and never born in the first place. Crossan thinks that is "transcendental terrorism." Then why read Paul? Because like every great "classic" (see Gadamer), which includes "religious classics" (see Paul Ricoeur and David Tracy),[3] Paul's letters are of enduring importance and are to be read and reread in every age. Accordingly, "resurrection" and "judgment day" are to be taken as *metaphors*, which is our task to *interpret*. Paul is a deep thinker, but his vision and insight are held captive by a premodern world full of angels and demonic powers and Judgment Days. His letters belong to a collective historical imaginary—which is true of everyone—whose contemporary relevance can only be discerned by a disciplined and interpretive reading.

To that end Crossan undertakes to read Paul "bi-lingually," by proposing three hermeneutic substitutions. (1) Substitute real-life

2. Aulén, *Christus Victor*.
3. Gadamer, *Truth and Method*, 193–94. Tracy, *The Analogical Imagination*; Tracy, *Plurality and Ambiguity*.

consequences for divine punishment. A punishment is like someone driving under the influence who is pulled over and given a ticket; a consequence is like the driver ending up in an accident. Punishments take place in legal-normative space; consequences take place in real-causal space. (2) Substitute the history of evolution for the history of salvation. (3) Replace forgiveness with our capacity to change, and mercy with the time we have left to change. The resulting (re)vision is this. We as a species have a collective responsibility to heed the consequences of our deeds. Why is that a problem? Because there is a built-in tension in our being between "I" and "we," between our individual being and social being, and we are strongly inclined to prefer the former over the latter. As a result we, as a species, have engaged in a three-fold violence against the earth—against the environment, against other species, and among ourselves (war), and judgment day is coming, not in a legal-normative way but a real causal crash that threatens to be the end of us. Paul thought the time had grown short, and we know neither the day nor the hour. Paul's timing was wrong, but his instincts were right. Today we also think the time is short, the end is near, but we are starting to get a rather good idea of the day and the hour, depending on how close we come to keeping the rise in the global temperature to 1.5 degrees Celsius. The time is now. The time has come to repent of this violence and to make real a vision of non-violence on all three fronts.

In the course of making this argument, Crossan acknowledges a number of contemporary philosophers who have engaged with Paul, using them as epigraphs to his chapters, but it would belong to another book, or several other books, to undertake a thematic discussion of what these thinkers have to say.[4] So, to some extent, these citations are like footnotes suggesting "further readings." Then, why not simply put them in the footnotes? Why draw attention to them like that? Maybe that is where they started out but they ended up as epigraphs because they are more important than footnotes. These thinkers are allies, fellow-travelers, partners in a central motive of *Paul as Pharisee*. With the exception of Jacob Taubes (1923–87),[5] a colorful and brilliant rabbi and professor of philosophical hermeneutics (Berlin), these philosophers are atheists and Marxists, but they are seriously interested in Paul and they have (mostly) done their historical-critical homework. Their importance is this. They

---

4. For an overview, see Caputo and Alcoff, eds., *St. Paul among the Philosophers*.
5. Taubes, *The Political Theology of Paul*.

think, as Alain Badiou (1937–) says, that Paul is trading in fables (see the epigraph to chapter 2).[6] What Paul is talking about, the resurrection of the dead, cannot be believed by a modern person—but that is not the end of it. That is only the beginning. Let us set that point aside and set about reading Paul seriously as a *thinker*. Let us put the distinction between "philosophy" and "theology" out of action and *read* what Paul has to say to us today, for our own situation, what he is saying about life and death, about justice and injustice. That is exactly what Crossan wants to do.

In addition to Taubes and Badiou, Crossan also mentions Giorgio Agamben (1942–),[7] whose book, like Taubes's, is a commentary on the letter to the Romans. I plan to treat these thinkers and their relation to Crossan's argument thematically, by singling out five issues they address—civilization and post-civilization, universality, time (*kairos* and *chronos*), conversion, and the law (*nomos*).[8]

I will conclude by briefly adding my own two cents, with all due caution. I am, after all, but a philosopher, not a New Testament historian, and, as Jacob Taubes would say, what do I know?

CIVILIZATION AND POST-CIVILIZATION

Let us start with Crossan's subtitle, *A Vision of Post-Civilization*, and with the seminal and tragic Jewish thinker Walter Benjamin (1892–1940), a figure who is not found in Crossan's text but in the context, or perhaps Crossan would say, belongs to the "matrix" for the philosophical line of thought that follows. Benjamin deeply influenced Taubes, and he is the principal source of Agamben's *The Time that Remains*, but he is also the source of what Crossan calls the "normalcy of this world," or "civilization" as a way to describe what Paul called the wisdom and power of the world as opposed to the wisdom and power of God. Against this Crossan poses the possibility of a *post*-civilization. I would like to take credit for this insight and say that I figured this out by myself and consider my work

---

6. Badiou, *Saint Paul: The Foundation of Universalism*, 4–5.

7. Agamben, *The Time that Remains*.

8. The figure who is not mentioned by Crossan who also plays a role in this movement is Slavoj Žižek, who sides with Badiou, whom he regards as a Trojan horse infiltrating religion who shows that God is dead and Christianity dissolves into Marxism. Both Badiou and Žižek attack postmodernism as a kind of liberal permissiveness, a skeptical dilly-dallying, political correctness, as opposed to radical Marxist politics, a resolute commitment to truth, which is hard and fast, which they both find in Marx and in Paul's apostolic zeal to fight the good fight.

done and my duties discharged. But honesty compels me to say that when I told Dominic that I thought I should start with Benjamin, he replied in an email, "it is precisely Walter Benjamin that haunts my use of post/civilization over, under, and around the book." Crossan inscribes a famous line from Benjamin— "There is no document of civilization which is not at the same time a document of barbarism"—over a painting of Paul in a video discussion of his book.[9] That is to say, first, there is no chance I am going to get ahead of John Dominic Crossan, and second, that we are right to start here.

Benjamin wrote a famous but short piece, just a few paragraphs, under the title "Theologico-Political Fragment," which begins, "Only the Messiah himself completes all history, in the sense that he alone redeems, completes, creates its relation to the messianic."[10] Benjamin portrays world history as a history of nihilism where what history calls progress is a headlong rush into catastrophe, a corruption and moral disorder so profound that it cannot be remedied by human hands. No historical era can effect this relation to the messianic of itself; the order of "immanence" (the world) collapses in on itself. For Benjamin, the kingdom of God is not the *telos* of history, not a goal, but an *end*, a break, an apocalyptic crisis, a time of destruction, annihilation. The profane order is erected on the principle of happiness, which runs in one direction, making forward progress, while the messianic direction, "the mystical conception of history," runs in another direction, backwards, brushes against the grain, looking back at the dead bodies accumulated in the past. So, the intensity of the messianic effect is a function of the friction of these conflicting forces. But in seeking progress and happiness in what is passing away, all that is earthly seeks (incurs) its downfall (*Untergang*), with the result that "world politics" is "nihilism." Taubes (and Agamben agrees with him) hypothesizes that this short piece is a close parallel to Rom 8, in which Paul speaks of the world as subject to futility, groaning for redemption and passing away.[11]

In 1940, Benjamin elaborated this densely concentrated fragment in a longer piece, entitled "On the Concept of History," which was earlier

---

9. Benjamin, "On the Concept of History," 4:392. Agamben has also written extensively about Benjamin. See Agamben, *State of Exception*.

10. Benjamin, "Theologico-Political Fragment," 3:305–6. The text is also reproduced in its entirety in Taubes, *The Political Theology of Paul*, 70–72, with a slightly different translation.

11. Taubes, *The Political Theology of Paul*, 70.

translated under the title "Theses on the Philosophy of History." Benjamin develops the concept of messianic history as a history of injustice and oppression standing in need of "redemption." The idea of the "past," Benjamin says, is "indexed" to "redemption."[12] The dead are not merely dead but *remembered*. Every day is a day of remembrance[13] when the dead *call* to us, asking *us* to make right the wrong that was done them, and we in turn must have the ears to hear, be tuned to their call, which Benjamin calls "the echo of the now silent ones."[14] There is a "secret agreement between past generations and the present one."[15] The subject of history is the oppressed, but universal history is written by the oppressors. The very idea of the Messiah, then, is to *right the wrongs* that were done to the dead, justification, to make right, *justus + facere, justificatio*, in German, *Rechtsfertigung* (*Rechts + fertigen*).

Consequently, every generation is endowed with "a *weak* messianic power," and the past has a "claim" on this power.[16] "Weak" is in italics? Why? Because if "strong," it will turn our head to dreaming of a coming future Savior, suggest an iron law of history, an inevitable outcome, and we will relax because rescue is coming no matter what and then we will fall into quietism. But if *weak*, then *we* must make up what is lacking. "Our coming was expected on earth"[17]—that is, *we* are the messianic generation, *we* are the ones the dead have been waiting for. We must step up, which is what Bonhoeffer was telling the German Lutheran church in the Third Reich.

Benjamin interprets a Klee painting ("*Angelus novus*") as the angel of history, facing the past with his back to the future, beholding a catastrophe, an accumulating wreckage. "The angel would like to stay, awaken the dead, and make whole what has been smashed," but the wind blowing from Paradise [that is, the forward movement of so-called progress] is too strong."[18] The Messiah cannot awaken the dead and change the past. The best we can do is act in the *present* and change the *meaning* of the past. That is the meaning of "Judgment Day," the day when the accounts

---

12. Benjamin, "On the Concept of History," 390.
13. Benjamin, "On the Concept of History," 395, 401.
14. Benjamin, "On the Concept of History," 390.
15. That is why Metz speaks of "the dangerous memory of suffering," of which the memory of the Cross is paradigmatic. Metz, *Faith in History and Society*, 109–15.
16. Benjamin, "On the Concept of History," 390.
17. Benjamin, "On the Concept of History," 390.
18. Benjamin, "On the Concept of History," 392.

of history will be settled, when wrongs will be made right, but Judgment Day is not some day at the end of time but every day, *today*. So, the idea of a "redeemed mankind" requires the (messianic) historian to record *every moment* in history—not a tear shall be lost—not just the major events but even the minor, minute, and everyday ones, so that nothing is left unredeemed. Even the most inconspicuous thing is like a flower turning toward the sun of history.[19]

The idea of messianic time comes to a head in what Benjamin calls "now-time," *Jetzzeit*—which, as Taubes and Agamben will argue, translates Paul's *ho nyn kairos*. "Now-time" is not a transition, the line dividing the past from the future (Aristotle) but a moment (*kairos, Augenblick*) where the *past* is "blasted out" of the continuum of time (*chronos*) and is made *present*, now. For example, he says, the French Revolution looked on Rome and saw itself as "Rome Incarnate."[20] Messianic time is conceived as the *break* in this historical time, an "interruption," which can be compared to a "tiger's leap," as the tiger slowly gathers itself up in order to lunge. Now-time is a "model of messianic time" and it "comprises the entire history of mankind in a tremendous abbreviation,"[21] a text also seized upon by Agamben, who relates it to Paul's time "grown short" (1 Cor 7:29), as we will see below. Messianic time is *kairotic*, like the moment of decision, the opportune time, the time to strike. Instead of a smooth transition (*chronos*) to the next moment, it *makes the clock stop*; it makes time *stand still*, blasting open the continuum, making the continuum of history "explode." In now-time there is a "constellation" of forces, a moment saturated with tensions, a shock, a "messianic arrest of happening," which means a "revolutionary chance in the fight for the oppressed past" (Benjamin, 396). The "normalcy" of the rush of progress is the true madness or exception and the messianic is a call to "stop" the madness and mayhem. In the final line of this text he says that in messianic time "every second is the narrow gate through which the Messiah might enter" (Benjamin, 397).

Benjamin's work is understandably dark. Like the Jews living under the under heel of Rome in the first century, Benjamin was a Jew in 1930s Germany living under the Nazis. This text is among his last, written shortly before his suicide, while attempting to escape on foot across the mountains from France into Spain. So, Benjamin's view of history

---

19. Benjamin, "On the Concept of History," 390.
20. Benjamin, "On the Concept of History," 395.
21. Benjamin, "On the Concept of History," 396.

is shaped by the memory of a long history of Jewish oppression, by the Nazi nightmare, but also by his Marxism, or his version of Marxism—he departs from Marx's view of an inevitable historical dialectic—as an accumulating history of capitalist exploitation of the workers. The tragedy of our times, Benjamin thinks, is that we accept this exceptional disorder (*Ausnahmsstand*) as normal, as the order of the day, and we must make the true state of exception take place, which is to take exception to that spurious normalcy in a revolutionary strike.[22] The secular counterpart to the "kingdom of God" for him is a classless society (which Taubes, Agamben, and Badiou all see in Gal 3:27–28).

When Heidegger said the meaning of Being is time, he meant that our understanding of Being is keyed to a temporal dimension. The Greeks thought that true being lay in eternal and unchanging presence (the present, the eternal now) and the Stoics in abiding by the eternal and necessary. The direction of the messianic for Benjamin is *back*, toward the past and its retroactive redemption. Jewish prayers are prayers of remembrance, he says, and should not be wasted on dreaming about the future.[23] We should be "nourished by the image of enslaved ancestors rather than by the ideal of liberated grandchildren."[24] Even when Benjamin speaks of hope, he means "hope in the past,"[25] redemption.

This leads me to pose a question to Crossan about just how closely Benjamin's messianic parallels Paul. While no one can fail to admire Benjamin's powerful elaboration of a weak messianic, I have always thought its construal of the now-time to be one-sidedly turned to the past. But is not the emphasis of both the prophets and Paul turned in a *creationist* way toward the future, *making all things new*? Is not the thrust of Crossan's chapters 8 and 9 to account for Paul's "new creation," where resurrection has already begun? Is "a vision of *post*-civilization" not an apocalyptic vision of what is possible, of what can come? Is not messianic time primarily a matter of a structural, irreducible "to-come"? Is the not messianic prayer, even in cultivating a memory of the dead, always praying for the kingdom to come? Even if the Messiah has already come, do we not—as long as we live in time—want the Messiah to come *again*? Is that not the very stuff of living in time?

---

22. Benjamin, "On the Concept of History," 392.
23. Benjamin, "On the Concept of History," 397.
24. Benjamin, "On the Concept of History," 394.
25. Benjamin, "On the Concept of History," 392;

THE UNIVERSALISM OF ST. PAUL

Crossan cites Badiou's *Saint Paul: The Foundation of Universalism* twice, in the epigraphs to chapters 2 (the resurrection is a fable) and 7 (the resolution of the Jerusalem conference was unstable). The title of Badiou's book is based on his reading of Gal 3:27–28, which he takes to be a recognition on the part of Paul of the universal essence of human being. This essence, he said, is arrived at by a process of "subtraction," by subtracting Greek and Jew, male and female, master and slave, which results in the remainder, the universally human. Badiou is unapologetic about the mathematical analogy. The more interesting part of his book, I think, is that he takes Paul as a paradigm of the "event," of a radical decision, the model of the "revolutionary subject," resolved to turn a personal revelation into a universal truth. But on his conception of *universality*, Badiou serves as a good example of why historians and theologians should keep plenty of light between themselves and philosophers, who have an endemic propensity to produce stone cold abstractions like this, like patients etherized upon a table. The only thing genuinely universal about Badiou's position on this point is that it is disputed by just about everyone else.

Taubes, whose lectures were given in 1987 and published in 1993, four years before Badiou's book, had already put this misunderstanding to rest. By wanting to include the Gentiles, Paul is not trying to be one of the Greco-Hellenistic "liberal" Jews, who were accommodating to Roman rule and could wave the flag of a *nomos* (law) theology, which was reassuring to Greco-Roman culture. Paul is not a "universalist," Taubes writes:

> Paul is a fanatic! Paul is a zealot, a Jewish zealot, and he has nothing to do with the "mishmash," the "blather" in the spirit of this great nomos liberalism. He is totally illiberal; of that I am certain.[26]

Gal 3:27–28 is not liberal accommodation; this is a revolution which turns "Jewish-Roman-Hellenistic upper-class theology on its head." So, if Paul is "universalist" this is not a Hellenistic universalism but an "eye of the needle" universal which overturns or transvalues the values of Hellenistic philosophy. Paul's universalism, Taubes thinks, "signifies the election of Israel." It is *pas* Israel! His universalism is not pan-Hellenism

---

26. Taubes, *The Political Theology of Paul*, 25.

or pan-globalism or pan-humanism but *pan-Israelism*. As Dale Martin points out, Paul says the Gentiles are being "grafted" on to the tree of Israel, so if you love mathematics, this is addition, not subtraction.[27] I think Crossan would agree with Taubes, not Badiou, but for his own reason:

> His [Paul's] own foundational vision of the universalism of Jews-and-Gentiles was not based on some Greek post-Alexander cultural universalism or some Roman post-Augustus imperial universalism. Pauline universalism was founded and grounded on—resurrection! What could be more absolutely universal than the resurrection-judgment-sanction of all the dead from his Pharisaic past or its already ongoing "first fruits" with Jesus from his Messianic/ Christic present?"[28])

According to Crossan, the *"foundation of universalism"* (Badiou's term) for Paul is the Pharisaic belief in the "general judgment," judgment day, the resurrection of the dead ones, when everybody, living and dead, is going to face the divine music![29] The crucifixion and resurrection meant cosmic injustice precipitated cosmic justice, and everybody (*pas*) is on the divine hook, *universally*!

THE TIME IS NOW

The Hellenistic universalism Badiou is trying to find in Paul is also rejected by Giorgio Agamben, where it is part of a larger and complicated theory of time. The contemporary interest of philosophers in Paul goes back a hundred years, to the young Heidegger's 1919–23 lectures at Freiburg on the "hermeneutics of facticity," in which Paul's letters and Augustine's *Confessions* played an important role.[30] After returning home from World War I, Heidegger, who had been a rising star in German Catholicism, converted to Lutheranism and became known as quite an expert reader of Luther. He was even invited by Bultmann to give a lecture on Luther's concept of sin in a Luther seminar conducted by Bultmann when Heidegger had accepted a position at Marburg. Heidegger

27. See Martin, "Teleology, Epistemology, and Universal Vision in Paul," 100–101, and also my "Introduction" to *St. Paul among the Philosophers*, "Postcards from Paul: Subtracting versus Grafting," 1–23.

28. Crossan, *Paul the Pharisee*, 249.

29. Crossan, *Paul the Pharisee*, 39.

30. Heidegger, *The Phenomenology of Religious Life*.

was particularly focused on Paul's experience of lived temporality (*Temporalität*) in a time when we know neither the day nor the hour. These lectures, he tells us, were pretty much the first draft of *Being and Time*. So, the "time" in the title of what is arguably (for my money) the most important book of European philosophy in the twentieth century goes back to Paul!

The epigraphs Crossan inscribes in both chapters 9 and 10 are taken from Agamben's *The Time that Remains*. Agamben dedicated the book to Taubes who, like Agamben, was working in the space that Benjamin had opened. Like Heidegger, Agamben is focused on Paul's *experience* of time, which he treats by distinguishing *kairos* and *chronos*.[31] He is particularly interested in 1 Cor 7:29-32 and the *hōs mē* (as though not) sayings, which "may be his [Paul's] most rigorous definition of messianic life."[32] These he characterizes in a typically enigmatic way as the "revocation of every vocation,"[33] where vocation is translating *klēsis* (19-23). These sayings do not demonstrate an otherworldly indifference to life here on earth; they are defining characteristics of living in "messianic time," of the "form of life" which he calls messianic. It is of no importance that, *historically*, Paul was mistaken to think that the world was about to end. What is important is the *structure* of "messianic time" that is on display here. While he got what time it is wrong, he got what time is right. At this moment, Paul says, the *kairos*, the time of the now (*ho nyn kairos*) has been foreshortened (1 Cor 7:29: *synestalmenos*), contracted, rolled up into a tight ball—we can hear the voice of Benjamin in this language—in which Agamben thinks the dynamics of messianic time are made visible.

To say that every vocation is lived under revocation is not to say it is abolished but rather struck through, marked with an asterisk, and made to tremble with the fundamental *tensions* of messianic time. Be a steward, not a lord; use the things of this world (*usus*) but do not take them as your possession (*dominium*) and identify with them. As Kierkegaard said, do not lace the garments of temporality too tightly. This both affirms the vocation and hollows out the vocation as having lasting worldly importance. It revokes the factual condition without undermining it. Paul concludes this passage by saying that the figure of this world (*schēma tou kosmou*) is passing away, which leads both Agamben and Taubes to think this lies behind Benjamin's notion of the fleeting passing away of the past.

31. Agamben, *The Time that Remains*, 68-69.
32. Agamben, *The Time that Remains*, 23,
33. Agamben, *The Time that Remains*, 23-26.

The messianic tension is immanent to time. Paul is not talking about a transition to another future world outside time. Make use of the world (*chrēsis*) but do not identify with it. If you are a slave, use your calling (slavery) as if you were free. Use here is contrasted with possession, *usus* not *dominium* [be a steward not an owner]. The messianic calling is not a right or a possession or a stable identity but a "potentiality." Whatever your worldly station, use it as if not. So, you become a new creature in the Messiah but nothing changes outwardly. That is why Agamben was also interested in Franciscan poverty which, by easy extension, should extend to Pope Francis's *Laudato Si* when it comes to using not owning the earth and to Crossan's concern with the ecological crisis.[34]

In Agamben's terms, to be made a new creature in the Messiah is to render our worldly vocation "inoperative," ineffective, which is a signature concept of his work. The calling is not abolished or abandoned but given new meaning. The content is unchanged but appropriated in a new way. The *what* is the same; the *how* has changed. This non-possession is why he sees here an anticipation of a Marxist classless society, a radical egalitarianism, which is, as Benjamin had said, the secularization of messianic time.[35] All creation is subject to futility and decay and is in need of redemption, even as we are deprived of identity and self-possession. Agamben does not see the *hōs mē* injunctions as nihilistic or quietistic but as emancipatory: *every worldly vocation is released for its free use* in the messianic moment, which I personally take to be a highlight of his book.

This analysis in turn throws light on the question of Paul's universalism. Agamben also rejects Badiou's claim that Gal 3:28–29 means that Paul is cutting through to a universal human essence of which Greek and Jew, male and female, master and slave, are accidental variations, differences which we "tolerate." That is what Agamben calls the "production of the same."[36] The messianic effect is to render these distinctions *inoperative*; it leaves them intact but deprived of their hierarchical and exclusionary power. This is not universalism but the production of the "remnant," which is not a mathematical quantity (Badiou's remainder), the seven thousand, but a qualitative category. By this Agamben means that a person is a complex of many identities, that no one is simply identical with oneself, that there is always an excess, a more to every life.

34. Agamben, *The Highest Poverty*; Pope Francis, *Praise Be to You*.
35. Agamben, *The Time that Remains*, 30.
36. Agamben, *The Time that Remains*, 51–52.

No one is simply, self-identically a Jew or a Greek. Hereafter we are Jews or Greeks as if we are not. We are all "non-non-Jews" in the Messiah who produces this shock, this dislocating, dispossessive effect on everyone who now lives not as themselves but lets the Messiah lives in them.[37] This compares to Derrida's concept of having an identity (a proper name, a driver's license, a passport, say) but not being "identical with oneself" (think of Rom 7:19–25) and Derrida's fear of an identitarian politics.[38]

Paul is not interested in the end-time, Agamben says—that is a remarkable claim to make—but in the time that remains, the time that is beginning to end—and for Crossan, what better way to describe the present political and ecological crisis? Messianic time is the time it takes to end,[39] the time that is rapidly passing away, foreshortened time, the *kairos* which represents an interruption (Benjamin) or *caesura* in chronological time. Now is the time! Messianic time is the time to seize the moment. We should not think of messianic time as the time of deferral (Scholem) or as merely transitional to the end-time. This is also Agamben's critique of Derrida's notion of the "messianic." Deconstruction, Agamben has persuaded himself, is a "thwarted messianism, a suspension of the messianic," inasmuch as the "trace" can never catch up with itself; there is infinite "deferment," no pleroma. But for Agamben the messianic is not waiting for fulfillment, but is a fulfillment *in* the moment. It is not an infinite task extended over an infinite future, as in Husserlian idealization or Derrida's deferral.[40] In messianic time we seize hold of the instant and bring it to fulfillment now, actualizing the voice from the past (potency) which we are called upon to actualize.

The notion of the inoperative (*non-oiu-in-opera*) is a central feature of Agamben's work, and it can be traced back to his interest in the Aristotelian categories of potency (*dynamis*) and actualization (*energeia*),

37. Agamben, *The Time that Remains*, 49–53.
38. Derrida, *The Other Heading*.
39. Agamben, *The Time that Remains*, 62–65.
40. *The Time that Remains*, 101–103. This criticism of Derrida is misguided. It cuts him off before he finishes explaining himself. In "The Force of Law: 'The Mystical Foundation of Authority,'" 255–58, Derrida emphasizes that the "urgency" of justice is constitutive of the *aporia* of the justice-*to-come*. Justice is always to-come—*and* justice is demanded *now*. "Yet justice, however unpresentable, does not wait." The force of the to-come is to insist on the impossibility of "good conscience," that we can never assure ourselves of a having fully met our responsibility to the other, and it has nothing whatever to do with procrastination, with putting off action for another day, or an idle daydream or anemic longing. In the second half of this same essay, Derrida offers his own analysis of an essay by Benjamin entitled "The Critique of Violence."

not-yet-at-work and at-work.⁴¹ The past is the sphere of the completed but in the *kairos*, we can render it *in*complete, give it back to the *potential*, and turn it toward actualizing the incomplete future. It is as if the Sabbath—Agamben's seven chapters are the six days of *work* plus one day of *rest* of Genesis—which is a model of messianic peace and rest, is not a seventh day added on but embedded in the six days as a messianic moment of rest/interruption. Messianic time is the interruption of chronological time (days of work) in which time can be arrested (day of rest), grasped and accomplished,⁴² a moment in which we gather ourselves together, gather our power/potency together, in order to strike, like Benjamin's tiger's leap.

Inoperative also serves as his translation of Paul's *katargein* and guides his reading of the faith and trust (*pistis*) in the promise (*epaggelia*) as related to the law, to the *works* of law. So Paul writes in Rom 7:5–6 that under the law our sinful passions were "at work," enacted in us (*enērgeito*), but now we are discharged (*katergēthēmen*), de-activatived, made inoperative, from the law. That is why power or potentiality is realized in weakness (2 Cor 12:9), and God choose the weak to confound the strong (1 Cor 1:27), which turns Aristotle's distinction upside down.⁴³ So, the messianic is not the destruction of the works of the law but their "deactivation." The Messiah abolishes all rule (*arche*) and authority (*exousiai*) and hands the Kingdom over to his Father, returning the power of the law to a state of potentiality.⁴⁴ What is deactivated is not destroyed but conserved and held onto for fulfillment, passing over to something better which brings it to fulfillment.⁴⁵ That is what Hegel meant by *Aufhebung*, which is also how Luther translated *katargēsis*, according to which the law is both abolished and preserved in messianic time.⁴⁶

---

41. Agamben, *Potentialities: Collected Essays in Philosophy*. In §14 (226–32) of this text, Agamben discusses his notion of "absolute immanence," in the medieval sense of an action beginning and ending in the subject, a "transcendental field beneath the cogito," a sphere of "inoperativity" where something is but does not act, which is a feature of "pure life," a netherland, like a comatose person hanging between life and death.

42. Agamben, *The Time that Remains*, 69–72.

43. Agamben, *The Time that Remains*, 96–97.

44. This same argument is made by Schelling in his theory of the three "potencies" which correspond to the three ages of the world, which in turn correspond to the Trinity. See Schelling, *Philosophy of Revelation*, 315–27.

45. Agamben, *The Time that Remains*, 97–99.

46. Agamben, *The Time that Remains*, 99–101.

By anyone's accounting, this is a fascinating analysis, but it imports a massive amount of theory and of etymological sophistication of which one must imagine Paul is perfectly innocent. Agamben is often too clever by half in his reliance on etymologies; a word's meaning is fixed by use and context, not etymology. To take one example, I flagged above his claim that Paul is interested in the *kairos*, but *not* the end-time, and hence that Paul is not an apocalyptic thinker.[47] That is true of Agamben and probably also of Benjamin, but it seems an odd, even bizarre claim to make about Paul! So, I wonder what Crossan makes of that? Is not "a vision of post-civilization" an apocalyptic unveiling of the end time?

CALLING NOT CONVERSION

Crossan makes use of citations from Taubes, whose approach to Paul is deeply Jewish and scriptural, on three occasions (chapter 1, 3, and 6). Like Crossan, Taubes disposes of one of the common misconceptions of Paul, the famous "unhorsing" (as in Tintoretto's painting), his road-to-Damascus "conversion" to "Christianity," the scare quotes signifying the misconception. For the Jews, he says, Jesus is a "nice guy,"[48] but Paul is a troublemaker.[49] Jesus is a son of Israel, but Paul is a heretic. But Taubes holds that Paul's delimitation of the law is profoundly Jewish and he sets about "gathering the heretic back into the fold."[50] Paul is not a heretical Jew who "converted to Christianity." There was nothing to convert *to*. Paul is a Jew speaking as a Jew in *answer to his calling*[51] by the God of Israel. This calling came by way of a vision of the heavenly Jesus, as Crossan insists, not a letter of recommendation from Peter or James, and it consisted in inviting the Gentiles to the table with the Jews (literally!), inviting them into the Jewish fold. For Taubes, Paul is a Jew, I will not say, first, last, and always, but rather first and last. In between, he is a heretical Jew, a *strategically* heretical Jew, risking becoming anathema from his brothers on the law, on dietary restrictions and circumcision, and he is deeply anguished about that. But this departure *from* the Jews is undertaken *for* the Jews, for the sake of the *true* Israel, for *all* (*pas*) Israel, which

---

47. Agamben, *The Time that Remains*, 62–65.
48. Taubes, *The Political Theology of Paul*, 5.
49. Taubes, *The Political Theology of Paul*, 16.
50. Taubes, *The Political Theology of Paul*, 11.
51. Agamben, *The Time that Remains*, 19–23, on *klēsis*.

includes folding the Gentiles into Israel. Everything that Paul is doing, Taubes says, is signaled by the word "all" (*pas*). That is the key, the crucial hermeneutical clue to understanding what Paul has in mind,[52] which is the end time, when the God of *Israel* will be *all in all*. For Taubes Paul is making a distinction between Jews and Israel, Jews being Jews according to the flesh (*sarx*), an ethnic group, but Israel being a community, a Ver-Bund, of the spirit (*pneuma*).

Paul thinks the time is short and his calling is to assist in the *fulfillment* of the promise God made to Israel by including the Gentiles. His "heresy," then, is strategic and not even his idea, but God's idea, who, having been angered and made jealous once before by the Jews who worshipped other gods, decided to repay them in kind. "So I will make them jealous with what is no people, provoke them with a foolish nation" (Deut 32:21). Taubes reads Paul on a parallel to Moses, as a new Moses who goes one step farther than Moses. According to Taubes, Paul thought the success of the Gentile mission would make Israel jealous, meaning the Jews who rejected Jesus.[53] He reads Rom 8:31–9:5 on an analogy with Moses's plea for mercy for Israel, which he elaborates by an analysis of the Yom Kippur liturgy. Paul faced the same problem: the people have provoked the wrath of God by rejecting the Messiah, and the Messiah was condemned according to the law, which means—Crossan is making the same point—so much the worse for the law.[54] This is all quite devastating to Paul personally, who would be accursed from the Messiah for his people. But critical (kairotic) times call for critical deeds. The people of God are at this moment no longer the people of God.

Taubes adds that understanding scripture by way of the liturgy is a Catholic idea, and he refers us to Hans Urs von Balthasar whom he admires, along with von Balthasar's friend and compatriot, Karl Barth, whose commentary on Romans Taubes also admires. Benjamin, Taubes, von Balthasar, Carl Schmitt, and Barth all have little confidence in the order of "immanence"—by which they mean mainly liberal Protestantism and would include what we today call "secular humanism," which they are sure is going under, breaking down—and look to transcendence, divine authorization, intervention and support for help. Taubes thinks that Benjamin is serving up a Barth-like "dialectical theology . . . outside

---

52. Taubes, *The Political Theology of Paul*, 21.
53. Taubes, *The Political Theology of Paul*, 28–38.
54. Taubes, *The Political Theology of Paul*, 38.

the Christian church ... lay theology ... no bayonets, no state stands behind it to collect the taxes."[55] About this, I invite Crossan's commentary.

Paul's heresy, his separation from the Jews, announcing the election of the Gentiles, is only an episode in God's efforts to win back his people in the end time. Taubes even make an odd comparison of Paul's mission to the "conversion" of Sabbati Sevi to Islam (Taubes, 8–9). This could be interpreted as a strategic planting of a kind of Trojan horse in Islam. Whatever it means, in general it means that when the Messiah shows up, it will be like a slap in the face, a catastrophe, part of a "paradoxical" messianic logic.[56] When the Messiah finally comes, it will be the coming of what we did not see coming (Derrida's definition of the "event"). This is not what we expected the Messiah to look like, and that is what first threw Paul off the track, which is also part of Crossan's argument.

Finally, like Crossan, Taubes also proposes that Paul's primary audience was the *sebomenoi*, the God-fearers, not outright polytheistic pagans, which would represent too great a stretch,[57] which explains what went wrong with Paul's Arabian mission.[58] For the most part, Crossan and Taubes seem to see eye to eye, but Crossan gets there by meticulous historical investigation and does not mention the logic of divine jealousy that Taubes proposes, the analogy of Paul with Moses, and Taubes's use of Yom Kippur liturgy, so I wonder what he makes of all that.

NOMOS

We have already discussed the interesting if idiosyncratic angle that Agamben has on faith and the works of the law. Taubes has a different take, one closer to Crossan and recalls the "political theology" in the title of his lectures. Taubes puts his position tellingly and succinctly:

> Judaism "is" political theology—that is its "cross," because theology finally cannot be broken down by dividing it by "political," because law is finally not the first and last after all, because there are "even" between man and man [a reference to Martin Buber] relationships that "exceed," "transcend" law—love, mercy, forgiveness (not at all "sentimentally," but "in reality"). I wouldn't

---

55. Taubes, *The Political Theology of Paul*, 75.
56. Taubes, *The Political Theology of Paul*, 9.
57. Taubes, *The Political Theology of Paul*, 20; Crossan, *Paul the Pharisee*, chap. 6.
58. Crossan, *Paul the Pharisee*, chap. 5.

know how to take a single step further in my wretched and often warped life . . . without holding fast to "these three," and this leads me again and again—against my "will"—to Paul.[59]

That, one might easily conclude, is Taubes confessing that he is a Christian, or in this case a Jew who has converted to Christianity, since that delimitation of the law in the name of love is an elemental Christian claim. But that is not the case. As he says elsewhere, "Now I of course am a Paulinist, not a Christian, but a Paulinist."[60] For Taubes, being a Pauline Jew—a Jew who is faithful to Paul and a Paul who is faithful to the Jews—is exactly what he and Paul have in common, and the reason is that Paul's delimitation of the law in the name of love and justice, mercy and forgiveness, is Jewish root and branch.

Taubes and Crossan are on the same page here. For both of them, Paul's talk of the law, *nomos*, is not restricted to Torah; it is just as much, and maybe more, Roman law, *lex Romana*, and also "natural law," in the name of which Jews are subordinated to Greeks, slaves to masters, and women to men.[61] Being "against nature," "violating the natural order" is history's oldest alibi for oppression, which Crossan identifies as the confusion of nature and custom. This delimitation of the law is political through and through. In a letter addressed to Rome, to the seat of the Roman Empire, he announces that the days of Roman rule are numbered. As Taubes puts it in his characteristic way, this "carries a political charge; it is explosive to the highest degree." "Has he gone *meshugge* [crazy], to be writing his condemnation to Rome of all places?"[62] Accordingly, Rom 13 is not a political theology of the divinely authorized sovereign; it speaks of a foreshortened time, not a permanent world order of divine authority or theocracy (Carl Schmitt), and Rom 8 describes a world in decline waiting for the glory of God. This is not what we call democracy, but anti-imperial, anti-Caesar, and all this in a letter to Rome.[63] The editors of Taube's the book call this a "negative political theology,"[64] that is, theology as critique without having a positive political program to propose as an alternate.

59. Taubes, *The Political Theology of Paul*, 110.
60. Taubes, *The Political Theology of Paul*, 88.
61. Crossan, *Paul the Pharisee*, 198.
62. Taubes, *The Political Theology of Paul*, 24.
63. Taubes, *The Political Theology of Paul*, 73.
64. Taubes, *The Political Theology of Paul*, 121.

For Crossan it was important to Paul that Jesus was crucified, not simply banished or tortured, that Jesus's mistreatment by the law be odious. If God's anointed was crucified "legally," by Roman law, if it was by and under the law that a degrading death was visited upon God's anointed one, then so much the worse for the law; the law is sin. As Taubes says, "It isn't *nomos* but rather the one who was nailed to the cross by *nomos* who is the imperator."[65] Crossan's position is so strong that he thinks Rom 13:1–7 is a later insertion while Taubes treats it as a kind *pro temp* arrangement: if the end is near, if Rome is going under anyway, don't make things difficult for yourselves. Pay your taxes and bide your time; do not stand out.[66] For Crossan, Paul's condemnation of the law is general, including in its sweep Torah, Roman law, natural law, human law as such. Crossan thinks "the purpose of law is the obstruction of justice, the effect of law is the circumvention of justice."[67](Cross

Paul's delimitation of the law is the "excess" Taubes speaks of; it renders the law "inoperative" in Agamben's terms, and, I would add, is the point of Derrida's "Force of Law"—a paper delivered to the Cardoza Law school—which distinguishes justice from the law. "Justice in itself, if there is such a thing" (*s'il y en a*), which is *not* deconstructible, is the "weak force" of a call. But the law is a real force and there is no doubt such a thing *exists*, and as such it *is* deconstructible. The universality of the law blinds it to the excess which is visible to the eyes of justice.

The point is, then, for these atheistic Marxists, deconstructionists, for this radical rabbi, and for Crossan, this delimitation of the law is not a Jewish heresy. This is Pauline Judaism, a radical, revolutionary Judaism conducted in the name of "all" Israel, as Taubes insists. Paul is not trying to start up a new religion; he thinks the world is about to end and he tells everybody to keep their present seat. His calling is to assist in the fulfillment of the primordial promise, in which we have *emunah*,[68] a faithful trust, made to Abraham before there even was a law. His is a calling which, as Taubes says, Paul "outbids" Moses[69]—they are both dealing with a God angered by the faithlessness of the Jews—by going where Moses would not go, to the Gentiles, so that God, meaning the God of Israel, may be all in all (1 Cor 15:28, *panta en pasin*).

65. Taubes, *The Political Theology of Paul*, 24.
66. Taubes, *The Political Theology of Paul*, 53–54.
67. Crossan, *Paul the Pharisee*, 137.
68. Taubes, *The Political Theology of Paul*, 6–7.
69. Taubes, *The Political Theology of Paul*, 39.

COSMIC EVOLUTION OR COSMIC FUTILITY?

In sum, in terms of the big picture, of the most general horizon, I would say that from a philosophical point of view, Crossan's book, like that of Taubes and Agamben, belongs to a space that Benjamin has cleared, to a time of crisis, of a world "subject to futility, of the rule of the dark powers of the world, which Crossan calls "civilization." As to particular points and particular readings, his work most closely approximates Taubes, who has no quarrel with Benjamin. I do not think Crossan has much in common with Badiou and I think the findings of Agamben are a bit exotic and would be interesting to him in themselves, particularly since they are mostly congenial with Benjamin and Taubes but might brush against his historical grain. The difference between Crossan and Taubes is that Taubes's work is fiery, intuitive, and sometimes confusing, strange, and hard to follow. Taubes was dying of cancer, his time was indeed short, and the book is a transcription of his lectures, so there is a fair amount of digression and improvisation. Crossan, by contrast, proceeds by way of a meticulous, disciplined historical investigation—charged by an imaginative philosophical leap, a "bilingual" reading which translates a Pauline vision into the contemporary crisis in which we today are caught up. Like Paul, we are thinking of the end of the world, facing an ecological apocalypse.

Again, speaking as a philosopher, I think Crossan brings his book to a perfect conclusion by invoking *ultimate* questions. To take Paul seriously, as a thinker from the ancient world who has something to say to us, which is relevant to us here and now, Crossan says, is to see that he is asking the oldest and most venerable questions. "Why is there being rather than nothing? Why is being dynamic rather than static? Why is that dynamic just rather than unjust?" Ultimately, Crossan says, the *mysterium tremendum et fascinans* is as terrifying and fascinating for Paul as for us. "Whether, therefore, you read it as a committed theist, an impatient atheist, or an indifferent none, you— we— live together within Evolution and Paul's Pharisaic vision of universal responsibility, and cosmic accountability in Messianic-Christic now-time can best be described as an intuition of Evolution presented as a revelation of God."[70]

To this perfect conclusion, I say amen, and the way philosophers say amen is to say, just as the service ends and everyone is heading for the door, "I have one more question."

70. Crossan, *Paul the Pharisee*, 260.

That is, "what if that dynamic becoming is running down?"

Crossan, like Paul, moves between the *human* dimensions of the messianic event, all Israel, all humankind, and its *cosmic* dimensions, all creation, or, human history and cosmic evolution. Now there is a big difference between those two. As Benjamin said about universal history and messianic history, they are *running in different directions*, the one, human evolution, negentropic (building up) and the other, cosmic evolution, entropic (running down), but the building up is *losing*. When Paul said that creation itself is subject to futility and decay, he had an extremely constricted picture of the cosmos in mind, but he spoke more truly than he knew, if we put it in a contemporary cosmological perspective. I refer to the widespread view of the astro-physicists that in a billion years or less, our sun, which Plato thought was eternal, will have imploded into a white dwarf, and eventually all the stars in the cosmos will undergo star death. Considered long term, cosmic evolution is really cosmic *devolution* (increasing entropy). Ultimately, the "big bang"—which is really a "big expansion" (there were no sound waves)—will have expanded into entropic oblivion, utter dissipation, and that will be that. The present form of the world really is passing away (1 Cor 7:31), period! The evolution of *life* on *earth* is a *local* negentropic episode in ever increasing *cosmic* entropy; earthly life is like a hot cup of *Star*bucks sitting out in a long cold cosmic winter night.

That is the ultimate *cosmic matrix*. That is the ultimate *cosmic judgment day*; that is the ultimate *cosmic accounting*; that is the ultimate "super-Sabbath" day of radical (re)quiescent *rest* (as in R.I.P) for all creatures great and small; that is the final "post-civilization." Then the question would be (were there anyone around to ask it), *why is there nothing rather than something*? That, of course, is not a "problem," because it is trillions of trillions of years off, so it is *not now, not yet*, and the time is *not short*, and there is nothing we can do about it anyway. But it is a "mystery," part of the *mysterium tremendum et fascinans*.

If so, are being and becoming, dynamic and static, justice and injustice, *ultimately*, that is, *cosmically*, a tale told by an idiot, signifying nothing? Why bother with justice and injustice? Do we really want to bring *cosmic* history into this discussion or are we better off if we just shut *cosmic* questions down and tend to our own *terrestrial* business? Can we avoid doing so? Do we not live in age in which the extra-terrestrial and the post-human are staring us in the face?

If we try to drop it, will this cosmic "futility" not still be quietly eating at us—when in an idle moment spooky thoughts creep over us unawares—we who say we are interested in "ultimate" matters, like being and becoming, like the *Deus absconditus* who caused Luther to lose a lot of sleep or the dark night of the soul that kept John of the Cross awake through the night? Cosmically speaking, it looks like crucifixion, a cosmic Golgotha, what Hegel called the "Golgotha of the Absolute Spirit," and not resurrection, has the last word.

Can Paul help us out here?[71]

---

71. I attempt to deal with this question in *Specters of God*.

21

Reflections on Resurrection and Redemption in Romans

PAMELA EISENBAUM

In his new book, *Paul the Pharisee*, Crossan begins by identifying four matrices: 1) the Christian Matrix; 2) Jewish Matrix; 3) Roman Matrix; 4) and the Evolutionary Matrix. These matrices do not constitute analytical categories or methodologies. Rather, they are frameworks that inform his approach to Paul in this book. This book, like so much of Crossan's work, is historically oriented, and the first three matrices reflect Crossan's historical commitment. Nevertheless, the evolutionary matrix is paramount. "My purpose in this book," he says, "is to conduct an experiment on Paul using the fourth or Evolutionary matrix . . . as the cumulative context of the other three."[1]

Crossan does not develop the evolutionary matrix in detail, but he clearly means a frame for reading Paul that makes the apostle's message meaningful beyond the historical and the Christian theological lens and that is capable of speaking to the severe challenges humanity faces at this moment, such as weapons of mass destruction, climate change, and the extinction of non-human species.

Crossan highlights three Twentieth century philosophers who have written on Paul: Girogio Agamben, Jacob Taubes, and Alain Badiou. Crossan appeals to them because their readings of Paul exemplify, or at least resemble, what he envisions for the evolutionary matrix. The three

---

1. Crossan, *Paul the Pharisee*, 27.

philosophers presumably give legitimacy to the claim that the apostle has wisdom for those of us living in this troubled age, whether we are Christian or not.[2]

In spite of his intention to foreground the evolutionary framework, Crossan never abandons historical analysis. He never lets go of the first three matrices, the Jewish, Roman, and Christian. I would expect nothing less, for Crossan's work is always grounded in history. But his faithfulness to Paul's historical context results in repeated return to interpretations informed by the other matrices, and this pattern sometimes gets in the way of the book's stated purpose to elevate the evolutionary matrix.

I am sympathetic to Crossan's aspirations to broach the temporal chasm to enable Paul to speak now and share his ethical concerns. We have reached a point in human evolution when technological, social, and cultural evolution have overtaken the workings of biological evolution and have sped up time to such a point that the extinction of humans—or the transformation of human life into something incomprehensibly different than what we know now—is a real possibility. The end of the world no longer seems like a crazy idea promulgated by religious fanatics that the rest of us can safely ignore.

The majority of my students at Iliff School of Theology, most of whom are progressive Christians with deep commitments to social justice, usually start my Introduction to the New Testament course hating Paul. One of my missions is to "convert" them to being Paul-friendly, perhaps even advocates for Paul's message. Sometimes I succeed. But the most frequent stumbling block is Paul's apocalypticism. They cannot connect with the apocalyptic Paul. While I once lacked an adequate response, now I find it ready at hand: His apocalyptic mindset motivated Paul to *do* something, not to wait passively for divine intervention (as we find in some apocalyptic texts). Apocalypticism is a form of eschatological thinking where the deadline for the final world-ending event has been

---

2. The three philosophers whom Crossan highlights do not, in my opinion, all serve his purpose equally well, partly because they each have a different relationship to the historical and their interpretations of Paul each have their own agenda. Agamben in *The Time that Remains* may be the most inspiring for reading Paul in the evolutionary matrix, precisely because his take on Romans centers on thinking eschatologically in the present moment, yet he remains exegetically tethered to Paul and cannot completely abandon his Catholic upbringing. Badiou's book, *Saint Paul*, provides the least compelling reading of Paul, in my view, in spite of the implied promise of its title: *The Foundations of Universalism*.

moved up. And imminent deadlines can be highly motivating: if you do not act with urgency when a lot is at stake, disaster may ensue.

Apocalyptic prophecies about climate change and the exponential scaling of AI have a high probability of coming true. If you read the daily reports, essays, articles, and books about AI, so many of them follow a narrative trajectory that looks very much like the theological history familiar to Christians: AI is either going to save us or damn us, but which ever it is, it is coming sooner than you think.[3] And the proposed dates for the point of no return when it comes to climate change keep getting moved up, too.

Thus, what was once the weirdest part of Paul's message—the end of the world is nigh and with it the final judgment—frankly makes sense at this time in the history of human evolution. Paul's message of indictment and accountability, as well as his urgency is a perfect match for the human-made doomsday scenarios at our doorstep.[4]

In this paper I use Romans 9–11 to experiment with the conjunctive use of the Jewish and evolutionary matrices. Together, these chapters function as Paul's vision of the end-time, a vision that encompasses the whole world, and yet it comes from a particularly Jewish perspective. In Romans 9–11 Paul draws deeply from the well of scripture and from his personal experience as a Jew.

For me the Jewish matrix is not merely a historical framework. Since I am a Jewish reader of Paul and Paul is a Jewish author, the Jewish matrix becomes transhistorical in my case, encompassing past, present, and future. The Jewish matrix in my construal is the historical time within which we locate the historical Paul *and* the continual genealogy of Judaism that may help all who have ears to reflect on Paul's message "in the time that remains," to borrow a phrase from Agamben.

As Crossan reminds us at several points, the resurrection as conceived by the Pharisees (and many other Jews), including Paul, is a universal event that happens at the end of time—everyone must be raised to be accountable to God. That all humans are resurrected does not mean, however, that Paul's eschatological vision constitutes "universalism." The

---

3. For an example of the view of AI as damnation, see Barrat, *The Final Invention*. For a view representing the salvific narrative, see Tegmark, *Being Human*.

4. I think Crossan recognizes the potential of Paul's apocalypticism for the evolutionary matrix, but his desire to give the historical Paul full coverage (by including discussion of Luke's Paul for example) diffuses the power of Paul's apocalyptic message, which is uniquely suited to the evolutionary matrix.

vast majority of readers do not regard Paul as having imagined everyone participating in a blissful eternal life. There are requirements for entry to that life. Over the centuries Christian theologians stipulated different requirements, but nearly all agreed that only *some* people would achieve eternal life in the presence of the divine.

One way to bring out the full universal potential of Paul's message is to root it historically in Jewish apocalypticism, while setting aside the Christian inflection that so pervades Pauline interpretation. In Romans 9–11 Paul not only envisions a universal event, he envisions a reconciliation of humans with God, creation, and other humans. Within the language of Judaism, Paul believes that all peoples have a place in the World to Come (*ha-olam haba*). It may come as a surprise, but I will argue that Paul did not believe that confessional belief in Jesus was a requirement for all people, any more than other Pharisees believed that all non-Jews were required to observe of all the laws of Torah to achieve a place in the world to come.[5] Moreover, the world-to-come is not located in the airy space above; the transformed world occupies the same space as this world, and we humans have a role to play in that transformation, though we will not all play the same role.

Jewish categories of thought—in Paul's time and today—remain mostly unknown to Christians and others. Although the Jewish matrix is even older than the Christian one, its unfamiliarity to the world-at-large provides an opportunity to hear Paul in new ways—ways that not only ameliorate the anti-Jewish bias but that may also appeal to those who are neither Christian nor Jewish but share the same ethical concerns. In my discussion of Romans 9–11, I do not entirely ignore the Christian interpretative framework. But I intend to use it only as reference point to help the reader perceive the difference between reading Paul within Judaism and reading Paul within Christianity.

In what follows, I engage Romans 9–11 in five "movements." As any experienced reader knows, Paul's logic is not always linear, hence my use of the language of movement. I have followed the order of the text for simplicity's sake, but I use each movement to focus on a theme which sometimes reaches beyond the immediate text selection. I have necessarily foregone attention to the finer points of textual exegesis, and I apologize in advance. I will, however, highlight snippets of text to illustrate key elements of Paul's vision of the end-time events.

---

5. Full disclosure: Even among my closest colleagues who work within the paradigm of Paul-within-Judaism, I have not convinced most of them of my position.

FIRST MOVEMENT, 9:1-29: PAUL AND ISRAEL

In case there was any doubt that Paul continued to understand himself as a Jew after his experience on the Damascus road, he opens chapter nine on a heartfelt and very personal note about many of his fellow countrymen: they have not embraced his gospel. They do not understand who Jesus Messiah is nor do they comprehend that his resurrection signals the beginning of the end. For Paul, everyone—Israel and the nations—stands on the event horizon, not yet engulfed by the gravity of the new creation, but not able to go back. For a Pharisee like Paul, history goes only one direction, and when it ends, it ends. Unfortunately, most of his fellow Jews do not recognize they have arrived at the event horizon.

There is no question Paul became a follower of Jesus, but that fact did not alter his identity as a Jew. I do not mean that he retained his Jewish identity in *ethnic* terms while in *religious* terms he became something else.[6] The distinction between religion and ethnicity does not work when it comes to ancient Judaism (or, frankly, modern Judaism).[7] In the ancient Roman world, to worship certain gods places you in a certain kin group, and this is unambiguously the case with Judaism. When Paul changed his mind about Jesus, he did not abandon Israel.

Like any other Jew, Paul divided the world into two kinds of people—one is either a Jew or a non-Jew. When he addressed his followers, they remain "non-Jews" (*ethnē*), though he does speak of them as having

---

6. This assertion is fundamental to understanding Paul within Judaism, and it is unambiguously endorsed by scholars who have collaborated under the label "Paul within Judaism" for the last thirty years (though the unmitigated endorsement of Paul's Jewishness has its origins much earlier, mostly famously in the work of Krister Stendahl). Paul is not merely a Jew according to the flesh; Paul is not a marginal Jew; and Paul has not rejected any of the core tenets of Judaism. Paul may have had some ideas we do not find in other early Jewish authors, but Paul is unique in the way every Jewish author is unique. Philo had some unusual things to say but he is no less Jewish for having said them. Works representing this perspective include my *Paul Was Not A Christian*; Fredriksen, *The Pagans' Apostle*; Nanos, *The Mystery of Romans*; Novenson, *Paul Then and Now*. That is a small sample. A broader sampling of scholarship may be found in a volume edited by Nanos and Zetterholm, *Paul Within Judaism*. Two scholars who remain in the tradition of seeing Paul as, at best, a marginal Jew, include Barclay, *Pauline Churches*; and Wright, *Paul*. Wright also adamantly denies that Paul possessed an apocalyptic eschatology. The views of Barclay and Wright represent the dominant position on Paul's identify.

7. See Buell, "Rethinking the Relevance of Race"; Fredriksen, "Judaizing the Nations"; Fredriksen, *The Pagan's Apostle*, 32–69; Johnson-Hodge, *If Sons, then Heirs*.

turned from their former gods to the God of Israel (see 1 Thess 2:10).[8] Interestingly, although conversion to Judaism was not uncommon in Paul's day, the apostle adamantly opposes the conversion of non-Jews to Judaism.[9] Paul's rejection of conversion as an option is notable, especially since as a Pharisee, the conversion of a non-Jew to Judaism was acceptable. The apostle's change of opinion was due to the apocalyptic perspective he adopts when he embraces Jesus as the one whom God anointed to initiate the process of redemption. While the apostle envisions world-wide reconciliation of peoples, he does not collapse the distinction between Jews and non-Jews. It would undermine the prophets' vision of all the world's various nations streaming to Jerusalem.[10]

In Romans 9 Paul argues that God chose only some of Abraham's descendants to be God's people, and that the favored ones did not do anything to earn that status. Isaac and Jacob are chosen; Ishmael and Esau are not. In the traditional Christian reading, these biblical stories serve as illustrations of a soteriological argument rooted in the Christian matrix, in which freewill and determinism (Augustine) or predestination (Calvin) focus on who will achieve salvation and who will not.[11]

Let us put the Christian matrix aside and stick with the Jewish one. Romans 9 looks mostly to the past to explain a theme in Israel's history rather than describing how salivation unfolds in the future. In vv. 4–5, Paul details the privileges and blessings Israel enjoys: They are the ones who were adopted by God as God's own, they received the Torah, the Messiah comes from Israel, etc. As God had said,

> For you are a people holy to the LORD your God; the LORD your God has chosen you out of all the peoples on earth to be his people, his treasured possession. (Deut 7:6)

But Paul then explains that Israel did not *earn* these privileges by being more righteous than other peoples. Although Paul does not make an explicit connection to Deuteronomy on this point (he will appeal to it several times in the subsequent chapters), it states more than once that Israel was not chosen by God because Israel was superior to the other

---

8. Scott, *The Real Paul*, 56–60, explains why translating *ethnē* as "gentiles" is inappropriate for ancient Jewish texts, so I use either "nations" or "non-Jews."
9. See Thiessen, "Paul's Argument"; and Thiessen, *Paul and the Gentile Problem*.
10. See the influential article by Fredriksen, "Judaism, the Circumcision of Gentiles."
11. Novenson, *Paul Then and Now*, 128.

nations or more righteous: "It was not because you were more numerous than any other people that the Lord set his heart on you and chose you—for you were the fewest of all peoples. It was because the Lord loved you and kept the oath that he swore to your ancestors" (Deut 7:7). And God, when preparing the people to take possession of the land God promised, says to them: "It is not because of your righteousness or the uprightness of your heart that you are going in to occupy their land; but because of the wickedness of these nations the Lord your God is dispossessing them before you" (Deut 9:5).[12]

Of course, Paul is not *only* thinking of Israel in making this theological point; God may reject or embrace any people for the sake of glorifying his name, as with Pharoah (Rom 9:17; Exod 10:1), or for demonstrating his mercy on those who do not deserve it (Rom 9:22–23; Exod 33:19).

In v. 6, Paul says "Not all who are born of Israel are Israel." Here we arrive at the question, Who is Israel? Many Christian readers of Paul have argued that Paul, as he progresses through these chapters, argues that Israel will be comprised of a new chosen people: those who call Jesus Lord. In historical Christian language: Israel now equates to the church. Later, when Paul says "all Israel will be saved" (Rom 11:25), the apostle has completed the redefinition of Israel.

But that is not Paul's argument. Rather, Israel did not become Israel because of a bond according to the flesh. For if Israel as a people was formed exclusively through a biological lineage, then Esau would have been chosen along with Jacob and Ishamel along with Isaac. Israel becomes Israel because God made a promise, and the children who received the promise belong to Israel. God's people have always been God's choice. If Israel's status as God's treasured possession was attained exclusively by divine choice, surely God has the prerogative of choosing others, too? Paul's quotation of Hosea makes that clear. "Those who were not my people I will call 'my people . . . And in the very place where it was said to them, 'You are not my people,' there they shall be called children of the living God" (Hosea 2:23). In other words, if Israel benefitted from God's benevolent justice not because they observed the commandments of Torah (which comes later as a consequence of their covenant with God),

---

12. The LXX translates the Hebrew *tzedek* (righteousness) with *dikaiosynē*. Significantly, it does not translate the Hebrew *rashah* (wickedness) as one would expect (i.e. *kakos*) but rather with *asebeia*, which means impiety or more specifically, idolatry.

and not because they were a righteous people, but because they trusted in God's promises after God first reached out to Abraham.[13]

SECOND MOVEMENT 9:30—10:4: ISRAEL AND THE NATIONS; JUSTICE AND FAITH

> "What shall we say now? That even though the nations did not pursue justice, they have attained (God's) righteousness, a righteousness that comes out of faithfulness, while Israel, having pursued the Torah's justice, did not fulfill the Torah. Why not? Because they did not seek it out of faith (in the promise); but as if it out of obligatory acts."[14]

Israel pursued "Torah of righteousness (*nomon dikaiosynē* [9:31]). In other words, Israel has observed the Torah. Within Paul's Pharisaic Jewish matrix, observing Torah is fine and good—it is in fact obligatory. The issue is Israel, collectively speaking, does not recognize that the promises made in the Torah regarding the end-time are being fulfilled now. They have failed to recognize what time it is. Now is the culmination of history, time for the dead to awaken, time for the final judgment, when everyone must account for him or herself, and time when God redeems this world and all the people in it. Jesus Messiah is God's intermediary who enables all the nations to stand righteous before God. In spite of their former worship of other gods, the nations may be counted with Israel as righteous before God. To be righteous entitles them to a share in World-to-Come. If not for the Messiah, the nations would stand condemned because their idolatry otherwise put them in violation of divine law.[15]

For Paul, Israel is "ignorant of the righteousness that comes from God" for the benefit of nations (10:3); Israel does not see that "Messiah is the fulfillment of the Torah so there may be justice for all who are faithful" (10:4). While the Apostle sees his mission to the nations as facilitating the

---

13. Gen 12:2–3; 15:5–5; 17:4 (cf. Rom 4 where the significance of God's promise to Abraham that he would be the father or many nations, and that the nations would be blessed because of him).

14. My translation. The word *dikaiosynē* appears four times in the quotation; twice I have translated it as "justice"; and twice as "righteousness." It is most often render as "justification," reflecting traditional Protestant theology (especially as rooted in Luther), in English translations of Paul.

15. See Hayes, *What's Divine about Divine Law?*

fulfillment of the divine promise made long ago to Abraham, Israel as a people is not living up to that role.

THIRD MOVEMENT 10:5–21: REDEMPTION FOR ALL NATIONS

Everyone who calls upon the name of the Lord shall be redeemed. Jews lived in a covenanted relationship with God by observing Torah, but that was not an option for the other nations. The nations must therefore confess Jesus as Lord—this commitment is how they express their gratitude to the God of Israel, who "grafts" them onto the Abrahamic genealogy and thereby grants them the inheritance of the World-to-Come. Since the nations do not have Torah, their only option rests in their trust in Jesus as Lord and their devotion to the God of Israel. But even this is not a substitute for accountability. The Torah may have been given to Israel, but everyone is accountable to God's law.[16] Other nations do not have to follow all the statutes and ordinances of the Torah, because, frankly, most of the commandments do not apply to the nations—a point often overlooked. *Not* doing the commandments to which Israel alone is obliged (e.g. circumcision) *is* following the Torah.[17] But, some commandments are non-negotiable. Worshipping the God of Israel, Creator of the Universe—everyone is obligated.

For the nations to have the opportunity to call upon the Lord and thereby express their faith, they must first have the opportunity to hear the gospel proclaimed, and that is Israel's responsibility, she was chosen to be the light to the nations. Unfortunately, mysteriously, she is not fulfilling her mission—when Paul critiques Israel for her lack of faith, that is what he is talking about.

FOURTH MOVEMENT 11:1-24: THE REMNANT AND AN EXTENDED DEADLINE

Although a hardening has come upon Israel, so that they are not keeping faith with God's promise of imminent redemption for all, God will never

---

16. Stowers, *A Rereading Romans*; Fredriksen, "The Question of Worship."

17. Indeed, Maimonides in the *Mishneh Toreh* says explicitly that no Jew should force a non-Jew to perform *mitzvot*, the commandments God imposed exclusively on Israel (*On Repentance* 8.1).

reject God's people and renege on the divine promises. God preserves a remnant so that reconciliation is always possible. While the tradition of the remnant is important in Romans 9–11, traditional Christian commentators too often miss its significance in Romans because the remnant is assumed to be the Christian elect.[18] In other words, only an elect few attain salvation (eternal life). But, in fact, the remnant serves only as an interim moment that enables God to find God's way back to the people, and vice versa, after there has been a breach or betrayal.[19]

The remnant in Paul's discussion refers to Paul and other Jews who understand Jesus as Messiah and recognize his significance for Israel. To be sure, the majority of Jews have not accepted Jesus as Messiah, but that does not put them outside Israel, and they are not without hope that they will participate in the World-to-Come. They are, however, not playing their part in the unfolding of the divine plan. They are not assisting Paul in his mission; Paul says they oppose his gospel (11:28). Fortunately for everyone, Paul and his Jewish companions function as the remnant—they ensure God's covenant and promises will not be broken until such time when all Israel is redeemed, for "the gifts and calling of God are irrevocable" (11:29).

In the meantime, Israel's seeming lack of faith serves a divine purpose—extending the time for the nations to prepare for their redemption. Israel's rejection of Christ enables God to show his great mercy—the deadline for the judgment has been extended, thus allowing Paul to extend his mission even further. Therefore, Israel's disobedience constitutes a protraction of the timetable, so that the nations have a chance to respond to God's call. As a result of Israel's "hardening," there is more time to preach the gospel, more time for the nations to heed God's call. But no one should lose faith that God will deliver on the promises—all must remain faithful, for God could still choose to withhold mercy to those who stray from the faithful course.

---

18. Stendahl, *The Final Account*, 75–77.

19. In 9:27b the NRSV reads "only a remnant shall be saved." But the "only" is not in the Greek. The NRSV reflects how the text as traditionally rendered links the remnant and those who will be "saved" in the end. But in 9:27 Paul is in the middle of his discourse casting how the end unfolds. The language of "all Israel" and "the full number of the nations" at the end of chapter 11 cannot equate to the "remnant." Both Isaiah and Paul mean that a remnant shall be saved to ensure—even when nearly all of Israel has gone astray—that all of Israel will be redeemed once she returns to God and recommits to the covenant. See also Jer 6:9. See the discussion by Fredriksen in *Pagans' Apostle*, 158–59.

FIFTH MOVEMENT 11:25–36: DIVERSITY AND INCLUSION

To appeal to Paul's famous words in vv. 25–26: "Once the full number of the nations has come in," says Paul, "all Israel will be saved" (*pas Yisraēl sōthēsetai*). The remnant Paul spoke of in the fourth movement should not be interpreted as the chosen few left standing at the end of time, predestined for salvation, while everyone else is damned (or destined to go extinct). "For the gifts and calling of God are irrevocable." By means of this unusual plan for redemption of the world, not only is Israel redeemed, but there will be full inclusion of all the nations who call upon the Lord.

Ultimately, we can call Paul's vision of redemption universal in that it includes all peoples. It is, however, not an imperialist universalism. Being part of this redemption does not mean everybody becomes Christian (or, for that matter, everybody becomes Jewish!). What is so attractive about this vision of redemption is that reconciliation between nations does not mean everybody becomes the same so that they all think alike and all difference has been erased. If everyone becomes like everyone else, then it cannot truly be a reconciliation. The beauty of the tradition of the ingathering of nations is that it represents the coming together of all the world's *different* peoples. To be sure, the nations are coming to Jerusalem to worship the God of Israel, but this is not a mass conversion.[20]

In Jewish tradition from the Bible till today, it is possible for non-Jews to have a share in the world-to-come. To say this in a way that resembles American Christian language, Jews do not believe that non-Jews must convert to Judaism to achieve salvation and have eternal life. Jews understand themselves as being bound to observe the requirements of Torah because of a special covenant between God and the people of Israel. Non-Jews are accountable to the divine law, but they do not have all the obligations incumbent on Jews. Ancient Israelites and many post-biblical Jews understand themselves as playing a distinct role in God's cosmic plan to reconcile all the world's peoples at the end of this world; others play different roles. This idea may be foreign to the traditional Christian view, but it is a longstanding tradition in Judaism.

Paul never leaves behind the binary of Israel and the nations, in spite of the unity that characterizes the world-to-come.[21] The Apostle

---

20. Fredriksen, *The Pagans' Apostle*, 73–77.
21. See Garroway, *Paul's Gentile-Jews*. Although I do not completely agree with

envisions all the various nations coming together to dwell in the new creation, but they are included in their variety as different peoples. In other words, Paul does not collapse Jews and non-Jews into one generic mass of eschatological humanity.[22] All will be kin, but non-Jews do not become Jews. Paul's vision of the end draws from the well of Jewish eschatological tradition wherein "the nations *join with* Israel; but they do not 'join' Israel." Put another way, "inclusion is not conversion."[23] Indeed, the binary of Jew and non-Jew is habituated language characteristic of Jews, but when Paul uses it in relation to the world-to-come, he is talking about a multiplicity of peoples; the binary of "Jews" and "the nations" is just a shorthand for speaking of the nations of the world. But "nations" does not refer to any specific people group, *ethnos*, and Paul does think there are only two peoples. Non-Jewish Greek speakers would hear the word *ethne* (plural) and think of a multiplicity of peoples. God created all humans from the first human (Gen 1:28–31)—indeed God created all living things—and a multiplicity of nations emerged. But in between creation and the end of time, the nations became alienated by their worship of other gods. At the end of this world, not only must Israel be reconciled to her creator, but all peoples must be reconciled. For Jews, to be sure, there are those who know the God of Israel and those who worship other gods, but that is a cultic distinction, not an ethnic one. When Paul speaks of solving the problem of idolatry in this world, Paul associates *ethnē* with idolatry, and he sometimes uses *ethnē* in derogatory ways. But more often than not, *ethnē* is a neutral term. When Paul addresses the people of Rome in his letter as *ethnē*, he is not trying to insult them.[24] On the contrary, the apostle may be conveying a sense of grandeur—"attention nations of the world!"

---

the language Garroway uses to describe the relationship between Jews and non-Jews, he brings out Paul's ambiguity as the apostle tries to both incorporate and distinguish the nations from Israel.

22. Fredriksen, "Judaizing the Nations."

23. Both quotations from Fredriksen, *The Pagans' Apostle*, 75.

24. Esler, *Conflict and Identity*, argues we should translate *ethnē* in Romans as "foreigners," but that has insulting connotations that do not make sense when Paul is obviously attempting to insinuate himself to his audience in Rome. Fredriksen's claim that the *ethnē* should be understood as "pagans" is more faithful to the issue of idolatry and idolatry is what alienates the nations from God, but I'm not sure it works in light of contemporary connotations. To be fair, Fredriksen acknowledges the issues raised by the choice of "pagans" (*The Pagan's Apostle*, 34).

THE TWO-WAYS

The interpretation of Romans 9–11 I have offered is sometimes mocked as "two-ways salvation"; *Sonderweg* in German.[25] It is a designation used by interpreters who defend the traditional reading of these chapters. The charge of "two-ways salvation" is meant to affect incredulity at the idea that the apostle believed there could be *two* ways to salvation, one for Jews and one for gentiles. It's non-sensical, they say. How could God have two different standards for achieving salvation, and two independent means for each of them to get there, since all human individuals share the same human condition and need the same remedy.[26]

The first mistake these critics make is assuming Paul is preoccupied with individuals and not peoples or nations. The alleged *Sonderweg* seems unfair if God is using one standard of measure for one person and a different standard of judgment for someone else. The Greek word *dikaiosynē* weaves together the meaning of equitable justice, and the righteousness that comes from the practice of justice, whether by God or humans. Insofar as Paul has individuals in mind, God is the "true judge" (an extremely common epithet in classical Jewish texts) and of course he uses the same standard, and that standard has to do with ethical behavior—were you a righteous person? Whether you belonged to Israel or not, the Pharisees would affirm all humans share the same human condition and all must stand before God for judgment. Of course, in the Jewish matrix, humans are not utterly hopeless sinners, even if they are flawed. Righteousness is *possible*. When God judges humans righteous, it does not mean they have attained moral perfection. The reason for sacrifices of atonement and the many laws of recompense that appear in the Torah indicates there is no expectation of perfect behavior. There is an expectation of loyalty to the one God, trust (*pistis*) in God's promises, and a faithful heart (Deut 9:5)

When a Jew learns of another's passing the first thing they are supposed to say to the bereaved is "Blessed be the true Judge." Rabbinic sources contain elaborate instruction about when God should be blessed as the true Judge, as opposed to another epithet. "He would say: Those that are born will die, and those that are dead will be revived, and the

---

25. See, for example, Zoccali, "And So All Israel Shall Be Saved"; and Zoccali *Whom God Has Called*. Stendahl addresses the charge directly in *The Final Account*, 76.

26. John Marshall has an excellent analysis of why so many interpreters fail to take seriously the possibility that Paul has an inclusive vision from both Israel and the nations in "Misunderstanding the New Paul."

living will be judged. [It is necessary] to know, to make known, and to become conscious that [God] is God ... [God] is the Judge ... the future Judge. And do not let your [evil] impulse assure you that the netherworld is a place of refuge for you; because against your will you were created, against your will you were born, against your will you live, against your will you die, and against your will you are destined to give account and reckoning before ... the Holy One, blessed be [God].[27]

The second mistake critics make is to think Paul's use of the familiar language of Jews and the nations indicates Paul is literally thinking about only two peoples, when he is in fact thinking about all the world's peoples or nations. Traditional Christian interpreters capitalized on the binary of Israel and the nations to justify the binary of Christians (the saved) and non-Christians (the damned). Redemption for Paul, however, is an all-inclusive cosmic process, both geographically and temporally. Time is collapsed, so that the "world's peoples" includes peoples of the distant past and an inconceivable future. Again, Paul's use of the binary of Israel and nations does not equate to the saved and the damned.

The rabbis sometimes ask themselves if *everyone* who ever lived will be resurrected (i.e. to stand for judgment, as one would expect). When they ask this question, they usually think about it in collective terms. The Talmud engages in a lengthy discussion/commentary on Mishnah *Sanhedrin* 10:1, which asks if all Israel has a share in the World-to-Come.[28] In the Talmud's lengthy commentary on this mishnah, someone asks if the generation of the flood will be raised to stand for God's judgment. The answer is no. They offer a couple reasons, but the upshot is one should not be tried twice for the same crime. Since it was such an ordeal the first time, that generation should not have to endure it again only to face the same judgment. The same goes for the people of Sodom. To generalize from these examples, in the early strata of rabbinic literature, the rabbis understand judgment as pertaining to groups not individuals.[29]

---

27. m. Avot 4:22. The English translation is by Joshua Kulp; see https://www.sefaria.org/Pirkei_Avot.4.22?lang=bi&with=all&lang2=en

28. This question comes up a lot. Most of the time the answer is something like Yes, of course! And this is followed by a list of exceptions. In this Mishnah the answer is indeed yes, except for "those who deny the resurrection of the dead, those who say the Torah is not from heaven, and an Epicurian," by which they most likely mean any idolators. See m. Sanhedrin 10.1; Talmudic elaboration can be found in y. Sanhedrin 10.1.1

29. Hirshman provides a good discussion of the nations and the World-to-Come in early rabbinic literature in "Rabbinic Universalism." Rabbinic discussions about resurrection and the final judgment sometimes do propose consideration of individuals. It

But Paul's Letter to the Romans is not in any case an answer to the question, How can I—that is me, in particular—be saved?[30] Rather, it is how will the multiplicity of peoples and all of creation be redeemed, and how do I faithfully participate in that redemption? Paul, thinking like a Pharisee, did not see humans, Israel especially, as passive recipients of salvation but rather as partners with God in redemption. There is no doubt that Paul envisions the world being redeemed as one world. And redemption certainly includes putting the whole world right, Jews and non-Jews, everybody. But there is no reason the participants have the same role to play in this climactic cosmic drama. Potentially all humans have some agency in bringing about redemption, for it is an act of reconciliation between humans and God *and* between different peoples.[31]

The rabbis did not think non-Jews needed to observe all the commandments of the Torah to be redeemed—in fact, they did not expect all *Jews* to keep all the commandments—hence the rituals of atonement. Similar to the rabbinic discussions above, Paul's description of the culmination of history is *not* a description of how each and every individual person gets "saved." That is the Christian model. Paul's Pharisaic question is, now that the end of time is at hand, *how* will God reconcile all people, Jews and non-Jews, collectively? Paul argues that the answer to this question lies in the prophetic tradition of the ingathering of the nations, and the imagery of that tradition is of the nations coming together in harmony and living in peace, just as "the lion lies down with the lamb." It is a vision of the world redeemed as a whole. Moreover, the transformed world will not be located in another space—like the heavens. Rather, this world will be transformed, as Paul describes so beautifully in Romans 8.

AN EVOLUTIONARY READING

This reading of Romans 9–11 was inspired by Crossan's experiment in *Paul the Pharisee*, in which he integrates into the default historical framework of biblical scholars a contemporary framework he calls the

---

is not always clear if the individual is a representative of a people or truly an individual. In any case, they often imply that, if you get resurrected, you will probably have a good outcome. Resurrection gives you the chance to plead your case and to have it heard without fear or favor. One may be assured of a righteousness judgment, which is likely imbued with mercy. The wicked (like the people of Sodom) don't deserve a hearing.

30. Stendahl, *Paul Among Jews and Gentiles*.

31. Stendahl, *Final Account*, sees in Romans 9–11 the seeds for a Pauline theology of pluralism.

"evolutionary matrix." Crossan attempts to energize Paul's message such that it stretches beyond the centuries of Christian theology and presumably beyond the first century. My Twenty-First Century Judaism differs greatly from Paul's first century Judaism, but there are threads of continuity that have enabled me to integrate the evolutionary matrix in particular ways. One of those ways was to facilitate a fairer portrayal of Judaism that strives to wrest Paul free of some of the more unpleasant constraints of the Christian matrix. Prior to Crossan's evolutionary matrix, the fight against anti-Judaism has long informed my work on Paul, and that goal still has relevance.

I have also offered a way for modern readers to embrace Paul's apocalyptic vision and his sense of urgency. Paul could never have imagined climate change or the rapid progression of AI. (Neither could he have imagined that his work would ferment the antisemitism of subsequent centuries.) But he did see and experience suffering on a grand scale. The grip of Rome probably seemed insurmountable, just as our challenges do now. How could things possibly be different? What is so inspiring about Romans 9–11 is how hopeful and inclusive Paul's vision of the end-time is, in spite of the dim reality in which he and so many others lived.[32] Many ancient Jewish authors engaged in apocalyptic speculation. Most of their writings make the end of this world look terrifying—not something to look forward to. Romans 9–11, however, is nothing like those other texts, such as Daniel, Ezekiel, 1 Enoch, or Revelation of John, to name a small number of examples. Obviously, these texts are of a different genre and speak to a different audience.[33] Nevertheless, Paul's rendering of the end-time in Romans is strikingly hopeful and inclusive. The use of the evolutionary matrix, at least as I have understood it, facilitated my enthusiasm for Paul's prophetic-apocalyptic message and its potential to inspire those of us facing such cataclysmic challenges, whoever we may be. It is important to note, however, that I could not have argued for an inclusive, universalist reading of Paul—surely a more attractive interpretation to many "outside" contemporary readers—without simultaneously maintaining the Jewish matrix.

32. Fredriksen, *Pagans' Apostle*, 26–28.

33 To be sure, I recognize the differences between texts we label "apocalypse" (like the Revelation of John or 1 Enoch) and Jewish authors who engaged in vivid eschatological expectations that were sometimes characterized with urgency. Nevertheless, when one considers the range of texts expressing apocalyptic intimations or vision of the end of the world, they are generally meant to inspire dread, not hope. See Collins, *The Apocalyptic Imagination*, for discussion of various modes of apocalyptic.

Bibliography

Achtemeier, Paul J. *An Introduction to the New Hermeneutic*. Philadelphia: Westminster, 1969.
Agamben, Georgio. *The Highest Poverty: Monastic Rules and Form of Life*. Translated by Adam Kotsko. Stanford: Stanford University Press, 2013.
———. *Potentialities: Collected Essays in Philosophy*. Translated by Daniel Heller-Roazen. Stanford: Stanford University Press, 2013.
———. *State of Exception*. Translated by K. Attell. Chicago: University of Chicago Press, 2005.
———. *The Time that Remains: A Commentary on the Letter to the Romans*. Translated by Patricia Dailey. Stanford: Stanford University Press, 2005.
Aulén, Gustaf. *Christus Victor: An Historical Study of the Three Main Types of the Idea of the Atonement*. Translated by A. G. Herbert. London: SPCK, 1931. Reprint, Eugene, OR: Wipf & Stock, 2003.
Aune, David E. *The Westminster Dictionary of New Testament and Early Christian Literature and Rhetoric*. Louisville: Westminster John Knox, 2003.
Badiou, Alain. *Saint Paul: The Foundation of Universalism*. Translated by Ray Brassier. Stanford: Stanford University Press, 2003.
Barclay, John. *Pauline Churches and Diaspora Jews*. Tübingen: Mohr Siebeck, 2009.
Barrat, James. *The Final Invention: AI and the End of the Human Era*. London: Saint Martins Griffin, 2015.
Beavis, Mary Ann. "Encountering the Parables: Appreciation and Critique." In *Encountering the Parables in Contexts Old and New*, edited by T. E. Goud et al., 240–56. T&T Clark Library of New Testament Studies. London: T. & T. Clark, 2022.
Benjamin, Walter. "On the Concept of History." In *Selected Writings*, edited by Howard Eiland and Michael W. Jennings, 389–411. Vol. 4. Cambridge: Harvard University Press, 2003.
———. "Theologico-Political Fragment." In *Walter Benjamin: Selected Writings*. Edited by Howard Eiland and Michael W. Jennings, 305–6. Translated by Edmund Jephcott. Vol. 3 of *Walter Benjamin: Selected Writings*. Edited by Howard Eiland and Michael W. Jennings. Translated by Edmund Jephcott. Cambridge: Harvard University Press, 2002.
———. "Theses on the Philosophy of History" ("On the Concept of History"), Translated by Harry Zohn in *Critical Theory and Society: A Reader*, edited by Stephen Eric Bronner and Douglas Mackay Kellner, 255–63. New York: Routledge, 1989.

Bessler, Joseph A. *A Scandalous Jesus: How Three Historic Quests Changed Theology for the Better*. Salem, OR: Polebridge, 2013.

Betz, Hans D., ed. *Christology and a Modern Pilgrimage: A Discussion with Norman Perrin*. Chicago: New Testament Colloquium, 1971.

Bloomquist, L. Gregory. "Aphorism" in *NIDB*, 1.188-89.

Borg, Marcus J. "Jesus, Teaching of in *Anchor Bible Dictionary*, 3.804-12.

———. "A Renaissance in Jesus Studies." *Theology Today* 45 (1988) 280-92.

———. "A Temperate Case for a Non-Eschatological Jesus." *Foundations & Facets Forum* 2 (1986) 81-102.

Bornkamm, Günther. *Jesus of Nazareth*. Translated by Irene and Fraser McLuskey with James M. Robinson. New York: Harper & Row, 1960.

Brown, Jerry Wayne. *The Rise of Biblical Criticism in America, 1800–1870: The New England Scholars*. Middletown, CT: Wesleyan University Press, 1969.

Brown, Raymond E. *The Death of the Messiah: From Gethsemane to the Grave*. 2 vols. New York: Doubleday, 1994.

———. "The Gospel of Peter and Canonical Gospel Priority." *New Testament Studies* 33 (1994) 321-43.

Buell, Denise Kimber. "Rethinking the Relevance of Race for Early Christian Self-Definition." *Harvard Theological Review* 94 (2001) 449-76.

Bultmann, Rudolf. *Die Geschichte der Synoptischen Tradition*. Göttingen: Vandenhoeck & Ruprecht, 1957.

———. *The History of the Synoptic Tradition*. Translated by John Marsh. New York: Harper & Row, 1963.

———. *Theology of the New Testament*. Translated by Kendrick Grobel. 2 vols. in 1. New York: Scribner, 1951.

Butler, Judith. *The Force of Non-Violence*. New York: Verso, 2020.

Buttrick, George Arthur, ed. *The Interpreter's Dictionary of the Bible*. 4 vols. New York: Abingdon, 1962.

Caputo, John D. *Hermeneutics: Facts and Interpretation in the Age of Information*. London: Penguin, 2018.

———. *Specters of God: An Anatomy of the Apophatic Imagination*. Bloomington: Indiana University Press, 2022.

Caputo, John D., and Linda Alcoff, eds. *St. Paul among the Philosophers*. Indiana Series in the Philosophy of Religion. Bloomington: Indiana University Press, 2009.

Carney, T. F. *The Shape of the Past: Models and Antiquity*. Lawrence, KS: Coronado, 1975.

Caruth, Cathy. *Unclaimed Experience: Trauma Narrative, and History*. Baltimore: Johns Hopkins University Press, 1996.

Case, Shirley Jackson. *Jesus: A New Biography*. Chicago: University of Chicago Press, 1927.

Charlesworth, James H. *Jesus within Judaism: New Light from Exciting Archaeological Discoveries*. Garden City, NY: Doubleday, 1988.

Collins, John J. *The Apocalyptic Imagination: An Introduction to Jewish Apocalyptic Literature*. 3rd ed. Grand Rapids: Eerdmans, 2015.

Colwell, Ernest C. "The Chicago School of Biblical Interpretation." Lecture delivered on February 26, 1969.

Cotter, Wendy. *Miracles in Greco-Roman Antiquity: A Sourcebook for the Study of New Testament Miracle Studies*. New York: Routledge, 1999.

Craddock, Fred B., Jr. *As One Without Authority*. Rev. ed. St. Louis: Chalice, 2001.

Crossan, John Dominic. "Anti-Semitism and the Gospels." *Theological Studies* 26 (1965) 189-214.

———. *The Birth of Christianity: Discovering What Happened in the Years Immediately after the Execution of Jesus*. San Francisco: HarperSanFrancisco, 1998.

———. "Bliss at Dawn, Darkness at Noon." Pages 148-151 in *Vatican II: Fifty Personal Stories*. Edited by William Madges and Michael J. Daley. Rev. and Expanded. Maryknoll, NY: Orbis, 2012.

———. *The Cross That Spoke, The Origins of the Passion Narrative*. San Francisco: Harper & Row, 1988. Reprint, Eugene, OR: Wipf & Stock, 2008.

———. *The Dark Interval: Towards a Theology of Story*. Niles, IL: Argus, 1975. Reprint, Sonoma, CA: Polebridge (Eagle Books), 1988.

———. *A Fragile Craft: The Work of Amos Niven Wilder*. Biblical Scholarship in North America. Chico, CA: Scholars, 1981.

———. *Finding Is the First Act. Trove Folktales and Jesus' Treasure Parable*. Semeia Supplements 9. Missoula, MT: Scholars; Philadelphia: Fortress, 1979. Reprint, Eugene, OR: Wipf & Stock, 2008.

———. *Four Other Gospels: Shadows on the Contours of Canon*. Minneapolis: Winston, 1985.

———. "The Historical Jesus & the Galilee Boat." Westar Wednesdays, April 26, 2023.

———. *The Historical Jesus: The Life of a Mediterranean Jewish Peasant*. San Francisco: HarperSanFrancisco, 1991.

———. *How to Read the Bible and Still Be a Christian*. New York: HarperOne, 2015.

———. *Imago Dei. A Study in Philo and St. Paul*. Rome: Gregorian University Press, 1961.

———. *In Fragments: The Aphorisms of Jesus*. San Francisco: Harper & Row, 1983. Reprint, Eugene, OR: Wipf & Stock, 2008.

———. *In Parables: The Challenge of the Historical Jesus*. New York: Harper & Row, 1973.

———. "It Is Written: A Structuralist Analysis of John 6." Pages 197–213. In of *Society of Biblical Literature 1979 Seminar Papers*. Edited by Paul J. Achtemeier. Vol. 1 of *Society of Biblical Literature 1979 Seminar Papers*. Edited by Paul J. Achtemeier. Missoula, MT: Scholars, 1979.

———. *Jesus: A Revolutionary Biography*. San Francisco: HarperSanFrancisco, 1994.

———. *A Long Way from Tipperary: What a Former Monk Discovered in His Search for the Truth*. San Francisco: HarperOne, 2000. Reprint, Eugene, OR: Wipf & Stock, 2020.

———. "Mark and the Relatives of Jesus." *Novum Testamentum* 15 (1973) 81–113.

———. "Parable and Example in the Teaching of Jesus." *New Testament Studies* 18 (1971–72) 285–307.

———. *Paul the Pharisee: A Vision Beyond the Violence of Civilization*. Salem, OR: Polebridge, 2024.

———. *The Power of Parable: How Fiction by Jesus Became Fiction about Jesus*. New York: HarperOne, 2012.

———. *Raid on the Articulate: Comic Eschatology in Jesus and Borges*. New York: Harper & Row, 1976. Reprint, Eugene, OR: Wipf & Stock, 2008.

———. *Render Unto Caesar: The Struggle Over Christ and Culture in the New Testament*. Standard Edition. New York: HarperOne, 2022.

---. "Responses and Reflections." In *Jesus and Faith: A Conversation on the Work of John Dominic Crossan*, edited by Jeffrey Carlson and Robert A. Ludwig, 142–64. Maryknoll, NY: Orbis, 1994.

---. *Sayings Parallels: A Wookbook for the Jesus Tradition*. Philadelphia: Fortress, 1986. Reprint, Eugene, OR: Wipf & Stock, 2008.

---. "Structuralist Analysis and the Parables of Jesus." *Linguistica Biblica* 29–30 (1973) 41–51.

---. "A Vision of Divine Justice: The Resurrection of Jesus in Eastern Christian Iconography." *Journal of Biblical Literature* 132 (2013) 5–32.

---. *Who Killed Jesus? Exposing the Roots of Anti-Semitism in the Gospel Story of the Death of Jesus*. San Francisco: HaperSanFrancisco, 1995.

Crossan, John Dominic, and Jonathan L. Reed. *Excavating Jesus: Beneath the Stones, Behind the Texts*. San Francisco: HarperOne, 2001.

Crossan, John Dominic, and Sarah Crossan. *Resurrecting Easter: How the West Lost and the East Kept the Original Easter Vision*. San Francisco: HarperOne, 2018.

Cuddon, J. A., ed. *The Penguin Dictionary of Literary Terms and Literary Theory*. 4th ed. New York: Penguin, 2000.

Denker, Jurgen. *Die theologiegeschichtliche Stellung des Petrusevangeliums: Ein Beitrag zur fruhgeschichte des Dokestismus*. Europaische Hochschulshriften 23/36. Bern: Lang. 1975.

Derrida, Jacques. "The Force of Law: 'The Mystical Foundation of Authority.'" Pages 228–297. In *Acts of Religion*. Translated by Mary Quantaince. Edited by Gil Anidjar. London: Routledge, 2002.

---. *The Other Heading: Reflections on Today's Europe*. Translated by Pascale-Anne Brault and Michael Naas. Bloomington: Indiana University Press, 1992.

Dewey, Arthur J. *Inventing the Passion: How the Death of Jesus Was Remembered*. Salem, OR: Polebridge, 2017.

Dodd, Charles H. *The Parables of the Kingdom*. New York: Scribner, 1935, reprinted 1961.

Donahue, John R., "Biblical Scholarship 50 years After *Divino Afflante Spiritu*: From September 18, 1993." *America: The Jesuit Review*. Sept 18, 1993 (https://www.americamagazine.org/issue/100/biblical-scholarship-50-years-after-divino-afflante-spiritu#:~:text=Divino%20Afflante%20Spiritu%20provided%20the,Catholic%20University%20of%20America%20and)

Ebeling, Gerhard. "The Significance of the Critical-Historical Method for Church and Theology in Protestantism." In *Word and Faith*, 17–61. Philadelphia: Fortress Press, 1963.

Eisenbaum, Pamela. *Paul Was not a Christian: The Original Message of a Misunderstood Apostle*. New York: HarperOne, 2009.

Esler, Philip. *Conflict and Identity in Romans: The Social Setting of Paul's Letter*. Minneapolis: Fortress, 2003.

Fathy, Ehud. "The Asàrotos Òikos Mosaic as an Elite Status Symbol." *POTESTAS. Estudios Del Mundo Clásico E Historia Del Arte* 10 (2017) https://doi.org/10.6035/Potestas.2017.10.1

Francis, Pope. *Praise Be to You—Laudato Si' On Care for Our Common Home*. San Francisco: Ignatius, 2015.

Fredriksen, Paula. "Judaism, the Circumcision of Gentiles, and Apocalyptic Hope: Another Look at Galatians 1 and 2." *Journal of Theological Studies* 42 (1991) 532–64.

———. "Judaizing the Nations: The Ritual Demands of Paul's Gospel." *New Testament Studies* 56 (2010) 232–52.

———. *The Pagans' Apostle*. New Haven: Yale University Press, 2017.

———. "The Question of Worship: Gods, Pagans, and the Redemption of Israel." In *Paul Within Judaism: Restoring the First Century Context to the Apostle*, edited by Mark D. Nanos and Magnus Zetterholm, 175–202. Minneapolis: Fortress, 2015.

Freedman, David Noel, ed. *The Anchor Bible Dictionary*. 6 vols. New York: Doubleday, 1992.

Funk, Robert W. "From Parable to Gospel: Domesticating the Tradition." *Forum* 1, 3 (1985) 3–24.

———. *Funk on Parables: Collected Essays*. Edited by Bernard Brandon Scott. Sonoma, CA: Polebridge, 2006.

———. "The Hermeneutical Problem and Historical Criticism." In *The New Hermeneutic*, edited by James M. Robinson and John B. Cobb Jr., 163–97. New York: Harper & Row, 1964

———. "The Issue of Jesus: The Opening Remarks of Jesus Seminar Chairman Funk." *Forum* 1 (1985) 7–12.

———. *Language, Hermeneutic, and Word of God: The Problem of Language in the New Testament and Contemporary Theology*. New York: Harper & Row, 1966.

———. "The Watershed of the American Biblical Tradition: The Chicago School, First Phase, 1892–1920." *Journal of Biblical Literature* 95 (1976) 4–22.

Funk, Robert W., Roy W. Hoover, and The Jesus Seminar, eds. *The Five Gospels: The Search for the Authentic Words of Jesus*. New York: Macmillan, 1993.

Funk, Robert W., and The Jesus Seminar. *The Acts of Jesus: Search for the Authentic Deeds of Jesus*. San Francisco: HarperSanFrancisco, 1998.

Funk, Robert W., Bernard Brandon Scott, and James R. Butts. *The Parables of Jesus: Red Letter Edition*. Sonoma, CA: Polebridge, 1988.

Gabler, Johann Philipp. "Oratorio de justo discrimine theologiae biblicae et dogmaticae regundisque utrisque finibus." *Kleine theologische Schriften* 2.4 (1831) 179–96. English translation in John Sandys-Wunsch and Laurence Eldredge. "J. P. Gabler and the Distinction Between Biblical and Dogmatic Theology: Translation, Commentary, and Discussion of His Originality." *Scottish Journal of Theology* 33 (1980) 135–58.

Gadamer, Hans-Georg. *Truth and Method*. 2nd ed. Translated by Joel Weinsheimer and Donald G. Marshall. New York: Crossroad, 1992.

Garroway, Joshua. *Paul's Gentile-Jews: Neither Jew nor Gentile, but Both*. New York: Palgrave Macmillan, 2012.

Häkkinen, Sakari. *The Gospel of the Poor*. London: Lambert Academic, 2017.

Harrington, Daniel. "The Jewishness of Jesus: Facing Some Problems." *Catholic Biblical Quarterly* 49 (1987) 1–13.

Hayes, Christine. *What's Divine about Divine Law?* Princeton: Princeton University Press, 2015.

Hedrick, Charles W. *Many Things in Parables: Jesus and His Modern Critics*. Louisville: Westminster John Knox, 2004.

———. *Nag Hammadi Codices XI, XII, XIII*. NHS 28. Leiden: Brill, 1990.

―――. *The Wisdom of Jesus: Between the Sages of Israel and the Apostles of the Church.* Eugene, OR: Cascade Books, 2014.

Heidegger, Martin. *The Phenomenology of Religious Life.* Translated by Matthias Fritsch and Jennifer Anna Gosetti-Ferencei. Bloomington: Indiana University Press, 2004.

Hirshman, Marc. "Rabbinic Universalism in the Second and Third Centuries." *Harvard Theological Review* 93 (2000) 101–15.

Hobsbawm, Eric J. *Primitive Rebels: Studies in Archaic Forms of Social Movement in the 19th and 20th Centuries.* Manchester: Manchester University Press, 1971.

Holman, C. Hugh. *A Handbook to Literature.* 3rd edition. Indianapolis: Odyssey, 1972.

―――. *A Handbook to Literature.* 6th ed. New York: Macmillan, 1991.

Hoover, Roy W., Marcus J. Borg, Kathleen E. Corley, John Dominic Crossan, Arthur J. Dewey, Robert T. Fortna, Robert W. Funk, et al. *Profiles of Jesus.* Santa Rosa, CA: Polebridge, 2002.

Hunt, Lynn. *History: Why It Matters.* Medford, MA: Polity, 2018.

Jackson, Glenna. "From Hippo to Hippos: Being on the Edge of Smash in Africa." In *When Faith Meets Reason: Religion Scholars Reflect on Their Spiritual Journeys*, edited by Charles W. Hedrick, 1–11. Santa Rosa, CA: Polebridge, 2008.

―――. "The Jesus Seminar in Africa." *Forum.* 6.1 (2003) 85–94.

―――. "Learning from Africans How to Read the Parables of Jesus." *The Fourth R* 34/5 (2021) 9–11.

―――. "Twenty Years of Experiencing the Parables in Africa." In *Encountering the Parables in Contexts Old and New*, edited by T. E. Goud et al., 235–37. T&T Clark Library of New Testament Studies, London: T. & T. Clark, 2022.

Jeremias, Joachim. *The Parables of Jesus.* Translated by S. H. Hooke. New York: Scribner, 1972.

"The Jesus Seminar: *Voting Records* Sorted by Gospels by Weighted Average." *Foundation and Facets Forum* 6.3/4 (1990) 245–99.

Johnson, Luke Timothy. *The Real Jesus.* New York: HarperCollins, 1996.

Johnson-Hodge, Caroline. *If Sons, then Heirs: A Study of Kinship and Ethnicity in the Letters of Paul.* Oxford: Oxford University, 2007.

Jülicher, Adolf. *Die Gleichnisreden Jesu.* Tübingen: Mohr Siebeck, 1888. 2nd ed., 1899.

Kartsonis, Anna D. *Anastasis: The Making of an Image.* Princeton University Press, 1986.

Käsemann, Ernst. "The Problem of the Historical Jesus." In *Essays on New Testament Themes*, 15–47. Studies in Biblical Theology 41. London: SCM Press, 1964.

Kermode, Frank. *The Sense of an Ending: Studies in the Theory of Fiction.* London: Oxford University Press, 1966.

King, Karen L. *The Secret Revelation of John.* Cambridge: Harvard University Press, 2006.

Kloppenborg, John S. *The Formation of Q: Trajectories in Ancient Wisdom Collections.* Philadelphia: Fortress, 1987.

―――. *The Tenants in the Vineyard: Ideology, Economics, and Agrarian Conflict in Jewish Palestine.* Tübingen: Mohr Siebeck, 2006.

Klosinski, Lee. "The Meals in Mark." PhD diss., Claremont Graduate School, 1988.

Laughlin, Paul Alan, and Glenna S. Jackson. *Remedial Christianity: What Every Believer Should Know About the Faith, but Probably Doesn't.* Sonoma, CA: Polebridge, 2000.

Lee, Margaret Ellen, and Bernard Brandon Scott. *Sound Mapping the New Testament.* Sonoma, CA: Polebridge, 2009.

Lenski, Gerhard. *Power and Privilege*. New York: McGraw-Hill, 1966.
Lewis, I. M. *Ecstatic Religion: An Anthropological Study of Spirit Possession and Shamanism*. Harmondsworth: Penguin, 1971.
Lillie, Celene. *The Rape of Eve*. Minneapolis: Fortress, 2017.
Loisy, Alfred. *The Gospel and the Church*. Edited by Bernard B. Scott. Translated by Christopher Home. 1903. Reprinted in Lives of Jesus Series. Philadelphia: Fortress, 1976.
Lopez, Davina. *Apostle to the Conquered*. Minneapolis: Fortress, 2008.
Mack, Burton L. *A Myth of Innocence, Mark and Christian Origins*. Philadelphia: Fortress Press, 1988.
Malina, Bruce J. *The New Testament World, Insights from Cultural Anthropology*. Atlanta: John Knox, 1981.
Marshall, John. "Misunderstanding the New Paul: Marcion's Transformation of the Sonderzeit Paul." *Journal of Early Christian Studies* 20 (2012) 1–29
Martin, Dale. "Teleology, Epistemology, and Universal Vision in Paul." In *St. Paul among the Philosophers*, edited by John D Caputo and Linda Alcoff, 91–108. Indiana Series in the Philosophy of Religion. Bloomington: Indiana University Press, 2009.
Mathews, Shailer. *The Social Teachings of Jesus*. New York: Macmillan, 1897.
McGaughy, Lane C. "The Search for the Historical Jesus: Why Start with the Sayings?" *The Fourth R* 9 (1996) 17–26.
Meier, John P. *A Marginal Jew: Rethinking the Historical Jesus*. Vol 1: *The Roots of the Problem and the Person*. Garden City, NY: Doubleday, 1991.
———. *A Marginal Jew: Rethinking the Historical Jesus*. Vol. 2: *Mentor, Message, and Miracles*. New York: Doubleday; 1994.
———. *A Marginal Jew: Rethinking the Historical Jesus*. Vol. 3: *Companions and Competitors*. New Haven: Yale University Press, 2001.
———. *A Marginal Jew: Rethinking the Historical Jesus*. Vol. 4: *Law and Love*. New York: Yale University Press, 2009.
———. *A Marginal Jew: Rethinking the Historical Jesus*. Vol. 5: *Probing the Authenticity of the Parables*. Illustrated edition. New Haven: Yale University Press, 2016.
Metz, Johann Baptist. *Faith in History and Society*. Translated by D. Smith. New York: Crossroad, 1980.
Metzger, Bruce M. *A Textual Commentary on the Greek New Testament*. New York: United Bible Societies, 1971.
Miles, Jack. "If Jesus Is God, What God Is He?" Westar Institute Lecture. Atlanta: November 22, 2015.
Miller, Robert, ed. *The Apocalyptic Jesus, A Debate*. Santa Rosa, CA: Polebridge, 2001.
Nanos, Mark D. *The Mystery of Romans: The Jewish Context of Paul's Letter*. Minneapolis: Fortress, 1995.
Nanos, Mark D., and Magnus Zetterholm. *Paul within Judaism: Restoring the First-Century Context to the Apostle*. Minneapolis: Fortress, 2015.
Neill, Stephen, and Tom Wright. *The Interpretation of the New Testament 1861–1986*. Oxford: Oxford University Press, 1988.
Nickelsburg, George W. E. *Resurrection, Immortality, and Eternal Life in Intertestamental Judaism*. Harvard Theological Studies 26. Cambridge: Harvard University Press, 1972.
Novenson, Matthew V. *Paul Then and Now*. Grand Rapids: Eerdmans, 2022.

Oakman, Douglas E. *Jesus and the Economic Questions of His Day.* Studies in the Bible and Early Christianity 8. Lewiston, NY: Mellen, 1986.
Ong, Walter J. *Orality and Literacy, The Technologizing of the Word.* New York: Methuen, 1982.
Palmer, R. R., and Joel Colton. *A History of the Modern World.* New York: Knopf, 1978.
Patterson, Stephen J. *The God of Jesus: The Historical Jesus and the Search for Meaning.* Harrisburg, PA: Trinity, 1998.
Pelikan, Jaroslav. "Dogma." In *A Handbook of Christian Theology*, 80–82. New York: Meridian Books, 1958.
———. *The Emergence of the Catholic Tradition (100–600).* Chicago: The University of Chicago Press, 1971.
———. *Jesus through the Centuries.* New Haven: Yale University Press, 1985.
Perrin, Norman. *The Kingdom of God in the Teaching of Jesus.* London: SCM, 1963.
———. *Rediscovering the Teaching of Jesus.* New York: Harper & Row, 1967.
Phipps, William E. "Eve and Pandora Contrasted." *Theology Today* 45 (1988) 24–48.
Pliny. *Natural History. Books 36–37.* Translated by D. E. Eichholz. Loeb Classical Library 419. Cambridge: Harvard University Press, 1962.
Powell, Mark Allen. *Jesus as a Figure in History: How Modern Historians View the Man from Galilee.* Louisville: Westminster John Knox Press, 1998.
Redfield, R. *Peasant Society and Culture.* Chicago: University of Chicago Press, 1969.
Reed, Jonathan L. *HarperCollins Visual Guide to the New Testament.* New York: HarperCollins, 2007.
Reimarus, Hermann Samuel. *Reimarus: Fragments.* Edited by Charles H. Talbert. Translated by Ralph S. Fraser. Lives of Jesus Series. Philadelphia: Fortress Press, 1970. Reprint, Scholars Press Reprints and Translations Series. Chico, CA: Scholars Press, 1985.
Robinson, James M. "Hermeneutic Since Barth." In *The New Hermeneutic*, edited by James M. Robinson and John B. Cobb Jr., 1–77. New York: Harper & Row, 1964. Reprinted in James M. Robinson, *Language, Hermeneutic, and History: Theology after Barth and Bultmann*, 69–146. Eugene, OR: Cascade Books, 2008.
———. *A New Quest of the Historical Jesus.* Studies in Biblical Theology 1/25. London: SCM, 1959.
———. "Robert W. Funk and Hermeneutics." In *Evaluating the Legacy of Robert W. Funk*, edited by Andrew W. Scrimgeour, 53–58. Atlanta: SBL Press, 2018.
Safrai, Ze'ev, and R. Steven Notley. *Parables of the Sages: Jewish Wisdom from Jesus to Rav Ashi.* Ann. ed. London: Tyndale, 2015.
Sakenfeld, Katharine Doob, ed. *New Interpreter's Dictionary of the Bible Volume.* 5 vols. Nashville: Abingdon, 2006.
Sanders, E.P. *Jesus and Judaism.* Philadelphia: Fortress, 1985.
Saunders, Ernest W. *Searching the Scriptures: A History of the Society of Biblical Literature, 1880–1980.* Chico, CA: Scholars, 1982.
Schelling, F. W. J. *Philosophy of Revelation (1841–42) and Related Texts.* Edited and Translated by Klaus Ottmann. Putnam, CT: Spring, 2020.
Schmidt, Daryl. "Fundamentally Pluralistic: An Odyssey." *The Fourth R* 8 (1995) 7–14.
Schweitzer, Albert. *The Quest of the Historical Jesus. A Critical Study of Its Progress from Reimarus to Wrede.* New York: Macmillan, 1968.
Scott, Bernard Brandon. "Essaying the Rock: The Authenticity of the Jesus Parable Tradition." *Forum* 2 (1986) 3–35.

———. "From Reimarus to Crossan: Stages in a Quest." *Currents in Research: Biblical Studies* 2 (1994) 253–80.
———. *Hear Then the Parable, A Commentary on the Parables of Jesus*. Minneapolis: Fortress Press, 1989.
———. *Hollywood Dreams and Biblical Stories*. Minneapolis: Fortress Press, 1994.
———. "Holmes Is on the Case: E. P. Sanders' Profile of Jesus." *Forum* n.s. 1 (1998) 261–74.
———. *Jesus, Symbol-Maker for the Kingdom*. Philadelphia: Fortress, 1981.
———. "New Options in An Old Quest." In *The Historical Jesus Through Catholic and Jewish Eyes*, 1–50. Harrisburg, PA: Trinity, 2000.
———. *The Real Paul: Recovering His Radical Challenge*. Salem, OR: Polebridge, 2015.
———. "To Impose Is Not / To Discover: Methodology in John Dominic Crossan's *The Historical Jesus*." In *Jesus and Faith: A Conversation on the Work of John Dominic Crossan*, edited by Jeffrey Carlson and Robert A. Ludwig, 22–30. Maryknoll, NY: Orbis, 1994.
Sharma, Kriti. *Interdependence: Biology and Beyond*. New York: Fordham University Press, 2015.
Stendahl, Krister. *The Final Account: Paul's Letter to the Romans*. Minneapolis: Fortress, 1995.
———. *Paul Among Jews and Gentiles*. Minneapolis: Fortress, 1976.
Stowers, Stanley K. *A Rereading of Romans: Justice, Jews, and Gentiles*. New Haven: Yale University Press, 1994.
Strauss, David Friedrick. *The Life of Jesus Critically Examined*. Translated by George Eliot. Lives of Jesus Series. 1838. Reprint, Philadelphia: Fortress, 1972.
Tannehill, Robert C. *The Sword of His Mouth*. Semeia Supplements. Philadelphia: Fortress, 1975. Reprint, Eugene, OR: Wipf & Stock, 2003.
Tate, W. Randolph. *Interpreting the Bible: A Handbook of Terms and Methods*. Peabody, MA: Hendrickson, 2006.
Tatum, W. Barnes. *In Quest of Jesus: A Guidebook*. Atlanta: John Knox, 1982.
Taubes, Jacob. *The Political Theology of Paul*. Translated by Dana Hollander. Stanford: Stanford University Press, 2004.
Taussig, Hal, ed. *A New New Testament: A Bible for the Twenty-First Century Combining Traditional and Newly Discovered Texts*. Boston: Mariner, 2015.
Tegmark, Max, *Being Human in the Age of Artificial Intelligence*. New York: Penguin, 2018.
Thiessen, Matthew. "Paul's Argument Against Gentile Circumcision in Romans 2:17–29." *Novum Testamentum* 56 (2014) 373–91,
———. *Paul and the Gentile Problem*. Oxford: Oxford University Press, 2016.
Tracy, David. *Plurality and Ambiguity: Hermeneutics, Religion, Hope*. San Francisco: Harper & Row, 1987.
Tracy, David. *The Analogical Imagination: Christian Theology and the Culture of Pluralism*. New York: Crossroad, 1981.
Vearncombe, Erin, Brandon Scott, Hal Taussig, and The Westar Institute. *After Jesus Before Christianity: A Historical Exploration of the First Two Centuries of Jesus Movements*. San Francisco: HarperOne, 2021.
Via, Dan. *The Parables: Their Literary and Existential Dimension*. Philadelphia: Fortress, 1967. Reprint, Eugene, OR: Wipf & Stock, 2007.

Walzer, Arthur E. "Audience in Historical Jesus Research: The Cases of Wright and Crossan." *Journal for the Study of the Historical Jesus* 19 (2021) 191–216.

Wilder, Amos. *Early Christian Rhetoric: The Language of the Gospel*. London: SCM, 1964. Reprint, Eugene, OR: Wipf & Stock, 2014.

Wilkins, Michael J., and P. Morland. *Jesus Under Fire: Modern Scholarship Reinvents the Historical Jesus*. Grand Rapids: Zondervan Academic, 1996.

Wilson, Bryan R. *Magic and the Millennium: A Sociological Study of Religious Movements of Protest among Tribal and Third-World Peoples*. New York: Harper & Row, 1973.

Wistrich, Robert S. *Antisemitism: The Longest Hatred*. New York: Schocken, 1994,

Wright, N. T. *Paul and the Faithfulness of God*. 2 vols. Minneapolis: Fortress, 2013.

Zoccali, Christopher. "'And So All Israel Shall Be Saved': Competing Interpretations of Romans 11:26 in Pauline Scholarship." *Journal for the Study of the New Testament* 30 (2008) 289–318.

———. *Whom God Has Called: The Relationship of Church and Israel in Pauline Interpretation 1920 to the Present*. Eugene, OR: Pickwick Publications, 2010.

John Dominic Crossan
Curriculum Vitae
March 1, 2025

EDUCATIONAL BACKGROUND

1934: Born in Nenagh, Co. Tipperary, Ireland, on February 17, 1934.

1939-45: Grade School with the Christian Brothers, Naas, Co. Kildare, Ireland.

1945-50: High School at St. Eunan's College, Letterkenny, Co. Donegal, Ireland.

1951-57: Undergraduate studies in philosophy and theology at Stonebridge Priory, the Major Seminary of the Servites, a Roman Catholic religious order, in Lake Bluff, IL, USA.

1957-59: Graduate studies at St Patrick's Pontifical University, Maynooth, Co. Kildare, Ireland. Doctorate in Theology granted in June 1959. Thesis published in required summary format as *Imago Dei A Study in Philo and St. Paul*. Rome: Gregorian University Press, 1961.

1959-61: Post-doctoral studies in exegesis at the Pontifical Biblical Institute, Rome. Diploma as Sacred Scripture Licentiate (S.S.L) granted in June, 1961.

1965-67: Post-doctoral studies in archeology at the École Biblique et Archéologique Française de Jérusalem (then in Jordan). Study-visits to all the main sites in Greece, Turkey, Cyprus, Lebanon, Syria, Iraq, Iran, Jordan, Israel, Egypt, Tunisia, Morocco. Diploma as Elève titulaire de l'Ecole Biblique granted in June,1966.

ACADEMIC APPOINTMENTS

1961-65: Assistant Professor of Biblical Studies at Stonebridge Priory, Lake Bluff, Illinois.

Guest lectureships at: St. Norbert's Abbey, De Pere, Wisconsin (1963-64); Barat College, Lake Forest, Illinois (1963-64); Loyola University, Chicago, Illinois

(1964–65); St. Mary's College Graduate School, Notre Dame, Indiana (Summers of 1964 and 1965).

1967–68: Assistant Professor of Biblical Studies at Mundelein Seminary, Illinois.

1968–69: Assistant Professor of Biblical Studies at the Catholic Theological Union, Hyde Park, Chicago.

1969–73: Associate Professor in the Department of Religious Studies, DePaul University, Chicago.

1973–95: Professor in the Department of Religious Studies, DePaul University, Chicago.

1995: Emeritus Professor in the Department of Religious Studies, DePaul University, Chicago.

1996 (Fall) Croghan Bicentennial Visiting Professor of Religion, Williams College, Williamstown, MA.

2006 (Spring) Distinguished Visiting Professor of Religious Studies, University of Central Florida, Orlando, FL

PUBLICATIONS

Books

1. *Scanning the Sunday Gospel*. Milwaukee: Bruce, 1966.

2. *The Gospel of Eternal Life*. Milwaukee: Bruce, 1967.

3. *In Parables. The Challenge of the Historical Jesus*. New York: Harper & Row, 1973.

   Pages 53–78 are translated as "Gleichnisse der Verkehrung." In *Die neutestamentische Gleichnisforschung im Horizont von Hermeneutik und Literaturwissenschaft*, edited by Wolfgang Harnisch, 126–58. Wege der Forschung 575. Darmstadt: Wissenschaftliche Buchgesellschaft, 1982.

   Paperback edition, San Francisco: Harper & Row, 1985.

   Reissued Sonoma, CA: Polebridge (Eagle Books), 1992.

4. *The Dark Interval: Towards a Theology of Story*. Niles, IL: Argus, 1975.

   Reissued Sonoma, CA: Polebridge (Eagle Books), 1988.

5. *Raid on the Articulate. Comic Eschatology in Jesus and Borges*. New York: Harper & Row, 1976.

   Reissued Eugene, OR: Wipf & Stock, 2008.

6. *Finding Is the First Act. Trove Folktales and Jesus' Treasure Parable*. Semeia Supplements 9. Missoula, MT: Scholars; Philadelphia: Fortress, 1979.

   Reissued Eugene, OR: Wipf & Stock, 2008.

7. *Cliffs of Fall. Paradox and Polyvalence in the Parables of Jesus.* New York: Seabury Press, 1980.

   Reissued Eugene, OR: Wipf & Stock, 2008.

8. *A Fragile Craft. The Work of Amos Niven Wilder.* Biblical Scholarship in North America 3. Chico, CA: Scholars, 1981.

9. *In Fragments. The Aphorisms of Jesus.* San Francisco: Harper & Row, 1983.

   Reissued Eugene, OR: Wipf & Stock, 2008.

10. *Four Other Gospels. Shadows on the Contours of Canon.* Minneapolis: Winston/Seabury, 1985.

    Reissued Sonoma, CA: Polebridge, 1992.

    Reissued Eugene, OR: Wipf & Stock, 2008.

11. *Sayings Parallels: A Workbook for the Jesus Tradition.* Foundations and Facets of the New Testament. Philadelphia: Fortress, 1986.

    Reissued Eugene, OR: Wipf & Stock, 2008.

12. *The Cross That Spoke: The Origins of the Passion Narrative.* San Francisco: Harper & Row, 1988.

    Given the 1989 Award for Excellence in the Study of Religion (Analytical-Descriptive Studies) by the American Academy of Religion.

    Reissued Eugene, OR: Wipf & Stock, 2008.

13. *The Historical Jesus: The Life of a Mediterranean Jewish Peasant.* San Francisco: HarperSanFrancisco, 1991. Paperback edition, 1993.

    In top ten of "Religious Bestsellers (Hardcover)" according to *Publishers Weekly* for 6 months in 1992: No. 2 on March 16; No. 6 on April 13; No. 3 on May 11; No. 1 on June 8; No. 8 on August 10; No. 10 on September 21.

    Translated into German, Spanish (Spain and Latin America separately), Italian, Portuguese (Brazil), Polish, and Korean.

14. *Jesus: A Revolutionary Biography.* San Francisco: HarperSanFrancisco, 1994.

    In top ten of "Religious Bestsellers (Hardcover)" according to Publishers Weekly for 8 months in 1994: No. 6 on April 11; No. 4 on May 9; No. 3 on June 13; No. 5 on July 11; No. 8 on August 15; No. 8 on September 12; No. 10 on October 10; No. 10 on November 14.

    Translated into Portuguese (Brazil), Italian, Spanish (Spain and Latin America separately), German, Dutch, Polish, Danish, Chinese, Japanese, Korean.

15. *The Essential Jesus: Original Sayings and Earliest Images.* San Francisco: HarperSan Francisco, 1994.

    Translated into Spanish, German, Portuguese, and Japanese.

    Reissued Eugene, OR: Wipf & Stock, 2008.

16. *Who Killed Jesus? Exposing the Roots of Anti-Semitism in the Gospel Story of the Death of Jesus*. San Francisco: HarperSanFrancisco, 1995.

   In top ten of "Religious Bestsellers (Hardcover)" according to Publishers Weekly for 5 months in 1995: No. 7 on May 8; No. 8 on June 12; No. 10 on July 10; No. 8 on August 14; No. 8 on September 11.

   Translated into Portuguese, German, Spanish (Latin America), Dutch, and Japanese.

17. John Dominic Crossan and Richard G. Watts, *Who Is Jesus? Answers to Your Questions about the Historical Jesus*. New York: HarperPaperbacks 1996.

   Translated into Korean and Japanese.

   Reissued Louisville: Westminster John Knox, 1999.

18. *The Birth of Christianity. Discovering What Happened in the Years Immediately After the Execution of Jesus*. San Francisco: HarperSanFrancisco, 1998.

   In top ten of "Religious Bestsellers (Hardcover)" according to *Publishers Weekly* for 3 months in 1998: No. 8 on May 11; No. 9 on June 15; No. 8 on July 13. It was also picked as one of the ten "Religion" titles among "PW's Best 98 Books." *Publisher's Weekly*, November 2, 1998. It is in a British edition and was adopted by Doubleday Reader's Subscription Book Club and the Quality Paperback Book Club.

   Translated into Portuguese (Brazil), Polish, Spanish, Korean versions.

19. *A Long Way from Tipperary: A Memoir*. San Francisco: HarperSanFrancisco, 2000.

   Reissued Eugene, OR: Wipf & Stock, 2020.

20. John Dominic Crossan and Jonathan L. Reed, *Excavating Jesus: Beneath the Stones, Behind the Texts*. San Francisco: HarperSanFrancisco, 2001 [London: SPCK, 2001].

   Received *Publishers Weekly* "Best Religion Books of 2001" Award.

   Translated into Spanish (and book club), German, Korean, Hungarian, and Portuguese.

21. John Dominic Crossan and Jonathan L. Reed, *In Search of Paul: How Jesus' Apostle Opposed Rome's Empire with God's Kingdom*. San Francisco: HarperSanFrancisco, 2004. Separate English edition by SPCK.

   In top ten of "Religious Bestsellers (Hardcover)" according to *Publishers Weekly* for 1 month in 2004: No. 10 on December 20, 2004, p. 19.

   Translated into Spanish and Portuguese.

22. Marcus Borg and John Dominic Crossan, *The Last Week: A Day by Day Account of Jesus's Final Week in Jerusalem*. San Francisco: HarperSanFrancisco, 2006.

   In top ten of "Hardcover Religion Bestsellers" according to *Publishers Weekly* for 1 month in 2006: No. 10 on April 10.

UK version by SPCK. Translated into Spanish, Portuguese, Chinese, Korean, Japanese, Russian.

23. *God & Empire: Jesus against Rome Then and Now*. San Francisco: HarperSanFrancisco, 2007.

   Translated into Spanish, and Korean.

24. Marcus Borg and John Dominic Crossan, *The First Christmas: What the Gospels Really Teach about the Birth of Jesus*. San Francisco: HarperOne. 2007. Separate English edition by SPCK.

   Translated into Japanese, Spanish, Portuguese (Brazil), Korean, and Russian.

25. Marcus Borg and John Dominic Crossan, *The First Paul: Reclaiming the Radical Visionary behind the Church's Conservative Icon*. SanFrancisco: HarperOne, 2009. Separate English edition by SPCK.

   Translated into Spanish and Korean.

   Fourth in "Top Ten Books on Religion and Spirituality." *Booklist*, November 15, 2009.

26. *The Greatest Prayer: Rediscovering the Revolutionary Message of the Lord's Prayer*. San Francisco: HarperOne, 2010. Separate English edition by SPCK.

   Translated into Korean, Spanish, and Japanese.

27. *The Power of Parable: How Fiction by Jesus became Fiction about Jesus*. San Francisco: HarperOne, 2012.

   Translated into Korean and Spanish.

28. *How to Read the Bible and Still Be a Christian. Struggling with Divine Violence from Genesis through Revelation*. San Francisco: HarperOne, 2015.

   Translated into Korean, Russian, Spanish, and German.

29. John Dominic Crossan and Sarah Sexton Crossan, *Resurrecting Easter: How the West Lost and the East Kept the Original Easter Vision*. San Francisco: HarperOne, 2018.

30. *Render Unto Caesar: The Struggle over Christ and Culture in the New Testament*. San Francisco: HarperOne, 2022.

   Translated into Korean.

31. *Paul the Pharisee: A Vision Beyond the Violence of Civilization*. Salem, OR: Polebridge, 2024.

Book Sections

1. "The Marian Significance of John 1,12–13." Pages 99–107 in *Maria in Sacra Scriptura. Acta Congressus Mariologici-Mariani 1965*. Vol. V. Rome: Pontificia Academia Mariana Internationalis, 1967.

2. Articles in *The New Catholic Encyclopedia*. 15 vols. New York: McGraw Hill, 1967: (1) Barabbas, (2) Hour of Jesus, (3) High-Priestly Prayer of Jesus, (4) Justice of Men; (5) Justice of God; (6) Justification in the Bible; (7) Logos in the Bible; (8) Paraclete, (9) Word of God.

3. "Divorce and Remarriage in the New Testament." In *The Bond of Matrimony: An Ecumenical and Interdisciplinary Study*, edited by W. Bassett, 1–41. South Bend, IN: Notre Dame University Press, 1968.

4. "Judges." In *The Jerome Biblical Commentary*, edited by R. E. Brown, J. A. Fitzmyer, and R. E. Murphy, 149–62. New Jersey: Prentice-Hall, 1968.

5. "The Presence of God's Love in the Power of Jesus' Works." In *The Presence of God*, edited by P. Benoit, R. E. Murphy, and B. Van Iersel, 65–79. Concilium 50: Scripture. New York: Paulist, 1969.

6. "Man in Society: The Biblical View." In *Man In Society: Facts and Visions*, edited by H. H. Loiskandl, 18–42. Dubuque, IA: Kendall-Hunt, 1971.

7. "Redaction and Citation in Mark 11:9–10,17 and 14:27." In *Society of Biblical Literature 1972 Proceedings*, edited by Lane McGaughy. Vol. 1, 17–61. First International Congress of Learned Societies in the Field of Religion, Los Angeles, California, 1–5 September 1972.

    "Redaction and Citation in Mark 11:9–10 and 11:17." *Biblical Research* 17 (1972) 33–50.

8. "The Servant Parables of Jesus." Pages 94–118 in *Society of Biblical Literature 1973 Seminar Papers*. Edited by George MacRae. Vol 1. Cambridge, MA: SBL, 1973.

    "The Servant Parable of Jesus." *Semeia* 1 (1974) 17–62.

9. "Jesus and Pacifism." In *No Famine in the Land. Studies in Honor of John L. Mc Kenzie*, edited by J. W. Flanagan and A. Weisbrod Robinson, 196–208. Missoula, MT: Scholars, 1975.

10. "Empty Tomb and Absent Lord." In *The Passion in Mark*, edited by Werner Kelber, 135–52. Philadelphia: Fortress, 1976.

11. "Parable, Allegory, and Paradox." In *Semiology and Parables*, edited by Daniel Patte, 247–81. Pittsburgh Theological Monograph Series 9. Pittsburgh: Pickwick, 1976.

12. "Hidden Treasure Parables in Late Antiquity." In *Society of Biblical Literature 1976 Seminar Papers*, edited by George MacRae, 359–79. Missoula, MT: Scholars, 1976.

13. "'Ruth Amid the Alien Corn': Perspectives and Methods in Contemporary Biblical Criticism." Pages 199-210 in *The Biblical Mosaic: Changing Perspectives*. Edited Robert M. Polzin and Eugene Rothman. Semeia Studies 10. Missoula, MT: Scholars Press; Pittsburgh: Fortress Press, 1982. Republished as "Perspectives and Methods in Contemporary Biblical Research." *Biblical Research* 22 (1977) 39-49.

14. "A Form for Absence: The Markan Creation of Gospel." In *The Poetics of Faith: Essays Offered to Amos Niven Wilder*. Edited by William A. Beardslee *Semeia* 12-13 (1978) 41-55.

15. "It Is Written: A Structuralist Analysis of John 6." In *Society of Biblical Literature 1979 Seminar Papers*,. Edited by Paul J. Achtemeier, 1.197-213. Missoula, MT: Scholars, 1979

    "It Is Written: A Structuralist Analysis of John 6." *Semeia* 26 (1983) 3-21.

    "A Structuralist Analysis of John 6." Pages 235-249 in *Orientation by Disorientation. Studies in Literary Criticism and Biblical Literary Criticism Presented in Honor of William A. Beardslee*. Edited by. Richard A. Spencer. Pittsburgh Theological Monograph Series 35. Pittsburgh: Pickwick, 1980.

16. "Stages in Imagination." In *The Archaeology of the Imagination*, edited by Charles E. Winquist, 49-62. Journal of the American Academy of Religion Thematic Series 48/2 (1981).

17. "The Hermeneutical Jesus." In *The Bible and Its Traditions*, edited by Michael Patrick O'Connor and David Noel Freedman, 237-49. Michigan Quarterly Review 22/3 (Summer 1983).

    In *Backgrounds for the Bible*, edited by Michael Patrick O'Connor and David Noel Freedman, 15-27. Winona Lake, IN: Eisenbrauns, 1987.

18. "Parables of Jesus." In *Harper's Bible Dictionary*, edited by Paul J. Achtmeier, 748-49. San Francisco: Harper & Row, 1985.

19. "Jesus and Gospel." Pages 106-130 In *The Biblical Heritage in Modern Catholic Scholarship. In Honor of Bruce Vawter, C.M., on His 65th Birthday*, edited by John J. Collins and John Dominic Crossan, 106-30. Wilmington, DE: Glazier, 1986.

20. "The Infancy and Youth of the Messiah." and "The Passion, Crucifixion and Resurrection." Pages 59-81 and 109-132 in *The Search for Jesus: Modern Scholarship Looks at the Gospels*, edited by Hershel Shanks, 59-81 and 109-32. Washington, DC: Biblical Archaeology Society, 1994 [see #50 under Invited Lectures]

21. "The Historical Jesus in Earliest Christianity" and "Responses and Reflections." Pages 1-21 and 142-164 in *Jesus and Faith. A Conversation on the Work of John Dominic Crossan*, edited by Jeffrey Carlson and Robert A. Ludwig, 1-21. Maryknoll, NY: Orbis, 1994.

22. "Itinerants and Householders in the Earliest Kingdom Movement." In *Reimagining Christian Origins: A Colloquium Honoring Burton L. Mack*, edited by Elizabeth A. Castelli and Hal Taussig, 113-29. Valley Forge, PA: Trinity, 1996.

23. "Jesus and the Kingdom: Itinerants and Householders in Earliest Christianity." In *Jesus at 2000*, edited by Marcus J. Borg, 21–51. Boulder, CO: Westview, 1997.

24. "Will the Real Jesus Please Stand Up?" In *Will the Real Jesus Please Stand Up? A Debate between William Lane Craig and John Dominic Crossan*. Moderated by William F. Buckley, Jr. Edited by Paul Copan, 24–76. Grand Rapids: Baker, 2001.

25. "Our Own Faces in Deep Wells: A Future for Historical Jesus Research." In *God, The Gift, and Postmodernism*, edited by John D. Caputo and Michael J. Scanlon, 282–310. Indiana Series in the Philosophy of Religion. Bloomington: Indiana University Press, 1999.

26. "Historical Jesus as Risen Lord." In *The Jesus Controversy: Perspectives in Conflict*, 1–47. Rockwell Lecture Series at Rice University, Houston, TX. Harrisburg, PA: Trinity, 1999. Translated into Korean (Christian Literature Center, Seoul, 2019).

27. "The Labour of Sharing." In *The Labour of Reading: Desire, Alienation, and Biblical Interpretation. Essays in Honour of Robert C. Culley*, edited by Fiona C. Black, Roland Boer, Erin Runions, 235–48. Semeia Studies 36. Atlanta: Society of Biblical Literature 1999.

28. "Why Is Historical Jesus Research Necessary?" In *Jesus Two Thousand Years Later*, edited by James H. Charlesworth and Walter P. Weaver, 7–37. Faith and Scholarship Colloquies Series. Harrisburg, PA: Trinity, 2000.

29. "A Future for the Christian Faith?" In *The Once and Future Jesus*, the Jesus Seminar, 109–29. Santa Rosa, CA: Polebridge, 2000.

30. "Eschatology, Apocalypticism, and the Historical Jesus." In *Jesus Then & Now: Images of Jesus in History and Christology*, edited by Marvin Meyer and Charles Hughes, 91–112. Harrisburg, PA: Trinity, 2001. [Papers from an international symposium at Chapman University, Los Angeles, CA, Fall 1999]

31. "The Power of the Dog." In *Postmodern Interpretations of the Bible–A Reader*, edited by A. K. M. Adam, 187–93. St Louis: Chalice, 2001.

32. "Troubling History at Oberammergau." In *Telling a Good Story: The Art of Narrative. Queen's Quarterly: A Canadian Review* 108.2 (2001) 223–31.

33. In *The Apocalyptic Jesus: A Debate* (Dale C. Allison, Marcus J. Borg, John Dominic Crossan, Stephen J. Patterson). Edited by Robert J. Miller, 48–69, 119–23, 137–42, and 157–60. Santa Rosa, CA: Polebridge, 2000.

34. "The Ashes of Memory." In *Irish Spirit: Pagan, Celtic, Christian, Global*, edited by Patricia Monaghan, 156–64. Dublin: Wolfhound, 2001.

35. "The Passion after the Holocaust." In *A Shadow of Glory: Reading the New Testament after the Holocaust*, edited by Tod Linafelt, 171–84. New York: Routledge, 2002.

36. "Bliss at Dawn, Darkness at Noon." In *Vatican II: Forty Personal Stories*, edited by William Madges and Michael J. Daley, 121–23. Mystic, CT: Bayard Twenty-Third Publications, 2003.

"Bliss at Dawn, Darkness at Noon." In *Vatican II: Fifty Personal Stories*, edited by William Madges and Michael J. Daley, 148–51. Rev. and exp. ed. Maryknoll, NY: Orbis, 2012.

37. "Jesus as a Mediterranean Jewish Peasant." In *Profiles of Jesus*, edited by Roy W. Hoover, 161–68. Santa Rosa, CA: Polebridge, 2002.

38. "The Historical Jesus and Divine Dissent." Pages 14–29 in *The Role of Dissenter in Western Christianity from Jesus through the 16th Century*, edited by Alicia McNary Forsey, 14–29. Berkeley: Starr King School for the Ministry, 2004.

39. "Hymn to a Savage God." In *Jesus and Mel Gibson's The Passion of the Christ: The Film, the Gospels and the Claims of History*, edited by Kathleen E. Corley and Robert L. Webb, 8–27. New York: Continuum, 2004.

40. "The Justice of God and the Peace of Earth." In *War or Words? Interreligious Dialogue as an Instrument of Peace*, edited by Donald W. Musser and D. Dixon Sutherland, 204–19. Cleveland, OH: Pilgrim, 2005.

41. "Paul and Rome: The Challenge of a Just World Order." In *New Testament and Roman Empire: Shifting Paradigms for Interpretation*. Special Issue of the *Union Seminary Quarterly Review* 59.3-4 (2005) 6–20.

42. "Appendix: Bodily Resurrection Faith." In *The Resurrection of Jesus: John Dominic Crossan and N. T. Wright in Dialogue*, edited by Robert B. Stewart, 171–86 and 216–17. Minneapolis: Fortress, 2006.

43. "Jewish Crowd and Roman Governor." Pages 59–67 In *Mel Gibson's Bible: Religion, Popular Culture, and The Passion of the Christ*, edited by Timothy K. Beal and Tod Linafelt, 59–67. Afterlives of the Bible. Chicago: University of Chicago Press, 2006.

44. "The Gospel of Peter and the Canonical Gospels." In *Das Evangelium nach Petrus: Text, Kontexte, Intertexte*, edited by Thomas J. Kraus und Tobias Nicklas, 117–34. Texte und Untersuchungen zur Geschichte der altchristlichen Literatur 158. Berlin: de Gruyter, 2007.

45. "Hope for Our World: God's Kingdom on Earth." In *Together in Hope: Proclaiming God's Justice, Living God's Love*, edited by Adrian Alker for the Inclusive Church Network, 24–30. Sheffield: St. Marks Center for Radical Christianity, 2008.

46. "Roman Imperial Theology." In *The Shadow of Empire: Reclaiming the Bible as a History of Faithful Resistance*, edited by Richard A. Horsley, 59–73. Louisville: Westminster John Knox, 2008.

47. "A vida do Jesus historico"; and "As duas vozes mais antgas du tradicã de Jesus." In *A descoberta do Jesus histórico*, edited by André Chebitarese and Gabriele Cornelli, 13–30. and 85–103. São Paulo, Brazil: Paulinas, 2009. [Keynote addresses to the I Simpósio Internacional do Jesus Historico, Universidade Federal do Rio de Janeiro (UFRJ), Brasil, Tuesday-Thursday, October 16–18, 2007]

48. "Divine Violence in the Christian Bible." In *The Bible and the American Future*, edited by Robert Jewett with Wayne L. Alloway Jr. and John G. Lacey, 208–36. Eugene, OR: Cascade Books, 2009.

49. "Jesus and the Challenge of Collaborative Eschatology." In *The Historical Jesus: Five Views*, edited by James K. Beilby and Paul Rhodes Eddy, 105–32. Downers Grove, IL: IVP Academic, 2009. [Winner of the 2011 Christianity Today Book of the Year Award in the Biblical Studies category.]

50. "A morte do Jesus histórico"; "A ressurreição de Jesus"; and "Hino a um Deus selvagem (Sobrë um filme de Mel Gibson, A Paixäo de Cristo)." In *Morte e ressurreicão de Jesus. Reconstrucão e hermenêuticz. Um debate com John Dominic Crossan*, edited by Paulo Augusto de Souza Nogueira and Jonas Machado, 13–26, 27–43, 44–66. São Paulo, Brazil: Paulinas, 2009.

51. "Context and Text in Historical Jesus Methodology." In *The Handbook for the Study of the Historical Jesus. Vol. 1: How to Study the Historical Jesus*, edited by T. Holmén and S. E. Porter, 59–81. Leiden: Brill, 2010.

52. "Honest to Jesus and Honest to Bob." In *Evaluating the Legacy of Robert W. Funk: Reforming the Scholarly Model*, edited by Andrew D. Scrimgeour, 177–83. Biblical Scholarship in North America 28. Atlanta: SBL Press, 2018.

53. "Christian Easter and Human Evolution." In *The Universal Christ Issue of Oneing: An Alternative Orthodoxy* 7.1 (2019) 21–26. Albuquerque, NM: Center for Action and Contemplation.

54. "The Parables of Jesus." In *Jesus in Global Perspective 1: Historical Afterlives of Jesus*, edited by Gregory C. Jenks, 22–38. Westar Studies. Eugene, OR: Cascade Books, 2023.

Articles

1. "Mary's Virginity in St. John—An Exegetical Study." *Marianum* 19 (1957) 115–26.

2. "The Biblical Poetry of the Hebrews." *The Bible Today* 13 (1964) 832–37.

3. "Anti-Semitism and the Gospels." *Theological Studies* 26 (1965) 189–214.

4. "Mary and the Church in John 1:13." *The Bible Today* 20 (1965) 1318–24.

5. "Biblical Truth as Dialectical Analysis." *Chicago Studies* 6 (1967) 297–316. Reprinted in *Insight* 6 (1968) 20–29.

6. "Structure and Theology of Mt. 1:18–2:23." *Cahiers de Joséphologie* 16 (1968) 119–35.

7. "The Parable of the Wicked Husbandmen." *Journal of Biblical Literature* 90 (1971) 451–65.

8. "Parable and Example in the Teaching of Jesus." *New Testament Studies* 18 (1971–72) 285–307. Reprinted in *Semeia* 1 (1974) 63–104.

9. "Parable as Religious and Poetic Experience." *Journal of Religion* 53 (1973) 330-58.

10. "Mark and the Relatives of Jesus." *Novum Testamentum* 15 (1973) 81-113. Reprinted as Pages 52-84 in *The Composition of Mark's Gospel* (Leiden: Brill, 1999)

11. "The Seed Parables of Jesus." *Journal of Biblical Literature* 92 (1973) 244-66.

12. "Structuralist Analysis and the Parables of Jesus." *Linguistica Biblica* 29-30 (1973) 41-51. Reprinted and expanded in *Semeia* 1 (1974) 192-221.

13. "A Basic Bibliography for Parables Research." *Semeia* 1 (1974) 236-74.

14. "The Good Samaritan: Towards a Generic Definition of Parable." *Semeia* 2 (1974) 82-112.

15. "Immortality as Idolatry: The Limits of Narcotic Theology." *Listening* 10 (1975) 21-29.

16. "Literary Criticism and Biblical Hermeneutics." *Journal of Religion* 57 (1977) 76-80. [Essay review of Norman Perin, *Jesus and the Language of the Kingdom*. Philadelphia: Fortress, 1976.]

17. "A Metamodel for Polyvalent Narration." *Semeia* 9 (1977) 105-47.

18. "Waking the Bible: Biblical Hermeneutic and Literary Imagination." *Interpretation* 32 (1978) 269-85.

19. "Paradox Gives Rise to Metaphor: Paul Ricoeur's Hermeneutics and the Parables of Jesus." *Biblical Research* 24 (1979) 20-37.

20. "Difference and Divinity." *Semeia* 23 (1982) 29-40.

21. "Mark 12:13-17." *Interpretation* 37 (1983) 397-401.

22. "Parable as History and Literature." *Listening* 19 (1984) 5-18.

23. "From Moses to Jesus: Parallel Themes." *Bible Review* 2/2 (1986) 18-27.

24. "The Cross that Spoke: The Earliest Narrative of the Passion and Resurrection." *Forum* 3/2 (June 1987) 3-22.

25. "Living Earth and Living Christ: Thoughts on Carol P. Christ's, 'Finitude, Death, and Reverence for Life.'" *Semeia* 40 (1987) 109-18.

26. "Pattern and Particularity in Suffering and Story: Response to Beth Burbank's, 'Vignette: The Blessing of the Wrestler.'" *Journal of Supervision and Training in Ministry* 9 (1987) 211-16.

27. "Aphorism in Discourse and Narrative." *Semeia* 43 (1988) 121-40.

28. "Divine Immediacy and Human Immediacy: Towards a New First Principle in Historical Jesus Research." *Semeia* 44 (1988) 121-40.

29. "Materials and Methods in Historical Jesus Research." *Forum* 4/4 (1988) 3-24.

30. "Thoughts on Two Extracanonical Gospels." *Semeia* 49 (1990) 155-68.

31. "Jesus as a Mediterranean Jewish Peasant." *The Fourth R* 4/2 (1991) 11-14.

32. "The Life of a Mediterranean Jewish Peasant." *Christian Century* 108/37 (1991) 1194–1200.

33. "The Historical Jesus: An Interview with John Dominic Crossan." *Christian Century* 108/37 (1991) 1200–1204.

34. "Open Healing and Open Eating: Jesus as a Jewish Cynic?" *Biblical Research* 36 (1991) 6–18.

35. "Lists in Early Christianity: A Response to Early Christianity, Q and Jesus." *Semeia* 55 (1992) 235–43.

36. "Jesus and the Leper." *Forum* 8 (1992) 177–90.

37. "The Challenge of Multicontextual Interpretation." *Semeia* 62 (1993) 149–55.

38. "The Challenge of Christmas: Two Views." *Christian Century*, December 15, 1993, cover and pages 1270–80. "He Comes as One Unknown" by Beverly R. Gaventa, and "A Tale of Two Gods" by John Dominic Crossan ("adapted from the first chapter of *Jesus: A Revolutionary Biography*"), with mutual responses following.

39. "Some Theological Conclusions from My Historical Jesus Research." *Living Pulpit* 3/1 (1994) 18–19.

40. "Why Christians Must Search for the Historical Jesus." *Bible Review* 12/2 (1996) 34–38 and 42–45.

41. "The Passion Narrative." *Fourth R* 9/5–6 (1996) 3–8.

42. "'What Victory? What God?' A Review Debate with N. T. Wright on Jesus and the Victory of God." *Scottish Journal of Theology* 50 (1997) 345–58.

43. "Against Anxieties: Thomas 36 and the Historical Jesus." *Forum* 10 (1994) 57–67.

44. "The Gospel of Peter and the Canonical Gospels: Independence, Dependence, or Both?" *Forum* n.s. 1 (1998) 7–51.

45. "Spirituality or Sanctity." *Tikkun* 13/6 (1998) 34.

46. "Earliest Christianity in Counterfactual Focus." *Biblical Interpretation* 8 (1999) 92–112.

"Earliest Christianity in Counterfactual Focus." In *Virtual History and the Bible*, edited by J. Cheryl Exum, 185–93. Leiden: Brill, 2000.

47. "Exclusivity and Particularity." *Buddhist-Christian Studies* 19 (1999) 97–99. Reprinted in *Buddhists Talk about Jesus. Christians Talk about the Buddha*, edited by Rita M. Gross and Terry C. Muck, 83–86. New York: Continuum, 2000.

48. "Die Akte Jesus." *NZZ Folio (Die Zeitschrift der Neuen Zürcher Zeitung)*. Special issue on "Jesus, 2000 Jahre danach." 12 (1999) 25–28.

49. "Den historiske Jesus og kristendommens fodsel." *Kritisk forum for praktisk teologi: Efter Jesu fodsel* 78 (1999) 30–47.

50. "The Final Word." *Colloquium* (1999) 141–52.

51. "'Blessed Plot': A Reply to N. T. Wright's Review of *The Birth of Christianity.*" *Scottish Journal of Theology* 53 (2000) 92–112 [see 72–91].

52. "The Parables of Jesus." *Interpretation* 56 (2002) 247–59.

53. "Historical Knowledge: A Response to Hal Childs." *Pastoral Psychology* 51 (2003) 469–75.

54. "Virgin Mother or Bastard Child?" *HTS/Teologiese Studies/Theological Studies* 59 (2003) 663–91.

    Reprinted in *A Feminist Companion to Mariology*, edited by Amy-Jill Levine with Maria Mayo Robbins, 37–55. London: T. & T. Clark, 2005.

55. "The Resurrection of Jesus in Its Jewish Context." *Neotestamentica* 37.1 (2003) 29–57. [Invited Opening Lecture. New Testament Society of South Africa, Potchefstroom, South Africa, Tuesday, April 9, 2002, 7:30–9:00 pm.]

56. "Loosely Based on a True Story: The Passion of Jesus in Verbal and Visual Media." *Tikkun* 19/2 (2004) 25–27, 32.

57. "On Asking the Right Question." *Axial* (Winter 2004) 6–8.

58. "Crowd Control." *Christian Century* 121/6 (2004) 18 and 21–22.

59. "A Woman Equal to Paul: Who Is She?" *Bible Review* 21/3 (2005) 29–31 and 46–47.

60. "New Testament and Roman Empire: Shifting Paradigms for Interpretation." *Union Seminary Quarterly Review* 59/3–4 (2005) 1–15.

61. "Violence and the Normalcy of Civilization." *Search* 29 (2006) 3–12.

62. Marcus Borg and John Dominic Crossan, "Jesus' Final Week: Collision Course." *Christian Century* 124/6 (2007) 27–31.

63. "The Message of the Historical Jesus and Contemporary American Imperialism." *Rivista di Teologia dell'Evangelizzazione* 11 (2007) 395–406.

64. "A Vision of Divine Justice: The Resurrection of Jesus in Eastern Christian Iconography." *Journal of Biblical Literature* 132 (2013) 1–32. [AAR/SBL Annual Meeting: SBL Presidential Address, International Ballroom North, Hilton Chicago Hotel, 7:00–8:00pm, Saturday, November 17, 2012.]

65. "From Abba-Cry to Father-Prayer." *Fourth R* 28/2 (2015) 14–15 and 24.

66. "It's the Theology: In Memory of Marcus J. Borg, 1942–2015." *Fourth R* 29/1 (2016) 23–25.

67. John Dominic Crossan and Sarah Sexton Crossan, "The Eastern Church's Communal Vision of Resurrection: Rising Up with Christ." *Christian Century* 135/3 (2018) 22–25. [Cover: Image with caption "Resurrection is communal"]

68. John Dominic Crossan and Sarah Sexton Crossan, "Resurrecting Easter: Hunting the Original Resurrection Image." *Biblical Archaeology Review* 45/2 (2019) 20–28 and 60 (notes). [Cover: Image with caption "The Earliest Easter Images"]

69. "Jesus at Easter. Individual Ascension or Universal Resurrection?" *The Fourth R* 36/3 (2023) 3-10 [Color photo on cover and black and white photo on p. 4 are by Sarah Crossan].

70. "The Jesus Seminar and Me: An Interview with John Dominic Crossan." Interviewed by Robert Miller. *The Fourth R* 53 (2025) 3-8.

Reviews

1. John A. T. Robinson, *Twelve New Testament Studies*. SBT 34. Naperville, IL: Allenson, 1962. In *Catholic Biblical Quarterly* 25 (1963) 217-19.

2. C. Larcher, *L'Actualité chrétienne de l'Ancien Testament*. Lectio Divina 34. Paris: Cerf, 1962. In *Catholic Biblical Quarterly* 26 (1964) 112-14.

3. *Studiorum Paulinorum Congressus Internationalis Catholicus 1961*. AnBib 17-18. 2 vols. Rome: Pontifical Biblical Institute, 1963 In *Catholic Biblical Quarterly* 26 (1964) 389-390.

4. Leo J. O'Donovan, SJ, ed. *Word and Mystery: Biblical Essays on the Person and Mission of Christ*. Glen Rock, NJ: Newman, 1968. In *Catholic Biblical Quarterly* 31 (1969) 284-85.

5. A. Weiser, *Die Knechtsgleichnisse der synoptischen Evangelien*. STANT 29 Munich: Kösel, 1971. In *Journal of Biblical Literature* 92 (1973) 136-37.

6. Dan O. Via, Jr., *Kerygma and Comedy in the New Testament*. Philadelphia: Fortress, 1975. In *Journal of Biblical Literature* 95 (1976) 486-87.

7. Kenneth E. Bailey, *Poet and Peasant: A Literary Cultural Approach to the Parables in Luke*. Grand Rapids: Eerdmans, 1976. In *Journal of Biblical Literature* 96 (1977) 606-8.

8. Howard Schwartz, ed. *Imperial Messages: One Hundred Modern Parables*. New York: Avon, 1976. In *Parabola* 2 (1977) 128-30.

9. William O. Walker, Jr., ed. *The Relationships Among the Gospels*. Trinity University Monograph Series in Religion 5. San Antonio, TX: Trinity University Press, 1978. In *Journal of American Academy of Religion* 47 (1979) 138.

10. Franz Schnider, *Die verlorenen Söhne: Strukturanalytische und historisch-kritische Untersuchungen zu Lk 15*. OBO 17. Freiburg: Universitätsverlag; Göttingen: Vandenhoeck & Ruprecht, 1977. In *Catholic Biblical Quarterly* 41 (1979) 349-350.

11. Daniel Patte and Aline Patte. *Structural Exegesis: From Theory to Practice. Exegesis of Mark 15 and 16. Hermeneutical Implications*. Philadelphia: Fortress, 1978. In *Catholic Biblical Quarterly* 42 (1980) 276-78.

12. Groupe D'Entrevernes (Jean Calloud, et. al.). *Signes et paraboles: Sémiotique et texte évangélque*. Avec une étude de Jacques Geninasca et une postface de Algirdas Julien Greimas. Paris: Seuil, 1977. And The Entrevernes Group (Jean Calloud, et al.). *Signs and Parables: Semiotics and Gospel Texts*. With a study

by Jacques Geninasca. Postface by Algirdas Julien Greimas. Translated by Gary Phillips. Pittsburgh Theological Monograph Series 23. Pittsburgh: Pickwick. In *Catholic Biblical Quarterly* 42 (1980) 591-92.

13. Pheme Perkins, *Hearing the Parables of Jesus*. New York: Paulist, 1981. In *Catholic Biblical Quarterly* 44 (1982) 688-89.

14. Northrop Frye, *The Great Code: The Bible and Literature*. New York: Harcourt Brace Jovanovich, 1982. In *Commonweal* 109 (1982) 475-79.

15. James G. Williams. *Those Who Ponder Proverbs: Aphoristic Thinking and Biblical Literature*. Bible and Literature Series 2. Sheffield: Almond, 1981. In *Journal of Religion* 63 (1983) 77-78.

16. John R. Donahue. *The Gospel in Parable. Metaphor, Narrative, and Theology in the Synoptic Gospels*. Philadelphia: Fortress, 1988, In *Journal of Biblical Literature* 109 (1990) 139-41.

17. Ronald A. Piper, *Wisdom in the Q-Tradition: The Aphoristic Teaching of Jesus*. SNTSMS 61. Cambridge: Cambridge University Press, 1989. In *Journal of Biblical Literature* 110 (1991) 522-25.

18. Bernard Brandon Scott. *Hear Then the Parable: A Commentary on the Parables of Jesus*. Minneapolis: Fortress Press, 1989. In *Catholic Biblical Quarterly* 54 (1992) 377-78.

19. Jonathan Z. Smith, *Drudgery Divine: On the Comparison of Early Christianities and the Religions of Late Antiquity*. Chicago: University of Chicago Press, 1990. In *Numen* 39 (1992) 233-35.

20. Henry Wansbrough, ed. *Jesus and the Oral Gospel Tradition*. JSNT Supplement Series, 64. Sheffield: Sheffield Academic, 1991. In *Interpretation* (1993) 310.

21. N. T. Wright, *Who Was Jesus?* Grand Rapids: Eerdmans, 1993. In *Biblical Review* 9/4 (1993) 10-11.

22. Raymond E. Brown, *The Death of the Messiah: From Gethsemane to the Grave. A Commentary on the Passion Narratives in the Four Gospels*. 2 vols. The Anchor Bible Reference Library. New York: Doubleday, 1994. In *Journal of Religion* 75 (1995) 247-53.

23. John T. Carroll and Joel B. Green, with Robert E. Van Voorst, Joel Marcus, and Donald Senior, C.P., *The Death of Jesus in Early Christianity*. Peabody, MA: Hendrikson, 1995. In *Journal of Biblical Literature* 116 (1997) 361-63.

24. Thomas Cahill, *Desire of the Everlasting Hills. The World Before and After Jesus*. New York: Doubleday, 1999. In *The Globe and Mail*, Section D: Books (December 18, 1999) D2-D3.

25. Hal Childs, *The Myth of the Historical Jesus and the Evolution of Consciousness*. SBLDS 179. Atlanta: SBL, 2000. In *Biblical Interpretation* 9 (2001) 440-44.

26. John S. Kloppenborg, *The Tenants in the Vineyard: Ideology, Economics, and Agrarian Conflict in Jewish Palestine*. WUNT 195. Tübingen, Germany: Mohr Siebeck. 2006. In *Biblical Theology Bulletin* 37 (2007) 37–38.

27. Elaine Pagels and Karen L. King, *Reading Judas: The Gospel of Judas and the Shaping of Christianity*. New York: Viking Penguin, 2007. In *The Washington Post Book World*, (Palm) Sunday, April 1, 2007. Page 11 ("Embracing Judas").

ACADEMIC LECTURES

1. Garrett-Evangelical Theological Seminary, Evanston, IL (10 Nov 1976).
2. DePaul University, Chicago, IL (14 November 1976).
3. Loyola University, Chicago, IL (21 April 1977).
4. Carleton University, Ottawa, Canada (27 October 1977).
5. York University, Ontario, Canada (7 February 1978).
6. Villanova University, Villanova, PA (8 March 1978).
7. Catholic University of America, Washington, DC (14 March 1978).
8. Iliff School of Theology, Denver, CO (20–21 March 1978).
9. University of Colorado, Boulder, CO (22 March 1978).
10. Wartburg Theological Seminary, Dubuque, IA (4–5 December 1978).
11. University of Oregon, Eugene, OR (2–4 May 1979).
12. University of Chicago, Chicago, IL (3–5 October 1979).
13. Perkins School of Theology, Southern Methodist University, Dallas, TX (19–20 March 1980).
14. Indiana University, Bloomington, IN (28–29 September 1980).
15. Rice University, Houston, TX (29 January 1981).
16. Institute of Religion, Texas Medical Center, Houston, TX (30 January 1981).
17. Canisius College, Buffalo, NY (7 April 1981).
18. Eastern Great Lakes Biblical Society Meeting (CBA-SBL), Invited Plenary Lecture, Columbus, OH (1 May 1981).
19. Bethany Theological Seminary, Oak Brook, IL (20–21 October 1981).
20. Wheaton College Graduate School, Wheaton, IL (22 April 1982).
21. Simpson College, Indianola, IA (28 April 1982).
22. Northwestern University, Evanston, IL (12 November 1982).
23. St. Xavier College, Chicago, IL (17 January 1983).
24. Midwest Division Meeting, American Academy of Religion, Invited Plenary Lecture, Lake Geneva, WI (8 April 1983).

25. The Humanities Institute, University of Southern California, Los Angeles, CA (10 September 1983).
26. Institute for Antiquity and Christianity, Claremont Graduate School, Claremont, CA (11-12 September 1983).
27. Central States Region Annual Meeting (SBL-ASOR-AAR), Invited Plenary Lecture, Westminster College, Fulton, MO (1 April 1984).
28. Syracuse University, Syracuse, NY (28 November 1984).
29. Millikin University, Decatur, IL (1-2 October 1985).
30. Bangor Theological Seminary, Bangor, MA (3-5 February 1986).
31. Institute for Ministry, Loyola University, New Orleans, LA (21-22 February 1986).
32. Buffalo Biblical Institute, Buffalo, NY. (17-19 October 1986).
33. Chicago Society of Biblical Research, Wheaton College, Invited Lecture (25 October 1986).
34. Society of Biblical Literature, Annual Meeting, Atlanta GA, Invited Lecture in "Biblical Scholarship in the 21st Century Series" (24 November 1986).
35. University of Notre Dame, Notre Dame, IN (7-8 April 1987).
36. Claremont Graduate School, Claremont, CA (27-28 April 1987).
37. College of Saint Thomas, St Paul, MN (29-30 September 1987).
38. Saint Mary Seminary, Cleveland, OH (10 February 1988).
39. Concordia College, Moorhead, MN (18 March 1988).
40. University of Alberta, Edmonton, Canada (23 October 1991).
[Inauguration of Annual Lecture on "Religion, Culture and the Imagination"]
41. College of St. Francis, Joliet, IL (24 March 1992).
42. Institute for Antiquity and Christianity, Claremont Graduate School, Claremont, CA (1 April 1992).
43. Graduate Theological Union, Berkeley, CA (3 April 1992).
44. Episcopal Divinity School, Cambridge, MA (6 April 1992).
45. Union Theological Seminary, New York, NY (9 April 1992)
46. Florida Southern College (The 1992 Willis Lecture in Religion), Lakeland, FL (6 November 1992).
47. Capital University, Columbus, OH (24-25 January 1993).
48. Winslow Lectures (two), Seabury-Western Theololgical Seminary, Evanston, IL (13-14 May 1993).
49. Craigie Memorial Lecture (Canadian Society of Biblical Studies), Annual Meeting of Canadian Religion Societies, Carleton University, Ottawa, Canada (8 June 1993).

50. Two lectures during a full-day symposium on "The Search for Jesus: Modern Scholarship Looks at the Gospels." Baird Auditorium, National Museum of Natural History, Smithsonian Institution, Washington, DC, Saturday, September 11, 1993 [see #20 under 3b above].

51. Thomas L. King Lecture in Religious Studies, Washburn University, Topeka, KS, Thursday, October 14, 1993.

52. Alumni/ae Days Lectures (two), McCormick Theological Seminary, Chicago, Monday, April 25, 1994.

53. Schmiechen Lectures (three), Eden Theological Seminary, St. Louis, MO, Wednesday, October 12, 1994.

54. Edward Robinson Bicenntenial Lecture, Hamilton College, Clinton, NY, Sunday, October 30, 1994.

55. Ward Lecture on Religious Imagination, Lancaster Theological Seminary, Lancaster, PA, Thursday, November 3, 1994.

56. Earl Lectures, Pacific School of Religion, Berkeley, CA, Wednesday and Thursday, January 25-26, 1995.

57. Lecture at Mercyhurst College, Erie, PA, Thursday, March 16, 1995.

58. Teleconference for St. Stephen's College, University of Alberta, Edmonton, Canada, Monday, April 3, 1995.

59. Evening Lecture and all-day Seminar at University of Minnesota, Duluth, Friday-Saturday, April 7-8, 1995.

60. Lecture series at St. Stephen's College, University of Alberta, Edmonton, Canada, October 11-12, 1995.

61. Lecture and seminar at Trinity College (University of Dublin), Dublin, Ireland, October 19-20, 1995.

62. Lecture and seminar at University of Winnipeg, Winnipeg, Canada, November 8-9, 1995.

63. Lecture and seminar at Moravian College, Bethlehem, PA, November 14-15, 1995.

64. Lecture and seminar at Oregon State University ("Jesus at 2000"), Corvallis, OR, February 8-10, 1996.

65. Lansdowne Lecture and Seminars at Centre for Studies in Religion and Society, University of Victoria, BC, Canada, February 11-12, 1996.

66. Calwell Lectures at Louisville Presbyterian Seminary, Louisville, KY, March 4-5, 1996.

67. Fifteenth Annual Forum on Jewish/Christian Relations, Christian Theological Seminary, Indianapolis, IN, March 25, 1996.

68. Teleconference for St. Stephen's College, University of Alberta, Edmonton, Canada, Monday, March 26, 1996.

69. Lecture at Williams College, Williamstown, MA, Monday, April 8, 1996.

70. Faculty seminar and public lecture at Northern Illinois University, DeKalb, IL, Tuesday, April 16, 1996.

71. Lecture at Garrett-Evangelical Theological Seminary, Evanston, IL, Wednesday, April 24, 1996.

72. Five lectures for Auburn-Union Continuing Theological Education Program ("The Historical Jesus and Contemporary Faith"), Auburn Theological Seminary, New York, NY, Tuesday, April 30, through Thursday, May 2, 1996.

73. Four public lectures as Croghan Bicentennial Visiting Professor of Religion, Williams College, Williamstown, MA, Sept 17 and 24, Oct 1 and 8, 1996.

74. Slater-Willson Lecture at St. Paul School of Theology, Kansas City, MO, February 13, 1997.

75. Rockwell Lectures (Lecture 1), Rice University, Houston, TX, October 5, 1997.

76. Gustafson Lectures, United Theological Seminary of the Twin Cities, New Brighton, MN, October 6–7, 1997.

77. Evening public lecture and all-day workshop, Graduate Division of Wholistic Spirituality, Chestnut Hill College, Philadelphia, PA, June 14–15, 1998.

78. Gates Lecture and Convocation Address at Grinnell College, Grinnell, IA, October 7–8, 1998.

79. Lecture in Boston College Humanities Series Lowell Lectures, Boston College, MA, October 22, 1998.

80. Lecture on "Law and the Sacred." Birkbeck College, University of London, Friday, February 5, 1999.

81. Lecture at Oregon State University, Corvallis, OR, Thursday, March 4, 1999.

82. Lectures at St. Stephen's College of the University of Alberta, in Edmonton and Calgary, June 2–3, 1999.

83. Invited Guest Lecturer at the annual meeting of the Australia and New Zealand Association of Theological Schools and the Australia and New Zealand Society of Theological Studies, Morpeth (Newcastle), NSW, Australia, July 5–9, 1999.

84. Inaugural Lecture for the Humanities and Social Sciences Division's participation in the Centennial Celebration of Victoria University of Wellington, New Zealand, August 2, 1999.

85. Lectures and seminars at the Universities of Copenhagen and Aarhus (Denmark), Lund and Uppsala (Sweden), Helsinki (Finland), and Oslo (Norway), September 1–13, 1999.

86. Public lecture at the University of Tulsa, October 8, 1999.

87. Classes and public lecture at Stetson University, Deland, FL, October 18, 1999.

88. Classes and public lecture at Rollins College, Orlando, FL, December 1–3, 1999.

89. Public lecture at Iowa State University, Ames, IA, February 4, 2000.

90. Public lecture and graduate seminar at Harvard University Divinity School, February 22–23, 2000.

91. Three-day mini-course (19 hours) at St. Stephen's College, University of Alberta, Calgary, Canada, June 11–13, 2000.

92. Public lecture at the Institute for Antiquity and Christianity, Claremont University, Claremont, CA, September 19, 2000.

93. Public lecture at San Francisco Theological Seminary, San Anselmo, CA, September 21, 2000,

94. Graduate colloquy and panel discussion at Perkins School of Theology, Southern Methodist University, Dallas, TX, September 25, 2000.

95. Public lecture at Princeton Seminary's Center for Theological Inquiry, Tuesday, October 10, 2000.

96. Hearst Lecture at University of Northern Iowa, Cedar Falls, IA, Monday, October 23, 2000.

97. Full-day seminar and public lecture at Warren–Wilson College, Asheville, NC, December 2, 2000.

98. Manfred O. Meitzen Outstanding Guest Theological Lecture, West Virginia University, Morgantown, WV, Wednesday, February 7, 2001.

99. Public lecture, class visit, and faculty seminar at University of Oregon, Thursday and Friday, February 22–23, 2001.

100. Public lecture at DePaul University, Chicago, IL, Wednesday, March 8, 2001.

101. Student seminar and public lecture at McNeese State University, Lake Charles, LA, Friday, April 20, 2001.

102. Public lecture and Convocation Address at Averett University, Danville, VA, Monday–Tuesday, September 10–11, 2001.

103. Buckham Visiting Professor, Department of English, University of Vermont, Burlington, VT, Monday–Thursday, October 15–18, 2001 (7 classes, graduate seminar, faculty seminar, public lecture).

104. Joint lecture with Jonathan L. Reed on *Excavating Jesus: Beneath the Stones, Behind the Texts*, University of California at Riverside, CA, Monday, October 22, 2001.

105. Fasnacht Lecture on "Historical Jesus and Contemporary Christianity" (morning) and joint lecture with Jonathan L. Reed and Balage Balogh on *Excavating Jesus: Beneath the Stones, Behind the Texts* (evening), University of LaVerne. LaVerne, CA, Tuesday, October 23, 2001.

106. Joint lecture with Jonathan L. Reed on *Excavating Jesus: Beneath the Stones, Behind the Texts*, Institute for Antiquity and Christianity, Claremont Graduate University, Wednesday, October 24, 2001.

107. Seminar at Lincoln Theological Institute, University of Sheffield, England, Friday, November 9, 2001.

108. Public lecture, student class, and faculty seminar at St. Bonaventure University, St. Bonaventure, NY, Thursday, January 31, and Friday, February 1, 2002.

109. Student seminar and public lecture at Amherst College, Amherst, MA, Thursday, February 21, 2002.

110. Mary Olive Woods Annual Lecture and Faculty Seminar, Western Illinois University, Macomb, IL, February 28–March 1, 2002.

111. Cecile and Gene Usdin Judeo-Christian Lecture, Flagler College, St. Augustine, FL, Thursday, March 14, 2002.

112. Lecture on "Virgin Mother or Bastard Son" at Vanderbilt University, Nashville, TN, Monday, March 18, 2002

113. Invited keynote lecture at the New Testament Society of South Africa's annual meeting, University (Seminary) of Potchefstroom, South Africa (4/9/02).

114. Graduate seminars and/or public lectures in South Africa at the University of Pretoria (4/8/02), University of South Africa (UNISA) in Pretoria (4/16/02), University of Stellenbosch (4/17/02), University of Cape Town (4/18/02), University of Natal in Pietermaritzburg (4/22/02), University of Durban in Westville (4/23/02), and Rand Afrikaans University in Johannesburg (4/24/02).

115. Annual Arthur C. Wickenden Lectures on Religion (two), Department of Comparative Religion's 75th Anniversary Celebration, Miami University, Oxford, OH, Monday and Tuesday, October 21 and 22, 2002.

116. Keynote Address, Fifth Early Morse Wilbur History Colloquium, Unitarian Universalist Starr King School for the Ministry, Graduate Theological Faculty, Berkeley, CA, Saturday, January 25, 2003.

117. Joint lecture with Jonathan L. Reed on *Excavating Jesus: Beneath the Stones, Behind the Texts*, Regional SBL-WJSA-ASOR, St. Mary's College, Moraga, CA, Monday, March 25, 2003.

118. Lecture for Roger Williams Symposium, Washington State University, Pullman, WA, November 2, 2003.

119. Didier Seminar Lecture at the at the University of Minnesota, St. Paul, MN, February 27, 2004.

120. Fifth Annual Hurwitz Presidential Lecture on Faith, Reason, and the Imagination in the Liberal Arts, Albright College, Reading, PA, Monday, March 8, 2004.

121. Ninth Nadine Beacham and Charles F. Hall, Sr., Lectures in New Testament and Early Christianity, University of North Carolina, Columbia, SC, Thursday–Friday, April 1–2, 2004.

122. Theologian in Residence Lecture for the Ecumenical Christian Ministries at the University of Kansas, Lawrence, KS, Monday, April 19, 2004.

123. Twenty-third Annual Thomas L. King Lecture in Religious Studies at Washburn University, Topeka, KS, Tuesday, April 20, 2004.

124. Three Kellogg Lectures at Episcopal Divinity School, Cambridge, MA, Thursday-Friday, April 29-30, 2004.

125. Ring Family Lecture: "The Execution of Jesus in Gibson, Gospel, and History." Oberlin College, Oberlin, OH, November 4, 2004.

126. Lecture with Jonathan Reed on *In Search of Paul* at the University of LaVerne, LaVerne, CA, Monday, November 29, 2004.

127. Lecture with Jonathan Reed on *In Search of Paul* at the Claremont Graduate University, Claremont, CA, Tuesday, November 30, 2004.

128. Lectures and classes at Centenary College, Shreveport, LA, Tuesday-Thursday, January 18-20, 2005.

129. Lecture and discussion for the "Theological Forum" at Mid-America Baptist Theological Seminary, Germantown (Memphis), TN, Tuesday, January 25, 2005.

130. Class and lecture at the Divinity School, Vanderbilt University, Nashville, TN, Monday, February 21, 2005.

131. Lecture at Doane College, Crete, Nebraska, Tuesday, April 5. 2005.

132. Lecture on "Gospel, Gibson, and the Death of Jesus" at the University of Central Florida, Orlando, Fl, Tuesday evening, April 12, 2005.

133. Lecture (in series at Wilmot Church of Canada), St. Thomas University, Fredericton, New Brunswick, Canada, Friday, April 29, 2005.

134. Matriculation Day Lectures at the Episcopal Divinity School, Cambridge, MA, Monday, September 26, 2005.

135, Lecture on "Paul Today" for Judeo-Christian Lectures at Tulane University, New Orleans, LA, Thursday, March 2, 2006.

136. Lecture on "Jesus and Empire" for the series on "Confronting Empire." DePaul University, Chicago, IL, Monday, May 15, 2006.

137. Annual B. Frank Hall Lecture, Department of Religion and Philosophy, University of North Carolina, Wilmington, NC, March 29, +2-hour class discussion. March 30, 2007.

138. Lecture and faculty responses at Union Theological Seminary, New York, NY, Monday. November 5, 2007.

139. First Philosophy and Religious Studies Department Scholarship Benefit Lecture, University of Northern Iowa, Cedar Falls, IA, Monday, September 29, 2008.

140. Three lectures for the Walter and Mary Tuohy Chair, John Carroll University, University Heights, OH, Thursday, October 9, 2008.

141. Lilly-endowed lecture (Program on Theology and Vocation) at Transylvania College, Lexington, KY, Wednesday, February 4, 2009.

142. Two lectures and seminar participations on "God & Empire, "Seminario Evangelico de Theologia, Matanzas, Cuba, Thursday-Friday, February 12-13, 2009.

143. Public lecture and class at Central Florida Community College, Ocala, FL, Tuesday-Wednesday, February 17-18, 2009.

144. Public lecture for Willis Wood Lecture Series and class, Amherst College, Amherst, MA, Tuesday-Wednesday, February 24-25, 2009.

145. Annual Robison Lecture, Culver-Stockton College, Canton, MO, Thursday, March 5, 2009.

146. Joint Lectures with Marcus Borg, Eden Theological Seminary, St. Louis, MO, Wednesday-Thursday, April 14-15, 2009

147. Lilly Foundation Lecture at Pacific Lutheran University, Tacoma, WA, Thursday, October 15, 2009.

148. Three lectures and seminar participations on "The First Paul, "Seminario Evangelico de Theologia, Matanzas, Cuba, Thursday-Friday, February 11-12, 2010.

149. Joint Lecture with Marcus Borg, La Grange College, LaGrange, GA, Monday-Tuesday, April 12-13, 2010.

150. Public Interview with John Dart (Friday evening) and Video presentation on "Resurrection of Jesus in Eastern Christianity." (Saturday morning) at the Twenty-Fifth Anniversary Meeting of the Jesus Seminar, Santa Rosa, CA, October 15-16, 2010.

151. Participation in HarperOne seminar with A.-J. Levine, Marvin Meyer, and Brent Landau on "Prophecies and Myths Surrounding the Birth of Jesus." SBL Annual Meeting, Marriott Marquis A707, Atlanta, GA, Saturday, November 20, 2010.

151. Seminar class at Northwest Christian University, Monday, October 10, 2011.

152. Seminar for Honors College, Seminar for Religion department, and Ira E. Gaston Public Lecture, University of Oregon, Monday, October 10, 2011.

153. Lecture and two classes for the Department of Philosophy and Religion, Central Michigan University, Mt. Pleasant, MI, Tuesday-Wednesday, October 25-26, 2011.

154. AAR/SBL Annual Meeting: SBL Presidential Address, International Ballroom North, Hilton Chicago Hotel, 7:00-8:00pm, Saturday, November 17, 2012. "A Vision of Divine Justice: The Resurrection of Jesus in Eastern Christian Iconography." Published as "A Vision of Divine Justice: The Resurrection of Jesus in Eastern Christian Iconography." *Journal of Biblical Literature* 132 (2013) 1-32.

155. Class Visit, Faculty Colloquium, Public Lecture at Gonzaga University, WA, Thursday, October 3, 2013.

SCHOLARLY CONFERENCES

1. Invited paper presented on "Methodology and the Jesus Seminar" to the Chicago Society of Biblical Research, Wheaton College (25 October 1986).

2. Participation in panel discussion of my book, *In Fragments: The Aphorisms of Jesus* at Society of Biblical Literature, Annual Meeting, Atlanta, GA (23 November 1986).

3. Invited paper presented on "The Cross that Spoke: The Earliest Narrative of the Passion and Resurrection in the *Gospel of Peter* " to inaugurate new series on "Biblical Scholarship in the 21st Century." Society of Biblical Literature, Annual Meeting, Atlanta, GA (24 November 1986).

4. Paper presented on "Materials and Methods in Historical Jesus Research" at the Sixth Meeting of "The Jesus Seminar." Luther Northwestern Theological Seminary, St. Paul, MN (15–18 October 1987).

5. Two papers presented at the AAR/SBL 1987 Annual Meeting, Boston, 5–8 December 1987: (a) "Multiple Attestation in Greco-Roman Aphorisms" to the Pronouncement Stories Group, and (b) "Tradition and Development in Q" to the Q Seminar.

6. Paper presented and participated in panel discussion on "Jesus and Apocalypticism" in the Historical Jesus Section at the AAR/SBL 1989 Annual Meeting, Anaheim, CA.

7. Participation in panel discussion of my book *The Cross that Spoke. The Origins of the Passion Narrative*. (San Francisco: Harper & Row, 1988) in the Consultation on Christian Apocrypha at the AAR/SBL 1989 Annual Meeting, Anaheim, CA.

8. Paper presented on "Methodology and Data-Base in Historical Jesus Research" to the Eleventh Meeting of "The Jesus Seminar." Xavier University, Cincinnati, OH. (October 18–21, 1990).

9. Paper presented and participated in panel discussion on "Jesus as Cynic?" in the Historical Jesus Section at the AAR/SBL 1990 Annual Meeting, New Orleans, LA. (17–20 November 1990).

10. Organization and hosting of Chicago Society of Biblical Research Centennial Celebration, at DePaul University, on Saturday, April 20, 1991, from 10:30 AM to 8:00 PM. Paper delivered on "Open Healing and Open Eating: Jesus as a Jewish Cynic?"

11. Participation and response-paper delivered at the meeting of "The Jesus Seminar." University of Alberta, Edmonton, Canada (24–27 October 1991).

12. Delivery of response-paper and participation in panel discussion for the "Historical Jesus Section" during the Society of Biblical Literature Annual Meeting, Kansas City, KS (23–26 November 1991) "In What Sense History? A Response to Craig Evans' paper "In What Sense 'Blasphemy'? Jesus before Caiaphas in Mark 16:61–62."

13. Delivery of response-paper and participation in panel discussion for the "Greco-Roman Religions Group" during the Society of Biblical Literature Annual Meeting, Kansas City, KS (23-26 November 1991) "Official Religion and Popular Religion: Thoughts about Jonathan Z. Smith's *Drudgery Divine.*"
14. Delivery of paper at "The Jesus Seminar." Rutgers University, New Brunswick, NJ (22-25 October 1992) "Orality and the Miracles of the Jesus Tradition."
15. Participation in panel discussion of my book *The Historical Jesus. The Life of a Mediterranean Jewish Peasant* (San Francisco: HarperSanFrancisco, 1991) in the Historical Jesus Section at the AAR/SBL 1992 Annual Meeting, San Francisco, CA.
16. Participation in panel discussion on "Christian Apopcrypha and the Arts" in the Intertextuality in Christian Apocrypha Seminar at the AAR/SBL 1992 Annual Meeting, San Francisco, CA.
17. Participation in panel discussion for the 1993 Historical Jesus Seminar, Canadian Society of Biblical Studies, Carleton University, Ottawa, Canada (Wednesday, June 9, 1993).
18. Participation in panel discussion with John P. Meier (Catholic University) and Roger Haight, S.J. (Weston School of Theology) on "Contrasting Approaches to the Historical Jesus" at the Fifty-Sixth General Meeting of the Catholic Biblical Association of America, Mount Community Center, Atchison, KS (Monday, August 16, 1993).
19. Delivery of paper, debate, and response for "The Historical Jesus: Conversations with John Dominic Crossan and Nicholas Thomas Wright." a six-hour session at the Society of Biblical Literature Twelfth International Meeting, Katholieke Universiteit Leuven, Belgium, 7-10 August,1994.
20. Participation on panel sponsored by the *ad hoc* Committee on the Public Understanding of Religion during the American Academy of Religion Annual Meeting, Chicago, IL (November 19-22, 1994), on "Reaching a General Audience."
21. Delivery of paper-response for joint session of Archaeology of the New Testament World and Historical Jesus Section during the Society of Biblical Literature Annual Meeting, Chicago, IL (November 19-22, 1994) "Issues in the Integration of Material and Literary Remains."
22. Delivery of paper for session of Intertextuality in Christian Apocrypha Seminar during the Society of Biblical Literature Annual Meeting, Philadelphia, PA (November 18-21, 1995) "The *Gospel of Peter* and the Canonical Gospels."
23. Delivery of response to four papers for "Women and the (Search for the) Historical Jesus." co-sponsored by the Women in the Biblical World Section and Historical Jesus Section, during the Society of Biblical Literature Annual Meeting, New Orleans, LA (November 23-26, 1996).
24. Invited participation on panel, "Method in Historical Jesus Research." Southeastern Region of the Society of Biblical Literature, Macon, GA (March 14, 1997).

25. Paper presented at International Conference on Religion and Postmodernism at Villanova University (September 25-27, 1997) "Our Own Faces in Deep Wells: A Future for Historical Jesus Research."

26. Participation on panel discussion of "Method in Historical Jesus Research." Historical Jesus Section, the Society of Biblical Literature Annual Meeting, San Francisco, CA (November 22-25, 1997).

27. Paper presentation and panel participation in Department of Religion Bible Symposium at Florida Southern College, Lakeland, FL (January 22-33, 1998) "Who Do You Say that I Am? Jesus Scholarship at the End of the Twentieth Century."

28. Paper presentation at the International Conference on the Images of Jesus, Chapman University, Orange, CA (November 15-17, 1999) "Eschatology, Apocalypticism, and the Historical Jesus."

29. Panelist for "Commercial Publishing and the Public Scholar" and for "Representations of Jews and Judaism in Current Work on the Historical Jesus" (Historical Jesus Section), during the Society of Biblical Literature Annual Meeting, Boston, MA (November 20-23, 1999).

30. Paper presentation at the International Conference on the Trial of Jesus, Netanya Academic College, School of Law, Netanya, Israel, March 7, 2000.

31. Paper presentation and panelist for "Special Session: The Historical Jesus and Galilean Archaeology in 2000." during the Society Biblical Literature Annual Meeting, Nashville, TN (November 18-21, 2000).

32. Response presentation to Adriana Destro and Mauro Pesce, *The Birth of a Religion: The Community of John and Its Early History* (Italian version), for the Italian Evening Reception, during the Society Biblical Literature Annual Meeting, Nashville, TN (November 18-21, 2000).

33. Response presentation to Hal Childs, *The Myth of the Historical Jesus and the Evolution of Consciousness: John Dominic Crossan's Quest in Psychological Perspective*, for the Psychology and Biblical Studies Section of the Society Biblical Literature Annual Meeting, Nashville, TN (November 18-21, 2000).

34. Response to N. T. Wright, *The Resurrection of the Son of God*, Evangelical Philosophical Society (I), AAR-SBL Annual Meeting, 7:00-10:00pm, Saturday, November 22, 2003 (Hyatt/Montreal-Vancouver), Atlanta, GA.

35. Response to Richard Swinburne, "On the Resurrection." Evangelical Philosophical Society (II), AAR-SBL Annual Meeting, 7:00-8:30pm, Sunday, November 23, 2003 (Marriott Marquis/Tigris), Atlanta, GA.

36. Panel discussion with Kathleen Corley and Jane Schaberg on "Women and the Historical Jesus" with paper on "Jesus and Women." Historical Jesus Section (I), AAR-SBL Annual Meeting, 9:00-11:30am, Monday, November 24, 2003 (Hyatt/Centennial III-IV), Atlanta, GA.

37. Five lectures (four hours apiece) for the GTU Cooperative Summer Session at the Pacific School of Religion, Berkeley, CA, Monday-Friday, July 12-16, 2004.

38. Seminar on "The Prospect of a World Community of Religions: Domination or Collaboration" (Arvind Sharma), Millsaps College and the D. L. Dykes, Jr., Foundation, Jackson, MS, Wednesday–Friday, October 13–15, 2004.

39. Seminar on "The New Testament and the Roman Empire" at Union Theological Seminary, New York, NY, Friday–Saturday, October 29–30, 2004.

40. Seminar on *The Resurrection of the Son of God* with Bishop N. T. Wright, Evangelical Theological Society Annual Meeting. San Antonio, TX, Friday (morning), November 19, 2004.

41. Response to paper on "The Historical Jesus and the Gospel of Thomas." Evangelical Theological Society Annual Meeting. San Antonio, TX, Friday (afternoon), November 19, 2004.

42. Participation in the Presidential Forum on Mel Gibson's *The Passion of the Christ*, American Schools of Oriental Research, Annual Meeting, San Antonio, TX, Friday (evening), November 19, 2004.

43. Response and participation on panel reviewing James D. G. Dunn, *Jesus Remembered*. Volume 1 of *Christianity in the Making* (Grand Rapids: Eerdmans, 2003), Historical Jesus Section, Session 1, AAR/SBL Annual Meeting, Monday, November 22, 2004.

44. Paper and panel participation on "The Authority of the Bible." Review of Bart D. Ehrman's *Misquoting Jesus* and N.T. Wright's *The Last Word*. SBL Annual Meeting, Philadelphia, PA, Saturday, November 19, 2005.

45. Paper, "Honest to Bob: In Memory of Robert W. Funk." SBL Annual Meeting, Philadelphia, PA, Monday, November 21, 2005.

46. Paper on "Text and Artifact: Paul and the Archaeology of Roman Imperial Theology," and panel participation for the SBL and Institute for Antiquity and Christianity Seminar on "The Future of the Past." SBL Annual Meeting, Philadelphia, PA, Monday, November 21, 2005.

47. Two Lectures on Jesus and Paul for the Japan Bible Society at the International Bible Forum, Tokyo, Japan, Wed–Fri, May 3–5, 2006.

48. Distinguished Visiting Professor for five lectures (three hours apiece), Chalmers Summer School, Week 4, Vancouver School of Theology, Vancouver, Canada, Monday–Friday, July 24–28, 2006.

49. Lecture at the King Fahd Center for Middle East and Islamic Studies, University of Arkansas, Fayetteville, AK, October 12, 2006.

50. Two lectures, one for the Honors College and one for the Center for the Study of Spirituality, Florida International University, Miami, FL, Thursday, November 9, 2006.

51. Three lectures on "Religion and Violence" (2/14, 2/28, 3/7), Program in Religious Studies, Department of Philosophy, University of Central Florida, Orlando, FL,

February 14 ("Civilization and Violence"), February 18 ("Bible and Violence"), March 7 ("Apocalypse and Violence").

52. Opening and closing lectures at the *I Simpósio Internacional do Jesus Historico*, Universidade Federal do Rio de Janeiro (UFRJ), Brazil, Tuesday–Thursday, October 16–18, 2007.

53. Faculty Seminar at the University of Brasilia (UnB) and public lecture at the Franciscan School of Philosophy and Theology, Brasilia, Brazil, Monday, October 22, 2007.

54. Three lectures for *"Jesus de Nazaré em Debate: Diálogo com John Dominic Crossan."* Universidade Metodista de São Paulo (UMESP), Tuesday–Thursday, October 23–25, 2007.

55. Lecture at Fortress Press Annual Breakfast for Lutheran Professors and Graduate Students, AAR–SBL Annual Meeting, San Diego, CA, Sunday, November 18, 2007.

56. Lecture on "Assessing the Legacy of Robert W. Funk." AAR–SBL Annual Meeting, San Diego, CA, Sunday, November 18, 2007.

57. Participation in AAR–SBL Annual Meeting, San Francisco, CA, Friday–Tuesday, November 18–22, 2011: (1) HarperOne Panel on *Believers, Scholars, and Culture: Assessing the Impact of Two Centuries of Critical Biblical Scholarship* [Crossan, Ehrman, Levine, and Wright]; (2) SBL Historical Jesus Section paper on "From Abba–Cry to Father–Prayer"; (3) SBL Christian Apocrypha Section, panel to review of Paul Foster's *Gospel of Peter*.

58. Participation in AAR–SBL Annual Meeting, Saturday–Tuesday, November 21–24, 2015: (1) Westar Institute Panel *on New Interpretations of Paul* to review Bernard Brandon Scott, *The Real Paul; Recovering His Radical Challenge* (Polebridge Press, 2015), Sunday, November 22, 4:00–5:00pm; (2) SBL–Westar Institute Public Lecture on *Interpreting Divine Violence in the Bible*, Tuesday, November 24, 9:30–10:30am.

59. Participation in AAR–SBL Annual Meeting, Saturday–Tuesday, November 19–22, 2016: (1) Historical Jesus Session 1. Panel on *Parables and the Historical Jesus: The State of the Question* (with John Meier, Klyne Snodgrass, R. Steven Notley, and Ruben Zimmerman; A.J. Levine, presider), Saturday, November 19, 1:00–3:30pm; (2) Joint Panel on Bible and Popular Culture with Bible and Film, to review Matthew S. Rindge, *Profane Parables: Film and the American Dream* (Baylor University Press, 2016).

PUBLIC LECTURES

1. "Two-days of Dialogue about Jesus." United Methodist Church, Arch Street, Philadelphia, PA, 7–8 May 1986.

2. "A Fifth Gospel: Peter Tells All." Sheil Center, Roman Catholic Campus Ministry, Northwestern University, 23 February 1989.

3. Panelist for Professor Milt Rosenberg on "The Historical Jesus." WGN Radio 720AM, 9:00–11:00 PM, Thursday, May 31, 1990.

4. Panelist (by conference call) for Fred Anderly, over National Public Radio via WOSU, Columbus, Ohio, on "The Historical Jesus." 2:30–3:45 PM, Tuesday, April 2, 1991.

5. Panelist for CBC (Canada) Radio discussion on the historical Jesus, Sunday, October 27, 1991.

6. For interactions with the media concerning my book *The Historical Jesus. The Life of a Mediterranean Jewish Peasant*. San Francisco: HarperSanFrancisco, 1991.

7. "Jesus the Jewish Peasant: Does Fact Challenge Faith?" *Ekklesia* 13th Lecture Series, Oak Park, IL, 9:30–12:00 noon, Wednesday, 18 March, 1992.

8. "The Historical Jesus." Chicago Authors Program, Union League Club, 11:30–1:30PM, Wednesday, 15 April 1992.

9. "The Historical Jesus and Christmas-time Stories." Annual Convention of the Religion Newswriters Association, Louisville, KT, Saturday, May 9, 1992.

10. "The Historical Jesus." monthly meeting of the Chicago area *Mensa* Society, Ramada Hotel O'Hare, IL, Sunday, May 31, 1992.

11. "The Jesus of History and Our Ministry Today." Catholic Conference of Illinois, Department of Campus Ministry, Continuing Education Workshop, at Carmelite Center, Aylesford (Darien), IL, Thursday–Friday, October 15–16, 1992.

12. "The Historical Jesus: The Life of a Mediterranean Peasant." Theology South Lecture Series, Saint Xavier University, Chicago, IL, Thursday, December 10, 1992.

13. "The Historical Jesus." Lake Shore Unitarian Society, Winnetka, Sunday, February 7, 1993.

14. "The Historical Jesus." Northminister Presbyterian Church, Evanston, IL, Sunday, March 28, 1993.

15. "Jesus, the Jewish Peasant." Ladies Theology of Park Ridge, Wednesday, March 31, 1993.

16. "Jesus: A Jewish Peasant." The Fourth Annual Consultation Sponsored by the Christian Associates of Southwest Pennsylvania, St. Nicholas Cathedral, Pittsburgh, Sunday, May 16, 1993.

17. About 40 radio programs (either taped for later broadcast or live with call-ins) on *Jesus: A Revolutionary Biography*, coast to coast in sixteen states, November 1993 to March 1994.

18. "The Parables of Jesus." Episcopal Church of the Holy Comforter Continuing Education, Kenilworth, IL Wednesday, February 9, 1994.

19. "The Historical Jesus and Contemporary Faith." A special satellite uplinked creative conversation with Burton Mack and Marcus Borg, sponsored by Grace Cathedral of San Francisco, Harper Collins, and Trinity Institute of New York, at the Mark Hopkins Hotel (3–5 PM) and Grace Cathedral (7–9 PM), Saturday, February 19, 1994.

20. Four lectures on *Jesus: A Revolutionary Biography* to the Associates of the Jesus Seminar, Santa Rosa, CA, Thursday, March 3, 1994.

21. Lecture on the historical Jesus at Heritage United Methodist Church, Littleton, CO, and the Tattered Cover Bookstore's Series on Spirituality, Sunday, November 13, 1994.

22. Lecture on the historical Jesus at Theology South Group, Saint Xavier University, Chicago, IL, Thursday, December 1, 1994.

23. Lecture on the historical Jesus at the Lake Shore Unitarian Society, Winnetka, Sunday, December 4, 1994.

24. Lecture on the historical Jesus at Glenview Community Church (United Church of Christ), Wednesday, February 15, 1995.

25. Lecture on the historical Jesus at St. Chrysostom's Church, Chicago, IL, Wednesday, March 15, 1995.

26. Lecture on the historical Jesus for Rabbi Samuel Gordon's Interfaith Family Network, Wilmette, IL, Wednesday, March 29, 1995.

27. Lectures on the historical Jesus at St. Joan of Arc and St. Stephen's Churches, Minneapolis, MN, Friday–Saturday, March 31–April 1, 1995.

28. Five lectures on the historical Jesus at Kirkridge Retreat and Study Center, Bangor, PA, Friday–Sunday, April 21–23, 1995.

29. Lecture on the historical Jesus for Rabbi Samuel Gordon's Interfaith Family Network, Chicago, IL, Monday, June 12, 1995

30. Panel with Rosemary Radford Ruether and Martin Marty on "Christianity and the Library" at the American Library Association's Summer Meeting, Hilton Hotel and Towers, Chicago, IL, Sunday, June 25, 1995.

31. Interviews filmed on location in Rome and Ravenna for four-part BBC series on The Historical Jesus, Monday and Wednesday, July 24 and 26, 1995.

32. Debate with Dr. William Lane Craig entitled "Will the Real Jesus Please Stand Up." moderated by Mr. William F. Buckley, Jr., Sunday, September 24, 1995, Moody Church, Chicago.

33. Full-day lecture to Associates on *Who Killed Jesus?* and participation in the meeting of the Jesus Seminar, Santa Rosa, CA (October 25–29, 1995).

34. Lecture on the historical Jesus at Grace Place (Jewish, Episcopalian, and Lutheran communities), Chicago, IL, Monday, April 15, 1996.

35. "The Historical Jesus and Christian Faith." Lake Shore Unitarian Society, Winnetka, Sunday, April 21, 1996.

36. "Jesus at 2000: The Conversation Continues." with Marcus Borg, Deirdre Goode, Luke Timothy Johnson, N. T. Wright, Episcopal Teleconferencing Network, Trinity Institute, New York, NY, Wednesday, May 1, 1996.
37. Two lectures and panel discussion for the Consultation XXII on Parish Ministry, United Church of Christ Annual Convocation, Orlando, FL, Tuesday-Thursday, January 7-9, 1997.
38. Three programs for Odyssey TV Channel, National Interfaith Cable Coalition, Trinity Place, NY, taped Nashville, TN (Stone and Associates), Monday, January 13, 1997.
39. Two lectures at United Church of Christ, Gainesville, FL, Friday and Saturday, January 17-18, 1997.
40. Lecture for Washington Hebrew Congregation's Sunday Scholar Series, Washington, DC, Sunday, 16 March, 1997.
41. Screening and discussion of excerpted summary from PBS' 4-hour *Frontline* series, "From Jesus to Christ: The First Christians." WMFE (PBS) and Rollins College, Orlando, FL, 7:00-9:00 PM, Tuesday, March 31, 1998.
42. Lecture for Unitarian Universalist Christian Fellowship at the Unitarian Universalist General Assembly, Rochester, NY, Monday, June 29, 1998.
43. Full-day seminar with Unitarian Universalist Ministers, San Pedro Retreat Centre, Orlando, FL, Tuesday, October 13, 1998.
44. Rising Lecture under ecumenical auspices of Methodist, Presbyterian, and Roman Catholic Churches, Pittsburgh, KS, November 1, 1998.
45. Seminars and sermons under the ecumenical auspices of Congregational, Methodist, and Lutheran Churches, Aurora, IL, November 7-8, 1998.
46. Lecture, seminar, adult forum, and sermon, and discussion at Christ Community Church, Spring Lake, MI, February 19-21, 1999.
47. Lecture, seminar, adult forum, and sermon at The Center for Spiritual Development, Trinity Episcopal Cathedral, Portland, OR, March 6-7, 1999.
48. Lecture at St. Matthew Catholic Church, Winter Haven, FL, Friday, March 12, 1999.
49. Lecture, seminar, adult forum, and sermon at Winnetka Congregational Church, Winnetka, IL, March 19-21, 1999.
50. Five lectures at Kirkridge Retreat Center, Bangor, PA, Friday-Sunday, May 21-23, 1999.
51. Two-days of lectures at Five Oaks United Church of Canada Education and Retreat Centre, Paris (west of Toronto), Ontario, Canada, June 4, 1999.
52. Lecture tour of New Zealand, July 13-31, 1999, with one-day seminars in Nelson (8/14), Dunedin (8/22), Napier (8/26), Hamilton (8/29), and two-day seminars in Christchurch (8/16-17), Wellington (8/23-24), and Auckland (8/30-31).

53. Lecture at the First United Methodist Church of Orlando, August 25, 1999.
54. All-day seminar at the Unitarian Church of Tulsa, October 9, 1999.
55. Lecture as part of Westar Institute's Conference on "The Once and Future Jesus." October 20-24, 1999.
56. Lecture, seminar, adult forum, and sermon at Myers Park Baptist Church, Charlotte, NC, November 12–14, 1999.
57. E-group seminar on Jesus and apocalypticism for BeliefNet.com, January 17–February 14, 2000.
58. Seminar, adult forum, and sermon at United Church of Christ Congregational, Ames, IA, February 5–6, 2000.
59. Lecture at Church of Our Savior, Arlington, MA, February 23, 2000.
60. Dialogue with A.-J. Levine on historical Jesus, Christ Community Church, Spring Lake, MI, March 17–19, 2000.
61. Seminar, adult forum, and sermon at First United Methodist Church, Orlando, FL, March 25–26, 2000.
62. Lecture, seminar, and sermons at St. Bartholomew's Episcopal Church, Yarmouth, ME, April 7–9, 2000.
63. Five lectures for Department of Religion, Chautauqua Institution, Chautauqua, NY, July 17–21, 2000.
64. Three lectures at St. Mark's Episcopal Church, Niagara-on-the-Lake, Ontario, Canada, July 21–22, 2000.
65. Two lectures at Center for Spiritual Development, Trinity Episcopal Cathedral, Portland, OR, September 15 and 17, 2000.
66. Lecture at Trinity Episcopal Cathedral, San Jose, CA, September 20, 2000.
67. Lecture at First Congregational Church, Berkeley, CA, September 22, 2000.
68. Interview for Grace Online, Grace Episcopal Cathedral, San Francisco, CA, September 24, 2000.
69. Lecture at Fourth Presbyterian Church, Michigan Avenue, Chicago, IL, Wednesday, October 3, 2000.
70. Lecture at Harvard University's Memorial Church, Cambridge, MA, Friday, October 6, 2000.
71. Lecture at Center for Religious Inquiry, St. Barth's Church, 109 East 50th Street, New York, NY, Wednesday, October 11, 2000.
72. Lecture at Madison Avenue Presbyterian Church, 921 Madison Avenue, New York, NY, Thursday, October 12, 2000.
73. Lecture for the Program and Ministries Department, Washington National Cathedral, Massachusetts and Wisconsin Avenues, NW, DC, Friday, October 20, 2000.

74. Talk and discussion with local ministers, Cedar Falls, IA, Monday, October 23, 2000.
75. Three lectures at the Sixteenth Annual Florida Winter Pastors' School, Stetson University, DeLand, FL, Tuesday and Wednesday, January 30–31, 2001.
76. Lecture, seminar, sermon, and forum at Sixth Presbyterian Church, Pittsburgh, PA, Friday–Sunday, February 9–11, 2001.
77. Lecture, seminar, sermon, and forum at First United Methodist Church, Eugene, OR, Friday–Sunday, February 23–25, 2001.
78. Lecture at St. James Episcopal Cathedral, Chicago, IL, Thursday, March 8, 2001.
79. Lecture, seminar, sermon, and forum at Grace Episcopal Church, Oak Park, IL, Friday–Sunday, March 9–11, 2001.
80. Four-lecture seminar at the Foundation for Contemporary Theology, Houston, TX, Friday–Saturday, April 27–28, 2001.
81. Sermon and three Craven-Wilson Lectures at St. Paul's United Methodist Church, Houston, TX, Sunday–Monday, April 29–30, 2001.
82. Lecture, seminar, sermons, and forum at St. James Episcopal Church, San Francisco, CA, Friday–Sunday, May 11–13, 2001.
83. Five lectures for the 33rd annual meeting of the Atlantic Seminar in Theological Education (ASTE), NS Agricultural College, Truro, Nova Scotia, Canada, Monday–Thursday, June 11–14, 2001.
84. Five lectures and five pastors' seminars for Department of Religion, Chautauqua Institution, Chautauqua, NY, Monday–Friday, July 16–20, 2001.
85. Lecture at Canisius College and workshop at Westminster Presbyterian Church for the College's Center for the Global Study of Religion and the Network of Religious Communities in its "Conversations in Christ and Culture Series." Friday–Saturday, July 20–21, 2001.
86. Joint conversation with A.-J. Levine on Judaism and Christianity, Washington National Cathedral, Friday, October 12, 2001.
87. Kendig Cully/Christian Century Lecture, Cathedral Church of St. Paul, Burlington, VT, Sunday, October 14, 2001.
88. Lecture, seminar, sermon, and adult forum at Myers Park Baptist Church, Charlotte, NC, Friday–Sunday, October 26–28, 2001.
89. Lecture, seminar, sermon and adult forum at St. Mark's Anglican Church, Broomhill, Sheffield, England, Friday–Sunday, November 9–11, 2001.
90. Joint lecture with Jonathan L. Reed on *Excavating Jesus: Beneath the Stones, Behind the Texts*, Additional Meeting (sponsored by HarperSanFrancisco), AAR-SBL Annual Meetings, Denver, CO, Sunday, November 18, 2001.

91. Joint lecture with Jonathan L. Reed on *Excavating Jesus: Beneath the Stones, Behind the Texts*, Center for Spiritual Development, Trinity Episcopal Cathedral, Portland, OR, Friday and Saturday, November 30 and December 1, 2001.

92. Five lectures at Kirkridge Retreat Center, Bangor, Friday–Sunday, March 8–10, 2002.

93. Three lectures, sermon, and adult forum at Christ Church Episcopalian Cathedral, Nashville, TN, Saturday–Sunday March 15–16, 2002.

94. Evening lecture at Christ the King Roman Catholic Church. Nashville, TN, Sunday, March 17, 2002.

95. Palm Sunday sermons at Grace Episcopal Cathedral, San Francisco, CA, Sunday, March 24, 2002.

96. Evening lecture at Kanata, Ottawa, and lecture series at Stewart House Retreat Center, Pakenham, Ontario, Canada, Thursday–Saturday, June 6–8, 2002.

97. Three-day lecture series with Marcus Borg, Center for Spiritual Development, Trinity Episcopal Cathedral, Portland, OR, Tuesday–Thursday, June 18–20, 2002.

98. Weekend of lectures at New Covenant Community (Disciples, UCC, and Presbyterian), Bloomington-Normal, IL, Friday–Sunday, September 6–8, 2002.

99. First Annual Judeo–Christian Relations Lectures (two), sponsored by Temple Sinai, Loyola University, Tulane University, and the University of New Orleans, New Orleans, LA, Wednesday and Thursday, October 9 and 10, 2002.

100. Two-day seminar at Five Oaks United Church of Canada Education and Retreat Centre, Paris (west of Toronto), Ontario, Canada, Monday–Tuesday, November 4–5, 2002.

101. Two-day seminar Growth Pointe Mental Health Center, Jacksonville, FL, February 7–8, 2003.

102. Sermons, adult forum, evening lecture, full-day seminar at Memorial Presbyterian Church, St. Augustine, FL, Sunday–Monday, February 23–24, 2003.

103. Full-day seminar and sermons at Cross Creek Community Church, United Church of Christ, Dayton, OH, March 1–2, 2003.

104. Evening lecture, all-day seminar, sermons, adult forum at United Methodist Church of Red Bank, Red Bank, NJ, March 7–9, 2003.

105. Two-days of joint lectures and adult forum with Tex Sample on "Preserving the Sacred while Engaging Biblical Scholarship" for the D. L. Dykes Jr. Foundation and St. Andrew's Episcopal Cathedral, Jackson, MS, March 14–16, 2002.

106. Evening lecture, all-day seminar, sermon, adult forum at Swarthmore Presbyterian Church, Swarthmore, PA, Friday–Sunday, March 21–23, 2003.

107. Single lecture at Unity of Naples, Naples, FL, Saturday, April 12, 2003.

108. Three lectures for Dimensions of Faith, St. Matthew's Episcopal Church, Louisville, KY, Sunday, April 27, 2003.

109. Three and a half-day lecture series with Marcus Borg, Center for Spiritual Development, Trinity Episcopal Cathedral, Portland, OR, Tuesday–Friday, June 23–July 1, 2003.

110. Evening lecture at Trinity Episcopal Cathedral, Cleveland, OH, Thursday, September 4, 2003.

111. Evening lecture, all-day seminar, sermon, adult forum, at St. Paul's Episcopal Church, Akron, OH, Friday–Sunday, September 5–7, 2003.

112. Evening lecture, all-day seminar, and adult forum for the Center for Spiritual Enrichment, Basking Ridge Presbyterian Church, Basking Ridge, NJ, Friday–Sunday, October 17–19, 2003.

113. Five lectures on the historical Paul at Kirkridge Retreat and Study Center, Bangor, PA, Friday–Sunday, October 24–26, 2003.

114. Three lectures at Pullman Presbyterian Church, Pullman, WA, Monday, November 2, 2003.

115. Four lectures at the Foundation for Contemporary Theology, Houston, TX, Friday–Saturday, November 7–8, 2003.

116. Three lectures on "Literalism and Fundamentalism" at Grace St.Paul's Episcopal Church, Tucson, AZ, Friday–Saturday, November 14–15, 2003.

117. Five lectures and sermons at Unity of Naples Church, Naples, FL. Friday–Sunday, December 5–7, 2003.

118. MacKenzie Lecture, Sermon, and Adult Education Class at First Congregational Church of the United Church of Christ, Boulder, CO, Saturday–Sunday, February 708, 2004.

119. Lecture at United Disciples Fellowship and First Congregational Church of San Jose, San Jose, CA, Sunday February 15, 2004.

120. Lectures for the Didier Seminar at the House of Hope Presbyterian Church, St. Paul, MN, February 28–29, 2004.

121. Three lectures for the Colonial Foundation for Contemporary Theology, Colonial United Church of Christ, Prairie Village, KS, March 12–13, 2004.

122. Three lectures and two discussion sessions for the SnowStar Institute of Religion Annual Conference, Sheraton Fallsview, Niagara Falls, ON, Canada, March 17–18, 2004.

123. Theologian in Residence Lectures at Plymouth Congregational Church, Lawrence, KS, Sunday, April 18, 2004.

124. Lecture on the Jesus Seminar at Central Congregational Church, Topeka, KS, Tuesday, April 20, 2004.

125. Inaugural David P. Lyons Lectureship in Theology, First United Methodist Church, Madison, WI (3 lectures, sermon, adult forum) Friday–Sunday, April 24–25, 2004.

126. Five lectures at Servanthood House, Asheville, NC, Friday–Sunday, May 7–9, 2004.

127. Three lectures for the Center for Spiritual Formation, St. James Episcopal Church, Baton Rouge, LA, Friday–Saturday, May 14–15, 2004.

128. Three-day seminar with Marcus Borg and James Wallis, "Toward a Theology of Power." Center for Spiritual Development, Trinity Episcopal Cathedral, Portland, OR, Tuesday–Thursday, June 22–24, 2004.

129. Five-day seminar with Marcus Borg at Ring Lake Ranch, Dubois, WY, Monday–Friday, August 2–6, 2004.

130. Five lectures and sermons at Wayside Presbyterian Church. Erie, PA, Friday–Sunday, October 8–10, 2004.

131. Five lectures and sermon at Knox United Church, Calgary, Alberta, Canada, Friday–Sunday, October 22–24, 2004.

132. Four lectures, sermon, and Adult Forum at Coral Gables Congregational Church, Coral Gables, FL, Friday–Sunday, November 12–14, 2004.

133. Evening lecture at the Free Library of Philadelphia, Philadelphia, PA, Tuesday, November 16, 2004.

134. Evening lecture at St. Bartholomew's Church's Center for Religious Inquiry, New York, NY, Wednesday, November 17, 2004.

135. Evening lecture with Jonathan Reed on *In Search of Paul* at the First Congregational Church of Berkeley, Berkeley, CA, Wednesday, December 1, 2004.

136. Evening lecture with Jonathan Reed on *In Search of Paul* at Saint Gregory of Nyssa Episcopal Church, San Francisco, CA, Thursday, December 2, 2004.

137. Four lectures with Jonathan Reed on *In Search of Paul* at the Center for Spiritual Development, Trinity Episcopal Cathedral, Portland, OR, Friday–Saturday, December 3–4, 2004.

138. Evening lecture with Jonathan Reed on *In Search of Paul* at St. Mark's Episcopal Cathedral, Seattle, WA, Monday, December 6, 2004.

139. Evening lecture with Jonathan Reed on *In Search of Paul* at University Temple United Methodist Church, Seattle, WA, Wednesday, December 8, 2004.

140. Four lectures, sermons, and Adult Forum at Center for Spiritual Development, Trinity Episcopal Cathedral, Portland, OR. Friday–Sunday, February 4–6. 2005.

141. Three lectures at St. Paul's Episcopal Church, Franklin (Nashville), TN, Friday and Sunday, February 18 and 20, 2005.

142. Three lectures, three sermons, and adult Forum at Christ Church Cathedral, Nashville, TN, Saturday–Sunday, February 19–20, 2005.

143. Five lectures and sermon for the Arizona Foundation for Contemporary Theology, Trinity Episcopal Cathedral, Phoenix, AZ, and Via de Cristo United Methodist Church, Scottsdale, AZ, Friday-Sunday, February 25-27, 2005.

144. Five lectures and sermons at St. Peter's Episcopal Church, Carson City, NV, Friday-Sunday, March 4-6, 2005.

145. The Greer-Heard Point-Counter-Point Forum on Faith and Culture, with N. T. Wright, Bishop of Durham, and responses to papers at the Southwest Regional meeting of the Evangelical Theological Society papers (Gary Habermas, Charles Quayle, William Lane Craig) New Orleans Baptist Theological Seminary, New Orleans, LA, Friday-Saturday, March 11-12, 2005.

146. Gregory Lecture at First-Plymouth Congregational Church, Lincoln, NE. Wednesday, April 6, 2005.

147. Four lectures, sermons, and Adult Forum for The Chrysalis Group and St. Paul's Episcopal Church, Richmond, VA, Friday-Sunday, April 8-10, 2005.

148. Four lectures, sermons, and Adult Forum for Horizons of Faith, First United Methodist Church, Omaha, NE, Friday-Sunday, April 15-17, 2005.

149. Seven lectures at Five Oaks Retreat Center, Paris, Ontario, Canada, Friday-Sunday, April 22-24, 2005.

150. Five lectures at Wilmot United Church of Canada (including one at St. Thomas University), Fredericton, New Brunswick, Canada, Thursday-Saturday, April 28-30, 2005.

151. Three lectures for the Southern Points Associations for Exploring Religion (SPAFER), Birmingham, AL, Friday-Saturday, May 6-7, 2005.

152. Four lectures and three sermons on Jesus at First Community Church, Columbus, OH, Friday-Sunday, May 13-15, 2005.

153. One lecture at Trinity United Church, Smith Falls, ON, and four lectures at Chalmers United Church, Kingston, ON, Canada, May 18-20, 2005.

154. Four lectures at Grace Episcopal Church, Nyack, NY, Friday-Saturday, June 3-4, 2005.

155. Three-day joint seminar on "Mysticism, Empowerment, and Resistance" with Marcus Borg and Sister Joan Chittester O.S.B. at the Center for Spiritual Development, Trinity Episcopal Cathedral, Portland, OR, Wednesday-Friday, June 15-17, 2005.

156. Two lectures for the Collegiate Peaks Forum Series, Buena Vista, CO, Friday-Saturday, July 22-23, 2005.

157. Introduction and four 3-hour lectures on the historical Jesus for CHARIS Program, Concordia College, Moorhead, MN, at Thunderbird Lodge, Rainy Lake, MN, Sunday-Thursday, August 7-11, 2005.

158. Five-day seminar with Marcus Borg at Ring Lake Ranch, Dubois, WY, Monday-Friday, August 20-26, 2005.

159. Formal debate with Dr. James R. White of Alpha and Omega Ministries (Golden Gate Baptist Theological Seminary), "Is the Orthodox, Biblical/Canonical Account of the Life of Jesus of Nazareth Authentic and Historically Accurate?" Seattle, WA, 7:00–11:00pm, Saturday, August 27, 2005.

160. Three lectures at Unitarian Universalist Church, Baton Rouge, LA, Friday–Saturday, September 16–17, 2005.

161. Three Lectures for the Salem Atheneum, Salem, MA, Saturday, September 24, 2005.

162. Annual Bentley Memorial Lecture at The First Church in Salem (Unitarian), Salem, MA, Sunday, September 25, 2005.

163. Five lectures and sermon at First Congregational United Church of Christ, Guilford, CT, Friday–Sunday, September 30–October 2, 2005.

164. Five lectures for the Carol Ann Wallace Distinguished Lectureship in Human Values at Winona State University Rochester Center and Christ United Methodist Church, Rochester, MN, Friday–Saturday, October 6–8, 2005.

165. Five lectures "In Search of Paul" at Kirkridge Retreat and Study Center, Bangor, PA, Friday–Sunday, October 14–16, 2005.

166. Sermons and lecture at Unity Church of Dallas, Dallas, TX, Sunday October 23, 2005.

167. Five lectures for Religious Studies Department, Millsap College, and David L. Dykes, Jr., Foundation, Jackson, MS, Thursday–Saturday, October 27–30, 2005.

168. The Annual Ann Evans Woodall Lecture, All Saints Episcopal Church, Atlanta, GA, Thursday, November 3, 2005.

169. Single lecture for the Philadelphia Theological Institute at the Episcopal Cathedral, Philadelphia, PA, Friday, November 18, 2005.

170. Two lectures for St Richard's Episcopal Church, Winter Park (Orlando), FL, Saturday, December 3, 2005.

171. Four lectures (Roley Series), sermon, and Adult Forum at Madison Square Presbyterian Church, San Antonio, TX, Friday–Sunday, January 27–29, 2006.

172. Two lectures at Presbyterian Church of the Covenant and First Lutheran Church, Greensboro, NC, Friday–Saturday, February 17–18, 2006.

173. Four lectures and sermon at the Unitarian Church, Baton Rouge, LA, Friday–Sunday, March 3–5, 2006.

174. Three annual Montview Lectures, sermons, and Churchwide Forum at Montview Boulevard Presbyterian Church, Denver, CO, Friday–Sunday, March 3–5, 2006.

175. Three lectures and joint discussions with Marcus Borg and Joan Chittester on "Mysticism, Empowerment, and Resistance." First Baptist Church, Austin, TX, Thursday–Saturday, May 18–20, 2006.

176. Three-day Summer Seminar on "The Bible in the 21st Century" with Marcus Borg and Barbara Rossing, The Center for Spiritual Development, Trinity Episcopal Cathedral, Portland, OR. Monday–Wednesday, June 19–21, 2006.

177. Four lectures, sermon, and forum at St. John the Divine, Victoria, BC, Canada, Friday–Sunday, July 21–23, 2006.

178. Single lecture at St Mary's Kerrisdale Anglican Church, Tuesday, July 25, 2006.

179. Introduction and four 3-hour lectures on the historical Paul for CHARIS Program, Concordia College, Moorhead, MN, at Thunderbird Lodge, Rainy Lake, MN, Sunday–Thursday, August 13–17, 2006.

180. Five-day seminar on "Jesus and Paul" with Marcus Borg at Ring Lake Ranch, Dubois, WY, Monday–Friday, August 26–September 1, 2006.

181. Four lectures and two sermons at Unity Church of Dallas, Dallas, TX, Friday–Sunday, September 22–24, 2006.

182. Sermon and two "Broward (Brad) Liston Memorial Lectures." First Congregational Church of Winter Park (United Church of Christ). Orlando, Fl, Sunday, October 1, 2007.

183. Four lectures, sermon, and Adult Forum at Waterloo First United Methodist Church, Waterloo, Iowa, Friday–Sunday, October 6–8, 2006.

184. Four Henrietta Perdue Memorial lectures, sermon, and Adult Forum at Stone Church (Presbyterian) of Willow Glen, San Jose, CA, Friday–Sunday, October 27–29, 2006.

185. Three lectures for the Foundation for Contemporary Theology, Houston, TX, Friday–Saturday, November 3–4, 2006.

186. Lecture at Holy Family Roman Catholic Parish, Inverness, IL, Wednesday. November 15, 2006.

187. Four lectures for the Ministers and Laity Week, Phillips Theological Seminary, Tulsa, OK, Tuesday–Wednesday, January 16–17. 2007.

188. Evening lecture for "A January Adventure in Emerging Christianity: JA 2007." Strickland Auditorium, Epworth-by-the-Sea, St. Simon's Island, GA, Monday, January 22, 2007.

189. Four lectures and sermon at Faith United Church of Christ, Clearwater, FL, Saturday–Sunday, February 17–18, 2007.

190. Three lectures and two sermons at Calvary Episcopal Church, Memphis, TN, Thursday–Saturday, February 22–34, 2007.

191. Four lectures on "The Contemporary Challenge of Celtic Christianity." The Center for Spiritual Development, Trinity Episcopal Cathedral, Portland, OR, March 16–17, 2007.

192. Three lectures, two sermons, and Adult forum at Westminster Presbyterian Church and Unitarian Universalist Church, Buffalo, NY, March 24–25, 2007.

193. Two Keynote Addresses for the annual "Keep Making Peace" Conference, Progressive United Methodist Pastors of Michigan, Central United Methodist Church, Lansing, MI, March 31, 2007.

194. Inaugural lecture for the Huron-Cronyn Lectures on Faith and Reason, Bishop Cronyn Memorial Anglican Church, and discussion at Huron University College, University of Western Ontario, London, Ontario, Canada, April 12–13, 2007.

195. Six lectures at the Five Oaks Retreat Center, United Church of Canada, Paris, Ontario, Canada, April 13–15, 2007.

196. Three lectures at the Presbyterian Church of Barrington, Barrington, IL, April 20–21, 2007.

197. Promotional lecture on *God & Empire*, First Annual Philadelphia Book Fair, Free Library of Philadelphia, Sunday, April 22, 2007.

198. Lecture at the Westminster (Presbyterian Church) Town Hall Forum, Minneapolis, MN, Thursday, April 26, 2007.

199. Four lectures at St. Mark's Episcopal Church and Madison Square Presbyterian Church, San Antonio, TX, Friday–Saturday, May 11–12, 2007.

200. Four-day Borg-Crossan Summer Seminar on "The Bible and Christian Formation Today." The Center for Spiritual Development, Trinity Episcopal Cathedral, Portland, OR, June 25–29, 2007.

201. Three lectures at the Summer School for Pastors and Laity, Furman University, Greenville, SC, Monday–Tuesday, July 30–31, 2007.

202. Four lectures and Adult Forum at St. Paul's United Methodist Church, Helena, MT. Friday–Sunday September 28–30, 2007.

203. Three lectures and joint discussions with Marcus Borg and Joan Chittester on "Mysticism, Empowerment, and Resistance." Christ Church Cathedral, Houston, TX, Thursday–Saturday, October 4–6, 2007.

204. Lecture at Church of the Immaculate Conception, Assumption University, São Paulo, Brazil, Friday, October 26, 2007.

205. Lecture for the THEO*logando* Internacional: Missão Cultura e Teologica, Centro de Convencóes Reboucas, São Paulo, Brazil, Friday, October 26, 2007.

206. Three lectures for "Revival 2007" of the Unitarian–Universalist Christian Fellowship, West Shore Unitarian–Universalist Church, Cleveland, OH, Saturday, November 3, 2007.

207. Four lectures and sermon on Remembrance Sunday at St. Mark's Centre for Radical Christianity, St. Mark's (Anglican Church), Broomhill, Sheffield, UK, Friday–Sunday, November 9–11, 2007.

208. Three Borg-Crossan Lectures on our book *The First Christmas*, The Center for Spiritual Development, Trinity Episcopal Cathedral, Portland, OR, November 16–17, 2007.

209. Panel discussion on "What's the Most Important Non–Biblical Text for Understanding Jesus?" for HarperOne Forum, AAR-SBL Annual Meeting, San Diego, CA, Sunday, November 19, 2007.

210. Five Borg-Crossan lectures on Jesus and Paul for "Epiphany Explorations: Journey in the Wintertime." First Metropolitan United Church, Victoria, B.C., Canada, Friday–Saturday, January 18–19, 2008.

211. Four lectures on "God and Empire." Religious Studies Department, University of New Mexico, Albuquerque, NM, David Dykes, Jr., Foundation, and other local sponsors, University of New Mexico Continuing education Center, Friday–Saturday, January 25–26, 2008.

212. Danforth Lecture, Hope College, Holland, MI, Tuesday, January 29, 2008.

213. Four lectures (God & Empire; Celtic Christianity), sermon, and Adult Education Class at University Congregational United Church of Christ, Seattle, WA, Friday–Sunday, February 1–3. 2008.

214. Annual Moon Lecture, St. Mark's United Methodist Church, Sacramento, CA, Sunday, February 10, 2008.

215. Four lectures at the First Reformed Church of Christ, Burlington, NC, Friday–Saturday, February 22–23, 2008.

216. Three lectures for the "Nu Class." United Methodist Church, FL, Saturday–Sunday, March 1–2, 2008.

217. Four lectures and two sermons at the Unitarian Church, Baton Rouge, LA, Friday–Sunday, March 7–9, 2008.

218. Five lectures at the SnowStar Institute of Religion, Stratford, Ontario, Canada, Thursday–Friday, April 3–4, 2008.

219. Four Lectures at Shalom Center for Continuing Education, Uplands Retirement Village and sermon at the United Church of Christ, Pleasant Hill, TN, Friday to Sunday, April 11–13, 2008.

220. Four lectures for the "Day of Grace." St. Matthew's Evangelical Lutheran Church, Wauwatosa, WI, Friday–Saturday, April 18–19, 2008.

221. Three lectures jointly sponsored by Centenary United Methodist Church and Wake-Forest Divinity School. Winston-Salem, NC, Friday–Saturday, April 25–26, 2008.

222. Five-day Summer Seminar with Marcus Borg (5 lectures apiece and joint discussion sessions) on "Radical Discipleship in an Unjust World." The Center for Spiritual Development, Trinity Episcopal Cathedral, Portland, OR, Monday–Friday, June 23–27, 2008.

223. Lecture and discussion for the Summer Lecture Series 2008 of the Highlands Institute for American Religious and Philosophical Thought (HIARP), in the Episcopal Church of the Incarnation, Highlands, NC, Monday–Tuesday, July 7–8, 2008.

224. Five lectures and three discussion sessions with Marcus Borg at the Chautauqua Institute, Chautauqua, NY, Monday–Friday, August 11–15, 2008.

225. Four lectures with Marcus Borg and two Adult Education sessions, First United Methodist Church, Downers Grove, IL. Friday–Sunday, September 12–14, 2008.

226. Four lectures at Knox United Church, Calgary, Alberta, Canada, Friday–Sunday, September 19–21, 2008.

227. Four lectures with Marcus Borg and Adult Education Session, Faith Explorations, First United Methodist Church, Waterloo, IA, Friday–Sunday, September 26–28, 2008.

228. Four lectures at the Foundation for Contemporary Theology, Houston, TX, Friday–Saturday, October 3–4, 2008.

229. Single lecture at Historic St. Peter Church, Cleveland, OH, Wednesday, October 8, 2009.

230. Four lectures and two sermons at Coral Gables Congregational Church, Coral Gables, FL, Friday–Sunday, October 10–12, 2008.

231. Lecture on "Roman Imperial Theology." Westar Institute's Fall Meeting of Jesus Seminar on Christian Origins, Santa Rosa, CA, Friday, October 17, 2008.

232. The Henrietta Perdue Memorial Lecture, Stone Presbyterian Church of Willow Glen, San Jose, CA, Friday–Saturday, October 24–25, 2008.

233. Three lectures at St. Paul's Episcopal Church, Orillia, Ontario, Canada, Thursday, October 30, 2008.

234. Six lectures at Five Oaks Retreat Center, Paris, Ontario, Canada, Friday–Sunday, October 31–November 2, 2008.

235. Annual Proudfoot Memorial Lecture, First–St. Andrew's United Church, London, Ontario, Canada, November 3, 2008.

236. Four lectures sponsored by St. Paul's Episcopal Church, New Albany, IN; Archdiocese of Louisville; Episcopal Diocese of Kentucky; Louisville Presbyterian Theological Seminary and Bellarmine University, at Bellarmine University, Friday–Saturday, November 7–8, 2008.

237. Participation in premiere of Randy Robertson's *Phos Hilaron* multimedia production, three lectures, and discussion session, all jointly with Marcus Borg, Lansing B. Lee, Jr. Conference, Kanuga Conferences, Hendersonville, NC, Saturday–Sunday, November 15–16, 2008.

238. Four lectures, sermon, and Adult Forum at Holy Cross Lutheran Church, Newmarket, Ontario, Canada, Friday–Sunday, December 5–7, 2008.

239. Participation in two performance of Randy Robertson's *Phos Hilaron* multimedia production, and four lectures, jointly with Marcus Borg, All Saints Episcopal Church, Atlanta, GA, Friday–Sunday, December 11–12, 2008.

240. Three lectures for the Second Annual Interfaith Clergy Seminar, Center for Judaic, Holocaust, and Human Rights Studies, Florida Gulf Coast University, and

three lectures for the Center for Sacred Unity, Lamb of God Church, Fort Myers, FL, Friday–Saturday, January 23–24, 2009.

241. Three lectures at St. Peter the Fisherman Episcopal Church, New Smyrna Beach, FL, Saturday, January 31, 2009.

242. Lecture on Jesus, Higher Institute for Biblical and Theological Studies (ISEBIT), Anglican Cathedral of the Holy Trinity, Havana, Cuba, Saturday, February 14, 2009.

243. Four lectures, Adult Education, and sermon at First United Methodist Church, Eugene, OR, Friday–Sunday, February 20–22, 2009

244. Joint Lectures on "Jesus and Paul" with Marcus Borg, Calvary Episcopal Church, Memphis, TN, Friday–Saturday, February 27–28

245. Adult Education class and two Lenten sermons, Calvary Episcopal Church, Memphis, TN, Sunday–Tuesday, March 1–3, 2009.

246. Four lectures for St. Bede's Episcopal Church and St. Dunstan's Episcopal Church, Atlanta, GA, Friday–Saturday, March 13–14, 2009.

247. Joint Lectures on "Mysticism, Empowerment, Resistance, and Non-Violence"" with Marcus Borg, Horizons of Faith, First United Methodist Church, Omaha, NE, Friday–Sunday, March 20–22, 2009.

248. Four lectures, Sermons, and Adult Education as Theologian in Residence, St. Peter's Episcopal Cathedral, St. Petersburg, FL, Friday–Sunday, March 27–29, 2009.

249. Four lectures, sermon, and Adult Education, Central Presbyterian Church, Denver, CO, Friday–Sunday, April 17–19, 2009.

250. Session 1, Summer Lecture Series 2009, Highlands Institute for American Religious and Philosophical Thought (HIARP), Highlands, NC, and Episcopal Church of the Incarnation, Monday–Tuesday, May 31–June 1, 2009.

251. Three lectures at the United Methodist Church, Ludington, MI, Friday–Saturday, June 12–13, 2009.

252. Four-day Summer Seminar with Marcus Borg (4 lectures apiece and joint discussion sessions) on "The 'First' Paul; Radical Apostle of Jesus." The Center for Spiritual Development, Trinity Episcopal Cathedral, Portland, OR, Monday–Thursday, June 15–18, 2009.

253. Session 2, Summer Lecture Series 2009, Highlands Institute for American Religious and Philosophical Thought (HIARP), Highlands, NC (Episcopal Church of the Incarnation), Monday–Tuesday, July 13–14, 2009.

254. Three lectures at Cherry Log Christian Church, Cherry Log, GA, Friday–Saturday, September 11–12, 2009.

255. Three lectures at Grace Episcopal Church, Chattanooga, TN, September 18–19.

256. Four lectures, sermon, and Adult Education for the Leona and Ed Bock Foundation Series, Messiah Community Church (Evangelical Lutheran Church in America), Denver, CO, Friday–Sunday, September 25–27, 2009.

257. Four lectures, sermon, and Adult Education, University Congregational First United Church, Seattle, WA, October 16–18, 2009.

258. Lecture on "Divine Violence in the Christian Bible" for the Conference on *The Bible and the American Future*, ST. Mark's United Methodist Church, Lincoln, NE, Monday 19, 2009.

259. Four lectures at First United Methodist Church, Richardson, TX, Friday–Saturday, October 23–24, and two lectures at the Cultural Activities Center, Temple, TX, Sunday, October 26, 2009.

260. Two-day seminar with Marcus Borg, University of Alberta and Christ Church (Anglican), Edmonton, Alberta, Canada, Friday–Saturday, October 30–31, 2009

261. CHARIS Lectures and Religion Department Lecture, Concordia College, Moorhead, MN, Thursday, November 5, 2009.

262. Seventh Annual "The Bible and the World" Lecture and three-hour clergy seminar, St. Paul's Episcopal Church, Rochester, NY, Sunday, November 8–9, 2009

263. Two lectures for the Gene Bennett Program for Life-Long Learning, Colgate Rochester Crozer Divinity School, Rochester, NY, Monday, November 9, 009.

264. Full weekend for the 150th Anniversary of at Pilgrim Congregational United Church of Christ, Cleveland, OH, Friday–Sunday, November 13–15, 2009.

265. Full weekend at Holy Cross Lutheran Church, Newmarket, Ontario, Canada, Friday–Sunday, November 20–11, 2009.

266. Full weekend at St Paul's Episcopal Church, Walnut Creek, CA, Friday–Sunday, December 18–20, 2009.

267. Four lectures—repeated twice—on "The Social Gospel in the First and Twenty-First Century" along with Paul Raushenbush for "A January Adventure in Emerging Christianity." Epworth-by-the-Sea, St. Simons Island, GA, Friday–Sunday, January 15–17 and Monday–Wednesday, January18–20, 2010.

268. Three lectures for the Twenty-Fifth Anniversary Winter Pastors' School, Stetson University, Deland, FL, Wednesday–Thursday, February 3–4, 2010.

269. Three lectures with Marcus Borg on Jesus—and sermon on Sunday—for the Word and Note Series, Plymouth Congregational Church, Wichita, KS, Friday–Sunday, February 5–7, 2010.

270. Lecture on Paul, Higher Institute for Biblical and Theological Studies (ISEBIT), Anglican Cathedral of the Holy Trinity, Havana, Cuba, Saturday, February 13, 2010.

271. Four lectures, two sermons, and Adult Forum as John C. and Elizabeth Smaltz Fellow. Episcopal Church of Bethesda-by-the-Sea, Palm Beach, FL, Friday–Sunday, February 19–21, 2010.

272. The Greer-Heard Point/Counter-Point Forum on Faith and Culture, with Ben Witherington, III, and responses to papers at the Southwest Regional meeting of the Evangelical Theological Society papers, New Orleans Baptist Theological Seminary, New Orleans, LA, Friday-Saturday, February 26-27, 2010.

273. Four lectures at Earlham School of Religion and Sunday sermon at Friends Meeting (Quakers), Richmond, IN, Friday-Sunday, April 16-18, 2010.

274. Four-day lecture series with Marcus Borg, Center for Spiritual Development, Trinity Episcopal Cathedral, Portland, OR, Tuesday-Thursday, June 21-24, 2010.

275. Ten-hour course on Jesus for the Institute for Adult Spiritual Renewal (South Bend, IN), Loyola University (Lakeshore Campus), Chicago, IL, Friday (2:00-6:00pm) and Saturday (9:00am-4:00pm), July 9-10, 2010.

276. Lecture and discussion-session for Summer Lecture Series 2010, Highlands Institute for American Religious and Philosophical Thought (HIARP), Highlands, NC at the Episcopal Church of the Incarnation, Monday-Tuesday, July 12-13, 2010.

277. Ten lectures for the Progressive Christian Network of Victoria, Melbourne, Victoria, Australia, Tuesday-Friday, August 31-September 3, 2010.

278. Four lectures at Piedmont College, Demorest, GA, for the EFM Groups at Grace-Calvary Episcopal Church, Clarkesville, GA, and Resurrection Episcopal Church in Sautee-Nacoochee, GA, Friday-Saturday, September 10-11, 2010.

279. Sermon at evening service for "Love Welcomes All" and full weekend of E. Ashley Memorial Lecture Series, Congregational United Church of Christ, Hendersonville, NC, Thursday-Sunday, September 16-19, 2010.

280. Breakfast address (15 minutes) on *The Greatest Prayer* at the Religion Newswriters Association Conference 2010, Denver, CO, Saturday, September 25, 2010.

281. Three Turner Lectures, Northwest Region of the Christian Church (Disciples of Christ), Yakima, WA, Monday-Tuesday, October 4-5, 2010.

282. "Radically Faithful." Joint Lectures with Joerg Rieger, Progressive Christians Uniting, D. L. Dykes, Jr. Foundation, Joe B. and Louis P. Cook Foundation, and All Saints Episcopal Church, Pasadena, CA, October 8-9, 2010.

283. Five lectures at Five Oaks United Church of Canada Education and Retreat Center, Paris, Ontario, Canada, Friday-Sunday, October 22-24, 2010.

284. Theologian in Residence, Congregational United Church of Christ, Plymouth, NH, and New Hampshire Bible Society, Friday-Sunday, November 5-7, 2010.

285. Two Sundays (Adult Education and Sermon) and five weekday lectures at the Congregational United Church of Christ, Coral Gables, Sunday-Sunday, FL, February 6-13, 2011.

286. Three lectures, jointly with Marcus Borg, for the 50th Anniversary of the Anderson School of Theology for Lay People, Anderson, SC, Friday–Saturday, February 18–19, 2011.

287. Lunch meeting-discussion with clergy and four lectures for the Foundation for Contemporary Theology, Houston, TX, Friday–Saturday, February 25–26, 2011.

288. Three lectures for the SnowStar Institute of Religion, Ottawa, Canada, Friday–Saturday, March 4–5, 2011.

289. Two lectures and sermon, Longboat Island Chapel, Longboat Key, FL, Friday–Sunday, March 11–13, 2011.

290. Four lectures at the Vancouver School of Theology, Vancouver, BC, Canada, Thursday–Friday, March 17–18, 2011.

291. Five lectures and sermon at St. John the Divine Anglican Church, Victoria, BC, Canada, Friday–Sunday, March 18–20, 2011.

292. Five lectures at Lawrence Park Community Church, Toronto, Ontario, Canada, Friday–Saturday, April 1–2, 2011.

293. Davis Lecture on Christianity, Ohio State University, Columbus, OH, Wednesday April 13, 2011.

294. Lecture at Otterbein University, Columbus, OH, and discussion at Church of Messiah, Westville, OH, Thursday, April 14, 2011.

295. Seeds of Faith Conference, Episcopal Church of the Mediator, Meridian, MS, Friday–Sunday, May 20–22, 2011.

296. Ten-hour course on Paul for the Institute for Adult Spiritual Renewal (South Bend, IN), Loyola University (Lakeshore Campus), Chicago, IL, Friday (2:00–6:00pm) and Saturday (9:00am–4:00pm), July 8–9, 2011.

297. Sanctuary Lecture Series, Episcopal Church of the Incarnation, Highlands, NC, Sunday and Monday, July 24 and 25, 2011.

298. Five lectures with Joerg Rieger on "Economic Justice and Christian Vision" for the Department of Religion, Chautauqua Institution, Chautauqua, NY, Monday–Friday, August 8–12, 2011.

299. Four lectures with Marcus Borg on "Saying and Praying Christian." at the Conference Centre, University of Alberta, Edmonton, Alberta, Canada, Friday–Saturday, September 9–10, 2011.

300. Four lectures and sermon for the Progressive Christianity Network Great Britain at St. Andrews United Reformed Church, Roundhay, Leeds, UK, Friday–Sunday, September 16–18, 2011.

301. Sunday sermon and three nights of the Davis Lectures, Grace Baptist Church, Statesville, NC, Sunday–Tuesday, October 2–4, 2011. [

302. Cornerstone Sunday (1911–2011) sermon at the First Christian Church; four lectures for the Lane Institute for Faith and Education (LIFE) at First

Congregational United Church of Christ, Eugene, Oregon, Sunday–Monday, October 9–20, 2011.

303. Three lectures, sermon, and adult forum, St. Mark's Episcopal Church, Niagara-on-the-Lake, Ontario, Canada, Friday–Sunday, October 14–16, 2011.

304. Four lectures for the Maine Conference of the United Church of Christ, Fall Learning Event at Falmouth Congregational Church of Christ, Falmouth, ME, Friday–Saturday, November 4–5, with sermon and adult education class at the same Church, Sunday, November 6, 2011.

305. Burchenal Lecture, Eckerd College, St. Petersburg, FL, Tuesday, November 8, 2011.

306. Four lectures Vanderbilt Presbyterian Church, Naples, FL, Friday–Saturday, November 11–12, 2011.

307. Two lectures, sermon, and adult education class for First Annual Goth Lecture, Metropolitan United Church, London, ON, Canada, Saturday–Sunday, November 26–27, 2011.

308. Three lectures for Stetson University's Florida Winter Pastors' School, Wednesday–Thursday, February 1–2, 2012.

309. Two lectures and Sunday Sermon for Randy Robertson's *Gladdening Light* Symposium 2012, Friday–Sunday, February 3–4, 2012.

310. Two lectures and Sunday Sermon, Boniface Speakers Program. St. Boniface Episcopal Church, Sarasota, FL, Saturday–Sunday, February 11–12, 2012.

311. Four lectures and Sunday Sermon, jointly with Marcus Borg, United Church of Christ, Irvine, CA, Friday–Sunday, February 17–19, 2012.

312. Price Lecture Series, Trinity Episcopal Church, Boston, Saturday–Sunday, March 3–4, 2012.

313. Three lectures at Lebanon Valley College, Annville, PA, Wednesday–Thursday, March 14–15, 2012.

314. Four lectures and two Sermons at Unitarian Church of Baton Rouge, Baton Rouge, LA, Friday–Sunday, March 23–25, 2012.

315. Two Otts-Maloney Lectures, Davidson College, Davidson, NC, Tuesday and Wednesday, March 27–28, 2012.

316. Two lectures and sermons for Lyons Lectures, First United Methodist Church, Madison, WI, Friday–Sunday, April 13–15, 2012.

317. Three lectures and sermon at Queen Anne United Methodist Church, Seattle, WA, Saturday–Sunday, May 26–27, 2012.

318. Keynote and second lecture for United Church of Christ Central Atlantic Conference, University of Delaware, Friday–Sunday, June 8–10, 2012.

319. Ten-hour course on "The Power of Parable" for the Institute for Adult Spiritual Renewal (South Bend, IN), Loyola University (Lakeshore Campus), Chicago, IL, Friday (2:00–6:00pm) and Saturday (9:00am–4:00pm), June 29–30, 2012.

320. Three lecture, sermon, and Adult Education Class for a FAITH *and* REASON Seminar and Scholar in Residence Weekend, First Presbyterian Church, Mt., Pleasant, IA, Saturday–Sunday, August 18–19, 2012.

321. Ten lectures—nine on "The Power of Parable" and a final one on "Divine Violence?"—for Common Dreams on the Road, Alliance of Progressive Christians, Sydney, Australia, Tuesday–Friday, September 4–7, 2012.

322. Three lectures for Wisdom House Retreat and Conference Center and St. Michael's Episcopal Church, Litchfield, CT, Friday–Saturday, September 21–22, 2012.

323. Holy Trinity Episcopal Church, Gainesville, FL, Tuesday–Wednesday, October 16–17, 2012.

324. Four lectures for Epiphany Explorations: Journey in the Wintertime, First Metropolitan United Church, Victoria, BC, Canada, Saturday–Sunday, January 19–20, 2013.

325. Four lectures for the Farstrup-Mortensen Lectures, Bethania Lutheran Church, Solvang, CA, Friday–Saturday, February 22–23, 2013.

326. Four lectures, sermon, and Adult Forum at Trinity Episcopal Church, Santa Barbara, CA, Friday–Sunday, March 1–3, 2013.

327. Sermon, Adult Forum, two evening lectures (Sun and Mon), Episcopal Church of the Holy Cross, Dunn Loring, VA; Monday morning with VA clergy, Monday afternoon at Virginia Theological Seminary, Sunday–Monday, March 10–11, 2013.

328. Four lectures at Episcopal School of Knoxville for St. Elizabeth's Episcopal Church, Knoxville, TN, Friday–Saturday, March 15–16, 2013.

329. Full weekend for Harrisena Community Church, Queensbury, NY, Friday–Saturday, April 12–14, 2013.

330. Borg-Crossan Seminar on *The Challenge of the Christian Bible*, Old Stone Church, Bend, OR (burned and changed to) Trinity Episcopal Church, Tuesday–Friday, June 18–21, 2013.

331. Sermon at the main service on Sunday and Monday-evening lecture in the Sanctuary Lecture Series at the Episcopal Church of the Incarnation, Highlands, NC, Sunday–Monday, July 28–29, 2013.

332. Three lectures for St. Pius X (Roman Catholic) Parish, Coeur d'Elene, WA, Friday, October 4, 2013.

333. Three Joint lectures with Marcus Borg and Joan Chittister, Christ Church Episcopal Cathedral, Houston, TX, Friday–Saturday, October 18–19, 2013.

334. Four joint lectures, doubled Sermons, and Adult Education Class, with Marcus Borg at Messiah Community Church ELCA, Denver, CO, Friday–Sunday, November 1–3, 2013.

335. Three "Mountain Top Lectures." Amicalola State Park Lodge, Dawsonville, GA; Adult Education Class and Sermon at the Disciple of Christ Christian Church, Cherry Log, GA. Friday–Sunday, November 8–10, 2013.

336. Four lectures for the Bass Lecture Series, First Presbyterian Church, Annapolis, MD Friday–Saturday, November 15–16, 2013.

337. Three lectures for the Institute for Christian Studies, St. John's Episcopal Cathedral (01/31) and Riverside Presbyterian Church (02/01), Jacksonville, FL, January 31–February 1, 2014.

338. Three lectures as the Inaugural Ella Dodd Lecture Series, Community United Church of Christ, Vero Beach, FL, Tuesday–Wednesday, February 5–6, 2014.

339. Three lectures for Mt. Carmel Lutheran Church, San Luis Obispo, CA, Friday–Saturday, February 7–8, 2014.

340. Four lectures as the Inaugural "Winter Forum" at Wisconsin Dells, Wisconsin Council of Churches, at (combined) Holy Cross Episcopal Church and Dells Delton United Methodist Church, Wisconsin Dells, WI, Friday–Saturday, February 21–22, 2014.

341. Three lectures at Village Presbyterian Church, Prairie Village, KS, Friday–Saturday, February 28–March 1, 2014.

342. Five lectures for First Community Church, Columbus, OH, Friday–Saturday, March 7–8, 2014.

343. Francis Lecture and four Founder's-day Lectures, Chapman University, Orange, CA, Thursday–Saturday, March 13–15, 2014.

344. Five lectures for the *Free to Believe* Conference, Hayes Conference Center, Swanwick, Derbyshire, UK, Thursday–Saturday, March 27–29, 2014.

345. Five lectures at College Street United Church of Canada, Toronto, Canada, Friday–Saturday, April 4–5, 2014.

346. Muslim/Christian Dialogue with Dr. Shabir Ally on "The Historicity of the Life of Jesus in the Gospels." Medical Sciences Auditorium, University of Toronto, 3:30–7:pm, Saturday, April 5, 2014. Co-sponsored by: (a)Emmanuel College, the theological school of Victoria University in the University of Toronto; (b) The Multi-Faith Centre at the University of Toronto; and (c) The Islamic Information and Dawah Centre International. http://youtu.be/oBlt7VBGjVA

347. Four lectures, sermon, and Adult Education Forum for New Visions at First, First United Methodist Church, Eugene, OR, Friday–Sunday, April 11–13, 2014.

348. *Awakenings* 2014, United Congregational Church of Christ, Holyoke, MA, Friday–Saturday, April 25–26, 2014.

349. Lecture for the Collegiate Peaks Forum Series, First Presbyterian Church, Salida, CO, Thursday, May 1, 2014.

350. Three lectures. sermon, and adult education for the James W. White Lectureship, First Congregational United Church of Christ, Colorado Springs, CO, Friday-Sunday, May 2–4, 2014.

351. Four lectures, sermon, and Adult Education Class as Theologian in Residence at Bryn Mawr Presbyterian Church, Bryn Mawr (and Old Pine Street Church), PA Friday-Sunday, June 13–15, 2014.

352. Joint Lectures with Marcus Borg and Joan Chittister on "The Dream of God: A World of Justice and Non-Violence." University Congregational United Church of Christ and University Temple Church of Christ, Seattle, WA, Thursday-Saturday, June 19–21, 2014.

353. Five lectures for the Institute for Adult Spiritual Renewal, Adult Spiritual Renewal and Empowerment, Institute for Adult Spiritual Renewal, Loyola University (Lakeshore Campus), Chicago, IL, Friday-Saturday, June 27–28, 2014.

354. Four lectures and two sermons at Plymouth Congregational United Church of Christ, Fort Collins, CO, Friday-Sunday, September 12–14, 2014.

355. Participation in two panels on "Confronting Poverty from the Heart of Faith, Faith *and* Reason Seminar, South Main Baptist Church, Houston, TX, Thursday-Friday, September 18–19, 2015.

356. Four lectures at First Congregational Church, Tacoma, WA, Friday-Saturday, October 10–11, 2015.

357. Class presence, "Three Wise Guys" Radio Interview, and public lecture at Valencia College, Orlando, FL, Thursday, October 23, 2014.

358. Two Marold Lectures at Moravian Theological Seminary, Bethlehem, PA, Friday, November 7, 2014.

359. Three lectures for Stetson University Florida Winter Pastors' School, Stetson University, DeLand, FL, Tuesday-Thursday, January 27–29, 2015.

360. Annual Christian theology Lecture, Department of Religious Studies, Stetson University, DeLand, FL, Thursday, January 29, 2015.

361. Four lectures, Adult Education and Sermon, College of Central Florida and Fort King Presbyterian Church, Ocala, FL, Friday-Sunday, January 30–February 1, 2015.

362. Four lectures and informal dialogue, Growth Pointe Seminar, Flagler College, St. Augustine, FL, Friday-Saturday, February 6–7, 2015.

363. Four lectures and three Sunday sermons at the Arizona Foundation for Contemporary Theology in Dayspring United Methodist Church, Tempe, AZ, Friday-Sunday, March 6–8, 2015.

364. The Francis X. Shea Memorial Lecture, College of Saint Scholastica, Duluth, MN, Thursday, April 8, 2015.

365. Sunstone Symposium, University of Utah, Salt Lake City, UT, Tuesday–Friday, July 28–31, 2015

366. Two lectures for the Roman Catholic and Lutheran Fellowship Group of Spring Hill, FL, Cristo Rey and All Saints Lutheran Church (ELCA), Orlando, FL Friday, 18 September 2015.

367. Two lectures and panel discussion, "The Unending Conversation: Progressive Christian Apologetics in the Twenty-First Century." The Canon Theologian Lecture Series in Honor of Canon Marcus J. Borg. Trinity Episcopal Cathedral, Portland, OR, Thursday–Saturday, September 24–27, 2015.

368. Three lectures, adult Education Class, and Sermon at Myers Park Baptist Church, Charlotte, NC, Friday–Sunday, October 16–18, 2015.

369. Halstead Lecture, Drew University, Madison, NJ, Thursday, October 29, 2015.

370. Four lectures at Good Shepherd United Church of Christ, Sahuarita, AZ. Friday–Saturday, February 19–20, 2016.

371. Four lectures at St. Paul's Episcopal Church, Newport, AR. Friday–Saturday, March 11–12, 2016.

372. Four lectures in the Noted Speakers Series, First Unitarian Church of Memphis (The Church of the River), Memphis, TN, Friday–Saturday, April 1–2, 2016.

373. Lecture during Seminar (with Mark Allen Powell and Dennis McDonald) on "The Historical Jesus and the Gospels." Florida Southern College, Lakeland, FL, Thursday, April 14, 2016.

374. Five lectures during *2015 Peace Week*, Manchester University, North Manchester, IN, Tuesday–Thursday, April 19–21, 2016.

375. Four lecture and sermon at Saint James United Church, St. Johns, Newfoundland, Canada, Friday–Sunday, May 13–15, 2016.

376. Two lectures at Cristo Rey and All Saints Lutheran Church (ELCA), Orlando, FL, Saturday, June 25, 2016.

377. Three lectures, three sermons, and Adult Education at First Christian Church (Disciples of Christ), Edmond, OK, Friday–Sunday, August 26–28; Conference-day with Minister Group, Monday, August 29, 2016.

378. Three lectures at Sandy Springs Christian Church, Sandy Springs, GA, Friday–Saturday, September 23–24, 2016.

379. Three at Windermere Union Church, United Church of Christ, Windermere, FL. Sunday evenings, October 2, 9, and 16, 2016.

380. Two Keynote lectures for the Inauguration of the Tanho Center for a New New Testament, First United Methodist Church, Boulder, CO. Friday–Saturday, October 21–22, 2016.

381. Three lectures and Sunday sermon at the Sisters of Loreto Motherhouse, Nerinx, KY, Friday–Sunday, November 4–5, 2016.

382. Four lectures for *A January Adventure in Emerging Christianity*. Strickland Auditorium, Epworth-by-the-Sea, St. Simons Island, GA, Friday–Sunday, January 3–15, 2017.

383. Four lectures at Good Shepherd United Church of Christ, Sahuarita, AZ, Friday–Saturday, February 17–18, 2017.

384. Four lectures, two sermons, and Adult Education at Naples United Church of Christ, Naples, FL, Friday–Sunday, February 24–26, 2017.

385. Four lectures, sermon, Adult Education and interview at Luncheon for the 10th Anniversary of The Lecture Series, University Congregational United Church of Christ, Seattle, WA, Friday–Sunday, March 3–5, 2017.

386. Sermon and afternoon lecture at Kingston Congregational Church, Kingston, RI, Sunday, March 12, 2017.

387. Four lectures, sermon, and adult education class at First Congregational Church, Winter Park, FL, Friday–Sunday, March 24–26, 2017.

388. *Christian Century* Magazine and Wisconsin Council of Churches Forum, Washington Island, Door County, WI. Monday–Friday, June 26–30, 2017.

389. Carl Lecture Series, First United Methodist Church, Schenectady, NY, Saturday–Sunday, September 23–24, 2017

390. Wesley-Knox United Church, London, Ontario, Canada, Friday–Sunday, October 20–22, 2017.

391. Awakening Soul Gathering, Lutheridge Conference Center, Arden, NC, Thursday–Sunday, November 9–12, 2017.

392. Three lectures at the First Reformed United Church of Christ, Burlington NC. Friday–Saturday, March 23–24, 2018.

393. Four lectures, Sunday class, and Sermon. May 4–6; Unitarian–Universalist Church of Lancaster, Lancaster, PA, Friday–Sunday, March 4–6, 2018.

394. Three lectures Pendle Hill, Quaker Retreat Center, Wallingford, PA. Friday–Saturday, August 10–11, 2018.

395. Two lectures and sermon, one each at University Christian Church, St. Paul's Episcopal Cathedral, and Mission gathering Christian Church, San Diego, CA, Saturday–Sunday, September 15–17, 2018.

396. Discussion on the historical Jesus with Professor Mark Licona for *Ratio Christi*, Kennesaw State University, Kennesaw, GA, Wednesday, October 24, 2018.

397. Marney Lectures, on God and Violence. First Baptist Church of Austin, Austin, TX, Friday–Saturday, January 11–112,2019.

398. Two lectures on Paul at Community United Church of Christ, Vero Beach, FL, Wednesday, February 27, 2019.

399. Four lectures on Jesus, at Mary, Mother of Jesus, Inclusive Catholic Community, at Saint Andrew United Church of Christ, Sarasota, FL, Friday-Saturday, March 8-9, 2019.

400. Four lectures at the United Church, Salt Spring Island, Ganges, BC, Canada. Friday-Saturday, March 22-23, 2019.

401. Three lectures for *The Universal Christ Conference* and Webinar, Center for Action and Contemplation, Albuquerque Convention Center, Albuquerque, NM, Thursday-Sunday, March 28-31, 2019.

402. Three lectures and panel discussion, Southminster Presbyterian Church, Beaverton, OR, Friday-Saturday, April 5-6, 2019.

403. Keynote lecture for the Annual Meeting of the Rocky Mountain Conference of the United Church of Christ, Convention Center, Grand Junction, CO, Friday, June 7, 20-19.

404. Three lectures and sermon for the Holmgren Lectureship, First Congregational United Church of Christ, Grand Junction, CO, Saturday-Sunday, June 8-9, 2019.

405. Interfaith Lecture on *Archaeology and Jesus, Science and Faith*, Hall of Philosophy, Chautauqua Institution, Chautauqua, NY, Tuesday, July 9, 2019.

406. One-day workshop on "The Challenge of Paul" with 100 invited pastors or educators, Trinity United Methodist Church, Austin, TX, Saturday, September 14, 2019.

407. One lecture, Christ Church Unity, Orlando, FL, Friday, October 18, 2019.

408. Two lectures and two sermons, United Congregational Church, Irvine, CA, Saturday-Sunday, October 27-28, 2019.

409. UCSB-Westmont Annual Lecture in New Testament, Westmont College, Santa Barbara, CA, Thursday, February 20, 2020

410. Four lectures at St. Andrew's Presbyterian Church, Santa Barbara, CA. Friday-Saturday, February 21-22, 2020.

411. Four online visual classes with Q&As on "The Christmas Stories" for Tripp Fuller's *Homebrewed Christianity*, asynchronically available on *YouTube* after December 2022.

412. Five online visual classes with Q&As on "The Easter Stories" for Tripp Fuller's *Homebrewed Christianity*, asynchronically available on *YouTube* after March 2023.

413. Five online visual classes with Q&As on "The Historical Jesus" for Tripp Fuller's *Homebrewed Christianity*, asynchronically available on *YouTube* after March 2024.

414. Visual on-site Lecture on "Resurrection Universality and Cosmic Responsibility." Friday, May 24, 7:30-9:00. Westar Institute Spring Conference: Confronting

Christian Nationalism (Little America Hotel, Salt Lake City, UT), May 23–25, 2024.

415. Three on-site visual lectures on "The Historical Jesus." as keynote speaker for the Annual Congress of the Coalition for Spiritual and Public Leadership, Chicago, IL, June 7, 8, and 9, 2024.

416. Five Visual Classes with Q&As on "Paul the Pharisee" for Tripp Fuller's *Homebrewed Christianity,* asynchronically available on *YouTube* after March 2025.

EDITORSHIPS

1. Member of Editorial Board of *Semeia. An Experimental Journal for Biblical Criticism*: 1973–1986.

Volume Editor for: *Semeia* 2 (1974) *The Good Samaritan*; *Semeia* 4 (1975) *Paul Ricoeur on Biblical Hermeneutics*; *Semeia* (1977) *Polyvalent Narration*; *Semeia* 10 (1978) *Narrative Syntax*; *Semeia* 17 (1980) *Gnomic Wisdom.*

General Editor of *Semeia. An Experimental Journal for Biblical Criticism*: 1981–86.

2. Member of Editorial Board of the *Journal of the American Academy of Religion*: 1977–87.

3. John J. Collins and John Dominic Crossan, Eds., *The Biblical Heritage in Modern Catholic Scholarship. In Honor of Bruce Vawter, C.M., on his 65th Birthday.* Delaware: Glazier, 1986.

4. General Editor for *Religious Worlds: Primary Readings in Comparative Perspective.* Department of Religious Studies, DePaul University. Dubuque, IA: Kendall/Hunt, 1991.

5. *The Historical Jesus in Context.* Edited by Amy-Jill Levine, Dale. C. Allison Jr., and John Dominic Crossan. Princeton Readings in Religions. Princeton, NJ: Princeton University Press, 2006.

MEMBERSHIPS AND POSITIONS

1. Catholic Biblical Association: since 1962.

2. Chicago Society of Biblical Research: since 1964.

   Executive Secretary: 1971–75; Vice President: 1977–78; President: 1978–79.

3. Society of Biblical Literature: since 1964.

   Chair of Parables Seminar, SBL Annual Meeting, 1972–76.

   Member of Research and Publications Committee: 1975–78 and 1983–85.

   Chair of Historical Jesus Section, SBL Annual Meeting: 1993–98.

   Vice President, 2010–2011.

President, 2011-2012.

4. American Academy of Religion: 1970-2012.

5. Studiorum Novi Testamenti Societas: since 1970.

AWARDS AND RECOGNITIONS

1986 Faculty Research and Development Summer Research Grant, College of Liberal Arts and Sciences, DePaul University, Chicago.

1988-89 University Research Council Sabbatical Grant for Winter Quarter, DePaul University, Chicago.

1989 American Academy of Religion Award for Excellence in Religious Studies. Presented at AAR/SBL Annual Meeting, New Orleans, LA (18 November 1990).

1991 Ninth Annual Rev. William T. Cortelyou-Martin J. Lowery Award for Excellence from the College of Liberal Arts and Sciences, DePaul University.

1992 Faculty Research and Development Summer Research Grant, College of Liberal Arts and Sciences, DePaul University, Chicago.

1992-93 University Research Council, DePaul University, Chicago, Sabbatical Grant for Spring Quarter, 1993.

1993 University Research Council, DePaul University, Chicago, Grant for Summer research in Rome, Italy, 1993.

1995 Via Sapientiae Award, DePaul University's highest honor.

2003 Doctor of Humanities. Honorary doctorate from Stetson University, DeLand, FL, `Saturday, May 10, 2003.

2007 The Albert Schweitzer Memorial Award for Outstanding accomplishment in the Critical Study of Religion, from the Center for Inquiry (CFI) and the Committee for the Scientific Examination of Religion (CSER), University of California at Davis, Thursday, January 25, 2007.

MEDIA REPORTS AND INTERVIEWS

1. Magazines

1. *The Christian Century*.

Cover of Vol. 108, No. 37, the Christmas issue of *The Christian Century*, December 18-15, 1991 announced "A Jewish Peasant: John Dominic Crossan on the Historical Jesus." The issue contained both a "summary" of the book by Crossan, "The Life of a Mediterranean Peasant" on pp. 1194-1200, and "The Historical Jesus: An interview with John Dominic Crossan" on pp. 1200-1204.

2. *America.*

John P. Meier, *America.* 166:8 (March 7, 1992) 198-99.

3. *Commonweal.*

Luke Timothy Johnson, "A Marginal Mediterranean Jewish Peasant." *Commonweal*, 24 April 1992.

4. *The Christian Century.*

David L. Bartlett, "The Historical Jesus and the Christ of Faith." *The Christian Century* 109:16 (6 May 1992) 489-493.

5. *Times Literary Supplement.*

J. Leslie Houlden, "Jesus before faith: Portrait of a Peasant Jewish Cynic?" *Times Literary Supplement,* September 25, 1992: 27.

6. *Utne Reader.*

Danny Duncan Collum, "Who Was This Man Jesus: New research offers a compelling portrait of Yeshu of Nazareth." *Utne Reader: The Best of the Alternative Press.* No. 54, Nov./Dec. 1992: 38-43.

7. *Publishers Weekly.*

William Griffin, "Viewing Jesus." and "The Jesus Factor." *Publishers Weekly*, April 13, 1992: 25, and November 9, 1992: 45.

8. *Mundo 21.*

José Alfonso Nino, "¿Quien fue realmente Jesus . . . un Judio Marginal . . . o un Idealista Revolucionario?" *Mundo 21,*4/4 (1993) 84-90.

9. *The Christian Century*

"The Challenge of Christmas: Two Views" in the Christmas issue, December 15, 1993, cover and pp. 1270-80. "He comes as One Unknown" by Beverly R. Gaventa, and "A Tale of Two Gods" by John Dominic Crossan ("adapted from the first chapter of *Jesus: A Revolutionary Biography*"), with mutual responses following.

10. *Time*

Richard N. Ostling, "Jesus Christ, Plain and Simple." *Time*, January 10, 1994: 38-39.

11. *Christianity and the Arts*

Marci Whitney-Schenck, "The Historical Face of Jesus." 1/1, Winter 1994: 8-9.

12. *Newsweek*

Russell Watson, "A Lesser Child of God." *Newsweek*, April 4, 1994: 53-54.

13. *Publishers Weekly*

Starred review ["books of special interest and merit"] of *Jesus: A Revolutionary Biography, Publishers Weekly*, December 13, 1993: 32; personal profile, *Publishers Weekly*, February 14, 1993: 49.

14. *GQ*

Russell Shorto, "Cross Fire." *GQ*, June 1994: 116-23.

15. *L'actualité*

Stéphane Baillargeon, "Interview: A`~ la recherche du vrai Jésus." *L'actualité*, 20/1, January 1995, title in band across top of front cover and Pages 12-14.

16. *Le Point*, France

Christian Makarian, "Une nouvelle facon de lire la Bible." *Le Point*, No. 1177, April 8, 1995: 30-44.

17. *Veja*, Brazil

Roberto Pompeu de Toledo, Cover Picture and "Especial" article. Front cover: picture of Jesus' body after deposition with caption, "Quem Matou Jesus? O que dizem os últimos estudios." Inside article on pages 66-79: "A Morte de Jesus." *Veja* (Ano 28, No. 15), April 12, 1995.

18. *Tikkun*

Claudia Setzer, "The Historical Jesus." *Tikkun. A Bimonthly Jewish Critique of Politics, Culture and Society.* 10.4 1995: 73-77 [on entire current debate].

19. *Time*

Cover (Jesus) on "The Search for Jesus: Some scholars are debunking the Gospels. Now traditionalists are fighting back. What are Christians to believe?" Inside article on pages 52-59 by David Van Biema, "The Gospel Truth?" (reported by Richard N. Ostling and Lisa H. Towle) *Time*, 147/15, April 8, 1996.

20. *Newsweek*

Cover (Jesus) on "Rethinking the Resurrection. A New Debate about the Risen Christ." Inside article by Kenneth L. Woodward, "Rethinking the Resurrection, " *Newsweek*, April 8, 1996: 60-70

21. *U. S. News & World Report*

Cover (Jesus) on "In Search of Jesus. Who was he? New appraisals of his life and its meaning." Inside article by Jeffery L. Sheler with Mike Tharp and Jill Jordan Seider, "In Search of Jesus. Some scholars seek answers in history and redefine the meaning of his life and deeds." *U. S. News & World Report*, April 8, 1996: 46-53.

22. *Publishers Weekly*

Henry Carrigan, "Scholars Search for the Historical Jesus." *Publishers Weekly*, May 13, 1996: 36-37.

23. *Publishers Weekly*

Starred review ["books of special interest and merit"] of *The Birth of Christianity*, *Publishers Weekly*, March 9, 1998: 63-64.

24. *Publishers Weekly*

Lynn Garrett, "Search for Jesus on TV." *Publishers Weekly*, April 13, 1998: 28.

25. *America*

Carolyn Osiek, *America*, November 14, 1998: 23-24.

26. *U. S. News & World Report*

Cover (Jesus) on "Why Jesus Was Killed: Scholars find new clues about the Crucifixion." Inside article by Jeffery L. Sheler. "Why Did He Die? Jesus put the kingdom of God against Caesar. And that act led to a political execution that launched a major world religion." *U. S. News & World Report*, April 24, 2000: 50-55.

27. *Bible Review*

Hershel Shanks, "Dom Crossan: The Bad Boy of Historical Jesus Studies." (Review of *A Long Way from Tipperary: A Memoir*) *Bible Review* 16, Oct 2000: 24-28 and 50.

28. *People*

Cover: "Inside Mel's Passion: His film about Jesus stirs faith and outrage." Inside: "The Gospel of Mel." Pp. 82-88 (quotes on Pages 84, 86).

29. *Broadview*

Alicia von Stamwitz, "Perspective/Interview: John Dominic Crossan." March 2020: 16-18. Photos by David Lawrence.

2. Newspapers

1. Peter Steinfels, "Peering Past Doctrine to Glimpse Jesus of History." *The New York Times*, Monday, December 23, 1991, started on the front page, A1, and was concluded on page A10. Steinfels' article was republished through the New York Times News Service in the following papers [that I know about]:

(1) "Historians follow their facts, not star, to birth, life of Jesus." *The Maui News*, Maui, HI, December 23, 1991: A1 (front page) and A4.

(2) "Life of Jesus re-examined." *South Bend Tribune*, South Bend, IN, December 23, 1991.

(3) "An elusive Jesus is sought by researchers: Two new books examine him through the lens of historical inquiry." *The Minneapolis Star Tribune*, Minneapolis, MN, December 24, 1991.

(4) "Historical Jesus Ever Elusive." *The International Herald Tribune*, December 24-25: 1 (the front page) and 4.

(5) "Getting to know Jesus, the historical figure: To many biblical scholars, his life still remains a mystery." *The Daily News and Record*, Greensboro, NC, December 25, 1991.

(6) "Jesus' life remains an enigma." *Times Union*, Albany, NY, [date not known].

(7) "Who Was Jesus? Man and Myth." *St. Petersburg Times*, St. Petersburg, FL, January 4, 1992.

(8) "Christianity: 'Historical Jesus remains issue." *The Vindicator*, Youngstown, OH, Saturday, April 18, 1992.

(9) "New Books underscore conflicting views of Christian, historical Jesus." *Woodland Hills Daily News* (Antelope Valley edition), Los Angeles, CA, Saturday, April 18, 1992.

2. Michael Steinhauser, "What was Jesus Really Like? A controversial new book portrays an itinerant cynic who had little use for the religious establishment." Toronto Star, Saturday, January 11, 1992: M9.

3. Dennis Polkow, "Seeking Jesus: Glimpsing the historical figure across the millenniums has been a controversial goal of DePaul's John Dominic Crossan." The Chicago Tribune, Tuesday, January 21, 1992 (lead article in the "Tempo" section: 1 and 5).

4. John Reumann, "Jesus, through scholars' eyes." *The Philadelphia Inquirer*, Sunday, March 15, 1992.

5. James E. Davis (*Fort Lauderdale Sun–Sentinel*), "Depiction of Jesus: Is it gospel? *News Sentinel*, Fort Wayne, IN, Friday, April 10, 1992.

6. Peter Steinfels, "BELIEFS. Reconciling the historical Jesus with the living Jesus of Christians' faith." New York Times, Saturday, April 11, 1992: 9.

7. Kathryn Marchocki, "Former Priest argues against the Resurrection." *Boston Sunday Herald*, Sunday, April 12, 1992: 24.

8. Rebecca Larsen, "Punching holes in miracles." *The Marin Independent Journal*, San Rafael, CA, (Palm) Sunday, April 12, 1992, under "Books" on page D4.

9. Don Lettin, "Authors Say Resurrection Didn't Happen. Books Present New Views of Jesus." The San Francisco Chronicle, (Good) Friday, April 17, 1992, on front page and A8.

10. Dennis Polkow, "The Jesus of history, the Christ of Faith. Separating one from the other stirs up storm of controversy, "(Good) Friday, April 17, 1992, in Chicago Suburban *Press Publications* (*The Addison Press, Bensenville Press, The Elmhurst Press, The Lombard Spectator, The Press, The Villa Park Argus, Wood Dale Press*), lead story in Section 2, "Family Living." pages 1 and 2.

11. Paul Turner, "Unconventional Views about Jesus. New interpretations raise eyebrows, ire in religious circles." The Spokesman-Review & Spokane Chronicle, (Easter) Sunday, April 19, 1992, on front page F1 of "Empire Life" section and F4).

12. Lois Kaplan, "Images of Jesus. Did he have dark skin or light? Blue eyes or brown? Through the ages, authors and artists have created differing pictures of Christ." *The Palm Beach Post*, West Palm Beach, FL, (Easter) Sunday, April 19, 1992, on front page 1F of "Accent" section and 7F.

13. Robert Lowman, "'The Historical Jesus,' an honest portrait." *The Woodland Hills Daily News* (Antelope Valley Edition), Los Angeles, Ca, in *L.A Life* section, Sunday, April 19, 1992: 10.

14. William H. Willimon, "The Search Continues for the Historical Jesus." *The Christian Science Monitor*, Tuesday, April 21, 1992.

15. Ed Golder, "Seeking Proof of Faith." *Grand Rapids Press*, MI, Saturday, April 25, 1992.

16. Bob Sanders, "Shedding new light and thoughts on Christ." *The Opelika-Auburn News*, Opelika, AL, Sunday, April 26.

17. Diane Wedington, "Author's historical survey depicts Jesus as peasant and revolutionary." *The Contra Costa Times*, Contra Costa, CA, Sunday, May 3, 1992.

18. John Dominic Crossan, "Why we must seek the historical Jesus: His message goes beyond the Gospels." *The Boston Sunday Globe*, Focus section [Religion and History], Sunday, July 26, 1992: 59.

19. Mary Beth Murphy, "Theologians challenged to discern real Christ." *The Milwaukee Sentinel*, Religion news, Saturday, February 13, 1993: 9A.

20. Bill Blankenship, "A question of faith." *The Topeka Capital-Journal*, Saturday, October 9, 1993: B1 (Religion).

21. Leslie Houlden (professor of theology, King's College, London), "No Superstar: This life of Christ sees him not as an apocalyptic prophet but as a peasant with a vision." *The New York Times*, Book Review section, Sunday, December 26, 1993.

22. Andrew Herrmann, "BIBLE BATTLE. Clerics Burn over Bible Revisionism: Ministers in N.W. Indiana Protest Scholar's New Testament Challenge." *Chicago Sunday Sun-Times*, December 26, 1993: 13.

23. Betty Neff, "No angel, no Magi: Scholar says the historical life of Jesus differs greatly from the biblical account." *The Huntsville Times*, Sunday, February 20, 1994: H6.

24. Mary Rourke, "Cross Examination." *Los Angeles Times*, View section, Thursday, February 24, 1944: E1 and E5.

25. Douglas Lowney, "Jesus: Rebel with a Cause." *SF Weekly*, Wednesday, March 2, 1994: 11–14, and cover picture entitled "The Battle for Jesus."

26 Michael McAteer, "Jesus: God or dangerous revolutionary?" *The Toronto Star*, Saturday, March 5, 1994: K14.

27. Mary Rourke, "What does Jesus mean to you." *Bannett Suburban Newspapers*, Los Angeles, CA, "Lifestyles" section, Thursday, March 10, 1994: 1C and 2c.

28. Richard Scheinin, "Re-visioning Jesus." *San Jose Mercury News*, CA, "Living: Religion and Ethics" section, Saturday, March 12, 1994: 1C and 11C.

29. Judith Cebula, "The Jesus Controversy." *The Indianapolis News*, Friday, April 1, 1994: A1 (front page) and A2.

30. Gordon Legge, "Scholars seek truth behind Jesus's life" and "In search of Jesus Christ." *Calgary Herald*, Canada, Saturday, April 2, 1994: A1 and A10–12.

31. *Chicago Tribune Magazine*, Sunday, July 17, 1994. On cover: Picture of large statue of Jesus as the Sacred Heart above smaller bust of Crossan with "Searching for Jesus: Can this man change what Christians believe? (John Dominic Crossan of De Paul University)." On pages 8–15, Jeff Lyon, "Gospel Truth. Will Christians accept a revolutionary portrait of Jesus that is based on scholarship, not faith?"

32. Darrell Hassler, "Seeing Jesus as a 'social revolutionary,'" *The Daily Times*, Ottawa, IL, Friday, August 19, 1994: 9 and 12.

33. Dawn Gibeau, "Color coding, by vote, what Jesus said." *National Catholic Reporter*, August 26, 1994: Cover and 6–7.

34. Gil Smart, "New Testament prof doesn't go by the book." *Sunday News*, Lancaster, PA, October 23, 1994: Cover and A4.

35. Jeff Lyon, "The Jesus case." For Starters Section, *Chicago Tribune* Magazine, Sunday, February 5, 1995.

36. David Crum, "Searching for the Gospel Truth." *Detroit Free Press*, Sunday, March 26, 1995: Section F, 1 and 6.

37. Susan Hogan, "The Controversial Theologian." *Duluth News-Tribune*, Thursday, April 6, 1995: 1 and 2.

38. Thomas Farrell, "'Gospel truth' may not be so gospel, book suggests." *Duluth News-Tribune*, Sunday, April 9, 1995: section 7E, 1.

39. Michael McAteer, "Doubting Thomases." *The Toronto Star*, Saturday, April 8, 1995, pages not known. See also "Correction." Saturday, April 29, 1995.

40.. Larry B. Stammer, "Good Friday Renews Focus on Roots of Anti-Semitism." *Los Angeles Times*, Friday April 14: 1 and 20.

41. Peggy R. Townsend, "The Faces of Jesus." *Santa Cruz County Sentinel*, Sunday, April 16, 1995: Section C, 1 and 3.

42. Marianne Sawicki, "Crossan's view of Jesus' death is jarring and may be healing." *National Catholic Reporter*, July 14, 1995: 12.

43. Mary Ann Fergus, "Scholar refutes Jesus stories." *The Pantagraph*, Bloomington, IL, Sunday, August 27, 1995: A1 and back page.

44. Mike Wilson, "Scholars seek truth about Jesus." *St. Petersburgh Times*, Saturday, December 23, 1995.

45. Jeff Lyon, "Update '95 . . . A look back at our cover stories . . . Searching for Jesus: John Dominic Crossan is still looking for the real Jesus." *Sunday Chicago Tribune*, Magazine section, Chicago, IL, Sunday, December 24, 1995, page 2.

46 Judith Cebula, "'Who Killed Jesus?' is focus of forum." *Indianapolis Star*, Indianapolis, IN, Tuesday, March 26, 1996: 1 and 5.

47. Frank Ramirez, "Theologian says killing of Jesus not so simple." *South Bend Tribune*, South Bend, IN, Friday, April 5, 1996: Section D (Faith), D1 and D2.

48. Bill Broadway, "What Really Happened to Jesus?" Metro: Religion, *Washington Post*, Washington, DC, Saturday, April 6, 1996, page B7.
49. Douglas Todd, "The Jesus Debate." *Ottawa Citizen*, Ottawa, Canada, Sunday, April 7, 1996: A1–A2.
50. Martin Levin, "Search for historical Jesus looses a tiger in the temple." *Globe and Mail*, Toronto, ON, Saturday, 13 April 13, 1996.
51. Robert Monroe, "Resurrection Revisited." *Inland Valley Daily Bulletin*, Ontario, CA, Sunday, April 28, 1966: Life Section, A13 and A16.
52. Bob Arndorfer, "Searching for Jesus: Researcher offers a Different View of Faith." *The Gainesville Sun*, Gainesville, FL, Easter Sunday, March 30, 1997: 1A and 8A.
53. Cary McMullen, "F[lorida]S[outhern]C[ollege] Symposium Focus is Inquiry into Jesus' Words, Deeds." *The Ledger*, Lakeland, FL, Friday, January 23, 1998.
54. David Crumm, "Books, documentary cast new light on Jesus." *The Detroit News and Free Press*, Saturday, April 4, 1998: 1 and 9.
55. Michelle Bearden, "Television series, book present provocative versions of Jesus' life." *The Tampa Tribune*, Saturday, April 4, 1998.
56. Bill Broadway, "Looking Anew at Jesus and early Christianity." *Washington Post*, Saturday, April 4, 1998.
57. Mary Rourke, "In the Spirit: Revisiting Jesus' Times." *Los Angeles Times*, Life and Style Section, Sunday, April 5, 1998: E1.
58. Gilles Delafon, "Du nouveau sur 'l'affaire Jésus.'" *Le Journal du Dimanche*, Paris, Sunday, April 5, 1998:32.
59. Carol McGraw (from *Orange County Register*, CA), "Scholars question Jews' role in the crucifixion." *The Orlando Sentinel*, Living Section, Saturday, April 11, 1998: D1 and D7.
60. T. F. Rigelhof, "Jesus and Christianity: interlocking puzzles." *The Toronto Globe and Mail*, Saturday, April 11, 1998.
61. William MacNeil, "Studying the Historical Jesus: Between resurrection and conversion." *Santa Fe*, NM, Sunday, April 12, 1998.
62. Don Lattin, "Looking for Jesus." *San Francisco Chronicle*, Book Review, Sunday, April 12, 1998: 1 and 8.
63. Richard Higgins, "Book Review: Reconstructing Christianity at its start." *The Boston Globe*, Saturday, May 2, 1998.
64. Tom DePoto, "Book Review: The Birth of Christianity." *The Star–Ledger*, Newark, NJ, Sunday, May 3, 1998.
65. Steven W. Lawler, "Christian scholars uses few secular tools." *St. Louis Post-Dispatch*, Sunday, May 31, 1998.

66. Victor Greto, "Resurrecting Jesus: Search for the Gospel truth examines facts and faith." *Colorado Springs Gazette*, "Lifestyle: Religion." Saturday, May 23, 1998: 1 and 3.
67. Ronnie Blair, "Book examines early-days of Christianity." *Tampa Tribune*, Saturday, June 13, 1998.
68. Robert L. Wilken, "The Greatest Story Ever Told." *Los Angeles Times*, Sunday, September 6, 1998.
69. David K. Nartonis, "Divining Currents in the Origin of Christianity." *Christian Science Monitor*, Thursday, August 20, 1998.
70. "Calvary and Damascus: First-generation Christians." *Trenton Times*, Trenton, NJ, Sunday, August 16, 1998.
71. Marcia Z. Nelson, "Authority on Jesus to bring theological challenge to Aurora." *The Beacon News*, Aurora, IL, October 31, 1998: F1 and 6.
72. Mark I. Pinsky, "Scholars take a new look at the Good Book." *The Orlando Sentinel*, Saturday, November 21, 1998: D1 and D7.
73. Trish Hollenbeck, "Reconstructing the life of Christ." *Pittsburg (KS) Morning Star*, Monday, November 2, 1998.
74. Virginia Sink, "Books for Oklahomans: Christmas more than Materialism." *Bethany Tribune* (Oklahoma City Metro Area), Thursday, November 5, 1998.
75. Mary Jane Henderson, "Crunching the numbers on this year's notable books." *St. Louis Post–Dispatch*, Sunday, November 29, 1998.
76. Mark I. Pinsky, "What really went on when Jesus arrived?" *The Orlando Sentinel*, Thursday, December 24, 1998: A4.
77. Clayton Hardiman, "Questioning the Faith." *The Muskegon Chronicle*, Friday, January 29, 1999, D1 and D3; "Jesus Scholar shares thoughts." *The Muskegon Chronicle*, Sunday, January 21, 1999, A1 and A2.
78. Charles Honey, "Controversial theologian brings his ideas to local church." *The Grand Rapids Press*, Saturday, February 13, 1999: B1 and B2.
79 Victor Greto, "Interpreting the Resurrection: For some Christians, faith in the risen Christ is a question of believing, not seeing." *Colorado Springs Gazette*, Saturday, April 3, 1999: Life 1 and 3.
80. John Blake, "Message of Rebirth." *Atlanta Journal Constitution*, Saturday, April 3, 1999.
81. Mark I. Pinsky, "Rebel theologian." *The Orlando Sentinel*, Living: Religion." Saturday, April 24, 1999: E1 and 6.
82. Gordon Legge, "John Dominic Crossan: Look for meaning behind parables, theologian urges." *Calgary Herald*: Religion and Spirituality, Saturday, June 12, 1999: OS9.

83. Stephanie Nolen, "Selling Jesus to the disenchanted: Gospel Truth?" *The Globe and Mail*, Toronto, Canada, Saturday, June 26, 1999: C17.

84. Ed Williams, "Justice is faith community's common ground." *The Charlotte Observer*, Sunday, November 14, 1999: C4.

85. Carol B. Cole, "Visions: A Look toward the Next Millennium." Supplement to the-daytona *Beach Sunday News-Journal*, Sunday, November, 1999: 3H and 9H.

86. Stephen Buttry, "Gospel messages get lost in search for literal truth." *The Des Moines Register*, Saturday, February 5, 2000

87. Clayton Hardiman, "Nearly 300 'eavesdrop' on debate about historical Jesus." *The Muskegan Sunday Chronicle* (Tri-Cities Edition), Sunday, March 19, 2000.

88. Jim Abbott, "Great Crusade." *The Orlando Sentine*, Sunday, June 18, 2000: F1 and F5.

89. Nancy Haught, "Soul-searching." *The Oregonian*, Wednesday, September 13, 2000: B1 and B3.

90. Rita Elkins, "Who Is Jesus?" Part 1 of 2. *Florida Today*, Saturday, September 14, 2000: 1D and 6D; "Believers Split on Historical Jesus." Part 2 of 2. *Florida Today*, Sunday, September 15, 2000: 1D and 5D.

91. Dale Neal, "Biblical scholar to teach, preach in Asheville." *Asheville Citizen-Times* (*Living*), Asheville, NC, Saturday, November 25, 2000; "Scholar preaches message of love, justice on first Sunday of Advent." *Asheville Citizen-Times* (*Mountains*), Monday, December 4, 2000.

92. Deborah Deasy, "Controversial theologian to lead workshops." *Pittsburgh Tribune-Review*, Pittsburgh, PA, Friday, February 9, 2001.

93. Ann Rodgers-Melnick, "Popular biblical scholar to speak in Squirrel Hill." *Pittsburgh Post-Gazette*, Pittsburgh, PA, Friday, February 9, 2001.

94. Faris Cassell, "Author preaches appreciation for the real Jesus." *Eugene Register-Guard*, Arts and Books, Eugene, OR, Sunday, February 18, 2001: 1B and 5B.

95. David Crum, "Resurrecting Jesus' Image." *Detroit Free Press*, Thursday, April 12, 2001: 1A and 8A.

96. Tim Funk, "Cure terrorism with justice, scholar says." *Charlotte Observer*, Charlotte, NC. Monday, October 29, 2001.

97. Andrew Kenneth Gay, "Scholar Crossan visits Flagler College." *The St. Augustine Record*, 1C-2C. St. Augustine, FL. Friday, March 22, 2002. "Crossan Engages, but also Enrages Flagler Students." *The St. Augustine Record*, 2C. St. Augustine, FL. Sunday, March 24, 2002.

98. Neels Jackson, "Die man met Bybel-ore." *Beeld*, Johannesburg, South Africa, Wednesday, April 17, 2002: 13.

99. Stephan Coan, "A different angle on Jesus." *The Natal Witness*, Durban, South Africa, Thursday, April 25, 2002:15.

100. Robert Neralich, "Archaeology, texts both explain Jesus in context." *Arkansas Democrat-Gazette*, Little Rock, AR, Saturday March 30, 2002.

101. Jennifer L. Grant, "Centerpiece: In Search of Jesus." *Naples News*, Saturday, April 5, 2003.

102. David Crumm, "Critics say Gibson film mimics a hateful book." *Detroit Free Press*, Thursday, February 19, 2004.

103. Larry Mitchell, "'Passion of the Christ' film draws mixed reviews from religious leaders." *Enterprise-Record*, Chico, CA, Thursday, February 19, 2004.

104. John Dominic Crossan, "The 'sin' of 'Passion.'" *Orlando Sentinel*, Insight section. Sun-day, February 22, 2004: G1 and G4.

105. John Blake, "Examining Jesus' death. Mel Gibson's 'The Passion of the Christ' raises anew the question of who was responsible." *The Atlanta Journal-Constitution*, Atlanta, GA, Monday, February 23, 2004: D1.

106. Frank Langfitt, "Issues of Faith and History." *Baltimore Sun*, Baltimore, MD, Saturday, February 28, 2004.

107. Jim Baker, "Biblical Scholar criticizes 'Passion,'" *Lawrence Journal-World*, Lawrence, KS, Sunday, February 29, 2004.

108. Sharon Boase, "Passion movie's theology is obscene, says Jesus scholar." *The Hamilton Spectator*, Toronto, Canada, Monday, March 15, 2004.

109. Ron Csillag, "Christian scholar questions Gibson's depiction of Jesus." *The Toronto Star*, Saturday, April 10, 2004

110. Jim Baker, "Biblical scholar visits area as Theologian in Residence." *Lawrence Journal-World*, Lawrence, KS, Monday, April 19, 2004

111. Phil Haslanger, "Author stresses 4 different Gospels." *The Capital Times*, Madison, WI, April 20, 2004.

112. Rush Barlow, "Putting Iraq into biblical perspective." *The Boston Globe*, Saturday, May 22, 2004.

113. Relma Hargus, "Scholar: God is just." *The Advocate*, Baton Rouge, LA, Saturday, May 22, 2004.

114. Phil Anderson, "Crossan tracks biblical history." *Topeka Capital-Journal*, Topeka, KS, Saturday, May 29, 2004.

115. Nancy Haught, "Striking Back at the Empires: A scholar sees lessons for America in Apostle Paul's challenge to Rome." Living section E1 and E8, *The Oregonian*, Portland, OR, Friday, December 3, 2004. Distributed by Newhouse and RNS.

116. Mark I. Pinsky, "What would Paul; say?" Life and Times, *The Orlando Sentinel*, Sunday, December 19.2004: F1 and F3.

117. Bob Reeves, "Who Was Jesus? Visiting scholar sees Christa as a revolutionary." *Journal Star*, Lincoln, NE, Section Con Values: Religion and Spirituality. Saturday, March 26, 2005: 1 and 4.

118. Nina Chiarelli, Who Was Jesus? Fredericton church plans three-day seminar next weekend." *New Brunswick Telegraph-Journal*, Fredericton, NB. Canada, Friday, April 22, 2005: B10.

119. Greg Garrison, "In Search of Paul. Theologian talks about his research into apostle's life." *The Birmingham News*. Religion, Friday, May 6, 2005: 1H and 4H.

=Greg Garrison, "Scholars chronicle Paul's lasting impact." *Biblical Recorder: NC Baptist News*, Tuesday, June 7, 2005 (Religion News Service]

120. Relma Hargus, "Author: Look at Jesus in light of first century." *Baton Rouge Advocate*, Living Values, Saturday, September 24, 2005: F1.

121. Paul Scott, "Jesus scholar brings food for new thought." *Post-Bulletin*, Rochester, MN, Tuesday, October 4, 2005.

122. Sam Hodges, "'Christianity was high treason: Q&A with John Dominic Crossan." *The Dallas Morning News*. Religion, Spirituality, and Values. Saturday, October 22, 2005: 1H.

123. Cori Bolger, "Controversial Jesus scholar to speak." Religion, *Clarion-Ledger*, Jackson, MS, Saturday, October 22, 2005: 1D-2D.

124. John Blake, "Rethinking Paul." *Atlanta Journal Constitution*, Faith and Values, Saturday, October 29, 2005: F2-F3.

125. Jay Rath, "Vetting the Jesus Parable." *Wisconsin State Journal*, Madison, WI, Saturday, February 25, 2006: C1 and C8.

126. Karris Goldeen, "Author to discuss Jesus' life, relation to politics in Roman times." *The Courier*, Waterloo-Cedar Falls, Iowa, Friday, September 29, 2006: A8.

127. Karen Heinselman, "Weekend explores history of Jesus, religion's future." *The Courier*, Waterloo-Cedar Falls, Iowa, Friday, October 6, 2006: A7.

128. Mark Pinsky, "New theories unlikely to influence believers." *Orlando Sentinel*, (Easter) Sunday, April 8, 2007 A3.

129. Keith Essenburg, "Author points to God's contrasts." Grand Rapids Press, Saturday, February 2, 2008.

130. Barney Zwartz, "Disturbing the Faith." *The Age* (Melbourne Life), Monday, September 6, 2010:20.

131. "Author's talk eyes parables and Jesus: Crossan to speak at Unitarian church." *The Advocate*, Saturday Edition, March 17, 2012: 2D and 8D.

132. Dve Mason, "'Our Father ...' Biblical scholar explores original meaning of the 'Lord's Prayer.'" *Santa Barbara News-Press*, Faith and Values. Saturday, February 25, 2013: D6.

(3) Radio

1. Live interview with call-ins on Milton Rosenberg's "Extension 720." WGN-AM, Chicago, IL, 9:00-11:00 PM, Thursday, May 31, 1990.
2. Panelist (by conference call) for Fred Anderly, over National Public Radio via WOSU, Columbus, Ohio, on "The Historical Jesus." 2:30-3:45 PM, Tuesday, April 2, 1991.
3. Panelist for CBC (Canada) Radio discussion on the historical Jesus, Sunday, October 27, 1991.
4. Live interview on "World Headquarters: The Jack Cole Show." WJNO-AM, West Palm Beach, FL, 5-6 PM, Thursday, December 26, 1991.
5. Live interview and calls-in on "The David Gold Show." KLIF-AM, Dallas, TX, 5-6 PM Tuesday, January 14, 1992.
6. Live interview and calls-in on "The Haymer and McNamee Show." WLS-AM and FM, Chicago, IL, 12-1 PM, Saturday, January 25, 1992.
7. Taped interview for "The Vicki Gabereau Show." Vancouver, BC, over Canadian Broadcasting System, 12-1 PM, Thursday, April 2, 1992.
8. Live interview and call-ins on "The Carole Hemingway Show." KGIL-AM, Mission Hills, CA, 4-5 PM, Thursday, April 2, 1992.
9. Live interview and call-ins on Larry Mantle's "Air Talk." KPCC-FM, Pasadena, CA, 6-7 PM, Thursday, April 2, 1992.
10. Taped interview with Leo Lee, Western Public Radio, for National Public Radio feed, San Francisco, CA, 10:00-10:30 AM, Friday, April 3, 1992.
11. Taped interview for Marita Dorenbecher's "Community Dialogue." KKHI-FM, San Francisco, CA, 2:30-3:00 PM, Friday, April 3, 1992.
12. Live interview with call-ins on "The Michael Krasny Show." KGO-AM, San Francisco, CA, 11:00-12:00 midnight, Friday, April 3, 1992.
13. Taped interview for Steve Moore's "Off the Shelf." WADN-AM, Boston, MA, 8:00-8:30 AM, Monday, April 6, 1992.
14. Live interview with call-ins on "The Gene Burns Show." WRKO-AM, Boston, MA, 10:00-12:00 noon, Monday, April 6, 1992.
15. Live interview with calls-in on "The Larry King Show." Mutual Broadcasting System, New York, NY, 12:00-1:00 AM, Thursday, April 9, 1992.
16. Taped interview with Roy Lloyd, Ecumedia News Network, New York, NY, for CBS and UPI Radio feed, 9:00-9:30 AM, Friday, April 10, 1992.
17. Taped interview for Reuben (Ben) Gums' "Interfaith Connection." WYNY-FM, New York, NY, 10-11 AM, Friday, April 10, 1992.
18. Live interview on Don Jackson's "One-Eyed Jack Show." WMAY-AM, Springfield, IL, 7:00-7:30 AM, Tuesday, April 14, 1992.

19. Taped interview for Gregory Hinz' "The Cutting Edge." WLUP-AM&FM, Chicago, IL, 11:00–11:30 AM, Thursday, April 16, 1992.
20. Live interview with call-ins on "The Gene Burns Show." WOR-AM, New York, NY, 3:00–5:20 PM, Friday, April 17, 1992.
21. Live interview with call-ins on "The Rick Barber Show." KOA-AM, Denver, CO, 12:00–5:20 PM, Friday, April 17, 1992.
22. Taped interview with Michael Joyce, *Voice of America*, Midwest bureau, Chicago, for 10-minute national and international feed, 10:00–11:00 AM, Wednesday, April 29, 1992.
23. Taped interview for John Walsh's "Book Shelf." WRHU-FM, Long Island, NY, 11:30–12:30 PM, Thursday, May 7, 1992.
24. Live interview with call-ins on "The Jeanine Graf Show." WEZE-AM, Boston, MA, 2–4 PM, Monday, July 20, 1992.
25. Two taped interview for two shows on Ronald Way's "Eye on Faith." KGLO-AM, Santa Inez, CA, 10–11 AM, Thursday, 23 July, and 10–11 AM, Thursday, 20 August, 1992.
26. Live interview with call-ins on Teddy Bart's "Beyond Reason." WWTN-FM, Nashville, TN, 10–11 AM, Sunday, 26 July, 1992.
27. Live interview on "The Wayne Larrivee Show." WGN-AM, Chicago, IL, 8:15–8:45 PM, Monday, September 7, 1992.
28. Live interview on Byron Schafer's "Religion on the Line." WABC, New York, 8–9 AM, Sunday, September 13, 1992.
29. Live interview on Dick Staub's "Chicago Talks." WYLL-FM, Elk Grove Village, IL, 3:30–4:00 PM, Wednesday, September 30, 1992.
30. Taped interview for National Public Radio with Ken Myers for use during "Weekend Edition" [over WBEZ, Chicago], 8:00–10:00 AM, Sunday, December 20, 1992.
31. Taped interview for the "Matthew Abraham Show." Radio 2CN, Canberra, Australia, 9:30–10:00 AM, Wednesday, 31 March, 1993.
32. Taped interview for the "Ramona Koval Show." Radio 3LO, Melbourne, Australia, 1:00–2:00 PM, Friday, April 2, 1993.
33. Taped interview for Rachael Kohn's "Religion Reports." Radio National, Sydney, Australia, 9:30–10:00 AM, Tuesday, April 6, 1993.
34. Live interview with call-ins on Fr. Ron Lengwin's "Amplify." KDKA-AM, Pittsburgh, PA, 10:00–11:00 PM, Sunday, April 4, 1993.
35. Taped interview for Judy Tierney's "Morning Program." Radio 7ZR, Hobart, Tasmania, Australia, 9:30–10:00 AM, Thursday, April 8 1993.
36. Live interview for the "Terry Lane Show." Radio 2BL, 2NC, 3LO, & 7ZR, from Melbourne, Australia, 1:00–1:20 PM, Wednesday, May 5, 1993.

37. Taped interview with Ron Way for "Eye on Faith." CBS Radio Network, Santa Ynez, CA, 4:00-6:00 PM, Monday, November 22, 1993.
38. Live interview with call-ins on the "Mark Davis Show." WCR-Radio, Washington, D.C., 11-12 AM, Tuesday, November 30, 1993.
39. Live interview with call-ins on the "Casey Stevens Show." WHCU-AM, Ithaca, NY, 3:00-3:40 PM, Thursday, December 2, 1993.
40. Live interview with Tom DiNanni for "Religion on the Line." KSTP-AM, Minneapolis, MN, 8:00-9:00 AM, Sunday, December 5, 1993.
41. Live interview with call-ins on "After Midnight, with Rick Barber." KOA-AM, Denver, CO, 12:00-2:00 AM, Monday, December 6, 1993.
42. Live interview with call-ins, on satellite across the country, for "The Paul Gonzales Show." the People's Radio Network, Tampa, FL, either 11:30 AM-1:00 PM, Monday, December 6, 1993.
43. Live interview with call-ins on the "Jack Ellery Show." WCTC-AM, New Brunswick, NJ, 7:10-20 Am, Tuesday, December 7, 1993.
44. Live interview with call-ins, on satellite across the country, on the "Jack Ellery Show." the People's Radio Network, from New Brunswick, NJ, 6:00-7:00 PM, Tuesday, December 7, 1993.
45. Taped interview for "Mix of Minds" with Deb Daigle. WZMX-FM, Farmington, CT, 8:30-9:00 AM, Wednesday, December 8, 1993.
46. Live interview with call-ins on the "Kevin McCarthy Show." KLIF, Dallas, TX, 11:00 AM-11:30 AM or 12:00 PM, Wednesday, December 8, 1993.
47. Live interview and debate on the "Jeanine Graf Show." WEZE-AM, Boston, MA, 1:00-2:00 PM, Thursday, December 9, 1993.
48. Taped interview for "Chatting with Betty [Stavis]" show. WESX-AM, Salem, MA, 1:30-1:35 PM, Tuesday, December 14, 1993.
49. Live interview with call-ins on Milton Rosenberg's "Extension 720." WGN-AM, Chicago, IL, 9:00-11:00 PM, Tuesday, December 14, 1993.
50. Taped interview with Carmen Jackson on "To the Best of Our Knowledge." WFMT-FM, Chicago, IL, for syndication over 140 Public Radio stations, 10:00-10:30 AM, Wednesday, December 15, 1993.
51. Taped interview with Steve Carpenter for the "Fresh Air and More" show. KCCK-FM, Cedar Rapids, IA, 11:00-11:30 AM, Wednesday, December 15, 1993.
52. Taped interview with Deborah Rowe for the "Talk of Chicago" show. WVON-AM, Chicago, IL, 11:30 AM-12:30 PM, Friday, December 16, 1993.
53. Taped interview with Marty Orgel for "Keep the Change" show. KCBS-AM, San Francisco, CA, for the CBS Radio Network, 4:00-4:10PM, Saturday, December 18, 1993.

54. Taped interview on the "Walter Dixon Show." WBIV-AM, Boston, MA, 6:00–6:30, Monday, December 20, 1993.
55. Live interview with Todd Feinburg for "Morning Talk with Rosalie and Todd." WSSH-AM, Boston, MA, for Talk America Radio Network, 8:20–8:40 AM, Tuesday, December 21, 1993.
56. Live interview on the "Pat McMahon Show." KTAR-AM, Phoenix, AZ, 12:00–2:00 PM, Tuesday, December 21, 1993.
57. Taped interview with Pat Nassan for UPI Audio, Tuesday, December 21, 1993.
58. Live interview with Tim Farley for the "Morning Show." WRVA-AM, Richmond, VA, 11:05–11:30 AM, Wednesday, December 22, 1993.
59. Taped interview for the "Tina Trenner Program." Colorado Springs, CO, syndicated by the American Forum Radio Network over 130 stations, 1:00–2:00 PM, Wednesday, December 22, 1993.
60. Live interview with call-ins on the "Gene Byrnes Program." WOR-AM Radio Network, New York, NY, syndicated to 85 stations, Wednesday, December 22, 1993.
61. Live interview on the "Late Afternoon" show with Jim Althoff. KING-AM, Seattle, WA, 7:00–7:30 PM, Wednesday, December 22, 1993.
62. Live interview with call-ins for Alex Ashlock's "Focus 580" show. WILL-AM&FM, University of Illinois at Urbana-Champaign (National Public Radio), 11:00 AM–12:00 PM, Thursday, December 23, 1993.
63. Live interview with call-ins on the "Roger Hedgecock Show." KSDO-AM, 4:00–5:00 PM, Thursday, December 23, 1993.
64. Live interview on the "Mark Kaufman Show." WWWE-AM, Cleveland, OH, 3:05–3:30 PM, Friday, December 24, 1993.
65. Live interview with call-ins on "Sound Off" with Lanny James, KMLB-AM, Monroe, LA, 5:00–6:00 PM, January 12, 1994.
66. Live interview with call-ins on "Jan Coleman Show." WGN-AM, Chicago, IL, 8:00–9:00 PM, January 15, 1994.
67. Taped interview with Paolo Longo for RAI, Radio Televisione Italiana (Radio), Washington, DC, 9:30–10:00 AM, Friday, January 22, 1994.
68. Live interview with call-ins on Bill Freeman's "The Morning Show." WGVU-AM, Grand Rapids, MI (National Public radio affiliate), 9:30–10:00 AM, January 24, 1994.
69. Live interview with call-ins on Barry Martin's "Double Talk.", KVON-AM, Napa, CA, 12:00–1:00 PM, Monday, January 24, 1994.
70. Live interview with call-ins on the "Wayne Larrivee Show." WGN-AM, Chicago, IL, 11:00–12:00 AM, Monday, February 21, 1994.

71. Live interview with call-ins on "Conversations with Jean Feraca." Wisconsin Public Radio (over 15 stations in WI and other states as well), Madison, WI, 10:00–11:00 AM, Monday, March 14, 1994.

72. Live interview on Dick Staub's "Chicago Talks." WYLL-FM, Elk Grove Village, IL, 5:00–6:00 PM, Monday, March 14, 1994.

73. Live interview with call-ins on the "Wayne Larrivee Show." WGN-AM, Chicago, IL, 10:00–12:00 AM, Monday, March 21, 1994.

74. Live interview with call-ins on John Nuzzo's "AM Beaver County." WBVP-FM, Beaver Falls, PA, 8:00–9:00 AM, Tuesday, March 22, 1994.

75. Live interview with David Alpern, "Newsweek on the Air." 1:15–1:30 PM, Saturday, March 26, 1994.

76. Taped interview with Terry Gross on "Fresh Air." National Public Radio, 1:00–1:45 PM, Wednesday, March 30, 1994.

77. Live interview on "Leigh McClusky Show." Radio 5AN, 7:30–7:45 AM, Adelaide, South Australia, Thursday, March 31, 1994.

78. Live interview on "Rob Hoskin Show." Radio Australia, 9:00–9:20 AM, Victoria, Australia, Radio Australia, Thursday, March 31, 1994.

79. Live interview on "Jennifer Byrne Show." Radio 2BL, 10:30–10:45 AM, Victoria, Australia, Thursday, March 31, 1994.

80. Live interview on "Annie Warburton Show." Radio 7ZR, Hobart, Tasmania, 2:30–2:50 PM, Thursday, March 31, 1994.

81. Live interview on "Philip Adams Show." Radio National, New South Wales, Australia, 2:30–2:50 PM, Thursday, March 31, 1994.

82. Live interview with call-ins on the "Kwesell and Crawford Show." WIVC-FM, Indianapolis, IN, 3:00–4:00 PM, Thursday, March 31, 1994.

83. Live interview with Jeff Schwarz's "Issues, Etc." St. Louis, MO, (Jubilee Radio Network Satellite Services) 11:05–11:25 PM, Sunday, April 3, 1994.

84. Live interview on "Verity James Show." Radio 6WF, Perth, Australia, 6:00–6:20 PM, Wednesday, April 13, 1994.

85. Live interview with Gary Wescott on "Wake Up the World." WSPO, Stephens Point, WI, 7:20–7:35 AM, Friday, April 15, 1994.

86. Live interview with Nicky Plummer and others on "The Breakfast Club." KLAS-FM, Kingston, Jamaica, 8:10–8:30 AM, Friday, April 15, 1994.

87. Live interview with Glen Mitchell on "Texas USA." KRLD, Dallas, TX, 10:00–11:30 PM, Thursday, May 12, 1994.

88. Taped interview with Ron Way for "Eye on Faith." CBS Radio Network, Santa Ynez, CA, 11:00–12:00 AM, Friday, May 13, 1994.

89. Live interview with Aaron Freeman on "Metropolis." WBEZ, Chicago, IL, 12:30–1:00 PM, Saturday, June 11, 1994.

90. Live interview with call-ins on the "Deborah Crable Show." WVON-AM, Chicago, IL, 10:35-12:20 AM, Thursday, July 14, 1994.

91. Taped interview on "Todd Pooser Show." KCMU-FM, National Public Radio, Seattle, WA, 12:00-1:00 PM, Monday, October 3, 1994.

92. Live interview with Jim Breedlove on "Breedlove and Co." KUDI, Yakima, WA, 8:30-8:45 AM, Monday, November 7, 1994.

93. Live interview with call-ins on Milton Rosenberg's "Extension 720." WGN-AM, Chicago, IL, 9:00-11:00 PM, Tuesday, March 7, 1995.

94. Live interview with call-ins, for Bill Freeman's "Morning Show." WGVU, a National Public Radio affiliate, Grant Rapids, MI, 9:00-10:00 AM, Wednesday, March 15, 1995.

95. Live interview with call-ins on Dick Staub's "Chicago Talks." WYLL-FM, Elk Grove Village, IL, 3:00-4:00 PM, Wednesday, March 22, 1995.

96. Live interview with call-ins on "Danny Bonaducce Show." 11:20-11:45 AM, WLUP Radio, Chicago, IL, Friday, March 24, 1995.

97. Live interview with call-ins on "Catherine Johns Show." WLS-AM&FM, Chicago, IL, 8:00-9:00 PM, Friday, March 24, 1995.

98. Live interview with call-ins on Tom Dinanni's "Religion on the Line." KSTP, Minneapolis, MN, 9:00-10:00 AM, Sunday, March 26, 1995.

99. Two taped interviews with Ralph Benmurghie for CBC's "Radio Noon." 11:00-11:30 AM, Thursday, March 23, 1995.

100. Taped interview with Gregory Hinz for "Chicago Street Talk." WLUP, Chicago, IL, 10:00-10:30 AM, Monday, March 27, 1995.

101. Taped interview for "Dave Baum Show." WBBM, Chicago, IL, 12:15 PM, Monday, March 27, 1995.

102. Live interview with Terry Gross for "Fresh Air." NPR, Chicago, IL, 12:00-1:00 PM, Monday, April 3, 1995.

103. Live interview for "The John Williams Show." WCCO-AM, Minneapolis, MN, 6:30-7:30 PM, Thursday, March 30, 1995.

104. Taped interview for KSJN-AM, "Minnesota Public Radio." 12:30-1:00 PM, Friday, March 31, 1995.

105. Live interview for "NY & Company." WNYC Radio, New York, NY, 12:45-1:15 PM, Wednesday, April 5, 1995.

106. Taped interview with Roy Lloyd for Ecumedia, New York, NY, 2:30-3:00 PM, Wednesday, April 5, 1995.

107. Taped interview with Marcel Dubois, O.P., Jerusalem for "Meridian." Australian Broadcasting Corp. at NPR Studio, Chicago, IL, 8:30-9:30 AM, Monday, April 10, 1995.

108. Taped interview for "Studs Terkel Show." WFMT, Chicago, IL, 11:00 AM, Monday, April 10, 1995.

109. Taped interview for "Mutual News." NBC Radio Network, Arlington, 1:00–1:30 PM, Monday, April 10, 1995.

110. Taped interview for "Page One." ATWITZEND, Washington DC, 11:30 AM–12:15 PM, Wednesday, April 12, 1995.

111. Taped interview for "Talk of the Nation." NPR, Washington DC, 3:00–4:00 PM, Wednesday, April 12, 1995.

112. Phone interview for "Countdown." Talk Radio News Service, Washington DC, 5:00–5:30 PM, Wednesday, April 12, 1995.

113. Taped interview for "Voice of America." Washington DC, 8:45–9:15 AM, Thursday, April 13, 1995.

114. Live interview for "WAMU-FM/Diane Rehm Show." American University Broadcast Center, 10:00–11:00 AM, Thursday, April 13, 1995.

115. Taped interview for "UPI Radio." 12:00–12:30 PM, Thursday, April 13, 1995.

116. Taped interview for "Between the Line.", A.P./WTOP, 1:00 PM, Thursday, April 13, 1995.

117. Taped interview with Barry Ian Fiore for "Everybody Knows." KKUP, Cupertino, CA, 10:00–11:30 AM, Sunday, April 16, 1995.

118. Live phone interview with Bill Kelly for CHML Radio, Hamilton, Ontario, Canada, 6:00–7:00 PM, Thursday, April 20, 1995.

119. Live interview with call-ins on Pat Cunningham's "Mid-Morning Show." WROK, Rock-ford, IL, 10:30–11:00 AM, Wednesday, April 26, 1995.

120. Geobald, WBAI, New York, NY, 10:15–10:45 PM, Tuesday, May 23, 1995.

121. Live interview on "Jack Cole Show." WJNO, West Palm Beach, FL, 2:00–3:00 PM, Tuesday, May 30, 1995.

122. Live interview with call-ins for Jack Brighton's "Focus 580" show, WILL-AM&FM (National Public Radio), University of Illinois at Urbana-Champaign, 11:00 AM–12:00 PM, Wednesday, June 7, 1995.

123. Live interview with call-ins on "The Michael Coren Show." CFRB-AM, Toronto, Canada, 10:00–11:00 AM CST, Friday, August 11, 1995.

124. Live interview on Teddy Bart's "Beyond Reason." WKDA, Nashville, TN, 5–6 PM, Wednesday, March 27, 1996.

125. Live interview on the Austrian Broadcasting Network, Vienna, 9:30–9:45 AM EST, Thursday, April 4, 1996.

126. Live interview with call-ins on "Conversations with Jean Feraca." Wisconsin Public Radio (over 15 stations in WI and other states as well), Madison, WI, 10:00–11:00 AM EST, Friday, April 4, 1996.

127. Taped interview with John Goldsmith, for Radio WSQR, DeKalb, IL, 2:300–3:00 PM, Tuesday, April 16, 1996.

128. Live interview with call-ins on "Terry Moore Show." Radio QR 77, Calgary, Alberta, Canada, 10:00–11:00 CST, Thursday, April 18, 1996.

129. Live interview with call-ins on "Al Wisk Show." WBAP, Dallas, TX, 8:30–9:00 PM, Wednesday, May 8, 1996.

130. Live interview in debate with Luke Timothy Johnson on Phillip Adams' show, "Late Night Live." ABC Radio, Sydney, Australia, 9:00–9:45 AM EST, Thursday, July 11, 1996.

131. Live interview with call-ins on "The Eliot Stein Show." United Broadcasting Network, 9:00–12:00 PM PST, Sunday, December 22, 1996.

132. Live interview with call-ins on Jonathan Overby's "Higher Ground." Wisconsin Public Radio, Madison, WI, 9:00–10:00 CST, Easter Sunday, March 30, 1997.

133. Live interview on Bryan LeBeau's "Talking History" (Creighton University), for National Public Radio over KIOS, Omaha, NE, and WRPI, Troy, NY, 4:30–5:00 PM EST, Wednesday, December 10, 1997.

134. Live interview with Aaron Freeman on "Metropolis." WBEZ, Chicago, IL, 2:00–2:15 CST, Saturday, December 20, 1997.

135. Live interview on Bryan LeBeau's "Talking History" (Creighton University), for National Public Radio over KIOS, Omaha, NE, and WRPI, Troy, NY, 3:30–4:00 PM EST, Wednesday, March 18, 1998.

136. Live interview on "Gene Burns Show." WKGO, San Francisco, CA, 6:30–7:00 PM EST, Thursday, April 2, 1998.

137. Taped interview with Roy Lloyd, Ecumedia News Network, New York, NY, for CBS and UPI Radio feed, 7:00–8:00 AM, Tuesday, April 7, 1998.

138. Taped interview for the "Morning Show." News 12 Long Island, Woodbury, NY, 9:00–9:20 AM, Tuesday, April 12, 1998.

139. Taped interview with Neal Lavon for "Voice of America." Washington, DC, 10:00–10:30 AM, Thursday, April 9, 1998.

140. Live interview with call-ins for "Talk of the Nation." NPR, Washington, DC, 2:00–3:00 PM, Thursday, April 9, 1998.

141. Live interview with call-ins on Milton Rosenberg's "Extension 720." WGN-AM, Chicago, IL, 9:00–11:00 PM, Thursday, April 9, 1998.

142. Live interview with call-ins on "Odyssey." WBEZ, Chicago, IL, Friday, April 10, 1998.

143. Live interview on Teddy Bart and Karlen Evins, "Beyond Reason." WKDA, Nashville, TN, from 1:00–2:00 PM, Tuesday, April 14, 1998.

144. Live interview with call-ins on "Jim McCrell's Show" (host: David Capes). KKTL, Houston, TX, from 8:20–9:00 PM EST, Friday, April 24, 1998.

145. Live interview on Dan Valenti's "Open Mike." WBRK, Pittsfield, MA, 9:00–9:30 AM EST, Monday, May 4, 1998.
146. Taped interview with Lyn Gallagher for Australian Broadcasting Corporation, Sydney, Australia, in studio of Florida Radio Network, 10:00–11:00 AM, Friday, May 29, 1998.
147. Live interview with call-ins for John Rabe's "Mid-Morning." KNOW, St. Paul, Minnesota Public Radio, 10:00–11:00, Monday, July 6, 1998.
148. Live interview with call-ins for Charles Brennan's "Morning Meeting." KMOX-AM (CBS), St. Louis, MO, 11:15–12:00 noon, Wednesday, July 8, 1998.
149. Live interview for Ed Johnson's "Profile." KOPB-FM, Oregon Public Radio, Portland, OR, 12:00–12:30 PM, Tuesday, July 21, 1998.
150. Live interview for Ed Roehling's "Conversations." WICR-FM, National Public Radio, Indianapolis, IN, 9:25–10:00 AM, Wednesday, July 22, 1998.
151. Taped interview for "Weekday" program. WUKY-FM, National Public Radio, Lexington, KY, 9:30–10:00 AM, Monday, July 27, 1998.
152. Taped interview for Marilee Richard's "Minnesota Morning." KMSU-FM, National Public Radio, Mankato, MN, 2:00–2:30 PM, Tuesday, July 28, 1998.
153. Live interview with call-ins for Susan Arbetter's "Vox Pop." WAMC-FM, Northeast Public Radio, Albany, NY, 2:00–3:00 PM, Tuesday, August 11, 1998.
154. Live interview for Vic Mickunas' "Book Nook." WYSO-FM, National Public Radio Springs), 2:00–3:00 PM, Wednesday, August 12, 1998.
155. Taped interview for Pat Nassan's "While We're on the Subject." For UPI Radio Network, 12:00–12:15 PM, Thursday, August 13, 1998.
156. Live Audio talk/interview for Eliot Stein's "Stein Online." CompuServe Interactive Radio, 7:00–8:20 PM, Friday, August 14, 1998.
157. Live interview with call-ins on "Conversations with Jean Feraca." Wisconsin Public Radio (over 15 stations in WI and other states as well), Madison, WI, 11:00–12:00 PM, Thursday, August 20, 1998.
158. Taped interview for "James, the Brother of Jesus"—Part 1: "The Missing Story." Produced by Lyn Gallacher, Australian Broadcasting Corporation's Radio National, July 26, 1998.
159. Live interview for "Forum with Michael Krasny." KQED (NPR), Berkeley, CA, 12:00–1:00 PM EST, Wednesday, February 24, 1999.
160. Taped interview for the "Tod Mundt Show." Michigan Public Radio, Ann Arbor, MI, 1:00–2:00 PM, Tuesday, April 27, 1999.
161. Live interview with call-ins on "Glen Beck Show." WFLA, Tampa, FL, 3:00–4:30 PM, Monday, March 20, 2000.
162. Live interview for Good Friday on "Glen Beck Show." WFLA, Tampa, FL, 4:00–5:30 PM, Thursday, April 21, 2000.

163. Live interview with call-ins on the "Kevin McCarthy Show." KLIF, Dallas, TX, 11:30 AM–12:00 PM, Tuesday, June 27, 2000.

164. Taped interview with Diana Jordan, "The Book Page and Between the Lines." KXL-AM Radio, Portland, OR, Friday, September 15, 2000.

165. Live interview with call-ins for "The Jeanine Graf Show." 96.9 Fm-Talk, Marshfield, MA, Wednesday, September 27, 2000.

166. Taped interview for Milton Rosenberg's "Extension 720." WGN-AM, Chicago, IL, 4:00–5:00 PM, Tuesday, October 3, 2000.

167. Live interview with call-ins for "WAMU-FM/Diane Rehm Show." American University Broadcast Center, 11:00 AM–12:00 noon, Wednesday, October 18, 2000.

168. Live interview with call-ins on Milton Rosenberg's "Extension 720." WGN-AM, Chicago, IL, 9:00–11:00 PM, Wednesday, March 7, 2001.

169. Taped interview on "Holy Land Experience Park" for "Nick News." Nickelodeon, 8:50–9:0pm, Sunday, May 27, 2001.

170. Live interview with call-ins for Mike Collins, Charlotte Talks." MFAE-FM (NPR), 9:00–10:00am, Friday, October 26, 2001.

171. Live interview with call-ins on "Conversations with Jean Feraca." Wisconsin Public Radio (over 15 stations in WI and other states as well), Madison, WI, 10:00–11:00 AM, Thursday, January 24, 2002.

172. Live interview with call-ins on "Interconnect" with John Hickenbergen and Cheri Lawson, National Public Radio, WMUB-FM, Miami University, 9:00–10:00am, Monday, October 21, 2002.

173. Live interview for Vic Mickunas' "Book Nook." WYSO-FM, National Public Radio for SW Ohio, Antioch University (Yellow Springs), 2:00–3:00 PM, Friday, February 28, 2003.

174. Taped interview, with Frs. Patrick Rogers and Patrick Comerford, for Vincent Browne's Tonight, RTE 1, Dublin, Ireland, Thursday, 3:00–4:00pm (USA-EST), April 10, 2003.

175. Live interview with Ron Insana (guest host) on the Laura Ingraham Show, Westwood One Radio, Arlington, VA, 9:00–9:30 (EST), July 29, 2003.

176. Live interview for "The Big Show with Bill Cunningham." News Radio 700 WLW, Cincinnati, OH, 1:30–1:45pm, February 17. 2004.

177. Live interview with Steven Feuerstein on "Speak Your Piece." WSNR 620AM, New York, NY, 1)45–11:15pm, Monday, February 23, 2004.

178. Live interview on "America's Radio Show with Andy Thomas." ESPN Radio WOIC 1230 AM, Columbia, SC, 4:30–5:00pm. Tuesday, February 23, 2004.

179. Live interview on "Mornings with Keith and Gail." KCOL 600 AM, 9:00–9:30am, Wednesday, February 25, 2004.

180. Live interview on "Ken Sasso Show." 850 KOA-AM, Denver, CO, 10:00–11:00pm, Wednesday, February 25, 2004.

181. Live interview on "Williams and Whisman." WJBC AM1230, Bloomington, IL, Thursday, February 26, 2004.

182. Live interview with call-ins for "Here on Earth" with Jean Feraca, Wisconsin Public Radio (over 15 stations in WI and other states as well), Madison, WI, 4:00–5:00 PM EST, Sunday, March 7, 2004.

183. Live interview with call-ins on "Interconnect" with John Hickenbergen and Cheri Lawson, National Public Radio, WNUB-FM, Miami University, Oxford, OH, 9:00–10:00am EST, Monday, March 15, 2004.

184. Taped interview with Terry Gross for "Fresh Air" on "Crucifixion as a Form of Execution." National Public Radio, April 1, 2004.

185. Live interview with Doug Fabrizio on "RadioWest." KUER FM90, NPR affiliate, 1:00–2:00pm ET, Monday, April 5, 2004.

186. Live interview on "Williams and Whisman." WJBC AM1230, Bloomington, IL, 3:00–4:00pm ET, Friday, April 9, 2004.

187. Live interview with Matthew Fox for "Spirit in Action." KPFA 94.1 FM, Berkeley, CA, Monday 1:00–2:00pm PST, May 3, 2004.

188. Taped interview with Terry Gross for "Fresh Air" on *In Search of Paul*, National Public Radio, November 16, 2004 [in Philadelphia studio].

189. Live interview for Dave Beck's, "The Beat." KUOW (NPR Affiliate), Seattle, WA, 2:00–2:30pm, Monday, December 6, 2004.

190. Live interview for "The Diane Rehm Show." WAMU-FM (NPR), American University Broadcast Center, 11:00 AM–12:00 noon, Friday, December 10, 2004.

191. Live interview with Marlene Smith, KBOO Community Radio, Portland, OR, 1:00–2:00pm EST, Friday, December 17, 2004.

192. Live interview Dr. Alvin Augustus Jones' "Morning Program." Paradise Radio Network, WCBQ-WHNC-AM, Oxford, NC, 8:45–9:00am, Friday, December 24, 2004.

193. Live interview on "The God Show" with Pat McMahon." NewsRadio 620 KTAR-AM, Phoenix, AZ, 2:00–3:00 PM EST, Wednesday, February 16, 2005.

194. Live interviews on "[Jim] Williams and [Beth] Whisman." WJBC AM1230, Bloomington, IL, Monday, April 18, 3:00–4:00pm. and Tuesday, April 19, 3:00–3:30pm, 2005.

195. Two taped interviews on "Common Threads" with Fred Stella for The Interfaith Dialogue Association WGVU AM&FM, Grand Rapids, MI, 1:00–2:00pm, Monday, February 20, 2006.

196. Live interview with Steve Fast and Beth Whisman." WJBC AM1230, Bloomington, IL, 4:40–5:00pm, Tuesday, May 23, 2006.

197. Taped interview with Todd Wilken for "Issues, Etc." KFUO, St. Louis, MO, 1:00–1:30pm, Wednesday, June 7, 2006.

198. Panelist on historical Jesus for *Tonight with Vincent Browne*, RTE Radio 1, Dublin, Ireland, 8:00–9:00pm, Wednesday, December 6, 2006.

199. Live interview with Andrea Jackson on The Daily Buzz, WKCF, Orlando, FL, 7:25–7:30am, Wednesday, February 28, 2007.

200. Taped interview (for Palm Sunday, April 1) on "The God Show" with Pat McMahon." NewsRadio 620 KTAR-AM, Phoenix, AZ, 1:45–2:45 PM est, Wednesday, March 28, 2007.

201. Live interview on "The Current." with Anna Maria Tremonti, 7:40–8:00am, Easter Mon-day, April 9, 2007.

202. Taped interview from the Westminster Town Hall Forum (from April 26) on Minnesota Public Radio. Monday, 12:00–1:00pm., Monday, April 30, 2007.

203. Taped interview with Rich Ficher's "StudioTulsa." KWGS 89.5 Radio (NPR), Tulsa, OK, 10:15–11:00am, Wednesday, June 13, 2007.

204. Live interview on "Open Line with Fred Anderle." WOSU Radio, NPR affiliate, Columbus, OH, 11:05–12:00pm, Wednesday, June 13, 2007.

205. Taped interview with Joe Donohue's "The Round Table." WAMC, National Productions, NPR, Albany, NY, 12:15–12:30pm, Wednesday, June 13, 2007.

206. Live interview on "Healthy Wealthy Wow" with Kim Power Stilson, KSRR-AM, Provo, UT, Wednesday, June 13, 2007.

207. Live interview with Diego Mulligan's "The Journey Home." KSFR Radio (NPR and BBC), Santa Fe and Albuquerque, NM, 7:10–8:00pm, Wednesday, June 13, 2007.

208. Live interview with David McMillan's "Strategies for Living." Newsradio710 KEEL, Shreveport, LA, 8:00–9:00am, Thursday, June 14, 2007.

209. Taped interview with Faiza El-Masry, News Feature, Voice of America International, Washington, DC, 9:30–9:50am, Thursday, June 14, 2007.

210. Live interview with David Bunte's "AM 920 Magazine." WBAA Radio (Purdue University), Indianapolis, IN (NPR), 9:50–10:10am, Thursday, June 14, 2007.

211. Taped interview with Jeff Schectman's "Morning Edition." KVON Radio, ABC Affiliate, Napa, CA, 10:30–11:00am, Thursday, June 14, 2007.

212. Live interview with Brandy Balkin's "Radio Active." Salt Lake City, UT, 2:00–3:00pm, Thursday, June 14, 2007.

213. Live interview for "Mark Dankof's America." Republic Broadcasting Network, Austin, TX, 9:00–10:00am, Friday, June 15, 2007.

214. Live interview with co-hosts Cheri Lawson and John Hingsbergen, "Interconnect." WMUB Radio, Oxford, Ohio, NPR affiliate, 9:00–10:00am, Monday, June 18, 2007.

215. Taped interview with Guy Rathbun's "Turning Pages." KCBX Public Radio FM 90, San Luis Obispo, CA, NPR affiliate, 1:00–1:20pm, Monday, June 18, 2007.
216. Live interview with Reggie Bryant's "In Pursuit of Truth." WURD Radio, Philadelphia, PA, 4:00–5:00pm, Tuesday, June 19, 2007.
217. Live interview on "The Diane Jones Show." KLPW Radio in Washington, MO, 9:35–9:55am, Monday, July 9, 2007.
218. Live interview with Jim Stowell's "The Idea Exchange." WBEV Radio, Madison and Central WI, 11:06–11:25am, Tuesday, July 10, 2007.
219. Live interview with Doug Fbrizio's "RadioWest." KUER FM 90/XM Public Radio, Salt Lake City, NPR affiliate, 1:00–2:00pm, Tuesday, July 10, 2007.
220. Live interview with Jean Feraca's "Here on Earth." Wisconsin Public Radio, Madison, WI, 4:00–4:00pm, Tuesday, July 10, 2007.
221. Live interview with Bob Johnson's "Second Saturday Magazine." Independent Public Radio, Bridgeport and Montauk, CT, 11:00–11:30am, Saturday, July 14, 2007.
222. Taped interview with Dave McMillan, "Strategies for Living." Newsradio710keel, Shreveport, LA, 6:00–7:00pm ET, Tuesday, November 20, 2007.
223. Taped interview with Cecilia Skidmore on "Open Mind." WGVU Radio, NPR Affiliate, Grand Rapids, MI, 2:00–2:30pm ET, Tuesday, November 27, 2007.
224. Taped interview with John Spalding on "The First Christmas" book for the "Busted Halo" and SoMa review on the Web.
225. Live interview with Chris Lawson and John Hingsbergen, "Interconnect." WMUB Radio, Oxford, OH, NPR affiliate (from Miami University), 9:00–10:00pm ET, Monday, December 3, 2007.
226. Live interview along with Marcus Borg, with guest-host Bob Singleton, "Open Line with Fred Anderle." WOSU Radio, NPR affiliate, Columbus, OH (Ohio State University), 11:00–12:00pm ET, Monday, December 3, 2007.
227. Live interview with Bob Johnson, "Second Saturday Magazine." WPKM Radio, Independent Public Radio, Bridgeport, CT and Montauk, NY, Saturday, December 8, 2007.
228. Live interview with Gena Edvalson and listener calls, "Radio Active." KRCL Radio, Salt Lake City, UT, 2:00–3:00pm ET, Thursday, December 13, 2007.
229. Taped interview with Faiza El-Masry, "News Feature." Voice of America International, Washington, DC, 9:30–9:50am ET, Friday, December 14, 2007.
230. Live interview with Ella Speaks, "The Ella Speaks Show." KTLR AM 890, Oklahoma City, OK, 10:00–10:30am ET, Monday, December 17, 2007.
231. Taped interview along with Marcus Borg, for Joe Donahue, "The Round Table." WAMC, National Productions, NPR, Albany, NY, 11:45–12:00pm ET, Monday, December 17, 2007.

232. Live interview with Krys Boyd, "Think." KERA Radio, NPR affiliate, Dallas, TX, 1:00–2:00pm ET, Monday, December 17, 2007.

233. Taped interview with Guy Rathbun, "Turning Pages." KCBX Public Radio FM 90, San Luis Obispo, CA, 3:00–3:20pm ET, Monday, December 17, 2007.

234. Live interview with Doug Fabrizio, "Radiowest." KUER FM 90/XM Public Radio, Salt Lake City, UT, 1:00–2:00pm ET, Wednesday, December 19, 2007.

235. Live interview along with Marcus Borg, for Jean Feraca, "Here on Earth." Wisconsin Public Radio, Madison, WI, 4:00–5:00pm ET, Wednesday, December 19, 2007.

236. Live interview with Diego Mulligan, "The Journey Home." Santa Fe Public Radio. KSFR Radio in Santa Fe/Albuquerque, NM, 6:00–6:30pm ET, Wednesday, December 19, 2007.

237. Live interview with Jim Bresnahan, "3XZ FM Newshour Show." Lexington, VA, 11:45–12:00pm ET, Thursday, December 20, 2007.

238. Live interview with Warren Pierce, "The Warren Pierce Show." WJR Radio, Detroit, MI, 7:35–7:45am ET, Saturday, December 20, 2007.

239. Live interview with Pete Braley, "The Peter Braley Show." WBSM Radio, Providence, RI, and New Bedford, Fall River, Southern MA, Cape Cod and the Islands, 7:35–7:50am ET, Monday, December 24, 2007.

240. Live interview with Dr. Michael Kell's "Mind, Brain and Body with the Doctor." on Voice of America's Global Health and Wellness Network, 10:00–11:00am ET, Friday, June 6, 2008.

241. Live interview and call-ins with Deborah Goodrich on "Debbie Daily." Cumulus Broad-casting, KMAJ-1440, 9:30–10:00am, Wednesday, June 18, 2008.

242. Live interview with Diego Mulligan, "The Journey Home." Santa Fe Public Radio. KSFR Radio in Santa Fe/Albuquerque, NM, 7:10–7:30pm ET, Thursday, June 19, 2008.

243. Live interview with e-mail questions, along with Bruce Chilton in France, for Kate Turkington's "Believe It or Not" on "The Apostle Paul: Saint of the Public Square." Talk Radio 702, Johannesburg, South Africa, Sunday, July 20, 2008, 7.30–8:30 pm (S.A. time).

244. Interview and call-ins with Katherine Perkins, "Talk@12." Public Radio Broadcasting Services of the University of Iowa and Iowa Public Radio, 1:00–2:00pm (est), Tuesday, September 23, 2008.

245. Live interview and call-ins with Julie Kredens, "State of Affairs." WFPL 89.3 FM, Louisville, KY, 11:00–12:00pm (et), Thursday, November 6, 2008.

246. Live interview along with Marcus Borg, for Jean Feraca, "Here on Earth." Wisconsin Public Radio, Madison, WI, 4:00–5:00pm ET, Wednesday, April 8, 2009.

247. Live interview with Diego Mulligan's "The Journey Home." KSFR Radio (NPR and BBC), Santa Fe and Albuquerque, NM, 7:35–8:00pm(EST), Wednesday, December 23, 2008.

248. Live interview along with Marcus Borg for Doug Fabrizio, "RadioWest." KUER FM 90/XM Public Radio, Salt Lake City, UT, 1:00–2:00pm ET, Monday, August 16, 2010.

249. Taped interview with John Cleary, "Sunday Nights." ABC Radio Religious Programs Department, Melbourne, Victoria, Australia, Tuesday, August 31, 2010.

250. Taped interview with Rachael Kohn, "The Spirit of Things." ABC National Radio, Melbourne, Victoria, Australia, Thursday, September 2, 2010.

251. Live interview for *The Greatest Prayer* with Father Dick Dwyer on "Busted Halo." 8:20–8:35pm, Tuesday, September 14, 2010.

252. Interview for *The Greatest Prayer* on the Nick and Josh Podcast, 5L00–5:30pm, Tuesday, September 21, 2010.

253. Taped interview with John Hall for the "John and Kathy Show." WORD-FM, 1:30–2:00pm, Tuesday, September 21, 2010.

254. Taped interview with Maureen Fielder On "Understanding Christianity's 'Strangest Prayer'" for *Interfaith Voices*, November 12–18, on http://www.interfaithradio.org.

255. Live interview with call-ins for Michael Kresny, *Forum*, KQED Radio (San Francisco NPR Affiliate), 10:00–11:00am, Wednesday, November 16, 2011 (with Willia Barnstone and N. T, Wright).

256. "Living on Purpose." Unity Online Radio, Unity Village, MO. 10:20–10:55am, Tuesday, June 11, 2013.

257. Live interview and call-ins (one other panelist) with Milt Rosenberg, WCGO-AM 1590, 12:00–2:00pm, Friday, June 19, 2015

(4) Television

1. Live interview on "Connie Martinson Talks Books." Continental Cablevision, Marina del Rey, CA, 2:00–2:30 PM, Thursday, April 2, 1992.

2. Live interview on Karen Anderson's "Light Works." KRON-TV, San Francisco, CA, 12:00–1:00 PM, Saturday, April 4, 1992.

3. Taped interview on "Chris Lydon and Company." WGBH-TV (PBS), Boston, MA, 2:00–3:00 PM, Monday, April 6, 1992.

4. Taped interview on Bob Hale's "Sunday Chronicles: The Interfaith Hour." WMAQ-TV (NBC), Chicago, IL, 6:00–7:00 AM, Sunday, May 24, 1992.

5. Quoted on-camera for various segments about the historical Jesus in "Mysteries of the Bible," a multi-unit series by Christy Connell Roos Entertainment Group shown on A&E and then distributed worldwide by Multimedia, since 1993.
6. Taped interview and debate on "Among Friends" with Jerry K. Rose, WCFC-TV (Christian Communications of Chicago), Channel 38, Chicago, IL. Aired 11–12 A.M. and 9–10 P.M, Wednesday, January 11, 1995.
7. Taped interview with Joan Wyatt for Vision-TV, 9:30–10:30 AM, United Church Television, Thursday, March 23, 1995.
8. Taped interview for CBC-TV, "Sunday Morning Live." 2:15–2:45 PM, Thursday, March 23, 1995.
9. Live interview on Chicagoland TV, 11:00–11:30 AM, Monday, March 27, 1995.
10. Taped interview for Metro Cable Network, "Northern Lights and Insights." Minnetonka, MN, 9:00–10:00 AM, Friday, March 31, 1995.
11. Live interview for "Radio City News." Minneapolis, MN, 1:30–1:45 PM, Friday, March 31, 1995.
12. Live interview for "News 12—Long Island Morning TV News." 7:30–9:30 AM, Thursday, April 6, 1995.
13. Taped interview for "Faces on Faith." Vision Cable Network, 2:00–3:30 PM, Thursday, April 6, 1995.
14. Live interview for "News Channel 8." Springfield, VA, 12:50–2:00 PM, Wednesday, April 12, 1995.
15. Live interview for "Talk Back Live." CNN TV Studio, Chicago, IL, Friday, April 14, 1995.
16. Quoted on-camera for "CBS Evening News." Easter Sunday, 1996.
17. Quoted on-camera for "The Mysterious Man of the Shroud." Landau Entertainment, CBS, 8:00–9:00 PM EST, Tuesday, April 1, 1997.
18. Quoted on-camera for "From Jesus to Christ: The First Christians." *Frontline*, PBS from WGBH, Boston, April 6 and 7, 1998 (Michael Sullivan, Executive Producer of *Frontline*; Marilyn Mellowes, Producer of 4-hour show).
19. Quoted on-camera for "Peter Jennings Reporting: The Search for Jesus." ABC-TV, Monday, June 27 (9–11pm ET), 2000.

Chat-room response to questions about "Peter Jennings Reporting: The Search for Jesus." on ABCNews.com, Tuesday, June 28, 2–3pm ET. (Moderator: Saira Stewart).

20. Quoted on-camera for "Who Is This Jesus?" Coral Ridge Media on PAX-TV, Monday, December 25, 8:00–9:00 PM ET, and on mainly CBS affiliates, Tuesday, December 26, 7:00–8:00 PM ET (infomercial for Dr. Kennedy and Christian fundamentalism).

21. Short segment in studio for Douglas Alexander on "CBC News Sunday." Toronto, Canada, Sunday, November 3, 2002 (on James ossuary).
22. Quoted on-camera for "The Last-days of Jesus." NBC Dateline, Monday, February 2, 2004.
23. Brief appearance for ABC's "PrimeTime Special" with Diane Sawyer on Mel Gibson's film *The Passion of the Christ*, Monday, February 16, 2004.
24. Appearance about Mel Gibson's film *The Passion of the Christ* for CBS' "Early Show." 7:45–7:60am, Thursday, February 19, 2004.
25. Appearance about Mel Gibson's film *The Passion of the Christ* for ABC's "Nightline." 11:30–12:00pm, Wednesday, February 20, 2004.
26. Appearances on NBC's "Dateline" special on "The Last-days of Jesus." 9:00–10:00pm, Friday, February 20, 2004.
27. Appearance on" Lester Holt Live." MSNBC, 4:45–5:00pm, Monday, February 23, 2004.
28. Appearance on "The Abrams Report." MSNBC, 6:45–7:00pm, Wednesday, February 25, 2004.
29. Quoted on-camera for "Peter Jennings Reporting: Jesus and Paul. The Word and the Witness." ABC-TV, 8:00–11:00pm ET, Monday, April 5, 2004.
30. Quoted on-camera for "The Trial of Jesus" on the History Channel, 8:00–9:00pm ET, Thursday, April 8, 2004.
31. Quoted on-camera for "In Search of Easter" on the National Geographic Channel, 9:00–10:00pm ET, Easter Sunday, April 11, 2004.
32. Taped-live interview on "The O'Reilly Factor" (8 minutes), Fox News, between 8:00–9:00pm ET, Thursday, April 8, 2004.
33. Live interview for "The Vicki Gabereauu Show." CTV, Vancouver, BC, Canada, 12:30–1:00pm, Wednesday, December 8, 2004.
34. Quoted for "The Birth of Jesus." Dateline NBC, Friday, November 11, 8:00–900pm EST, 2004.
35. Quoted for "The Mystery of Christmas." CBS 48 Hours, Tuesday, December 20, 109–11pm EST, 2004.
36. Taped interviews for "The Birth of Jesus." Fox News Special, 9:00pm and 12:00am, Sunday, December 19, and 9:00pm and 12:00am, Saturday (Christmas-day), December 25, 2004 [bottom-of-screen news streamed news from Iraq].

www.ingramcontent.com/pod-product-compliance
Lightning Source LLC
Chambersburg PA
CBHW030433300426
44112CB00009B/978